American
Dharma

American Dharma

*Buddhism
Beyond
Modernity*

ANN GLEIG

Yale UNIVERSITY PRESS/NEW HAVEN & LONDON

Yale University Press books may be purchased in quantity for
educational, business, or promotional use. For information,
please e-mail sales.press@yale.edu (U.S. office) or
sales@yaleup.co.uk (U.K. office).

Set in Minion type by Newgen North America, Austin, Texas.
Printed in the United States of America.

Library of Congress Control Number: 2018943194
ISBN 978-0-300-21580-9 (hardcover : alk. paper)

A catalogue record for this book is
available from the British Library.

This paper meets the requirements of ANSI/
NISO Z39.48-1992 (Permanence of Paper).

10 9 8 7 6 5 4 3 2 1

This book is dedicated to my first lineage:
My nan, Annie Kennedy Walters (1914–1994)
and my mum, Ann Gleig
"the three Annies"

Contents

Acknowledgments

B ecause that exists, this exists . . ." There are few things like writing a book to convince one of the basic insight of the Buddhist concept of dependent-origination: the mutual dependence of phenomena. I owe an immense debt of gratitude to the many practitioners who generously gave their time to be interviewed and, in many cases, provided important feedback on the chapters in which they are featured. Whether named in these pages or not, each one was essential in forming my understanding of current developments in American Buddhism. In particular, I thank Martin Aylward, Klia Bassing, Tara Brach, David Chapman, Jennifer Hawkins, Eleanor Hancock, Vince Horn, Josh Korda, Mushim Patricia Ikeda, Sumi Loundon Kim, Tenku Ruff, La Sarimento, Lama Karma Justin Wall, Gina Sharpe, Kate Lila Wheeler, and Larry Yang. I also acknowledge Michael Stone (1974–2017) and Aaron Lee (1983–2017). Each of them significantly affected the landscape of American Buddhism, and their tragic early deaths are a great loss for the sanghas they nurtured.

I am grateful to my colleagues Brooke Schedneck, Elizabeth Williams-Oerberg, and Jane Compson for their helpful feedback on different chapters in this book. I am grateful also to Cristina Rocha, Martin Baumann, and Jovan Maud, the editors at the *Journal of Global Buddhism,* for permission to reproduce my research and for the constructive feedback I have received from them. From the University of Central Florida, I am appreciative of Claudia Schippert for teaching me how to say "no" to other projects so I could stay focused on this one, and my undergraduate students who helped with interview transcriptions: Kelsi, Hania, Vanessa, and Samantha. I am also grateful to friends and mentors who supported me during the emotional vicissitudes that preparing a manuscript entails: Harvey Aronson, Gina Crago, Anne C. Klein, Anna Snow, Terry Stevens, Sabine O'Laughlin, Willem Overwijk, Lianne Wynne, Claire Villarreal, and Amanda Yoder. As well as the Viau family—my wonderful in-laws—who never complained about my missing family events because I had to work on this manuscript.

I offer my deepest gratitude to Jennifer Banks, my editor at Yale University Press. Jennifer saw the potential in the project when it was in its very infancy. Her confidence in it kept me going through the periods of doubt and insecurity that inevitably accompany one's first monograph, and her astute editorial suggestions made the chapters cleaner and more cohesive. I also thank Heather Gold, assistant editor at Yale University Press, for her patience with my many email requests, and Jessie Dolch for her absolutely meticulous copyediting. The attention and care she put into this manuscript were extraordinary. Extra special thanks are due to Franz Metcalf, without whom there would be no manuscript. Franz was the first person to encourage me to expand my research on Buddhism in postmodernity into a book-length project, and his thorough, thoughtful review of the first draft was indispensable. Most of all, though, I thank and recognize Jeanine Viau, my beloved, whose love, care, and patience make all things possible for me. She is my refuge.

American
Buddhism
After
Modernity

Introduction

A beautiful white blonde female, eyes closed, face tilted upwards, radiating joy and tranquility, decorated the cover of the February 3, 2014, edition of *Time* magazine. Across her slender upper body were the words "The Mindful Revolution: The Science of Finding Focus in a Stressed Out, Multitasking Culture." If this announcement on a national magazine known for its iconic cultural covers alone did not convince one of the arrival of mindfulness in North America, the accompanying article surely did. "The Mindful Revolution" interweaved the authors' experience of an eight-week mindfulness-based stress reduction (MBSR) program with a discussion of the increasing adoption of mindfulness meditation in a range of secular spheres such as medicine, education, business, and the military. It attributed the success of mindfulness to its scientific legitimation and its strategic marketing, revealing that, at the last count, Americans had spent $4 billion on mindfulness-related medicine. *Time* was just one of many popular news sources, including the *New York Times,* to cover the mindfulness boom, suggesting that mindfulness was already well on its way to becoming established in American mainstream life.[1]

One might imagine that American Buddhists would celebrate the endorsement of mindfulness in one of their nation's most established magazines. After all, the "revolution" had been pioneered by some of the most well-known American Buddhist teachers. *Time*'s title had first appeared as the title of a 2011 edited collection, *The Mindfulness Revolution*, published by the leading Buddhist press, Shambhala, which contained contributions by figures such as Joseph Goldstein, Jack Kornfield, and Jan Chozen Bays, promoting the use of mindfulness in a range of daily activities and secular contexts.[2] These teachers had established the first wave of American Buddhist meditation-based convert communities and had helped fashion a distinctively modern form of Buddhism that had given birth to the mindfulness movement. The response of the wider American Buddhist community to the *Time* feature, however, was far from celebratory. Both the cover image and the story became the subject of much critical commentary and debate.[3] A large part of the discord was due to the fact that almost a decade earlier the August 4, 2003, edition of *Time* had also featured a slim white blonde, accompanied by the caption "The Science of Meditation," which proclaimed meditation's health and fitness benefits. Taken together, the two covers gave a clear message of what type of Americans practiced mindfulness and what they practiced it for.

In response, Joanna Piacenza questioned why *Time* had chosen twice to represent mindfulness and, by association, Buddhism with an image of a white American when the majority of American Buddhists were actually Asian Americans. She declared this to be the result of meditation retreats being so expensive that only affluent white people could afford them. Distinguishing between those who were born into Buddhist families and those who converted to Buddhism, she accused the latter "elite" group of superficially appropriating Buddhism. As she put it, "In Western modernity, Buddhism has become something that you can fit into your life, not something you shape your life around." This new approach to Buddhism negated the wider institutional, ethical, and communal dimensions of the religion. Lamenting this thoroughly truncated vision, Piacenza's parting line was, "I suppose the question is, then, do you want the whole story?"[4]

Responses to the success of mindfulness in mainstream North America suggest that in fact many *do* want the whole story. Articles heralding its scientifically proven benefits have been followed by other commentaries expressing concern at various aspects of its secularization. Critiques range from traditionalist laments over the richness and complexity of a twenty-five-hundred-year-old tradition being reduced to one component of the Noble Eightfold Path to Marxist-inspired analyses of the elite hijacking of mindfulness and its complicity in neoliberal ideology and global capitalism.[5] Critics draw on distinctions between right and wrong mindfulness as decreed by the Pali Canon and differentiate between sincere individual intentions and the institutionalization of self-disciplines as informed by Michel Foucault. These unusual bedfellows of religious conservatives and critical theorists, premodern and poststructuralist perspectives, are united by a suspicion of the distinctively modern discourses that have overtaken Buddhism.

Indeed, resistance to the mindfulness movement and the American meditation-based convert Buddhist communities that it grew out of is part of a wider critique of Buddhist modernism, a historically unprecedented form of Buddhism that arose out of the encounter between traditional Buddhism and Western modernity under colonialism. As David McMahan has traced, Buddhist modernism is the result of modernization and reform processes that have been happening in Asia and the West for more than a century. It has been shaped by an engagement with the major discourses of Western modernity—science, Romanticism, and liberal Protestantism—and is marked by a number of distinctively modern values such as individuality, democracy, pluralism, and the privileging of meditation experience as the core of the tradition.[6]

While McMahan advances a generally sympathetic reading of Buddhist modernism, seeing it as a legitimate form of Buddhism that has been fashioned by both Asian and Western Buddhists as a response to the questions and concerns of modernity, a number of other scholars have targeted some of its core modern premises. Robert Sharf, for example, problematizes the modern emphasis on individual meditation experience, which has resulted in a loss of connection with traditional Buddhist lineage, community, and ritual. Donald S. Lopez's pointedly titled *The Scientific Buddha: His Short and Happy Life* suggests that it is time to retire the highly selective modernist vision of the Buddha as an early empiricist and its reduction of Buddhism to a scientific paradigm. Joseph Cheah challenges the white supremacy he sees at the heart of American Buddhist modernist communities, such as the Vipassana movement, which have been founded upon their ethnocentric distinction between essential (i.e., modern Western) and cultural (i.e., traditional Asian) Buddhism.[7]

I followed this disquiet over Buddhist modernism and its offshoots across popular and scholarly audiences with much interest because it confirmed and substantiated patterns I uncovered through my own ethnographic research with meditation-based convert American Buddhist groups. While external critiques of Buddhist modernism illustrate important trends in contemporary American Buddhism, they often fail to acknowledge that many convert communities have already been wrestling with and attempting to address certain limitations of Buddhist modernism. My research reveals, however, that key modernist features— such as the privileging of individual meditation practice, the neglect of elements discarded in the modernization process such as sangha and ritual, the psychologization of Buddhism, the distinction between "essential" and "cultural" Buddhism, and the overwhelmingly white, liberal middle- and upper-middle-class demographic—have increasingly come under scrutiny within American convert communities.

Taken together, such developments suggest that American Buddhist meditation-based convert communities are undergoing significant transformation and displaying features more characteristic of postmodern rather than modern cultural conditions. One distinctively postmodern pattern, for example, is the simultaneous appearance of an increasing decontextualization and modernization of traditional Buddhism *and* a renewal of interest in and revalorization of traditional Buddhism. At one end of the spectrum, there is much evidence of the further radicalization of trends initiated in Buddhist modernism: alongside the secularization of mindfulness, a wide array of phenomena has emerged from multiple configurations between Buddhism and new technologies, such as the emergence of meditation apps, to the growth of communities that promote a secular revisioning of Buddhism, such as the Secular Buddhist Association. At the other end, there has been considerable resistance to modernization trends: alongside critiques of the secular mindfulness movement, there has been a renewal of interest in traditional aspects of Buddhism such as sangha, ritual, and cosmology and a questioning of key components of Buddhist modernism, such as its reduction of Buddhism to a scientific paradigm. These two seemingly contradictory trends—innovation and preservation, radicalism and recovery—are indicative of postmodernity in which a revalorization of tradition appears alongside an acceleration of secularization and various hybrid combinations of the traditional and modern.

These multiple developments show that Buddhist modernism is undergoing significant transformation in North America. Much has changed since sociologist James William Coleman's enthusiastic portrayal in 2002 of the "new Buddhism" produced by the Western baby boomer converts since the 1960s.[8] Richard Hughes Seager glances at some of these new developments in the 2012 revised version of his book *Buddhism in America.* He notes, for example, that a new generation of dharma teachers has emerged during the first decade of the twenty-first century who have explicitly distanced themselves from the first generation of baby boomer teachers. Figures such as Dharma Punx founder Noah Levine, Pragmatic Dharma teacher Daniel Ingram, and Buddhist Geeks cofounder Vince Horn have rejected the "hippie" counterculture that initially shaped American meditation-based convert Buddhism and have drawn instead from the punk and digital cultures of Gen X and Gen Y. Similarly, Seager notes the shift from an explicit emphasis on Buddhism to Buddhist-inspired secular practice in the mindfulness movement.[9] Jay Michaelson offers a more expanded analysis of this shifting territory—the mainstreaming of mindfulness, the emergence of new post-boomer convert communities, and tensions between traditional and secular Buddhists—in his entertaining and informative first-person reflection *Evolving Dharma: Meditation, Buddhism and the Next Generation of Enlightenment.*[10] However, *American Dharma* is the first scholarly and ethnographic account to specifically focus on current shifts within meditation-based convert Buddhist modernist lineages in North America and to consider them within the framework of Buddhist modernism. It has two main aims: first, to identify these key developments, and second, to locate and analyze them within the wider cultural shift from the modern to the postmodern. The central claim of this book is that within American Buddhist meditation-based convert lineages, there is an increasing interrogation of Buddhist modernism and the emergence of characteristics that are more associated with the postmodern than the modern. Hence, it concludes that American Buddhism is witnessing the emergence of a new period marked by enlightenments *beyond* the (European) Enlightenment.

In arguing that American Buddhism is witnessing a shift from the modern to the postmodern, I pick up a thread in this book that was left at the end of McMahan's influential study *The Making of Buddhist Modernism*. In his concluding chapter "From the Modern to Postmodern," McMahan briefly discusses the appearance of trends that are more suggestive of postmodern than modern conditions, such as a renewed interest in tradition, increased pluralism, and various combinations of modernism and traditionalism. McMahan responds in the affirmative to Martin Baumann's earlier question of whether a new developmental stage was emerging in the history of Buddhism in the West. As Baumann put it: "I would like to ask whether at the close of modernity and at the beginning, or rather on-going, of so-called post-modernity, developments are determinable that point to a new and different form of Buddhism. Is it possible to extend the suggested periodization of Buddhism's history? And what might qualify as a distinctive characteristic, shaping Buddhism in the period after modernity, that is, post-modernity?"[11]

Baumann also suggests that Buddhism has taken a postmodern shape because it displays characteristics such as plurality, hybridity, and globality. In this book I follow the preliminary efforts of McMahan and Baumann by fully fleshing out the distinctive characteristics that are shaping Buddhism in postmodernity. Through a geographical focus on North American meditation-based convert communities, particularly those deriving from Theravada and Zen Buddhism, I draw attention to the specific ways in which Buddhist modernism is being transformed. First, though, it is necessary to clarify my two central categories: American meditation-based convert Buddhism and postmodernity.

Buddhist Modernism in America:
Meditation-Based Convert Buddhist Lineage

The category of convert Buddhism should be adopted cautiously as it has appropriately come under critical academic scrutiny, and many of the developments uncovered in this book put further pressure on it.

Chapter 1 analyzes the convert lineage in more detail, but for now some brief clarification is needed. Convert Buddhism is one part of a commonly employed typology to understand the different varieties of Buddhism in North America.[12] The most basic rendering of this taxonomy distinguishes between "immigrant," "ethnic," or, the more recently employed, "heritage" Buddhism (as practiced by Asian Americans) and "convert" or "white" Buddhism (as practiced predominantly by Euro-Americans). These two distinctive groups have been historically associated with a specific style of practice and goal: immigrants are concerned with cultural preservation, and their main forms of practice are ritual and devotional merit-making activities; while converts are concerned with seeking enlightenment and focus heavily on meditation practice.[13] In order to distinguish between American Buddhist convert groups that do not privilege meditation and have more diverse populations, I add the qualifier "meditation-based."[14] Following Joseph Cheah, I employ "Asian American Buddhists" as an umbrella term to refer to both recent ethnic Buddhists and those Buddhists of Asian ancestry who have been in the United States for many generations. I also follow Cheah in adopting the term "American Buddhists" to refer to both heritage Buddhists and convert Buddhists.[15]

In order to enable a thicker description and a more nuanced analysis of the rethinking of Buddhist modernism, I pay attention exclusively to meditation-based convert lineages. In particular, I focus on communities derived from Theravada and Zen Buddhist traditions, which as McMahan notes are the two lineages that have been at the forefront of Buddhist modernism.[16] Readers might be disappointed to find little direct consideration of Tibetan Buddhism, which Coleman correctly identifies as the third major tradition to make up American meditation-based convert lineages.[17] Although I had initially planned to include a Tibetan Buddhist community in the project, fieldwork complications prevented this, so I limit coverage to Gen X Tibetan Buddhist teachers only.

Finally, I must stress that I am not claiming meditation-based convert communities as exclusive iterations of Buddhist modernism in North America. Although the commonly employed convert-immigrant distinction between Buddhist groups in North America has positioned converts as "modern" and immigrants as "traditional," as I discuss in more detail, this mapping is highly problematic on a number of counts, including the fact that modernization processes have also characterized many Asian American heritage communities.[18]

The Cultural Shift to Postmodernity

The notoriously slippery and multivalent signifier "postmodernity" has led to much confusion and dissent. Much of the debate revolves around the exact relationship of postmodernity to modernity. Some cultural theorists argue that almost all of the features identified as "postmodern" have obvious precursors in what is conventionally considered the modern age, especially in the movement of modernism.[19] Hence, they argue, it should be seen less as signifying a definitive split with modernity and more as an extension of certain traits of modernity. I am in agreement here with sociologist David Lyon, who sees postmodernity as indicating a reshaping rather than replacing of modernity. This restructuring includes both an extension of modernity and a critique of modernity. As Lyon puts it, "rather than denote some type of ultimate replacement or split with modernity the prefix 'post' is attached to 'modernity' in order to alert us to the fact that modernity itself is now in question."[20] Following Lyon, I adopt the term cautiously and strategically as a general signifier to draw attention to significant economic, sociocultural, and intellectual shifts under way in Western modernity since the 1970s.

Although the term "postmodern" appeared as early as 1947, Colin Campbell locates its impact to the 1960s and 1970s, during which time it came to represent an antifoundational philosophical orientation and a body of sociocultural and political thought that was characterized by a critique of modern theories of epistemology.[21] The major proponents of this current are sociologists Jean-François Lyotard and Jean Baudrillard, together with poststructuralist thinkers such as Jacques Lacan, Roland Barthes, Michel Foucault, and Jacques Derrida. A number of scholars have put postmodern philosophy into conversation with Buddhist thought. Jin Y. Park has drawn on Derrida, Lyotard, and Mahayana philosophy to craft a new Buddhist postmodern ethic, while Carl Olson has compared the philosophy of Zen thinkers Dogen and Nishitanti to that of Lacan, Foucault, and Derrida.[22]

My use of postmodernism focuses not on its philosophical expressions, however, but on the more general economic and sociocultural shifts dated from the 1970s in which Western society is seen to have transitioned from a modern industrial age to a postmodern postindustrial age, marked by increasing globalization, the rapid development of new communication and information technologies, the restructuring of capitalism, and the rise of consumer culture. These dramatic social and cultural shifts have significantly altered the contours of modernity and produced a distinct intellectual and aesthetic postmodern culture.[23] At the base of this culture is what Lyotard identified in his seminal text on postmodernity, *The Postmodern Condition,* as "incredulity towards metanarratives."[24] Lyotard claimed that there had been a loss of faith in the absolute explanations and universal foundations of modernity, such as science, reason, and continual progress. According to James K. Smith, the problem is that science and reason dismiss and erase other narratives of meaning in claiming objective truth and demanding universal acceptance.[25] Resistance to the totalizing framework of modernity has resulted in the emergence of a plurality of epistemologies and an awareness of the historicity, contingency, and relativity of each worldview. It has produced a postmodern cultural sensibility that celebrates diversity and difference, and a critical, ironic, and self-referential form of consciousness.

One expression of the postmodern celebration of diversity is its embrace of hybridity and bricolage. Much artistic and intellectual production in postmodernity is marked by the combination of symbols from disparate cultural contexts and temporal periods and the celebration of fragmentation, playfulness, and irony. Closely related to this is the dedifferentiation of modern spheres of society and the blurring of boundaries between the private and public.[26] Jean Baudrillard attributes much of the boundary dissolution to the information age, which has produced an erasure of high and low culture as well as the phenomenon of the "hyperreality" in which the distinction between the real and its referents is undermined.[27]

Another expression of the postmodern affirmation of difference is found in postcolonial critiques of Eurocentrism and Western ethnocentrism. Postcolonialism aims to challenge modern epistemological frameworks, unravel Eurocentric logics, and interrogate stereotypical cultural representations and the dichotomies on which they depend.[28] As David Tracy argues, one of the marks of postcolonialism is the retrieval of those voices that had been muted, forgotten, and erased by the grand narratives of Eurocentric modernity.[29] Postcolonialism has seen the interrogation of the so-claimed "universal" humanist modern subject and a recovery of marginalized and oppressed populations. This has often gone hand in hand with a renewed respect for traditional worldviews and cultures that had been dismissed as "primitive" and "superstitious" in modernity.

Religion in Postmodernity and Postmodern Religion

The shift from modernity to postmodernity has also produced distinctive religious patterns and activities. Classically expressed in the secularization thesis, the long-standing consensus in sociology that religion was undergoing an inevitable process of decline in modern Western societies has been proved wrong. Contrary to predictions, postmodernity has witnessed not the demise but the resurgence of religion.[30] In tracking this revitalization, sociologists of religion have identified two distinct strands: the rise of global fundamentalism and the rise of deinstitutionalized forms of alternative and new spiritualities. Sociologists have also drawn attention to the dramatic relocation of religion and spirituality into secular spheres. Each of these three trends is observable in contemporary developments within American Buddhist meditation-based convert communities.

The global growth of fundamentalism, particularly Christian and Islamic fundamentalism, has received significant attention from scholars of religion. Many interpret this growth as being a response to the anxiety generated by the uncertainty and relativity of postmodernity.[31] This has resulted in the revalorization of a premodern religious past seen not only in fundamentalist forms of religion but also in the recovery of traditional religion and the incorporation of premodern elements in new religions. For example, Lyon notes that "nostalgic" forms of religion need not be fundamental and that traditional religion is flourishing, while Paul Heelas highlights the profusion of traditional symbols within New Age religion.[32]

Alongside this growth in fundamentalism, new, innovative forms of deinstitutionalized spirituality have emerged that directly display many of the characteristics associated with postmodernity. This has led a number of sociologists to categorize these alternative religious expressions as "postmodern religion." According to Heelas, postmodern religion is characterized by an intermingling of the religious and secular, a consumer approach in which religions are viewed as products and engagement is seen as a matter of personal choice, a willingness to combine high and low culture and draw from disparate frameworks of meaning, and an orientation toward pragmatism and relativity.[33] Similarly, in their exploration of different forms of postmodern spirituality, Lynne Hume and Kathleen McPhillips describe postmodern religion as being marked by fluid parameters, spiritual bricolage and inventiveness, discovery of the sacred in unlikely places, and a sense of playfulness.[34]

A third major trend in religion in postmodernity is a relocation of religion to secular spheres. As Lyon notes, there has been a significant deregulation and dedifferentiation of religion in contemporary culture. This has resulted in a considerable amount of religious activity occurring outside of conventional settings of churches and temples. Religion and spirituality now permeate contexts such as the Internet, business, and entertainment. This blurring of boundaries shows the insufficiency of analyses of religion that rely on the modern dichotomy of the religious and the secular.[35] As Courtney Bender and Ann Taves discuss, there has been a shift within sociology from theories of secularization to secularism, which involves a dramatic rethinking of the categories of the "religious" and the "secular," leading some theorists to talk of the "postsecular."[36]

In summary, the religious and spiritual landscape of postmodernity is fertile and variegated. The postmodern questioning of modernity's dismissal of the traditional and its embrace of diversity, hybridity, and pluralism have resulted in an environment in which many different forms of religious belief and activity have flourished. Alongside the recovery and revalorization of traditional models of religion is the profusion of new unconventional expressions of religiosity that often disrupt boundaries between the religious and the secular. Forms of spirituality that embrace and express popular culture and consumerism appear side by side with forms of religion that protest the commodification of the sacred. Hence, just as postmodernity simultaneously extends and resists modernity, so its religious expressions both radicalize and rebuke modern forms of religiosity.[37]

Map, Method, and Location

In this book I argue that contemporary developments in American Buddhist meditation-based convert lineages cannot be adequately explained within the category of Buddhist modernism. After providing historical and theoretical contexts on the emergence of Buddhist modernism in Asia and its transmission to North America, I offer a series of case studies that show both an interrogation of modernist features and the appearance of characteristics more associated with the postmodern, postcolonial, and postsecular within these communities. In chapters 2, 3, and 4, I successively explore challenges to three key components of Buddhist modernism—the scientific-rational lineage, the Romantic lineage, and the privileging of meditative experience—currently under way in American Buddhist convert communities. In chapters 5, 6, and 7, I shift focus to examine new developments within these communities: the growth of racial diversity and justice initiatives; the impact of new technologies, social media, and the digital age; and generational differences between baby boomer teachers and Gen X teachers. I identify in chapter 8 three emerging sensibilities or "turns"—critical, collective, and contextual—within American meditation-based convert Buddhist communities, particularly across online communities and spaces. I argue in the conclusion that these three turns and the other patterns I document across these case studies cannot be contained within the paradigm of Buddhist modernism and consider what new theoretical frameworks—postmodern Buddhism, postcolonial Buddhism, or postsecular Buddhism—might better express them.

In terms of methodology, my general approach is inspired by George Marcus's concept of multisited ethnography in which researchers follow a topic across various geographical and social sites rather than the conventional ethnographic approach of immersing themselves in a specific site. Multisited ethnography enables researchers to track the data under analysis—be it populations, ideas, or material objects—across multiple time-space boundaries as well as form connections across disparate sites. Because my interest was on tracking the various permutations of Buddhist modernism across the different facets and networks—communities and texts, actual and virtual—constituting it rather than any one specific American convert Buddhist community, this approach fit well. Similarly, multisited ethnography takes seriously unbounded spaces such as social media as valuable ethnographic sites, which perfectly aligns with the increasing emergence and influence of transnational online Buddhist communities and the lively Buddhist blogosphere.[38]

One critique of multisited ethnography is that it spreads researchers "too thin" and does not produce enough "depth" or empirically rich data.[39] To counter this, I have aimed at a thick descriptive account of the communities under analysis. I have also intentionally employed this detail-heavy approach as an alternative to some of the popular commentaries on American convert Buddhism, and its offshoot secular mindfulness, which are too often excessively polemic and one-dimensional, revealing as much about the ideological bent of authors as the lived experiences of their subjects. In order to illuminate more dimensionality and complexity, I have utilized the dual methodology of ethnography and discourse analysis. My ethnography consisted of a mix of structured and open-ended interviews, ranging on average from one to three hours long, and participant observation at a number of Buddhist teachings, retreats, and conferences both physical and virtual. I began interviews in 2011 with concentrated periods for each chapter individually indicated. The foundation for the present project, however, was an earlier period of fieldwork undertaken in 2008 on Spirit Rock Meditation Center, one of the two main North American centers of the Insight community.[40] This research started my thinking about how new developments initiated by Spirit Rock, as well as being continuations of modernist themes, were also attempts to counter and correct certain limitations of their immediate Asian Buddhist modernist lineages.[41]

Discourse analysis consists of analyzing numerous primary sources such as in-house materials produced by specific convert communities; popular American Buddhist magazines such as *Tricycle, Buddhadharma,* and *Lion's Roar* (formerly *Shambhala Sun*); and Western Buddhist books published by well-known American Buddhist teachers such as Jack Kornfield, Sylvia Boorstein, and Joseph Goldstein. The ever-expanding Buddhist blogosphere—the profusion of Buddhist websites, blogs, and discussion forums on the Internet—has also provided a rich resource of primary materials. These virtual spaces and materials are playing a significant role in both reflecting and creating contemporary understandings and formations of American meditation-based convert Buddhism.

Making transparent my own location as researcher is also necessary here. I have participated sporadically in convert meditation-based Buddhist groups for more than twenty years, beginning as a teenager in the United Kingdom and continuing to the present in the United States. During my ethnographic research, I have shared this and identified jokingly at times as a "rogue Buddhist," in acknowledgment of my on-off participation in Western Buddhist communities. This transparent dual identity functioned in a number of ways. Most significantly, my personal immersion in convert communities significantly enabled access to and acceptance from research populations. For example, a number of interviewees expressed comfort at knowing that I have been a practitioner for periods of time, and many of them said things such as "As a practitioner yourself, you will be familiar with . . ." These assumptions and experiences of shared worldviews and cultures often function to lubricate the ethnographic encounter, which, as Karen McCarthy Brown has pointed out, is above all a human relationship.[42]

My fieldwork approach can be located in the anthropological lineage, influenced by feminist and postmodern thought, of researching groups with which the ethnographer shares sociocultural, political, and religious sensibilities. An early articulation of this position is Ruth Behar's call for a "native anthropology" in which scholars claim a personal connection to the places in which they work and view identification rather than difference as the key defining image of anthropological research.[43] Nancy Scheper-Hughes builds on this principle of identification to forward a radical anthropology of witnessing in which fieldwork is intentionally undertaken as a militant act of empathy and protest.[44]

My particular location is also representative of a general fluidity between scholars and practitioners of Buddhism. There is a considerable crossover between the two groups, and this has significantly shaped the academic study of Buddhism. Charles Prebish has labeled the phenomenon of Buddhist scholar-practitioners as the "silent sangha" and reveals that in his 1999 survey at least a quarter of Buddhist scholars openly declared their personal commitment to Buddhism. He believes that another 25 percent were also practicing but remained closeted for fear of being perceived by their colleagues as apologetic and insufficiently critical.[45]

With respect to the study of Buddhist modernism and American Buddhist convert communities, however, many Buddhist scholar-practitioners such as Robert Sharf and Richard Payne have taken a critical rather than an apologetic stance.[46] This is in line with what Natalie Quli identifies as a strong trend toward the dismissal of Buddhist modernism and American Buddhist converts in the field of Buddhist studies. She attributes this to nostalgia, guilt, and misguided attempts by scholars to protect traditional Asian Buddhism from the "contamination" of Western-influenced Buddhist modernism.[47] Nonetheless, other practitioner-scholars have been much more affirmative about the modernization processes under way in American convert Buddhism. Sociologist James William Coleman, who practices within the Insight community, for example, has written enthusiastically about the "new Buddhism" it has fashioned.[48] In earlier research, I have also argued against automatically dismissing such communities as mere dilutions of traditional Asian Buddhism and concluded that they are legitimate, if historically unprecedented, forms of Buddhism.[49]

Another strong current of fluidity between scholars and practitioners of Buddhism is occurring on the Internet and in the popular Buddhist press. There are numerous references to and sharing of academic research among practitioners on the Buddhist blogosphere. Awareness of such research is facilitated by Buddhist websites such as Buddhist Geeks and the Secular Buddhist podcast, which have featured interviews with Buddhist scholars.[50] A further avenue of interaction is occurring in popular Buddhist magazines such as *Tricycle,* which has run a series of interviews with either Buddhist scholars or other academics researching Buddhism and meditation.[51] In addition to access to academic scholarship, practitioners also have access to scholars. There is a considerable presence of Buddhist scholars on the Buddhist blogosphere.[52] In the main, these scholars have forwarded critical perspectives on contemporary American Buddhist developments and in certain cases even engaged in combative debate with practitioners.[53]

Access to scholarship and scholars is having a substantial effect on the shaping of contemporary American Buddhism. A cursory glance at the Buddhist blogosphere shows practitioners making frequent reference to academic articles and texts. Two books that have been particularly influential are David L. McMahan's *The Making of Buddhist Modernism* and Erik Braun's *The Birth of the Insight Movement.* One of the primary functions these texts are serving is to make practitioners aware that certain "traditional" forms of Buddhism they have inherited are in fact not so traditional after all, but are rather earlier iterations of Buddhist modernism. In some cases, as I later examine, this is causing practitioners and communities to rethink and reformulate their approaches to Buddhism.

The fluidity between academic and practice communities within American Buddhism is not uncommon in contemporary American spirituality. In her study *The New Metaphysicals* Courtney Bender noted that her respondents' religious practices and experiences were significantly shaped by their conversations and engagements with academicians and academic studies. She concluded that ongoing interactions between scholars and practitioners were forging contemporary forms of religiosity and that scholars were more participants than observers of contemporary spirituality.[54] This pattern is becoming increasingly evident in the study of Buddhism in North America and is another example of the disruption and blurring of boundaries that characterize postmodernity.

Buddhist Modernism
from Asia to America

The World's Parliament of Religions held in Chicago in 1893, and organized by liberal Protestants, was the first major public event in which Asian Buddhist teachers represented their tradition in North America. One of these was a Sri Lankan monk and the first Theravadin Buddhist missionary to the United States, Anagarika Dharmapala (1864–1933). He captivated the audience with his speech "The World's Debt to Buddhism," which presented the Buddha as a religious reformer of "priestly selfishness" and the dharma as a universal system of philosophy that systematically laid out an evolutionary unfolding toward the perfection of humankind.[1] Another was the non-English-speaking Japanese Rinzai Zen Buddhist Shaku Soen (1859–1919), whose contribution, translated by D. T. Suzuki and read out by John Henry Barrows, explained karma as a principle of causation and emphasized the compatibility of Buddhism with science. Both of these Asian teachers presented Buddhism as a universal and rational religion, one that was eminently compatible with science and other modern values such as tolerance, social reform, and the "brotherhood of man." A few days after the conference, Dharmapala presided over the conversion of Charles T. Strauss, a Jewish businessman from New York who became the first person to convert to Buddhism on American soil.[2]

American Buddhist scholars have often identified the 1893 World's Parliament as a pivotal event in the history of the Euro-American convert adoption of Buddhism. This is not surprising, given that not only was it a "first" of its kind on multiple levels, but it also set in motion numerous events that would shape convert Buddhism in North America. After the conference, both Dharmapala and Soen, for example, embarked on tours of the United States that marked the first Buddhist missions in the country. While Dharmapala would eventually grow weary of "the self-indulgent quest for easy mysticism" that he found among Americans, Soen inspired Paul Carus (1852–1919) to become the first major Buddhist publisher in the US, and three of his students—Nyogen Senzaki (1878–1958), Shaku Sokatsu (1869–1954), and particularly the prolific Zen popularizer D. T. Suzuki (1870–1966)—would significantly influence the practice and representation of Zen in America.[3]

Yet, although delivered directly by Asian Buddhists, the picture of Buddhism presented at the World's Parliament was far from "traditional." Rather, it had emerged from the encounter between traditional Buddhism and Western modernity in Asia under the conditions of colonialism. Dharmapala was the protégé of Henry Steel Olcott (1832–1907), a Theosophist who had played a major role in the revitalization of Buddhism in Ceylon and helped fashion the form of "Protestant Buddhism" that Dharmapala faithfully presented at the World's Parliament.[4] Similarly, Soen was a proponent of the Japanese "New Buddhism" that had constructed a form of Buddhism influenced by Western modernity in the service of Japanese nationalism. In short, the rational and scientific vision of Buddhism presented at the World's Parliament had already been forged through the lens of Western modernity. To understand the story of American convert lineages in the US, therefore, one must turn attention to the meeting of traditional Buddhism and the various forces of Western modernity occurring in Asia during colonialism, an encounter that produced an historically unprecedented and unique form of Buddhism, commonly referred to as "Buddhist modernism."

Three Stages of Buddhism:
Canonical, Traditional, and Modernist

To understand Buddhist modernism, one first needs to know what it developed from and how it differs from classical forms of Buddhism. As Donald S. Lopez notes, however, the relation between modern and classical Buddhism is complex and more than a matter of simple historic chronology.[5] Yet, as Martin Baumann observes, a number of scholars have adopted a tripartite model of Buddhism that divides the history of Buddhism into three stages based on the history of Theravada Buddhism in particular: canonical, traditional, and modernist.[6] Following this model provides some helpful historic context to the emergence and distinct characteristics of Buddhist modernism.

In his examination of the modern Buddhist revival in Sri Lanka, George Bond divides Theravada into three historical stages: (1) canonical Buddhism, the early Buddhism reflected in the Pali Canon; (2) traditional Buddhism, the postcanonical Theravada established during the Ashokan period (ca. 268–233 BCE) and continued by the Pali Commentaries; and (3) modern Theravada, the twentieth-century Buddhism of revival and reformation.[7] Canonical Buddhism is rooted in the Pali Canon, which is the only complete canon of an early Buddhist school that survives in its original Indian language. It consists of three sections and, for this reason, is known as the *Tipitaka,* or the "Three Baskets," all of which are claimed to have come directly from the Buddha or from teachings he approved. The first basket is the *Vinaya Pitaka,* which treats issues of monastic discipline. The second is the *Sutta Pitaka,* which contains the discourses or sayings of the Buddha. The third is the *Abhidhamma Pitaka,* or the higher teaching, which contains philosophical teachings on such things as the nature of causation and analyzes the building blocks, or *dhammas,* that constitute the psychophysical world. It is of later origin than the first two baskets and represents a systematization and clarification of the suttas.[8]

According to Bond, canonical Buddhism is the most difficult form to define because of the size of the Pali Canon, the diversity of its teachings, and the absence of a set of precise criteria for distinguishing early from later material. Following Max Weber, scholars often represented early Buddhism as a religion of individual liberation for ascetic renounc-ers. Kitsiri Malalgoda, for example, describes it as "asocial and apolitical in its orientation."[9] S. J. Tambiah, however, has properly warned that this picture represents an oversimplification, since the Pali Canon indi-cates that early Buddhism had well-developed views of social and politi-cal matters. He persuasively argues that Weber overstated the extent to which early Buddhism was limited to ascetics.[10] Still, as Paul Williams points out, the Buddha was an ascetic renouncer whose main teaching was a soteriology concerned with individual liberation from the cycle of life, death, and rebirth.[11]

Traditional Theravada refers to the development of Buddhism af-ter the early canonical period, beginning from the time of the Indian emperor Ashoka around 268–233 BCE. The primary source for tradi-tional Theravada is the commentarial literature, particularly the *Visud-dhimagga* (*The Path of Purification*), attributed to the fifth-century Sri Lankan monk Buddhaghosa (409–431 CE). Drawing on the work of Louis Dumont, Bond explains traditional Theravada as developing in response to a particular kind of social context consisting of two catego-ries of people: renouncers and householders. Each group had its own corresponding religious practice and goal. The renouncers followed ascetic "disciplines of salvation," which aimed for the supramundane goal of liberation from the cycle of rebirth. The householders practiced religious forms such as ritual and morality that were associated with the mundane plane and aimed at worldly benefits and the accruing of karmic merit for good future rebirths.[12]

Bond claims that tensions between the two groups served as a ma-jor catalyst for the development of traditional Theravada. While early Buddhism was chiefly concerned with renouncers, as the tradition de-veloped it was increasingly called on to address the needs of people in the world. The hermeneutic strategy employed by traditional Theravada to balance the different needs of renouncers and householders was Bud-dhaghosa's *Visuddhimagga*. This text accommodates both groups by subsuming the mundane goals of the householders under the supra-mundane goal of *Nibbāna* (Nirvana) and its ideal religious type, the arahant, or the perfected being.[13] This is illustrated in one of its main features—the threefold trainings or perfections that must be developed for liberation: morality, concentration, and wisdom. In traditional Theravada, the layperson can train only in morality, and the higher perfections of concentration and wisdom are reserved for monastics. Central to traditional Theravada, therefore, is the strict separation of two levels: the mundane (*lokiya*) and the supramundane (*lokuttara*). One can enter the supramundane level only when one has advanced sufficiently on the mundane path. In short, *Visuddhimagga* maps out an arduous gradual hierarchical trajectory that posits Nirvana and arahantship as remote and implausible transcendental goals even for renouncers.

The cosmological hierarchy of the gradual path was reproduced institutionally, with the monastics given elite status as representatives of the Buddha and mediators of his teachings, the *dhamma*. Michael Ames describes two types of monk in traditional Theravada: hermit monks devoted (in theory) to meditation, and village monks devoted (in theory) to scholarship. In practice, however, Ames notes that most monks were more concerned with the mundane rather than the supramundane levels of the path and were focused on merit-making rituals. With Nirvana cast as such a remote ideal, both monastics and householders needed ways to address their immediate worldly concerns and future rebirths.[14] More recent studies by Erik Braun (2013) and Brooke Schedneck (2015) confirm that in traditional Theravada, meditation was rarely practiced, with much more emphasis on scholastic and devotional activities among monastics. Monks acted as fields of merit who generated good karma for laypeople through generosity, virtuous behavior, and devotion to the Buddha.[15]

Buddhist Modernism

The nineteenth-century encounter between traditional Asian Buddhism and Western modernity, much of which occurred under the conditions of colonialism, has produced a distinct form of Buddhism that has been referred to as "Protestant Buddhism," "reform Buddhism," and "modern Buddhism." More recently, however, scholars have settled on "Buddhist modernism," a term first used by German scholar Heinz Bechert in 1966. Bechert described Buddhist modernism as an Asian reformist movement spanning a number of geographical areas and schools that demythologized Buddhism and reinterpreted it as a rational religion that was linked to social reform and nationalist movements, especially in Burma and Sri Lanka.[16] Following Bechert, George Bond (1988), Richard Gombrich and Gananath Obeyesekere (1990), and Donald Swearer (1995) have also examined the emergence of forms of Buddhist modernism across Southeast Asia in the late nineteenth and early twentieth centuries. Swearer investigates how Theravada sanghas in Burma, Sri Lanka, and Thailand underwent unprecedented historical reforms that included the implementation of stricter monastic regulations, the revival of meditation practice, and the emergence of a mass meditation movement for both the lay and monastic communities.[17]

Simultaneously demonstrating accommodation and resistance to colonialism and modernity, the vision of Buddhism that emerged from these reforms selectively privileged aspects of Buddhism that were compatible with modern Western discourses and discarded elements that were incompatible. Common characteristics include (1) a claim to return to the "original" and "pure" teachings of the Buddha that were distorted by cultural and institutional overlays; (2) a framing of Buddhism as a rational and scientific religion; (3) a rejection of the traditional Theravada separation of the mundane and supramundane levels and a blurring of the roles of the layperson and the monk; (4) a revival of meditation practice and a claim that Nirvana is an attainable goal in this lifetime for both monastics and the laity; and (5) an interest in social reform issues such as gender equality.

As David McMahan states, "much of what is considered Buddhism today is inevitably part of, or at least deeply influenced by, these modernist forms that emerged over a century ago."[18] To understand American meditation-based convert lineages, therefore, it is necessary to look more closely at the forms of Asian Buddhist modernism that gave birth to them. Given space restrictions, I focus on the Asian variations of Buddhist modernism that have been most influential on convert lineages: Theravada Buddhism in Burma and Thailand, and Zen Buddhism in Japan.

Buddhist Modernism in Burma: The Birth of Insight

A 2013 study by Erik Braun has placed Burma at the forefront of the Theravada meditation revival that characterizes Buddhist modernism. In his aptly titled book *The Birth of Insight* he identifies the monk Ledi Sayadaw (1846–1923) as the pioneer of mass *vipassanā,* or insight, practice. Before the nineteenth century, interest in meditation practice in Burma was very rare, with monastics devoted to scholarship or devotional merit-making activities. Braun situates Ledi's work as containing the "first pervasive and influential call to meditate."[19] He developed a mass meditation movement in order to protect Buddhism from the threat of colonialism. Between 1824 and 1885, Burma had come under control of the British, and this occupation was seen as posing a great threat to the safety of the dhamma. With the king no longer able to serve as protector of the dhamma, as traditionally had been the case, Ledi believed that the responsibility fell to the Burmese Buddhist population, both monastics and the laity. One of his solutions was to popularize the study of Buddhist doctrine, particularly the *Abhidhamma,* which had traditionally been the elite pursuit of scholastic monastics. However, while the cultivation of virtue and studying the dhamma was essential, Ledi believed it was not sufficient and that meditation practice was also necessary.

In order to offer a simple and accessible meditation practice for a wide range of people, Ledi turned to both the *Abhidhamma* and Buddhaghosa's *Visuddhimagga.* Whereas the traditional approach set out here was to develop proficiency in *samatha,* or calming meditation, before beginning *vipassanā,* Ledi took the "second option" of beginning directly with the "dry path" of insight.[20] As Braun explains, Ledi did not discard the preliminary stages of cultivating generosity or concentration but made them less of an obstacle to beginning insight practice.[21] Further, in order to persuade a wide variety of people to meditate, Ledi emphasized the multiple benefits of meditation, and he affirmed mundane worldly life as a valid location for both meditation and awakening. In short, Ledi creatively drew from his traditional elite scholasticism to radically transform the hierarchy between the mundane and supramundane that marked traditional Theravada and to reframe meditation as a

mass monastic and lay phenomenon rather than a rare monastic practice. Although he maintained distinctions between monastics and the
laity, Ledi made meditation and realization available to the laity in a
systematic way that was unprecedented in Buddhist history. As Braun
notes, "This marked the birth of insight meditation as a popular movement that would reshape notions of Buddhism in modern Burma and
eventually grow into a global phenomenon."[22]

Indeed, Ledi's influence on modern Theravada meditation movements, which, in turn, have significantly shaped American convert lineages, can hardly be overstated. Several Burmese practice lineages trace
their origins to him, including two—the lay lineage of U Ba Khin and
the monastic lineage of Mahasi Sayadaw—that have been instrumental in bringing Vipassana practice to the United States.[23] One of Ledi's
most influential students was the lay teacher Saya Thetgyi (1873–1945),
who taught Sayagyi U Ba Khin (1899–1971), the accountant general of
Burma. U Ba Khin continued the domestication of Vipassana by en-
couraging its adoption as part of a daily routine for householders. Like
Ledi, he drew on the *Abhidhamma* to formulate his distinct approach
to Vipassana practice, but he downplayed its importance for lay practitioners, who might not have the time or interest in studying Buddhist
doctrine. He presented Vipassana as a form of "practical Buddhism"
that could be practiced by anyone regardless of his or her religious or
cultural affiliations.[24]

U Ba Khin's most influential student was S. N. Goenka (1924–2013),
a successful businessman and one of the leaders of the Hindu community in Burma. Goenka studied with U Ba Khin for fourteen years before returning to India in 1969, where he began teaching U Ba Khin's
distinct "scanning" style of Vipassana. Goenka further radicalized the
modern reconstruction of Buddhist Vipassana practice by presenting
it as a nonsectarian, scientific "method of mental purification" that is
distinct from organized religion. The Buddha, Goenka declared, did not
teach Buddhism, but rather the dhamma, which is "a universal remedy
for universal ills."[25]

The most influential of Ledi's students was the renowned forest-
dwelling monk Mingun Jetawan Sayadaw (1870–1955). Mingun was
the first person to set up a center to teach meditation to laypeople in

a group setting in 1911.[26] His student Mahasi Sayadaw (1904–1982) became the most famous meditation teacher in Burma, and his method
of "dry Vipassana" has become the most commonly adopted form of
Vipassana in the United States. Ingrid Jordt offers a close examination of
Burma's largest meditation center, the Mahasi Thathana Yeiktha in Ran-
goon, which was established by Mahasi with the support of the wealthy
philanthropist Sir U Thwin and Burma's first prime minster U Nu. She
shows that Mahasi Thathana Yeiktha greatly differs from the traditional
Burmese monastery, with its exclusive focus on meditation, the massive
participation of the laity, and the principle role of monastics as meditation teachers. Mahasi Thathana Yeiktha also contravenes traditional
Burmese religious ideals in that its model religious figure is not the
forest-dwelling monk but the layperson engaged in full-time pursuit of
Nirvana in an urban bureaucratically organized center. This mass-scale
pursuit of enlightenment primarily by laypeople who are educated but
not trained in the scriptures is unprecedented in Buddhist history.[27]

Drawing from the Pali suttas and the *Abhidhamma,* as well as his
own meditative practice, Mahasi aimed to discover the quickest method
for attaining liberation. Like Ledi, he eschewed the traditional preliminary practice of calming meditation in favor of the "dry practice" of
insight meditation as prescribed in the *Mahasatipatthana Sutta.*[28] He
advocated the intensive practice of Vipassana during silent retreats that
could last up to several months, with a daily schedule of between sixteen
and eighteen hours of sitting and walking meditation. The primary aim
of Mahasi's approach was to attain *sotapanna,* or stream entry, the first
of the four stages leading to Nirvana. He believed that the laity could
directly experience advanced stages of realization without studying the
scriptures or renouncing the world. With his exclusive focus on Vipassana, Mahasi downplayed or eliminated many traditional Theravadin
practices, such as scholarship, devotional exercises, and merit-making
activities.

Within a few years of Mahasi's arrival at Mahasi Thathana Yeiktha, a number of similar meditation centers with Mahasi-trained monastic teachers were established all over Burma. At Mahasi Thathana
Yeiktha and its branch organizations more than one million people are
said to have reached the first stages of enlightenment. Centers in which

Mahasi's method was taught also appeared in neighboring Theravadin countries such as Thailand and Sri Lanka, as well as Indonesia and India. As Braun states, the mass lay meditation practice that was first developed in Burma has had a strong influence on many other Southeast Asian countries.[29]

Buddhist Modernism in Thailand: The Thai Forest Tradition

Unlike Burma, the Kingdom of Siam, later Thailand, was never formally occupied by a colonial power. Nonetheless, the influence of Western modernity was far reaching, and, like other Southeast Asian countries, Thailand witnessed significant political, social, cultural, and religious reforms during the nineteenth century. As Brooke Schedneck discusses, in mid-nineteenth-century Siam, the intellectual elites became interested in modern science and began to see certain traditional Buddhist practices as superstitious and counter to modern progress. In response to Western modernity, they fashioned a distinctively modern interpretation of Thai Buddhism. Over the course of the successive reigns of King Rama IV (1851–1868), Rama V (1868–1910), and Rama VI (1910–1925), they and other prominent figures claimed that early Buddhism had been free of magical folk practices and was essentially a rational and empirical religion. As Schedneck explains, this elite Siamese presentation of Buddhism discarded the traditional cosmological context of Buddhism to make it compatible with modern discourses of science and rationality and to counter Christian critiques.[30]

The modern reformation of Theravada Buddhism in Thailand can be traced to when Prince Mongkut, the future Rama IV, initiated the Thammayut sect while he was a monk (1824–1851). During his monastic tenure, Mongkut sent a number of monks to Sri Lanka to bring back Pali scriptures, and he also adopted the strict monastic lineage of the Mon people of Burma. As its name, Thammayut, or "those adhering to the law," suggests, the sect was characterized by a strict adherence to the rules of monastic *vinaya* (discipline) and the practice of forest meditation practices revived from the Pali Canon. Combining these features with a modern perspective on Buddhism as a rational religion, the Thammayut sect disparaged local faith practices as cultural accretions on the original tradition.[31]

Two Thammayut monks, Ajahn Sao (1859–1941) and his student Ajahn Mun (1870–1949), brought the Thammayut approach to the monastic lineages of northeast Thailand, whose forest monastics had become known for their magical powers and lax discipline. To reform these lineages, Sao and Mun not only reinstated the *vinaya,* but they also taught a rigorous meditation practice and affirmed that Nirvana was attainable in the present life.[32] Although the Mun lineage attracted a wide following in Thailand, as Schedneck notes, it never became a mass meditation movement there. Rather, the lay meditation movement that developed in Thailand came from a second sect, the Mahanikai, which adopted the Vipassana approach of Ledi Sayadaw.[33] Nonetheless, the Thai forest tradition would have a significant impact on the American Insight movement through Mun's disciple Ajahn Chah (1918–1992) and another Thai forest monk, Ajahn Buddhadasa (1906–1993).

After receiving teaching instruction from Mun, Chah spent seven years practicing in the ascetic forest tradition in the jungle. In 1954, he was invited back to his village to establish a monastery, now known as Wat Pah Pong, from which more than one hundred other branch monasteries have since developed in Thailand. In 1967, the American Ajahn Sumedho (1934–) became ordained under him, followed by a number of other Westerners, and in 1975, Wat Pah Nanachat, the first English-speaking monastery in Thailand, was established, with Sumedho as its abbot.[34] Sumedho and a number of other monks trained by Chah have since established monasteries in North America, Australia, New Zealand, and Europe.

Ajahn Buddhadasa began to systematically reinterpret Theravada Buddhism in the 1930s and came to national prominence in the 1970s. He demythologized Theravada Buddhism and made it compatible with scientific rationalism and social reform. Rejecting the traditional Buddhist separation of the mundane and supramundane realms, Buddhadasa located the everyday world as the true site of Buddhist practice and rendered its highest goals of realization accessible to ordinary people.[35]

Buddhist Modernism in Japan: The New Buddhism

Like Thailand, Japan was never directly colonized by a European nation-state; however, in the mid-nineteenth century, it began engaging the intellectual and cultural discourses of Western modernity as well as opening trade with the United States and sending elites to European universities. This period also witnessed significant threats to Japanese Buddhism from both the internal religious "other" of state Shinto and the external religious "other" of Christianity. In response, Western-influenced Japanese Zen priests and lay figures created the "New Buddhism," a thoroughly modernist presentation of Zen as the pure transhistoric and transcultural essence of Buddhism that was superior to Christianity and compatible with scientific advancement and social progress.

Robert Sharf offers a close examination of the historical and ideological emergence of New Buddhism, the distinctively Japanese iteration of Buddhist modernism.[36] The early years of the Meiji period (1868–1912) witnessed dramatic political and cultural changes and rapid modernization and industrialization. Against this backdrop, Shinto government officials mounted a strong campaign called "abolishing Buddhism" against the Tokugawa Buddhist establishment. They accused Japanese Buddhism of being both antimodern—institutionally corrupt, superstitious, and holding Japan back from scientific advancement—and antinationalist—a foreign religious import that did not reflect the innate cultural and spiritual sensibilities of the Japanese.[37]

In response to the dual challenges of Shinto government opposition and Western discourses of modernity, a group of elite, university-educated Japanese Buddhists fashioned a distinctively modern form of Buddhism. They admitted that Buddhism had become corrupt but attributed this to institutional and cultural accretions that had distorted the pure spiritual core of the tradition. In what came to be known as the New Buddhism, reformers presented a picture of a pure Buddhism that was rational, empirical, and compatible with modern science and social reform. One proponent of the Meiji reformist movement, Kosen Soen (1816–1892), for example, promoted a "nonsectarian" and "socially engaged" form of Buddhism and actively encouraged lay participation in Zen.[38] His student was Shaku Soen, who presented his vision of Buddhism as a universal scientifically compatible religion at the World's Parliament of Religion and who also devoted much of this time to training lay practitioners.[39]

Sharf points out that the typically cosmopolitan and intellectual proponents of New Buddhism were educated at universities that were highly influenced by modern Western discourses, and he identifies the determinative influence of Romantic critiques of institutional religion and Enlightenment values of universalism, science, and reason.[40] He claims, for example, that the framing of Zen as "pure experience" reflected the understanding in the works of Friedrich Schleiermacher, Rudolph Otto, and William James of the core of religion as a sui generis unmediated experience. This Western-influenced reconstruction of Zen as pure spirituality was then presented to unsuspecting Westerners as an historically authentic picture of Zen, which, moreover, was claimed to be superior to Christianity. According to Sharf, therefore, Meiji Buddhist reform figures subversively appropriated key values of Western modernity to form a modern picture of Zen that was used to challenge the religious and cultural hegemony of the West.[41]

Sharf has shown that the New Buddhism was distinct from traditional or classical Zen on multiple levels. He disputes the notion of a "pure experience" that can be uncoupled from its institutional and doctrinal constraints, noting that classical Zen is one of the most scholastic and ritualistic forms of Buddhist monasticism and that enlightenment in Zen is "constituted in elaborately choreographed and eminently public ritual performance."[42] He has also questioned the legitimacy of New Buddhist proponents, pointing out that they were largely laypeople who were not trained in traditional Zen monastic settings. Nonetheless, this modernist vision of Zen was largely embraced by Western scholars and lay practitioners as an historically accurate picture of traditional Zen until recent studies such as Sharf's illuminated its specifically modernist and nationalist contextual origins.[43]

Buddhist Modernism and Tibet

Because of its relative geographical isolation, unlike other Asian Buddhist cultures, Tibet did not encounter modernist influences. Tibet did not come under colonial control nor did Tibetans make any efforts toward modernization such as establishing Western-style universities, sending elites to be educated in Europe, or adopting modern technologies such as the printing press. As Lopez bluntly puts it: "Modern Buddhism did not come to Tibet. There were no movements to ordain women, no publication of Buddhist magazines, no formation of lay Buddhist societies . . . no efforts by Tibetan Buddhists to found (or join) world Buddhist organizations."[44] He does, however, identify one monk, Gendun Chopel (1903–1951), as a Buddhist modernist because on his travels to India and Ceylon, during the years 1934–1946, he encountered many aspects of modern Buddhism, and his travel journals contain Buddhist modernist musings on topics such as the compatibility of Buddhism and science and support for Dharmapala's Maha Bodhi Society.[45]

It was not until Tibetans traveled West after the 1950s Chinese occupation that they began to engage Buddhist modern discourses in any significant way. In 1959, the Fourteenth Dalai Lama escaped to India and has since become the most well-known Tibetan spokesperson for Buddhist modernism. His modernizing activities include promoting compatibility between Buddhism and science, calling for gender equality and democratization in Tibetan Buddhism, and advocating for the global adoption of universal ethics beyond religious particularity.[46] Chögyam Trungpa Rinpoche (1939–1987) was another key Tibetan diasporic figure in the construction of Buddhist modernism. Through his prolific and accessible writings, Trungpa's psychological interpretations of Buddhist cosmology and teachings on "secular enlightenment" were disseminated to a large Western audience. He also established a series of meditation centers that become known as the Shambhala lineage as well as Naropa University in Boulder, Colorado, which have served as influential Tibetan Buddhist modernist hubs.[47]

Buddhist Modernism as a Transnational Sect and New Historic Form of Buddhism

Several scholars examined specific Asian iterations of Buddhist modernism, but Donald S. Lopez took the study of "modern Buddhism" in a new direction by demonstrating its transnational character. Lopez dates the birth of modern Buddhism to August 26, 1873, when a public debate was held between a Wesleyan clergyman, Rev. David de Silva, and the Buddhist monk Gunananda in the town of Panadure outside Colombo in Ceylon during British colonial occupation. Gunananda, an educated monk who was learned in both the Pali Canon and the Bible, was declared the winner of the debate after presenting a philosophical version of Buddhism that was more rationally sound than Christianity. Lopez identifies Gunananda as the first recorded representative of modern Buddhism and then traces distinct but overlapping local varieties of modern Buddhism across Southeast and East Asia to Europe and North America, "where they have combined, sometimes uneasily, and condensed not into a particular variety of Buddhism, such as Burmese Buddhism or Korean Buddhism, but rather something simply called Buddhism."[48]

This transnational Buddhism shares a number of characteristics: it is rational, universal, socially engaged, free of cultural and institutional accretions and devotional and ritual practices, and it privileges meditation as an empirically verifiable practice at its center.[49] As we have seen, however, rather than being an accurate reflection of traditional Buddhism, this vision of Buddhism largely originated with Buddhist reformers responding to modernity and colonialism. Hence Lopez concludes: "It is perhaps best to consider modern Buddhism not as a universal religion beyond sectarian borders, but as itself a Buddhist sect. . . . Like other Buddhist sects, modern Buddhism has its own lineage, its own doctrines, its own practices . . . [and] its own canon of sacred scriptures."[50] He presents selections from this canon, or what he ironically dubs the "modern Buddhist Bible," from the writings of Asian Buddhist teachers such as Shaku Soen, Mahasi Sayadaw, the Dalai Lama, and Thich Nhat Hanh and Western figures such as Henry Steel Olcott, Paul Carus, Alan Watts, and Jack Kerouac.

Analyzing the representations of Buddhism that emerge from the works of these influential modern figures and their contemporaries, David McMahan reaches a conclusion similar to that of Lopez in calling for the recognition of Buddhist modernism as an historically new and unique form of Buddhism. His groundbreaking book *The Making of Buddhist Modernism* (2008) was one of the first academic works to treat and respect Buddhist modernism as a legitimate form of Buddhism with its own communities of practice rather than to see it as a mere dilution or Western misrepresentation of more authentic traditional forms of Buddhism. As he states, although Buddhist modernism is not historically found in classical Buddhist texts and lived traditions, it is not merely the fantasy of an educated elite Western Buddhist population. Rather, this new form of Buddhism has been fashioned by modernizing Asian Buddhists and Westerners deeply engaged in creating Buddhist responses to modernity. McMahan offers a nuanced understanding of Buddhist modernism that does not reduce it to the simple accommodation of Buddhism to Western modernity but respects the agency of its major Asian architects and highlights the ways in which it has been utilized to critique Western ethnocentrism and resist colonialism.[51]

McMahan was also the first scholar to tease out and analyze the specific modern discourses that have interacted with Buddhism to create a uniquely modernist form of the tradition. He draws from Charles Taylor to parse modernity into three major strands: scientific-rationalism of the Enlightenment, Romantic expressivism, and Western monotheism. Across these three discourses run two major modern themes: (1) a world-affirming stance located in everyday life and a subjective turn toward interiority and self-reflexivity and (2) the key modern values of individualism, egalitarianism, liberalism, democracy, and the importance of social reform. Examining the work of early Asian and Western Buddhist modernists such as Paul Carus and D. T. Suzuki and contemporary figures such as Thich Nhat Hanh and Mark Epstein, McMahan shows how these modern themes have combined with classical Buddhist doctrine to produce a new form of Buddhism that is marked by the cultural processes of detraditionalization, demythologization, and psychologization.[52]

The modern lineage of scientific-rationalism, for example, has created what McMahan calls "the discourse of scientific Buddhism," which is founded on the core claim of the essential compatibility of Buddhism and modern science. He traces the genealogy of this lineage through the early figures of Dharmapala, Henry Steel Olcott, and Paul Carus, showing how their presentation of Buddhism framed it as scientific and rational and presented the Buddha as an early empiricist. This lineage has flourished and matured in contemporary times as dialogues between Buddhists and scientists have been established through organizations such as the Mind and Life Institute. McMahan identifies two broad themes in this scientific lineage: the careful tracking of complementarities between the sciences and Buddhism, and the precise mapping of their respective spheres, often configured as the mind (Buddhism) and the material world (science). Both of these occur within a wider framing of Buddhism as a "science of the mind," which complements the empiricism of Western science.[53]

The other major discourse of modernity to shape Buddhism is Romanticism, with its themes of interconnection, mysticism, nature, spontaneity, and creativity. McMahan traces the American Romantic lineage from the Transcendentalists to the countercultural movements of the Beat Generation and hippies. He lingers on the pivotal work of D. T. Suzuki in constructing and facilitating a Romantic version of Buddhism. Suzuki was a senior student of Soen, who, as we have already seen, was a proponent of the Japanese modernist New Buddhism movement. In 1897, Soen sent Suzuki, who had been his translator at the World's Parliament of Religions, to live and work with the publisher Carus. A prolific writer and lecturer, Suzuki furthered the process begun by Soen of attempting to extrapolate the essence of Zen from the religious institution of Buddhism. He presented Zen as the pure experience of an unmediated encounter with reality and a spontaneous living in harmony with that reality. Rather than being an historical religious tradition, Zen was depicted as a universal mystical essence that resided at the core of all religious traditions and authentic creativity. Artists such as John Cage and literary figures from the Beat Generation embraced Suzuki's experiential, mystical, and aesthetic presentation of Zen. Alan Watts, Allen Ginsberg, Jack Kerouac, Philip Whalen, and Gary Snyder extended this Romantic lineage through their heavily selective portrayal of Buddhism that stressed its experiential and creative elements and discarded its ethical and communal contexts.

One prominent site in which both scientific-rational and Romantic lineages are evident is the modern transformation of meditation. As McMahan notes, one of the central characteristics of Buddhist modernism is the detachment of Buddhist meditation from its wider cosmological, ethical, and social contexts. The "detraditionalization of meditation" can be traced from the presentation of Vipassana as a universal and nonsectarian practice, seen, for example, in the teachings of Burmese teacher U Ba Khin and his Indian student Goenka, to contemporary secular iterations of mindfulness such as Jon Kabat-Zinn's mindfulness-based stress reduction, which is presented as a practice of "pure awareness." McMahan highlights the *decontextualization* of meditation from its cosmological and ethical religious context; the *individualization* of meditation, in which the practice has been transformed from a communal endeavor embedded within the sangha and wider community of laity to a private individual spiritual practice; and the *psychologization* of meditation, in which it has been rendered as a psychotherapeutic technique.[54]

McMahan takes North America as his main geographical site to examine Buddhist modernism and focuses particularly on the modernization of Theravada and Zen as the two traditions that established many of the enduring motifs of Buddhist modernism.[55] As his focus is on textual analysis, however, he does not engage the sociological or ethnographic scholarship on American Buddhist meditation-based convert lineages to any significant degree. I therefore offer a review of these communities to see the ways in which they continue the modernization of Buddhism begun during colonialism and display Buddhist modernist characteristics identified by McMahan.

Buddhist Modernism in America: Meditation-Based Convert Lineages

Although a couple of academic studies treating the emergence of Buddhism in North America were published in the 1970s, the study of Buddhism in America as a subfield of Buddhist studies took off around the turn of the twenty-first century.[56] Influential books include Charles S. Prebish and Kenneth Tanaka (eds.), *The Faces of Buddhism in America* (1998); Charles S. Prebish, *Luminous Passage: The Practice and Study of Buddhism in America* (1999); Duncan Ryuken Williams and Christopher S. Queen (eds.), *American Buddhism: Methods and Findings in Recent Scholarship* (1999); and Richard Hughes Seager, *Buddhism in America* (1999).

An early common distinction made in this scholarship was between two forms of Buddhism in America: one associated with Asian American immigrants and their descendants and one associated with largely white Euro-American converts. Prebish had coined the term "two Buddhisms" in 1979 to delineate between a conservative Buddhism that "places primary emphasis on sound basic doctrines shared by all Buddhists, and on solid religious practice" and a "flashy, opaquely exotic and 'hip'" form associated with new religious movements and the counterculture.[57] In a later article, "Two Buddhisms Reconsidered," he redefined the former to denote the type of Buddhism practiced by Asian American communities and the latter to signify that practiced mostly by white Euro-American converts.[58] Three years later, in his 1999 book *Luminous Passage,* Prebish followed Paul Numrich, who delineated between two ethnic groups: Asian immigrants and American converts who "pursue largely separate and substantively distinct expressions of a common religious affiliation."[59] The former were engaged in communal devotional and merit-making activities, and the latter were focused on meditation and Buddhist philosophy.

Seager reiterated the immigrant/convert distinction, noting that there was a "gulf" between the two communities. Whereas immigrants tended to be informed by cosmology and focused on ritual practice, converts tended to psychologize transcendental aspects of Buddhism and pursue meditation practice as a therapeutic technique.[60]

As Jan Nattier pointed out, however, this twofold typology was limited. For one, not all converts were Euro-American. There were also African American and Latino converts as well as Asian Americans who came from other religious or secular backgrounds. Hence, she suggested shifting focus away from race and ethnicity to the modes by which various forms of American Buddhism were transported to the United States. This resulted in a threefold typology: import, export, and "baggage" Buddhism. Of particular concern to us here is import Buddhism. Import religion requires two essential resources: money and leisure time. Hence, Nattier labels import Buddhism as "elite" Buddhism because groups of the import variety are founded and populated by people who are "mostly well-educated, financially comfortable, and overwhelmingly European-American."[61] She notes that the most striking feature of elite Buddhism, which cuts across its various denominational forms of Tibetan, Zen, and Vipassana, is the privileging of meditation practice. While Nattier's threefold typology offers a more comprehensive and nuanced understanding of different forms of Buddhism in North America, her category of "elite Buddhism" confirms the existence of a distinct meditation-based, largely white-populated convert form of American Buddhism.

Although the focus of the present book is on current developments in this "convert" or "elite" Buddhist lineage in North America, a few words of qualification are essential. First, both the "two Buddhisms" and the "three Buddhisms" typologies have come under necessary and warranted critique. Wakoh Shannon Hickey, for example, has demonstrated how racism and white privilege have operated in three ways under this distinction: (1) the presumed authority of white convert Buddhists to define what counts as real "American Buddhism," (2) the assumption that "white Buddhism" is authentically American and Asian Buddhism is a foreign tradition located in North America, and (3) the fact that white American Buddhists have received a disproportionate amount of attention from both academic and popular quarters.[62] Hickey's convincing critique points to the importance of using the categories of "convert" and "immigrant" carefully in order not to reproduce the white privilege that has undoubtedly operated within them.

Second, as I examine in this book, significant demographic shifts are occurring within meditation-based convert lineages that disrupt the immigrant/convert distinction. While American meditation-based convert communities have been overwhelmingly populated by Caucasians, they are becoming increasingly racially diversified. Chenxing Han's recent research, for instance, extends critiques of the two Buddhisms typology by showing the tremendous variety of approaches taken toward Buddhism by young adult Asian Americans. She shows that both Asian Americans from heritage Buddhist backgrounds and those from non-Buddhist backgrounds practice in meditation-based lineages.[63] The demographic picture is further complicated by the fact that some first-generation white converts have brought up their children as Buddhists, thereby rendering the label of "convert" redundant. Among these "dharma brats," as they are sometimes jokingly called, are two of the most popular younger American Buddhist teachers—Ethan Nichtern and Lodro Rinzler.

Third, although I identify meditation-based convert lineages as a case study for Buddhist modernism, this certainly does not mean that heritage (or other types of convert) communities have not been the agents and subjects of modernization processes. As Natalie Quli points out, a problematic consequence of the immigrant/convert split is the positioning of immigrant communities as a static, conservative, traditional "other" against which progressive, innovative, modern American Buddhism is defined and celebrated. However, Asian American heritage communities such as the Buddhist Churches of America have changed significantly over time and have also been shaped by and adopted certain features of Buddhist modernism.[64] Further transnational Asian Buddhist traditions such as Fo Guang Shan, Dharma Drum Mountain, and Soka Gakkai could also serve as fruitful sites for exploring Buddhist modernist themes. My decision to focus on meditation-based convert communities is solely a pragmatic one and certainly does not claim an exclusive modern status for these communities.[65] Nonetheless, as Lopez and McMahan suggest, North American meditation-based convert communities have been a particularly fertile ground for the growth of Buddhist modernism. I turn now to a closer focus on the ways in which such communities demonstrate modernist features.

Meditation-Based Convert Lineages: Core Characteristics and Issues

Emma Layman's *Buddhism in America* (1976) was the first book to hint at the emergence of a distinct form of American Buddhism. In her introduction, Layman asks, "Is there a characteristically American style of Buddhism?" While she acknowledges that American Buddhists were "directing [their] attention to how they may fashion an *American* Buddhism," she answers her question in the negative.[66] By comparison, journalist and Tibetan Buddhist practitioner Rick Fields has no hesitation in delineating a distinct white and middle-class lineage of Buddhism in America. In *How the Swans Came to the Lake: A Narrative History of Buddhism in America*, Fields traces the history of convert lineages from the eighteenth-century Orientalist scholar William Jones, whose work influenced the American Transcendentalists, to the Fourteenth Dalai Lama's popular tour of the United States in the early 1990s during which he declared that Buddhism was becoming part of American life.[67]

In later work, Fields provisionally adopted the term "white Buddhists" to refer to the fact that "the so-called missionary or Euro-American Buddhism, in all its bewildering variety, is largely white and middle-class."[68] He presents white Buddhism as largely influenced by the counterculture and heavily focused on gaining enlightenment through the intensive practice of meditation. It is marked by a "bent-for-enlightenment zeal" and "a bias towards hard-style monastic and yogic practice."[69] Fields identifies six general trends of white Buddhism: (1) it is largely a lay movement, (2) it is focused on intensive meditation practice, (3) it incorporates Western psychology as an adjunct to Buddhist practice, (4) it is shaped by a strong feminist current, (5) it values social justice action, and (6) it is marked by democratic approaches to power and authority.[70] He also comments on the absence of those aspects of Buddhism, such as devotion, gratitude, and ritual, that he places under the general category of "faith" and the lack of a strong communal context.

Charles Prebish, a pioneer in the academic study of Buddhism in North America, fleshes out Fields's characteristics with his delineation of five main developmental issues in American Buddhism. He begins by taking up the question of how to define a Buddhist in North America. He opts for self-identification rather than the traditional Buddhist criterion of "taking refuge." He agrees with Jan Nattier that Americans are "notorious non-joiners" and follows her adoption of sociologists Rodney Stark and William Bainbridge's models of "audience client," requiring nothing more than minimal commitment, such as occasional event attendance, and "client cult," in which a participant has more committed membership within a group. The important point Prebish makes is that American Buddhists tend to be individualistic and do not value or promote community participation.[71]

The first developmental issue is *ethnicity* and the "extremely tense and complex relationship" between Asian American Buddhists and non–Asian American Buddhists.[72] Prebish notes that heated debates have occurred between the two communities as white American converts present themselves as the sole creators and representatives of "American Buddhism," to be distinguished from the "Buddhism in America" practiced by Asian Americans. In 1991, for example, *Tricycle* editor Helen Tworkov claimed that Asian American Buddhists "have not figured prominently in the development of something called American Buddhism" and its proponents have been "almost exclusively, educated members of the white middle class."[73] Many Asian Americans were offended by this suggestion, which both ignored the contributions of their communities and also implied that Buddhism became truly American only when taken up by white Americans.[74]

Although Prebish problematizes the ways in which the convert/ immigrant split plays out and points to ways it might blur in the future, he accepts it as a core characteristic of Buddhism in America and identifies the second developmental issue as the *different modes of practice* associated with Asian immigrant and American convert communities. He claims that there is a consensus among researchers that "American converts gravitate towards the various meditation traditions of Japanese or Korean Zen, Vajrayāna, and *vipassanā*," whereas Asian immigrants maintain ritual or devotional activities. He sees such an exclusive focus on Buddhist meditation within American convert communities that he declares it has become a "onefold path" and its "own subculture."[75] Prebish negatively compares the privileging of meditation with Asian Buddhists who practice within a wider and more balanced context that values ethics and community.[76]

The third developmental area is *democratization*. Prebish categorizes Asian Buddhism as primarily hierarchical and authoritarian and contrasts this with the democratization and egalitarianism under way in American Buddhism. He delineates three key aspects to this "radical democratization" process: (1) shifting patterns of authority in Buddhist sanghas, particularly between monastic and lay communities; (2) increasing gender equality, with women in positions of leadership and authority; and (3) the presence of individuals pursuing a nontraditional lifestyle, particularly in regard to sexuality.[77]

The fourth developmental area is *engagement,* which focuses on the emergence of socially engaged Buddhism. He sees Buddhist social and political engagement as owing much to the work of Thich Nhat Hanh and highlights the prominence of the Buddhist Peace Fellowship in the United States. While socially engaged Buddhism is a "radical revisioning" of traditional Buddhism, Prebish celebrates it as providing creative responses to daily life issues and societal problems in the contemporary world.[78]

The fifth issue is *adaptation* or *acculturation*. On one hand, there are a number of American convert Buddhists who are enthusiastically engaged with fashioning a distinctively American form of Buddhism, freed from Asian cultural elements. Take, for example, Lenore Friedman's reflection: "In what unique and perfect form would the Dharma flourish *here, now?* In some places, there has already been a shaking-free from Asian forms and a collective searching for more authentic, indigenous ones."[79] On the other hand, there is considerable resistance toward this Americanization process, which critics label as a dilution of traditional Buddhism that demonstrates American cultural imperialism and arrogance. Canadian Rinzai Zen monk Victor Sogen Hori, for instance, wrote an article in *Tricycle* which concluded that calls for an Americanization of Zen were unnecessary and harmful.[80]

In the same year that Prebish published *Luminous Passage* (1999), Richard Hughes Seager also published a book on Buddhism in America that painted a very similar picture. He claims that during the 1980s, as the first generation of native-born teachers emerged, observers adopted the phrase "American Buddhism" to denote expressions of the dharma that had developed among converts and given rise to a uniquely American form of Buddhism.[81] Seager observes that the first generation of converts had put family-centered lay practice, gender equality, and the integration of Buddhism with psychology center stage. He also highlights a secularization process in which "the transcendent goal of practice is itself often psychologized or reoriented to social transformation."[82]

Sociologist James William Coleman's 2002 book *The New Buddhism: The Western Transformation of an Ancient Tradition* provided an early ethnographic study of the "new Buddhism" being fashioned across American meditation-based lineages.[83] He sees Western Buddhism as being most influenced by three forms of Asian Buddhism—Zen, Tibetan, and Theravada—so correspondingly bases his qualitative study on two Zen, two Tibetan, and two Vipassana Buddhist centers in North America, as well as one unaffiliated. Coleman claims that his data show a radical new Buddhism developing in the West, which has five main characteristics: (1) the distinction between monk and layperson has been almost completely erased; (2) there is a very strong focus on meditation practice; (3) there is a move toward gender equality and an increasing number of women in positions of authority and leadership; (4) there is broad-ranging eclecticism, which includes both a borrowing and a mixing of teachings across Buddhist and non-Buddhist lineages; and (5) there has been a restructuring of power and authority in response to the sexual scandals that have afflicted various American Buddhist communities.[84]

Coleman's analysis of the new Buddhism echoes the earlier findings of Fields, Prebish, and Seager, but he is unique in claiming a striking resemblance between the "new Buddhism" and "original Buddhism." As Coleman states, "In both the newest and the oldest Buddhism, the highest goal is not faith and belief, proper behavior, or ritual devotion, but the direct experience of enlightenment. Both attach great importance to the practice of meditation and both feel that liberation must spring from each individual's own life and practice, not the intercession of supernatural beings who have assumed such great importance in some forms of Asian Buddhism."[85]

Coleman also presents a clear demographic picture of the participants of the new Buddhism. Ethnically, the members are overwhelmingly white, tend to be from the middle and especially the upper-middle class, and are highly educated. Politically, they are very liberal and drawn to progressive causes such as environmental and human rights issues. Coleman finds that this population is attracted to Buddhism because of personal problems and that participants tend to use meditation as a form of therapy. Like Prebish, he also observes that they have little interest in relational or community building. As he noted, "The members of groups I surveyed did not assign particularly great importance to building new relationships or a sense of community."[86]

Coleman's study is of great value in offering one of the first sociological studies of American convert Buddhism, but it is limited in that it fails to recognize that this new Buddhism is a form of Buddhist modernism. One of the main problems is Coleman's lack of awareness of the historical emergence of the Asian Buddhist modernist movements from which the new Buddhism has developed. He offers a survey of the three main forms of traditional Buddhism but completely ignores the modernization of Asian Buddhism that occurred during colonialism. Instead, he divides Buddhism into two broad camps: a small monastic elite that has continued the quest for enlightenment, and forms of popular Buddhism that were concerned with faith, devotion, and merit making.[87] He then aligns Western convert Buddhism with the former and Asian American immigrant communities to the latter. As Quli notes, this essentially positions Asian immigrants as static foils for progressive Western Buddhists.[88]

Coleman unreflexively reproduces many of the tropes of modern Buddhism such that his book blurs the line between examining and performing Buddhist modernism. Take, for example, Coleman's claim that "the Buddha was . . . not a Buddhist. It was the institutional structures and traditions that grew up around Siddhartha Gautama's teachings that made Buddhism into what we traditionally call a religion."[89] Similarly, in numerous places, he talks dismissively of "the cultural baggage from the East."[90] As we have examined, a distinction between the universal teachings of the Buddha and religious/cultural features of Buddhism appears in Asian forms of Buddhist modernism. Coleman, in short, performs what he presents: a thoroughly modernist understanding of Buddhism.

In 2005, Wendy Cadge produced a rich, detailed ethnographic comparative study of Theravada Buddhism in the United States. She examines two Theravada-associated sites: Wat Mongkoltepmunee (known as Wat Phila), a Thai temple in Philadelphia, and the Cambridge Insight Meditation Center (CIMC), a convert center in Cambridge, Massachusetts, focused on the practice of Vipassana meditation. Her study is somewhat unique in that it undermines the distinction between immigrant and convert forms of American Buddhism by positioning each community on a shared spectrum and emphasizing similarities rather than differences between the two. Nonetheless, her data on CIMC present a clearly modernist form of Buddhism: the center focuses on individual meditation practice, which is largely taught divorced from Buddhist history and religious context, and participants tend to be suspicious of

what they consider ritual and devotional practices. Similarly, she finds
a great deal of flexibility around formal organizational or communal affiliation, with many people practicing at CIMC who have no interest in
religious forms of Buddhism.[91] That said, Cadge does gesture toward the
emergence of new patterns in convert meditation-based Buddhism. For
example, as counterbalance to the individualism, she finds informal but
strong networks of relationships. Similarly, she observes that although
CIMC initially focused on meditation practice, the center is increasingly
coming to recognize other aspects—rituals and ceremonies, ethical precepts, and communal gatherings—as support for it.[92]

Cadge frames her book by drawing from an encounter with the
Sri Lankan monk Bhante Henepola Gunaratana, who established the
Bhavana Society, a monastery and meditation society in West Virginia.
Gunaratana, an heir to Buddhist modernism in Southeast Asia, told
her about the Heartwood sutta, in which a number of people are trying
to find the core of a tree, but only one finds the heartwood. As Cadge
explains, "The true heartwood that the people in this sutta seek is the
perpetual, timeless emancipation from suffering." Whereas Gunaratana
sees the mostly white Americans practicing intensive meditation as the
practitioners who are truly seeking this heartwood, Cadge claims to
make no normative argument herself about the essence of Buddhism.
Nonetheless, like Coleman she unreflexively reproduces Buddhist
modernist rhetoric in the conclusion of her study by claiming that the
greatest challenge facing immigrants is keeping the dharma "from being crowded out by ethnic and cultural events," thereby reproducing the
essential split between dharma and cultural accretions.[93]

White Privilege and Buddhist Modernism
in North America

As discussed above, a common feature of American meditation-based
Buddhism has been to extend and align with the Asian Buddhist modernist trope of distinguishing between essential and cultural Buddhism
onto convert and Asian American immigrant communities. According
to Joseph Cheah, this has produced a hierarchical racialized split, which
has received scant and insufficient attention in scholarship on American

Buddhism. As a corrective, Cheah draws from critical race theory to illuminate a legacy of Orientalism and white supremacy from the Western Orientalists of the Victorian era to the contemporary Vipassana movement.[94] Cheah borrows from Lori Pierce to define white supremacy as "the conscious or unconscious promotion and advancement of the beliefs, practices, values and ideals of Euroamerican White culture, especially when those cultural values are represented as normal."[95] As a largely invisible hegemonic discourse, white supremacy operates as a standard of normality in convert lineages. For example, bell hooks has discussed how African Americans feel marginalized in white convert communities, and for some, participating within them "has been synonymous with choosing whiteness."[96] Both Cheah and hooks argue that white supremacy, as an unconscious cultural discourse, has largely shaped Euro-American convert communities.

Crucial to Cheah's argument is the distinction made by Michael Omi and Howard Winant between cultural and racial rearticulation.[97] Cheah extends their work to define "cultural rearticulation" as "a way of representing religious tradition from another's culture into ideas and practices that are familiar and meaningful to people of one's own culture."[98] Such a process is inevitable when religions travel across cultural contexts, and examples from Buddhist history include the sinicization of Buddhism in China. By contrast, "racial rearticulation" is "the acquisition of the beliefs and practices of another's religious tradition and infusing them with new meanings derived from one's own culture in ways that preserve the prevailing system of racial hegemony."[99]

Cheah's basic claim is that alongside cultural rearticulations there have been numerous examples of racial rearticulation in the Western adaptations of Buddhism. Cheah traces white supremacy in Euro-American convert lineages to Western Orientalists' racial rearticulations of Asian Buddhism in the late and middle Victorian era. He argues that Orientalist constructions of Buddhism are inextricably linked to and reflect racist discourses and colonial projects of that period. Orientalists were writing at a time in which Enlightenment, Social Darwinist, and eugenic conceptions of race were prevalent in Europe and North America. These conceptions naturalized and essentialized sociocultural and political differences between races and positioned white people at the top of racial hierarchies. It was the "white man's burden" to educate and civilize nonwhites, and one major avenue by which this occurred was through the critique of the religious traditions of colonized people from the perspective of reason and science. Cheah argues that these racial discourses were operative within the interpretive framework of an Orientalist construction of Buddhism. First-generation scholars such as Eugene Burnouf and Brian Houghton Hodgson and second-generation scholars such as T. W. Rhys Davids dismissed the ritual, merit-making, and devotional aspects of Asian Buddhism as "superstitions" and presented textual canonical Buddhism as "real" or "pure" Buddhism. Further, they arrogantly assumed that Asian Buddhists were ignorant of "true" Buddhism, which only the objective scholarship employed by philologists and classicists could uncover. For Cheah, therefore, the Orientalist reshaping of Buddhism along textual Protestant lines was not only an inevitable cultural rearticulation, but also "rooted in the racial ideology of white supremacy that privileges Euro-American cultures and religions over those of Asians."[100]

Cheah sees a continuation and preservation of this racial hegemony in contemporary American convert iterations of Buddhism and argues that there are numerous places of slippage between cultural and racial rearticulations in Euro-American Buddhist modernism. He identifies three places in which adaptation occurs in a way that reinforces the superiority and legitimacy of white experience. One of these is the existence of a racial hierarchy in American Buddhism seen in the "two Buddhisms typology." One articulation of this typology is between "convert" and "ethnic" Buddhism. As Wakoh Shannon Hickey points out, the term "ethnic" is applied only to people of color, as though white converts were free of ethnicity. Similarly, the adjective "American" in "American Buddhism" almost always refers to white Americans. A second way in which white supremacy manifests is the authority to define what constitutes "true" Buddhism. Many white American Buddhists present their forms of Buddhism in which meditation is the central component as the "true" Buddhism and elevate it over the "cultural baggage" Buddhism of Asian immigrants.[101] Cheah acknowledges that these claims are not intentionally racist, but he sees them as arrogant remarks that flow naturally from the ideology of white supremacy. A third place where white supremacy

manifests is the repurposing of Buddhist meditation to fit with and af-
firm Western cultural values. One example is the decontextualization
of mindfulness meditation from its soteriological and ethical context
and its repackaging and marketing as a secular "tool" in the arenas of
business and medicine. Cheah argues that this demonstrates the cultural
power of whiteness in which one can appropriate the religious practices
of another culture without any acknowledgment of their origins. As an
example, he points to Daniel Goleman, a *New York Times* best-selling
author, who commented that within his work on emotional intelligence,
"The Dharma is so disguised that it could never be proven in court."[102]

The text-based Buddhism of the Orientalists in the Victorian era
and the meditation-centered Buddhism of white convert lineages are
united in claiming authority on what constitutes true Buddhism. For
Cheah, such value judgments are rooted in and reflect white supremacy
and cultural imperialism and mark such positions as racial rather than
cultural rearticulations. Hence, he concludes, "Race has been the central, if latent, factor in the ways in which white Buddhists and sympa-
thizers have translated Buddhist texts and adapted Buddhist practices to
the Western context."[103]

The work of Cheah and others such as Hickey and Quli who have
problematized the racialized dimensions of the immigrant/convert typology in American Buddhism raises the question of whether whiteness
as a discourse of modernity should be seen as a distinct and core characteristic of Euro-American Buddhist modernist lineages. As we have
seen, the distinction between "real" and "cultural" Buddhism is a key
component of Asian Buddhist modernism. Cheah recognizes that Asian
modernizers bequeathed their Western students a rationalized and demythologized form of Buddhism and in many cases taught Vipassana
meditation in a nonsectarian manner. For Cheah, the difference between Asian and Western modernizers, however, is that while the former downplayed the cultural aspects of their tradition, their meditation
practice remained firmly rooted in daily observance of the Triple Gem
(Buddha, dharma, and sangha) and devotional and ritual activities of
traditional Buddhism. However, he acknowledges that by making meditation available to the laity, Burmese and Thai Buddhist modernists,

"perhaps inadvertently, had set the stage for separating the practice of Buddhist meditation from the rest of religious life."[104]

Cheah also recognizes that Southeast Asian Buddhist figures used this modern distinction subversively to resist colonialism and Western ethnocentrism. In the racialized context of the United States, however, one way this distinction has functioned has been to promote a hegemonic racialized discourse. Hence, even if one does not agree with Cheah that race is the *central* factor in Euro-American adaptations of Buddhism, it is indisputable that white privilege has been a core factor in shaping North American meditation-based convert communities. Hence, in addition to McMahan's characteristics of Buddhist modernism, I add white privilege as a distinct characteristic of Buddhist modernist meditation-based communities in the United States.

Recent Developments in Meditation-Based Convert Lineages

As Scott Mitchell and Natalie Quli have recently observed, numerous dramatic changes have occurred in the social and cultural landscapes of North America since the first wave of academic studies on American Buddhism were done more than a decade ago.[105] One massive change has come through the growth of the Internet and social media, which have fundamentally altered patterns of communication. How have information culture and the digital age affected American convert lineages? Another significant development is the explosion of the secular mindfulness movement, which has been accompanied by both enthusiasm and resistance from the wider American Buddhist community. On one hand, the mindfulness movement demonstrates a radical extension of Buddhist modernist narratives; on the other, the backlash to it from certain quarters of the Buddhist world shows an interrogation of those narratives. Also of note is the increasing impact of Buddhist racial diversity and inclusion initiatives, which, reflecting wider cultural conversations on racial justice in the United States, are moving from the margins to the mainstream in certain meditation-based Buddhist communities. Finally, as the first generation of American boomer teachers

nears retirement, a new generation of Gen X and millennial practitioners is fashioning new approaches to Buddhism.

Jay Michaelson has tracked some of the changes, or what he calls
the "evolution of dharma," in a post-boomer American Buddhist landscape. As Michaelson notes, Western dharma discourse has been largely
shaped by the culturally specific framework of the boomer generation.
However, despite these communities being marked by democratic and
egalitarian trends, they have been "slow to catch up with the post-white,
post-modern, post-conventional and fully wired world of younger Buddhists (and post-Buddhist) practitioners."[106] Michaelson discusses the
ways in which new communities such as the Dharma Punx, Pragmatic
Dharma, and Buddhist Geeks, which are heavily populated by Gen X,
Gen Y, and millennial practitioners, are offering alternatives to the type
of dharma fashioned by the boomers. He identifies two main avenues of
change—online communities and posttraditional teachers—by which
the dominant modern liberal culture of American Buddhist convert lineages is being challenged and transformed.

Michaelson's reflections on the convergence of American Buddhism and postmodern identities and digital culture resonated with
my fieldwork data on two American Buddhist convert communities:
the East Bay Meditation Center in Oakland, California, and the virtual
network of Buddhist Geeks. In both cases, I identified the emergence
of patterns more associated with postmodern and postcolonial rather
than modern discourses. For example, I found that the center's culture
of diversity interrogated several elements of modern liberal convert
Buddhist communities and discourse. Its commitment to diversity and
intersectionality challenged the white, middle-class hegemonic demographic of convert lineages. It also undermined the common convert
distinction made between "essential dharma" and "cultural Buddhism,"
with a number of participants rendering visible and critiquing the racist
and colonialist underpinnings of such a distinction.[107]

As explained in the introduction, in interpreting these emerging
patterns within convert communities as more reflective of the postmodern than modern, I picked up a thread laid down by McMahan in
the conclusion of *The Making of Buddhist Modernism*. To explore how
American meditation-based convert lineages have been influenced by

and reflect the wider cultural shift from the modern to the postmodern, I offer six case studies of recent developments within these communities. The first three of these examine the unfolding of three of the main characteristics of Buddhist modernism: the Enlightenment-scientific lineage, the Romantic–depth psychology lineage, and the privileging of individual meditation practice. The following three identify some of the most pressing emerging issues in convert lineages: racial diversity and inclusion, technology and social media, and generational changes in teacher and practitioner demographics. Although these six case studies are by no means comprehensive or exhaustive of all of the shifts occurring in convert lineages, they should indicate whether it is useful and necessary to think of American meditation-based convert Buddhism as having entered a new period, what McMahan, extending Martin Baumann, dubs a "globalized postmodern Buddhism."[108]

From the Mindfulness Revolution
to the Mindfulness Wars

Hosted annually in San Francisco since 2010, the Wisdom
2.0 conference brings together tech entrepreneurs, ven-
ture capitalists, and various Buddhist and mindfulness lu-
minaries to investigate how to live and work with greater
awareness, compassion, and wisdom in the digital age. At the 2014 conference, a panel on Google's flagship Search Inside Yourself mindfulness program was just about to begin when three protestors strode onto
the stage. Later revealed to be members of the housing rights advocacy
group Heart of the City, they unraveled an "Eviction Free San Francisco"
banner and announced "Wisdom means not displacement," "Wisdom
means not surveillance" before repeatedly chanting "San Francisco: not
for sale." Conference organizer Soren Gordhamer and staff quickly es-
corted the protestors off the stage, with an awkward struggle ensuing as
one of them attempted to wrestle the banner out of a protestor's hands.
The audience appeared confused as to how to respond: some clapped,
others laughed nervously, and one person shouted, "I'd like to listen to
the presenters, please." Bill Duane, one of the three panelists, took charge
of a tense situation by inviting participants to use the disruption as a
"moment of practice" to see what it was like to come into contact with
people who had "heartfelt ideas" that might be different from their own.
Leading an impromptu body-scan meditation, Duane ended with a call

to meet conflict with compassion rather than judgment and extend this compassion to the protestors, panelists, and audience members alike. Enthusiastic applause followed, and there was no further discussion of the issues raised as attention returned to the advertised panel topic.

Much discussion ensued, however, as news of the protest erupted on Buddhist social media and press. On one side, Engaged Buddhists expressed support for the disruption and highlighted the unjust and dangerous working conditions of many of the Asian workers manufacturing technology as well as the devastating effect gentrification processes bound up with the tech boom were having on working-class San Francisco residents. Regardless of how much benefit individuals and corporations were gaining from bringing mindfulness techniques to the workplace, critics argued that these wider structural inequalities conflicted with Buddhist notions of wisdom and ethical principles of "nonharming" and "right livelihood." In a reflection for *Tricycle*, protest organizer and practicing Buddhist Amanda Ream explained that the protest was not only directed at the gentrification of San Francisco but the gentrification of the dharma itself. While professing respect for the American Buddhist teachers such as Sharon Salzberg who had taught at the conference, she called on Buddhists to investigate who was being excluded as the dharma went mainstream in a capitalist society.[1]

In response, Wisdom 2.0 released a statement that praised the Google panelists for responding to the protestors with mindfulness and compassion and thereby ensuring that an "emotionally jarring interruption was transformed into a moment of awareness and peace."[2] While the statement made no reference to the issues of gentrification, it emphasized a narrative of skillful wisdom that started with individual mindfulness practice and naturally expanded to transform organizations and the world. Similar sentiments appeared in comment threads across the Buddhist blogosphere. Many voices expressed appreciation for the mindful leadership modeled by Duane; others referenced Buddhist teacher Thich Nhat Hanh's reflection that if practiced with correct intention, mindfulness had the potential to positively transform corporate culture.

The Wisdom 2.0 disruption and the debates that followed capture many of the wider trends and tensions surrounding the secular mindfulness movement. The participation of luminaires such as Salz-berg, Jack Kornfield, and Joan Halifax at the conference suggests a stamp of approval from the American Buddhist establishment. As the protests indicated, however, not all practitioners are happy about this movement. This chapter examines the ambivalent relationship between American Buddhist convert communities and the mindfulness move-ment and tracks some of the major patterns around mindfulness that have emerged from within those communities.

American Buddhism and the Mindfulness Revolution

In 2011, leading Buddhist press Shambhala Publications published *The Mindfulness Revolution*. Edited by Barry Boyce, a longtime practitioner of Tibetan Buddhism, the anthology featured reflections on mindfulness practice from many of the heavyweights of American Buddhism such as Joseph Goldstein, Jack Kornfield, Pema Chodron, Thich Nhat Hanh, and Chögyam Trungpa Rinpoche, as well as prominent psychologists and scientists such as Daniel Goleman and Daniel Siegel. Boyce's introduc-tion simultaneously established a strong connection between Buddhism and mindfulness and uncoupled the two: on one hand, the Buddha was historically the most well-known mindfulness practitioner and the practice was at the very basis of Buddhism; on the other, similar prac-tices existed before the time of the Buddha, and over the previous thirty years, mindfulness, as pioneered by Jon Kabat-Zinn, had blossomed as a secular practice detachable from Buddhism. Mindfulness is able to cut across religious and secular worlds because it is based "on fundamen-tal mental and physical capabilities that all humans have, irrespective of any ideological views they may hold."[3] The universality of mindfulness accounted for the growing scientific acceptance of the practice as being beneficial to physical and emotional well-being across a variety of con-texts ranging from education to sport, health care to business.

Across the essays in the book, Buddhist and secular, particularly scientific, perspectives blended seamlessly. This was achieved primarily by separating Buddhism as a religious and cultural particularity, and dharma as the universal truth underlying and ultimately separate from that historic particularity. The only hint of discord raised was by Zen

Buddhist Norman Fischer, who confessed that as a "religious person" who had spent most of his adult life in monasteries and who saw the Buddhist soteriological goal of Nirvana at odds with ordinary goals such as well-being, he had initially viewed Kabat-Zinn's work with some skepticism. His suspicion was soon overcome, however, because "I learned from him that what I read in the ancient Buddhist texts was true: the path is available to everyone and must be shared, and to guide others effectively, you must be willing to use whatever comes to hand ('skillful means')."[4] In short, Fischer legitimated mindfulness as an expression of the Mahayana concept of *upaya*, or skillful means: it was a pragmatic modality that rendered an "esoteric" practice accessible to a much wider range of people. Alongside the framing of mindfulness as universal dharma, skillful means was the primary Buddhist concept used to legitimate mindfulness as Buddhist in the collection.

In the first academic text to present a cultural history of the American mindfulness movement, Jeff Wilson offers a more substantial fleshing out of Boyce's basic trajectory of mindfulness from Buddhism to the boardroom vis-à-vis Asian and American Buddhist modernist lineages. Wilson defines the mindfulness movement as "the widespread and growing collection of people who practice (and, especially, those who actively promote) techniques of awareness derived originally from the Buddhist cultures of Asia, which are typically grouped under the label 'mindfulness' in 21st century America."[5] He correctly notes that it was the nineteenth-century British Orientalist scholar Thomas William Rhys Davids (1843–1922), founder of the Pali Text Society, who first translated the Pali word *sati* as "mindfulness." In the early Pali texts, such as the *Satipatthana Sutta*, mindfulness was presented as a component of the Noble Eightfold Path, which was aimed toward the soteriological goal of Nirvana and was taught exclusively to the monastic community. However, the practice of meditation fell into decline in traditional Buddhism and by the tenth century CE had mostly died out in Theravada Buddhism. It was revived and refashioned only through the Buddhist modernist reforms that occurred across Southeast Asia during colonialism. As examined in chapter 1, following the Burmese leader Ledi Sayadaw, Southeast Asian Buddhist teachers began teaching mindfulness en masse to a lay audience for the first time in Buddhist history.

Wilson charts how mindfulness practices came to North America vis-à-vis the major Asian Buddhist modernist teachers and their American students starting at the beginning of the twentieth century.[6] He identifies the 1970s as the main turning point for the mindfulness movement as during this decade the three major players and institutions dedicated to disseminating mindfulness emerged. One of these was the Insight Meditation Society (IMS), which was established on May 19, 1975, to provide a retreat environment for the intensive practice of Theravada Buddhist meditation. The four American cofounders of IMS—Joseph Goldstein, Jack Kornfield, Sharon Salzberg, and Jacqueline Schwartz—had all recently returned to North America after spending several years in Asia training under Asian Buddhist monastic and lay teachers. They extended the modernization process initiated by their Asian teachers by discarding what they saw as Asian "cultural baggage" and rendering the dharma in a form that was most accessible for an American lay audience. As Kornfield explains, "We wanted to offer the powerful practices of insight meditation, as many of our teachers did, as simply as possible without the complications of rituals, robes, chanting and the whole religious tradition."[7]

In the 1980s, Kornfield and other Insight teachers decided they wanted to focus less on intensive retreat practice and more on integrating practice with daily life. They opened Spirit Rock Meditation Center in Woodacre, California, in 1996, which offers classes such as "Mindfulness and Everyday Life," alongside more classical Buddhist presentations such as "The Four Foundations of Mindfulness." As well as being at the forefront of teaching mindfulness in a Buddhist context, teachers from IMS and Spirit Rock have played a central role in the secular mindfulness movement.[8] Diana Winston, a member of the Teachers Council at Spirit Rock, for example, is the director of mindfulness education at the Mindfulness Awareness Research Center at the University of Southern California, one of the major mindfulness research institutions in the United States.

Wilson identifies the Vietnamese Buddhist modernist monk Thich Nhat Hanh as the second major figure in the mindfulness movement. Hanh was trained in the Thien tradition, which is influenced by both Japanese Zen and Theravada Buddhism, and was influenced by Asian

Buddhist reformists such as the Chinese monk Taixu. He began teaching meditation to Westerners in the 1970s after being exiled from Vietnam and founding Plum Village monastery in France. As exemplified in his 1976 book *The Miracle of Mindfulness,* Hanh's teaching emphasizes the application of mindfulness to daily activity. He is a prolific author of mindfulness texts and has built a massive international network of practice groups known as the Community of Mindful Living and a monastic and lay community, the Order of Interbeing, both of which place mindful living at their center. The Order of Interbeing, for example, is committed to following the Fourteen Mindfulness Trainings, which are described as a distillation of the Bodhisattva teachings of Mahayana Buddhism, and members of the community also produce a journal, *The Mindfulness Bell,* which is dedicated to "the art of mindful living." Although based in France, Hanh has three monasteries in the United States and, since his exile from Vietnam, toured the US nearly every year since until he suffered a stroke in 2014. He is often featured in Buddhist and mainstream magazines as a seminal mindfulness leader and has visited corporations such as Google and the World Bank headquarters to teach mindfulness.[9]

The third and arguably most influential figure in the mindfulness movement is scientist and meditation teacher Jon Kabat-Zinn, who took mindfulness completely out of a Buddhist context through pioneering mindfulness-based stress reduction (MBSR), the first and most well-known of medical mindfulness modalities. Kabat-Zinn's Buddhist background fits the typical profile of first-generation American convert Buddhists. White, upper-middle class, and highly educated, he trained both with the Korean Zen modernist teacher Seung Sahn, who founded the Providence Zen Center, and with Goldstein, Salzberg, and Kornfield at IMS. It was on a Vipassana retreat in 1979 that Kabat-Zinn had a vision of bringing mindfulness to the University of Massachusetts Medical Center, where he was doing his postdoctoral research working with people who had chronic pain. In 1979, he founded the Stress Reduction Clinic at the medical center, which offered a ten-week program, later remodeled into eight weeks, that was originally named the "Stress Reduction and Relaxation Program" but was renamed MBSR. Recontextualizing mindfulness from a Buddhist practice to a mainstream medical one,

Kabat-Zinn discarded all religious terminology and redefined mindfulness as a simple, systematic practice of cultivating awareness that could be used for physical and mental pain management.

The growth of MBSR has been extraordinary. By 2015, more than twenty thousand people had participated in the program at the University of Massachusetts Medical Center, which had produced one thousand certified MBSR instructors; MBSR programs appeared in about 720 medical settings in more than thirty countries. MBSR is taught not only in medical and therapeutic settings, but also in educational, military, corporate, and prison settings. Following its success, other forms of mindfulness-based therapy have been developed, such as mindfulness-based cognitive therapy. Kabat-Zinn's 1995 book *Wherever You Go, There You Are: Mindfulness Meditation in Everyday Life* became a best seller, and since then the number of books on mindfulness, ranging in topics from medicine to creativity, has exploded.[10]

Reflecting on how mindfulness transitioned from being a popular Buddhist modernist practice to a mainstream secular one, Wilson notes three interrelated trends: (1) the loss of Buddhist control over mindfulness as it became increasingly detached from its Buddhist context; (2) the application of mindfulness to a wide range of pragmatic concerns, from increasing work productivity to having better sex; and (3) the marketing of mindfulness to a non-Buddhist audience. These secular iterations have not replaced Buddhist-based mindfulness, but they exist alongside it.[11] Wilson's narrative ends with very little commentary on how American Buddhists have responded to these secular iterations.

In texts such as *The Mindfulness Revolution*, the crossover between Buddhist and secular mindfulness communities appears seamless and mutually supportive. Yet not all Buddhist practitioners have been positive about the relationship between the two.

"McMindfulness": The Buddhist Backlash

With mindfulness appearing on the cover of *Time* and news anchor Dan Harris's mindfulness guide *10% Happier* reaching number 1 on the *New York Times* best-seller list in April, the *New Republic* declared 2014 to be the "Year of Mindfulness."[12] Even quicker than the embrace of mindfulness in the mainstream media, however, was the backlash against it. As the *Guardian* sympathetically put it, "If 2014 was the year of Mindfulness, 2015 was the year of fruitlessly trying to debunk it."[13] Buddhist commentators had reported similar patterns even earlier. In December 2013, Justin Whitaker, author of the popular Buddhist blog *American Buddhist Perspective* (now *Perspectives*), published a short overview of the increasingly heated exchange between critics and defenders of mindfulness.[14] Hence, when Per Drougge published a review of mindfulness critiques under the title "Notes Towards a Coming Backlash" in March 2016, the "coming" appeared both understated and dated.[15]

In fact, concerned Buddhists had delivered critiques of mindfulness much earlier. Targeting the form of mindfulness taught within the Western Insight movement, a 2006 conversation between Bhikkhu Bodhi and Alan Wallace, whose conclusions were reiterated in a 2008 *Tricycle* article, highlights many of the concerns that came to the forefront of the secular mindfulness debates.[16] The authors pointed out that the common understanding of *sati* within the Vipassana community as nonjudgmental "bare attention" is not supported in the Pali Canon, which defines "right mindfulness" not as an ethically neutral state, but as a form of awareness that clearly distinguishes between wholesome and unwholesome mental states. Classical mindfulness, they emphasized, is always practiced within the ethical and soteriological context of the Noble Eightfold Path. While Bodhi quoted the Pali Canon, "The Tathāgata [Buddha] has no closed fist of a teacher," as license for teachers to use mindfulness as an aid to reduce suffering, he was concerned that proponents claimed that present-centered awareness contained the whole of the dharma. Wallace went further in his critique, lamenting that the modernization of Buddhism had produced inexperienced teachers, the dismissal of Buddhist philosophy as dogmatic "mumbo-jumbo," and the dilution of meditation into a therapeutic technique. Taken together, he declared, these signified a "degradation of the whole Buddhist tradition."[17]

The affective tones of concern and outrage expressed in the conversation between Bodhi and Wallace were to be echoed and extended in Buddhist critiques of the secular mindfulness movement. Many of these have been signified in the rhetorical trope "McMindfulness," which was coined by Miles Neale, a Buddhist psychotherapist and codirector of the Nalanda Institute for Contemplative Science. In a December 2010 *Shambhala Sun* interview, Neale expressed some concerns about mindfulness in an overall enthusiastic reflection on its adoption in education. While affirming the value of making mindfulness widely accessible as a universal mental training technique rather than a particular religious activity, Neale acknowledged that meditation was only one of the three components of the Buddhist path and asked what might be lost when mindfulness was uncoupled from wisdom and ethics. He identified the emergence of "McMindfulness," which he defined as "a kind of compartmentalized, secularized, watered-down version of mindfulness" that was following a trajectory similar to that of the commodification of yoga in the United States and becoming part of "the commercial self-help supermarkets."[18]

Although coined by Neale, the term was launched into popular currency by David Loy and Ronald Purser in "Beyond McMindfulness," a July 2013 *Huffington Post* blog that went viral.[19] The authors critique mindfulness from a canonical perspective, noting, like Bodhi and Wallace before them, that the Pali Canon distinguishes between "right mindfulness" (*samma sati*) and "wrong mindfulness" (*miccha sati*). The former is a state of awareness inseparable from wholesome intentions and is represented by a figure such as the Dalai Lama. The latter is an ethically neutral state that could be cultivated in figures such as "a terrorist, mindful assassin and white collar criminal." Hence for all of its individual therapeutic benefits, the authors maintain, uncoupling mindfulness from its ethical and soteriological context amounts to a "Faustian bargain." This canonical critique then takes a sharp sociocultural turn by contextualizing the adoption of mindfulness in business in relationship to the culture of corporate wellness. Purser, who is a professor of business, compares corporate mindfulness to training programs that have been discredited for attempting to pacify employees' complaints without changing the corporate structures responsible for those complaints. He argues that corporate mindfulness is little more than the latest individualist method for self-fulfillment, which deflects attention away from the structural injustices of capitalism.

"Beyond McMindfulness" is a significant marker of Buddhist critiques of mindfulness on multiple levels. It was the first to reach an extremely large audience, and it initiated a wave of analyses, many of which were also published online, which taken together constitute a substantial mindfulness backlash. The authors of these commentaries, for the most part, are not Buddhist teachers but rather lay practitioners with academic backgrounds who often identify as "Engaged Buddhists" and have formed an active network. Hence alongside the increase in mindfulness critiques has been the emergence of the mindfulness critic. At the forefront of these is Purser, who has taken on an active public and professional identity as a mindfulness critic. The article also moves seamlessly from a traditional critique, which problematizes mindfulness as canonically unsound, to a sociocultural one, which problematizes mindfulness primarily on the grounds of its complicity with socioeconomic structural injustices—a switch in register that was to gain considerable momentum in the following critiques.

One persistent critique of secular mindfulness from Buddhist quarters is that the popular understanding of mindfulness as nonjudgmental bare awareness is unsupported in the Pali Canon. This criticism is the same one leveled at Insight practice in the Western Vipassana community by Bodhi and Wallace and has been reiterated by a number of Buddhist scholars and monastics. American-born Theravadin monk Thanissaro Bhikkhu provides an example of a classical canonical critique of mindfulness. In *Right Mindfulness: Memory and Ardency on the Buddhist Path* (2012), Thanissaro takes aim at two misconceptions: the understanding of mindfulness as bare attention and the belief that mindfulness practice alone is sufficient to achieve awakening. As a corrective, he offers a close reading of mindfulness in the Pali Canon that emphasizes its intractable relationship to the other components of the Noble Eightfold Path and maintains attention on liberation as the soteriological goal of the practice.[20]

Closely related to the canonical critique is that of the ethics of teaching mindfulness in contexts that might conflict with core Buddhist teachings of nonharm, right livelihood, and interdependence. This criticism tends to denounce the adoption of mindfulness in corporations and the military and revolves around two main rhetorical tropes: the "mindful sniper," that is, military personnel who have been trained to be more effective killers, and the "mindless worker," or employees who passively accept unjust economic systems. In "Abusing the Buddha: How the U.S. Army and Google Co-Opt Mindfulness," for example, Buddhist teacher Michael Stone confesses that he has become concerned that a practice originally rooted in an ethics of nonharm is now being used in institutions that are complicit in violence and greed.[21]

While canonical critiques seek to problematize secular mindfulness by measuring it negatively against Buddhism, Buddhist scholar-practitioner Robert Sharf takes a different route by assessing it as a problematic form of Buddhism. In "Is Mindfulness Buddhist? (And Why It Matters)," Sharf situates the mindfulness debates as a contemporary iteration of earlier tensions within Buddhist history.[22] Reiterating that the definition of mindfulness as present-centered awareness is at odds with the Pali Canon, Sharf acknowledges, however, that a similar understanding of meditation was present in both eighth-century Chan Buddhist and Tibetan Dzogchen lineages. As with contemporary mindfulness, Sharf notes that movements with Chan and Dzogchen also aimed to render Buddhist practice accessible to laypeople who were not trained in Buddhist scholasticism or renunciation and that they also promised quick and powerful results from their simplified practices. Underlying these popular currents was the Buddhist innatist view of awakening that one could spontaneously realize one's inherent Buddhahood. Sharf sees a similar innatist view—a belief in a universal mystical state ultimately detachable from Buddhism as religious institution—operating within the mindfulness movement. Like mindfulness proponents, Chan popularizers were met with suspicion and criticism from traditional Buddhists for devaluing ethical, ritual, philosophical, and institutional components of the path. Although written for an academic audience, Sharf's work circulated across the Buddhist blogosphere, and his rhetorical trope of "mindlessness" reappeared in popular critiques.

Sharf focuses on the ways in which mindfulness and its predecessors conflicted with traditional Buddhism and then draws sociocultural conclusions. He argues that the experiential approach to Buddhism seen in medieval Chan, Japanese Buddhist modernism, and the secular mindfulness movement lends itself to passive assimilation into dominant and oppressive sociocultural structures. To explore the sociocultural critique in more detail, it is useful to break it down into three main interrelated components: capitalism, scientism, and colonialism.

The underlying thread of sociocultural Buddhist critiques of mindfulness is a problematizing of how mindfulness has become assimilated to and complicit in Western materialism rather than providing an alternative and challenge to it. Many of these critiques draw more on Marxist critical theory than Buddhism to target the intersections between capitalism, neoliberalism, and corporate mindfulness. They echo cultural critic Slavoj Žižek's 2001 critique of Western Buddhism as providing the perfect ideological supplement for the smooth functioning of global capitalism. Žižek argues that Asian religious teachings of renunciation and acceptance illustrate Marx's theory of religion as the opium of the people. As he puts it, "The 'Western Buddhist' meditative stance is arguably the most efficient way for us to fully participate in capitalist dynamics while retaining the appearance of mental sanity."[23]

In their article "Corporate Mindfulness Is Bullsh*t: Zen or No Zen, You're Working Harder and Being Paid Less" Ronald Purser and Edwin Ng apply Žižek's critique to secular mindfulness. They highlight structural inequalities and injustices that persist across educational, prison, and military settings despite the "mindfulness revolution" and claim that mindfulness has been adopted as a "cultural idea" to facilitate capitalism. They argue that rather than encourage workers to question the social and economic conditions that produce stress, mindfulness discourse locates stress within the individual mind and puts the responsibility on the individual rather than the corporation to cope with it. Identifying as "socially engaged Buddhist critics," the authors say they are neither dismissing the individual therapeutic benefits of mindfulness nor defending traditional approaches to mindfulness but rather "stressing the need to collectively address systematic problems that generate stressful conditions in the first place."[24]

A major part of the marketability of mindfulness has come from its scientific reframing and validation. In a series of *Tricycle* interviews, contributing editor and Tibetan Buddhist Linda Heuman has questioned both the science and scientism operating within the mindfulness movement. In dialogue with scientists and cultural critics, Heuman laments that scientific studies of mindfulness lack rigor and produce inconclusive results yet have been overhyped and irresponsibly marketed. Further, she raises concerns about how Buddhism is becoming assimilated to science with little attention to the many fundamental incompatibilities between its metaphysical worldview and the materialism underlying scientific perspectives.[25]

Purser and Buddhist editor and writer Andrew Cooper see this scientism as a form of neocolonialism, arguing that not only is scientifically legitimated mindfulness pushing traditional Buddhism out of the picture, but mindfulness proponents are engaging rhetorically in a "war on the Buddhist tradition." They target claims from mindfulness proponents that the science has liberated mindfulness from "the flaky, foreign, irrational, outdated and spooky metaphysics of religious tradition." At the core of this dismissal of traditional Buddhism as outdated and irrelevant is the belief that the dharma as universal essence can be uncoupled from Buddhism as a religious institution. The authors locate this search for the universal core of religion within Western perennialism and argue that it is inseparable from the colonial enterprise.[26]

Purser and Cooper's targeting of mindfulness as a form of neocolonialist cultural appropriation is further developed in a dialogue between Purser and Ng titled "White Privilege and the Mindfulness Movement." Ng argues that the separation of the universal dharma from the religious-cultural tradition of Buddhism erases the history of colonialism by which the former was "extracted" from the latter. As he puts it, this uncoupling "effaces the longstanding relations of domination and exploitation that allow one to receive the gift of the Dharma in the first place, a gift inherited from generations upon generations of non-Western, non-white others who have dutifully maintained the teachings for millennia." Furthermore, he questions the universality of the dharma, noting that in places, Kabat-Zinn's discourse situates white people outside of culture and takes their particular experience as the universal human model. Purser and Ng identify this as evidence of the "whiteness" and "white privilege" of the mindfulness movement and see analogous patterns of "white fragility" in the responses of mindfulness proponents when faced with such critiques.[27]

Buddhist Defenses of Mindfulness

The mindfulness critiques were directly countered by leading mindfulness proponents such as Jon Kabat-Zinn and *Mindful* magazine editor Barry Boyce. For example, in their pointedly titled article "This Is Not McMindfulness by Any Stretch of the Imagination," Edo Shonin and Kabat-Zinn reiterate that secular mindfulness is an authentic expression of the dharma and that when it is taught by an experienced teacher, it has the same transformative potency as in a traditional context.[28] Similarly, Boyce has emphasized teacher quality and argued that mindfulness practice could lead to real positive change in the workplace.[29] The first substantial Buddhist responses came in the Spring 2015 edition of *Buddhadharma: The Practitioner's Quarterly*, whose cover featured a woman in medical scrubs sitting cross-legged on a hospital floor with the title "The Mindfulness Movement: What Does It Mean for Buddhism?"[30] Jenny Wilks, an Insight meditation teacher and a mindfulness-based cognitive therapist, introduced the accompanying forum with an acknowledgment that although one might assume that Buddhists would be delighted at the success of secular mindfulness, many, in fact, had responded with ambivalence and criticism. Four Buddhist teachers who had been heavily involved with mindfulness attempted to allay such concerns: Melissa Myozen Blacker, the abbot of Boundless Way Zen Temple, who directed programs at the Center for Mindfulness; *Mindful* magazine editor Barry Boyce, who is a longtime Vajrayana practitioner; Diana Winston, a member of the Teachers Council at Spirit Rock and director of mindfulness education at UCLA's Mindful Awareness Research Center; and Trudy Goodman, the founder of InsightLA, which offers training in MBSR as well as Vipassana classes.

The panelists rebutted what they saw as the three main Buddhist concerns: that mindfulness is a diluted form of Buddhism for the masses, that it has no ethical orientation, and that it fosters compliance with unjust social and economic systems. Both Winston and Goodman dismissed these concerns, arguing that they did not reflect the actual work being done "on the ground." Attributing critiques to "more fundamentalist Buddhists," Goodman pointed out that in Asia as well as in the West, only a minority of practitioners were doing what "dyed-in-the-wool

Buddhists would recognize as pure practice." Referring to Zen texts, she pointed out that Buddhism has always offered a range of pragmatic benefits such as better health and prosperity. Moreover, she concluded, the dharma could not be diluted because, "If it really is our true nature to be clear, calm, sane, and good," practice would eventually lead to realization.

Blacker did sympathize with concerns that mindfulness was becoming reduced to a self-help technique. She attributed this to teachers "not quite getting the nondual aspect of mindfulness" and focusing on self-improvement rather than self-awakening. Goodman and Boyce agreed that the problem was a focus on easy, instant results rather than on developing a different relationship to suffering. Their main concern was ensuring the quality of teachers, who would embody and enact an ethical approach to mindfulness that maintained the integrity of practice and not promise "quick fixes." Whereas earlier mindfulness trainings had been largely led by people with Buddhist backgrounds, more people without sufficient meditation experience were teaching mindfulness. Winston dubbed this the "Wild West of Mindfulness" and advocated for quality control, standardization, and professionalization of the field. Moreover, she felt that Buddhists "have profound gifts to help the new generation of mindfulness teachers preserve what's possible in deep practice." Stressing complementarity rather than competition between mindfulness and Buddhism, participants claimed that mindfulness not only had made Buddhist practice accessible to a much wider non-Buddhist population, but had also stimulated interest in many people in learning more about Buddhism. The panelists' ultimate concern, however, was neither Buddhism nor mindfulness but rather a universal capacity for awakening, which preceded both systems. As Goodman put it, "realization is our birthright as human beings—it's not Buddhist, or any '-ist.'"[31]

Buddhadharma's forum illustrates the four main Buddhist counters to mindfulness critiques: (1) a *canonical legitimation* argument that draws on Buddhist concepts such as *upaya,* or skillful means, to legitimate secular mindfulness as having Buddhist precedence; (2) an *historic continuity* argument that emphasizes continuity and compatibility rather than discontinuity and contrast between Buddhism and mindfulness (for example, the claim that Buddhism has always offered a range of pragmatic benefits alongside its elite soteriological goal of liberation and that it has always been embedded in unjust sociocultural and economic systems); (3) an *experiential/functional* argument that privileges "on-the-ground" narratives of the ways in which mindfulness works to reduce individual suffering and, in some cases, positively affects wider institutional systems; and (4) an *ontological/religious* argument that uncouples a universal awakening from Buddhism and privileges it over Buddhism or any particular religious system. As with the *Buddhadharma* forum, these distinct arguments are often interlaced in Buddhist defenses of mindfulness. Below, however, I provide examples in which one argument is most dominant.

Some Buddhists have sought to legitimate secular mindfulness through recourse to canonical Buddhism, drawing on both the Pali Canon and the Mahayana sutras. Such Buddhists do not dispute that the understanding of mindfulness as bare attention is not congruent with its description in the Pali Canon, but they have still turned to the latter to provide Buddhist legitimation for the practice. For example, Lynette Monteiro, R. F. Musten, and Jane Compson, who have strong ties to both Buddhist and mindfulness communities, have drawn on a close reading of the Pali Canon and Buddhist scholar Rupert Gethin's reading of it to argue that the path of liberation reflects a universal law that transcends Buddhism. While Buddhism provides a particular set of trainings to align oneself with this law, they argue that there is no reason why other trainings that are not explicitly Buddhist, such as secular mindfulness, cannot also provide this function. The authors further point out that the concept of Buddhism as a reified bounded religious tradition is itself a result of Western colonialism. They do acknowledge ethical concerns around possible negative consequences of introducing mindfulness in military and corporate settings but point out that the Pali Canon emphasizes the role of intentionality as the key factor in the karmic outcome of an action as wholesome or unwholesome. In conclusion, they call for a mutually enriching dialogue between Buddhist and mindfulness communities, suggesting that the challenge is for contemporary mindfulness teachers to develop universal ethics that are in accord with but not identical to Buddhist ethics. According to these authors, "To essentialize mindfulness as a religious, Buddhist practice not only closes the door to such dialog, but it is also to misrepresent the Dhamma taught by the Buddha, which presents the Eightfold Path to the cessation of suffering as his discovery, not his creation, with the law of the Eightfold Path having universal applicability."[32]

Monteiro, Musten, and Compson's reading of the Pali Canon found support from Theravadin monastic Ajahn Amaro, who directly responded to their work. While offering some linguistic clarification and conceptual nuance around the concepts of *sati* and *sila*, Amaro basically affirms their reading of the dharma as a universal law that transcends a particular religious rendering. He argues that within the Pali Canon, the Buddha takes a pragmatic rather than dogmatic approach to freedom from suffering and that there is "no reason in principle why familiarity with explicitly 'Buddhist' teachings are a necessary condition for such liberation." He also accepts their claim that Buddhism makes meta-ethical assumptions that are not tradition-specific and have universal application as an accurate representation of traditional Buddhism. He concludes that for traditional Buddhists, the classical teachings can be freely practiced by anyone without expectation of that person becoming Buddhist. Amaro points out, however, that while Theravada Buddhism does not have an exclusive or proprietary claim on mindfulness, it does offer a "holistic mindfulness" that includes the well-being of others and can provide a useful model for developing secular mindfulness.[33] Therefore, like Monteiro, Musten, and Compson, Amaro proposes a dialogical rather than an oppositional relationship between the two. His response is significant because it comes from a monastic who moreover explicitly states that he is representing the "traditionalist standpoint," thereby undermining the common framing of the mindfulness debates as reflecting conflict between traditional and secular perspectives.

Secular Buddhist Doug Smith also applies pressure to the traditional/secular oppositional framework through appeal to the Pali Canon. Smith agrees that secular mindfulness does not contain all that is of value in the early Buddhist path, pointing particularly to the emphasis on dukkha and renunciation in the latter. However, he notes that many mindfulness critics overlook and misrepresent much of the Buddha's earliest recorded teachings. He argues that the Buddha was not opposed to profit and that nothing in the Pali Canon suggests he would be necessarily against market capitalism. Far from being an ethical puritan, Smith continues, the Buddha allowed for "a slightly off-kilter or 'dumbed down' Dhamma within the lay community." Hence, Smith concludes that if people's concern is with recovering Buddhism's original liberative purpose as recorded in the Pali Canon, Engaged Buddhist critiques are misrepresentative, and their "fictional view" of the early teachings actually reflect the teachings of the historical Jesus rather than the historical Buddha. In short, while not unsympathetic to critiques of the commodification of mindfulness, Smith finds little support within early Buddhism for socially engaged Buddhist critiques.[34]

Other Buddhists have looked to the Mahayana and Vajrayana sutras to support the mindfulness movement, pointing out that there are understandings of mindfulness in Zen and Tibetan traditions that are more congruent with contemporary modalities. John Dunne, a Buddhist scholar-practitioner, for example, delineates between two distinct Buddhist approaches toward mindfulness: one rooted in the *Abhidhamma* in the Pali Canon and the other in the nondual teachings of the Tibetan Mahamudra tradition. He suggests that MBSR adopts a nondual approach to practice and finds support and Buddhist legitimacy from Mahamudra and other nondual Buddhist lineages.[35] Another Mahayana concept that mindfulness proponents draw on is *upaya,* or skillful means. As noted earlier, alongside mindfulness as "universal dharma," *upaya* is one of the primary strategies advanced by Jon Kabat-Zinn in his framing of mindfulness as congruent with Buddhism. Reiterating this, editor Rod Meade Sperry introduced the September 2016 "Buddhist Guide to Mindfulness" issue of *Lion's Roar* by declaring: "Our feeling here at *Lion's Roar* is very much in line with the Buddha's teachings on *upaya,* or 'skillful means.' Boiled down, this means that it takes all kinds, so you share teachings accordingly, trying to deliver to people whatever works best for them."[36]

Closely related to the canonical legitimacy argument is the view that rather than represent a contemporary aberration or denigration of Buddhism, mindfulness actually continues many of its historic patterns. This argument aims at destabilizing an ahistorical and romantic version of Buddhism as always being concerned with liberation and above worldly matters such as health and wealth. Seth Zuiho Segall, a Zen priest and mindfulness researcher who runs a popular Buddhist blog titled *The Existential Buddhist,* provides an example of this. In reflecting on criticism directed at the participation of Buddhists and mindfulness teachers in economic gatherings such as the World Economic Forum in Davos, Switzerland, he argues that such involvement is historically congruent with a tradition that has always been entangled with the ruling class. As he explains:

> Some people react as if this is a kind of betrayal, as if the Dharma was solely the possession of the dispossessed. This, in fact, has always been the way the Dharma has percolated through societies. The Buddha advised kings and Brahmans. It was King Ashoka who spread the Dharma throughout India. In China and Japan, Buddhism was adopted by elites before it disseminated throughout the broader culture. Seminal figures like the Buddha, Nagarjuna, Shantideva, and Dogen were members of their respective aristocratic classes by birth, and often taught and advised other members of their class.[37]

Similarly, in response to Buddhist critiques of *Time*'s "Mindful Revolution" edition, Buddhist scholar-practitioner Pierce Salguero points to the similar promises and advertisements of health and well-being benefits of Buddhist practice that were forwarded by practitioners in medieval China. Salguero is not necessarily defending mindfulness, however; he is pointing out the historical inaccuracy of seeing its emphasis on pragmatic benefits as somehow incongruent with traditional Buddhism.[38] On the same note, mindfulness proponents have also pointed to occasions in which Buddhism has been complicit in nationalism and state violence, such as Japanese Zen's role in World War II and present-day Buddhist violence against Muslims in Southeast Asia. In short, these defenses of mindfulness understand it as continuing rather than disrupting historic Buddhist patterns and thereby attempt to undermine an oppositional framework between the traditional and secular that often undergirds critiques of the practice.

The experiential argument places ultimate value on the fact that secular mindfulness *works* to reduce suffering. Defenders claim that people working on the ground rarely share Buddhists' alarm around mindfulness because they witness firsthand the many transformative effects it has in a variety of contexts. *Tricycle* editor Wendy Joan Biddlecombe, for example, offers snapshots of people who have taken an MBSR course. One of these is a cancer survivor who says that she felt "transformed from the get-go"; another is a police lieutenant who reports that mindfulness helped him be more compassionate with the people he encounters in his work. While acknowledging the value of critiques, Biddlecombe directs attention to what she sees as the more pressing questions: "How have these people's lives been impacted? What do *they* have to say about the effects of mindfulness practice?"[39] Chris McKenna, program director at Mindful Schools, makes a similar point: "You go into a public elementary school in Oakland, and you see the lack of resources and regulation and time, the pile of mandated programming that these educators have to sort through, and then you get some basic mindfulness training up in that joint, and you see a classroom of kids go silent for two minutes, and you feel what's happening in the room—the cynicism goes away."[40]

In some cases, these first-person experiential narratives are accompanied by empirical data. Segall states in his blog "In Defense of Mindfulness": "The more important question isn't semantic, but empirical: Is mindfulness, as currently construed, useful or not? Does it reliably and meaningfully impact matters that human beings care deeply about, things like the perennial Buddhist concerns of sickness, old age, and death?" Segall draws on both his own experience of teaching mindfulness and a number of scientific studies to argue that mindfulness reduces both physical and psychological pain. Furthermore, he rejects what he labels as a "purist" approach to Buddhism and argues that the reduction of suffering and an increase in happiness are as valid aims for Buddhists as the search for liberation.[41]

Secular Buddhist and mindfulness facilitator Mark Knickelbine also takes a pragmatic route by declaring he is "dismayed by the fact-free nature of the mindfulness backlash," which he believes is driven largely by fear and not rooted in any specific evidence. He has written a number of articles defending mindfulness, which draw authority from his experience teaching mindfulness and privilege the experiential perspective with phrases such as "as every MBSR student knows."[42] An even stronger pushback comes from his colleague Ted Meissner, who is the founder of the Secular Buddhist Association and teaches at the Center for Mindfulness. Meissner is an ardent defender of mindfulness and decries what he sees as the "evidence-free fear mongering" underlying critiques of mindfulness in business and the military. He lambasts critics for trying to prevent mindfulness reaching populations that have a need and right to benefit from its scientifically proven results in reducing psychological and physical pain.[43]

Central to the experiential "mindfulness works" argument is a faith in the *intrinsic* power of mindfulness—often rendered here as equivalent to or an expression of the dharma—without the explicit context of Buddhism. As Knickelbine puts it: "My sense is that too many people have been introduced to the transformative power of dharma practice for it to be eradicated at this point. Trying to live mindfully, to embrace all of the suffering and joy of life, is the most difficult thing I have ever attempted, and I believe this is true for others as well. That we are still doing it is an indication that this is more than a fad. I trust the dharma."[44]

Another common response to Buddhist critiques of mindfulness has been an assertion of the distinction between awakening as a universal capacity and Buddhism as one particular but not exclusive vehicle for that expression. Take for example Sperry's rebuke to Buddhist critiques: "When the concern is that those who take up secular mindfulness practice will never become Buddhists, well, so what? Buddhists shouldn't want more Buddhists. Buddhists should want more enlightenment for more people. And enlightenment is hardly for only Buddhists."[45] This argument is an extension of mindfulness as "universal dharma" and should be identified as an alternative religious view—a perennialist nondual mystical approach—rather than a view that transcends religions. Although scholars correctly track the origins of the Western perennialist approach to the Romantic embrace of Asian religions during colonialism and its flowering in the 1960s counterculture, as Sharf pointed out, one finds Buddhist parallels in Buddhist Chan and Dzogchen lineages.[46]

One significant consequence of this perspective is that it positions Buddhism and mindfulness as both able in varying degrees to access this awakening. In most cases, advocates of this view tend to see mindfulness as a more accessible but less transformative practice. For example, my interviews with thirty-three Buddhist Gen X teachers, a large percentage of whom taught secular mindfulness, revealed two common rhetorical tropes for talking about mindfulness—"entry-level dharma" and a "doorway to the dharma"—both of which were used to express the view that although MBSR was less potent than Buddhist practice, it could still open people to "profound experiences" and serve as an "expression of awakening."[47] In other cases, proponents place them as different but essentially equivalent practices of awakening and propose a mutually beneficial dialogue between the two. Knickelbine, for instance, states that he has great respect for traditional Buddhism and does not want to replace it with mindfulness but rather put the two in conversation.[48] More unusual, among Buddhist-identified figures at least, is the view that mindfulness is superior to Buddhism. Meissner, for example, sees mindfulness as an "evolutionary advance" over Buddhism and says that he has found MBSR teachers to be "far more skillful and authentic than some of my traditional teachers."[49]

In addition to these four distinct defenses of mindfulness, Buddhists have responded in two main ways to Neo-Marxist socioeconomic critiques of corporate mindfulness. The most common response is that systematic transformation is ultimately rooted in individual transformation and that the latter is likely, albeit not guaranteed, to positively affect institutional contexts. Mirabai Bush's reflection on teaching mindfulness in ethically problematic corporations such as Monsanto captures this position well. As she puts it: "The corporation is a legal structure, based on return for investors, and that basic nature is unlikely to change until we develop a new economic system. But it is people who make the decisions, create the products, determine the profit margin."[50] Closely related to this argument is that the charge of the "mindless worker" misrepresents the nature of mindfulness practice, which does not encourage passivity and compliance but rather fosters a deeper engagement with the world. Also related is the concept of "stealth Buddhism," a term introduced into Buddhist/mindfulness circles by Trudy Goodman. In a 2014 Buddhist Geeks interview, Goodman suggested that through secular mindfulness, implicit, transformative Buddhist teachings were being disseminated into secular spaces such as businesses.[51] Stealth Buddhism is often linked to the "Trojan horse" approach, which proposes that mindfulness practice has an implicit ethical dimension that will inevitably influence the wider institutional context in which it is taught.

A second main response to socioeconomic critiques is to argue that it is neither the intention nor the function of mindfulness to overcome capitalism so it is not fair to judge it against this standard. In some cases, respondents are sympathetic to anticapitalist critiques but do not believe that mindfulness should be singled out as the problem. Theravadin monk Ajahn Sujato, for example, states that "mindfulness is what it is" and should not be measured against its capacity to change an unjust world.[52] In other cases, respondents are more dismissive of the charges. Segall, for instance, points out, "The Buddha, after all, taught that life is suffering, not that capitalism is suffering."[53]

Beyond Mindfulness: Emerging Buddhist Trajectories

While early reflections from Buddhists involved in the secularization of mindfulness included acknowledgment of some of its potential problems, the mindfulness backlash has affected a deeper consideration from the American Buddhist community across a range of forums. In *Tricycle* articles, Buddhist teachers such as Joseph Goldstein and Phillip Moffitt clarified differences between traditional and secular mindfulness and emphasized the importance of the ethical and soteriological context of the former.[54] Similar points were raised at an online Shambhala Buddhist conference, "Beyond Mindfulness: Explore Mindfulness as a Path to Wisdom and Transformation," cohosted by Fleet Maull and angel Kyodo williams, for which more than twenty-four hundred people registered. In several places, Maull emphasized the "provocative" title of the conference and said that there were valid concerns among Buddhists about whether the fullness of tradition was being represented in the mindfulness movement. As indicated by their descriptions, presentations tackled some of the popular misunderstandings of mindfulness: "Hear why 'mindfulness' means more than just being in the present," and "Learn why mindfulness is not all that we need, and clarify potentially harmful misunderstandings of mindfulness."[55]

Just as clarifications of mindfulness have been occurring in public Buddhist forums, Buddhist teachers have been bringing these conversations to mindfulness trainings. Diana Winston, for example, has been tackling concerns about mindfulness at the annual Mindfulness Facilitators Retreat she coteaches at Spirit Rock. In a 2014 talk titled "The 12 Myths of the Mindfulness Movement," she addresses many misperceptions of mindfulness, such as its false marketing as an ultimate panacea and the unreliability of many of the scientific studies exploring it.[56]

An explicit affirmation of a new "beyond" stage in mindfulness comes from Vince Horn, cofounder of Buddhist Geeks and Meditate.io. Horn identifies what he calls "the 2nd Generation of mindfulness" and borrows from the "hype cycle of technology" model to distinguish three stages in mindfulness: the peak of inflated expectations, which expresses the optimism of the mindfulness revolution; the trough of disillusionment, which concerns the mindfulness backlash; and the plateau of enlightenment, which looks forward to emerging approaches to mindfulness. Horn counts himself as one of many—Buddhists and non-Buddhists—who are "starting to reimagine mindfulness as an imperfect tradition which can incorporate its criticisms and evolve in response to the most valid points." He predicts that this evolution will result in more relational forms of mindfulness taught by teachers who are more cognizant of the ethical dimensions of the practice and more critical of capitalism.[57]

In general, Buddhists such as the "Beyond Mindfulness" presenters, Winston, and Horn remain optimistic about the transformative power of mindfulness yet fully acknowledge the challenges it faces as it goes mainstream in consumerist culture. I have distinguished four main responses to these challenges: (1) an engagement with social justice, (2) an explicit engagement with Buddhism, (3) an implicit engagement with

Buddhism, and (4) a movement to fully distinguish between Buddhism and mindfulness. Although these responses often overlap, examples that focus on each response individually are useful.

One distinctive pattern emerging among American Buddhists is an attempt to enrich mindfulness through more engagement with diversity and inclusion and social justice perspectives. The most vocal proponents within the Buddhism community have been socially engaged Buddhists. Maia Duerr, former director of the Buddhist Peace Fellowship, for example, suggested that Buddhists develop a "Socially Responsible Mindfulness Manifesto," which would emphasize mindfulness as a tool for collective and personal liberation and include a pledge not to teach mindfulness in unjust conditions.[58] She contacted Theravadin monastic and Engaged Buddhist Bhikkhu Bodhi for feedback, and he responded that the development of socially just forms of mindfulness requires not only a significant departure from individualistic secular models of mindfulness, but also from the classical Pali form. Bodhi has produced a document titled "Modes of Applied Mindfulness" that differentiates four types of mindfulness: classical, secular therapeutic, secular instrumental, and socially transformative. Each mode has its own function, ultimate aim, and problem. For example, the function of classical mindfulness is to facilitate insight, its ultimate aim is liberation from the cycle of rebirth, and its problem is that it may lead to narcissistic self-absorption and indifference to socioeconomic inequities. The function of socially transformative mindfulness is to foster greater social and economic justice in order to promote the realization of a just and peaceful world. Bodhi stresses that mindfulness practice alone is not sufficient to bring about these transformative societal conditions and has offered a teaching called "conscientious compassion," which combines mindfulness with the responsibility to take effective action to ameliorate the suffering of others. For Bodhi, a sense of justice—which he defines specifically as "the objective decree that holds we have to establish a social and economic order and a political system which [are] respectful to every human being, and which [enable] every human being to unfold their full potential and capacities"—is too often missing from mindfulness training.[59] He believes that there are neglected suttas within the Pali Canon that provide Buddhist support for combining justice and mindfulness perspectives and has recently published an anthology of the Buddha's teachings on social and communal harmony.[60]

Another iteration of the social justice turn includes Buddhist teachers and communities that offer mindfulness to activists and people of color. One example is Kaira Jewel Lingo, who was an ordained nun for fifteen years in Thich Nhat Hanh's Order of Interbeing and now teaches mindfulness and compassion as a lay dharma teacher. Lingo offers secular mindfulness training as well as trainings in the engaged mindfulness tradition of Thich Nhat Hanh for specific audiences, including environmental activists and people of color. Another is Insight Buddhist teacher Ruth King, who has developed "Mindful of Race," a training that combines mindfulness with an exploration of racial conditioning, which she offers for groups and organizations.[61] The East Bay Meditation Center in Oakland, California, is also a central hub for mindfulness from an Engaged Buddhist perspective. Senior teacher Mushim Patricia Ikeda teaches mindfulness to social justice activists and uses Bhikkhu Bodhi's applications of mindfulness in her training curriculum. She affirms the multiple ways that mindfulness can function within an overarching Engaged Buddhist framework from short-term stress reduction to facilitating insight not only into the conditioned nature of the self, but also into unjust structures of society that can be transformed into more liberating collective spaces.[62]

In addition to the emergence of specific Buddhist teachers and communities promoting socially just iterations of mindfulness, initiatives and conversations around diversity and inclusion have become more common in the Buddhist-mindfulness networks. These include such things as attempts to ensure diverse faculty representation in mindfulness organizations, to offer diversity and inclusion trainings for mindfulness teachers, and to provide scholarships for people of color to participate in trainings and programs. I interviewed four directors of mindfulness-training organizations who had backgrounds in Buddhism, and they all shared ways in which they incorporated diversity and inclusion concerns into their organizations: Peace in Schools, the Mindfulness Institute, Inward Bound Mindfulness Education, and SATI: Mindfulness Workshops and Coaching. For example, Jessica Morey, cofounder of Inward Bound Mindfulness Education and long-term Insight practitioner, said: "I think the ethical, social justice, and societal aspects of these teachings will be emphasized. What's the role of mindfulness practice in social justice, climate change, and capitalism? These questions are so immediate and critical we have to focus on them."[63]

A second distinctive pattern emerging among American Buddhists includes efforts to enrich mindfulness through an explicit engagement with its wider Buddhist ethical and soteriological context. Against the Stream Buddhist teacher Dave Smith, who teaches secular mindfulness in prisons, youth detention centers, and addiction facilities, provides an example of such a Buddhist turn. Smith has called on the secular mindfulness community to engage more with the foundational teachings of Theravada Buddhism. He feels that secular mindfulness is at a "critical juncture" and wants to see more collaboration between mindfulness and Buddhist communities.[64] Smith's book *Ethical Mindfulness* opens with the strong endorsement that mindfulness meditation saved his life, but he was able to fully heal only through practicing the complete Buddhist path. Similarly, he reports that in his work with vulnerable populations, he has had a greater transformational impact when he has been able to offer a range of Buddhist teachings and practices. Drawing on the Four Noble Truths, the *Brahma-viharas* (sublime abodes), and the five lay precepts, Smith has developed "ethical mindfulness"—an approach that adds the *intention* of the nonharming of self and others to the emphasis on *attention* in secular mindfulness. Smith believes it is irresponsible to discard the Four Noble Truths because mindfulness is intrinsically a Buddhist practice and it is disingenuous not to be transparent about its origin. He identifies honesty and pragmatism as factors in his decision to "come fully out of the closet" as a Buddhist teacher in his secular mindfulness work.[65]

Lama Karma Justin Wall, the resident teacher at Milarepa Dzong Retreat Center in Tennessee, proposes that a dialogue with Tibetan Buddhism can enrich mindfulness. Wall completed a yearlong training certification at the Mindful Awareness Research Center at UCLA in 2015, and although positive about the program, he feels that the lack of engagement with the deeper wisdom teachings of Buddhism in mainstream secular mindfulness limits its transformative potential. "I want to see the mindfulness movement being enriched and informed by Tibetan

Buddhism," he explained. "Its metaphors are naturalistic and experiential. It would make a very easy transition."[66] Wall sees his response as part of an emerging trend to incorporate compassion into mindfulness programs, such as at Stanford University's Compassion Cultivation Training program and Emory University's Cognitively Based Compassion Training. Both of these programs draw on the Tibetan Lojong, or mind training tradition, but Wall notes a reluctance to include the theory and practice of groundlessness that permeates the Mahayana source tradition of mind training. He wants to harness groundlessness as the basis of globally sustainable ethical action and develop a "groundless ethics of wisdom and compassion." Wall sees a similar approach in the work of Denys Rinpoche, who has pioneered the method of Open Mindfulness Compassion, which is a secular adaptation of Dzogchen, Mahamudra, and Lojong practices.[67]

Lisa Dale Miller has also drawn from Tibetan Buddhism to reintroduce the soteriological context of mindfulness. A psychotherapist, Miller has trained in both Insight and Tibetan lineages and feels that, as "someone steeped in both worlds," she has something important to contribute to the Buddhist-mindfulness debates. She rejects Kabat-Zinn's claims that MBSR is an expression of the Buddhadharma as "too grandiose" and argues that MBSR is too stripped down to qualify as an authentic expression of Buddhism. In order to "bring the dharma back, to teach the actual dharma to clinicians," she wrote *Effortless Mindfulness: Genuine Mental Health Through Awakened Presence,* a book that draws heavily on various but particularly Tibetan Buddhist teachings to promote a soteriologically explicit form of nondual mindfulness. Miller says the aim of the book is to reunite clinical mindfulness with its source—Buddhist psychology and philosophy—and thereby move beyond mindfulness as a practice of symptom reduction to one grounded in and pointing to the liberating recognition of the emptiness of all phenomena.[68]

Zen Buddhist teachers Robert Meikyo Rosenbaum and Barry Magid suggest that secular mindfulness can benefit from an encounter with both the philosophical depth of Zen Buddhism and the pragmatic experience of American Zen Buddhists. Their pointedly titled coedited collection *What's Wrong with Mindfulness (And What Isn't)* claims that

the American Zen teachers featured in the collection are uniquely quali-
fied to offer models for how to adapt Buddhist practices to the contemporary world without "contaminating" them.[69] The first half of the book
echoes concerns about the decontextualization, commodification, and
instrumentalization of secular mindfulness. Magid and Marc R. Poirier
argue that the modernization processes that mark mindfulness—secularization, instrumentalization, and deracination—have cut off too
much of its religious roots. Rather than call for a return to a traditional
monastic context, however, they suggest that a laicized Zen that engages
psychological and social realities but does not discard its religious core
can serve as a model for a "more genuinely Buddhist no gain approach"
to mindfulness. In contrast to a "secular, for gain approach," the former is not a technique but a religious practice that demands a lifelong
commitment.[70] Poirier points out that some MBSR teachers are reintro-
ducing some of the components that were taken out of the eight-week
module and concludes that there seems to be "a movement back toward
a religion-like frame within which to secure practice."[71]

   A third emerging pattern includes the efforts of American Buddhists to draw on their Buddhist training to offer deeper, more transformational iterations of mindfulness. In these cases, teachers are generally
positive about the use of mindfulness as "stress reduction," which is a
necessary first step for many people, but they want to offer mindfulness
teachings that have more depth because they rely on other Buddhist
teachings. These teachers tend to frame mindfulness as a practice that
expresses the "deeper truths" or the "nature of reality" that are contained
in but not exclusive to Buddhism. Hence, to a large degree, this trend
continues Kabat-Zinn's framing of mindfulness as universal dharma in
that it uncouples the truths within Buddhism and the institutional religious traditions of Buddhism. Teachers, however, stress that they are
not just teaching mindfulness as bare attention but are including ethical
and relational aspects of Buddhist teachings, although presented in a
way, and with a vocabulary, that is more accessible and useful for non-
Buddhist audiences. The emphasis here, then, is on how to communicate in pragmatic ways without losing the depth of the dharma.

   One example of this comes from Insight teachers Martin Aylward
and Mark Coleman, who cofounded the Mindfulness Training Institute

in 2012 as a direct response to criticisms of mindfulness within Buddhist circles. As Buddhists, they felt that they had a responsibility to contribute to improving secular mindfulness if they were complaining that important aspects of the tradition were being left out. Alternating annually between the United States and Europe, they offer a one-year mindfulness teacher training program that is currently in its fourth iteration. One of their goals is to provide solid retreat experience as well as give trainees grounding in the Buddhist teachings that underlie mindfulness. Although they do include the *Satipatthana Sutta,* most of this is done implicitly rather than explicitly through presenting traditional Buddhism in a vocabulary that will resonate most with their audience. Aylward said, for example, that they "used the spirit rather than the letter of the precepts" by emphasizing kindness and respect as essential boundaries for mindfulness practice. He did not see this as a clear Buddhist/ secular distinction, however, because he actually employed the same approach when teaching in Buddhist contexts. Pointing out that the word "Buddhism" was a colonial Western construction, he shared that teachings on the dharma were best brought alive in everyday experience and language rather than dry and technical Buddhist terms.[72]

Another example comes from Jessica Morey, cofounder and executive director of Inward Bound Mindfulness Education (iBme), a nonprofit organization that offers mindfulness training for youth and the people who support them. Morey is a longtime Insight practitioner and also teaches in the Dharma Punx community. She began volunteering at Insight teen meditation retreats in 2007 and was invited to teach in 2009. iBme adopted the retreat model from the Insight-Theravada tradition, but the group made an early decision to teach mindfulness in a secular way to make it accessible to a wider range of teens. The decision was an easy one, Morey said, because they were already teaching mindfulness in a nondogmatic way that did not rely on Buddhist doctrine. Nonetheless, she added, "On teen retreats we also point out the truths of suffering in life, impermanence, the basic nature of our thoughts and emotions, and the reality of interdependence. We also emphasize compassion, loving-kindness, and ethics." For Morey, these were perspectives at "the heart of reality" and "intrinsic to the human condition" that were present in other wisdom traditions as well as in Buddhism. She had begun calling her approach "deep mindfulness" because it is concerned with supporting a deeper transformation to less egocentric ways, a process that was often uncomfortable and challenging. As she explained, "We are committed to teaching 'depth' and not just 'stress reduction' in the way that secular mindfulness can be taught today."[73]

Craig and Devon Hase are the cofounders of SATI: Mindfulness Workshops and Coaching. They have both trained in multiple Buddhist lineages and teach at an Insight meditation group in Madison, Wisconsin. While professing great respect for Kabat-Zinn, Craig disagrees with his assertion that he has taken the essentials of Buddhist practice and made them secular. As he put it, "Who's to say what the pith of the practice is? Why mindfulness more than ethics or ritual?" Similar to Vince Horn's second generation of mindfulness perspective, Craig believes that it is time to bring more relational and ethical contexts of "Buddhism/dharma" into secular mindfulness, and he and Devon offer the parts of "Buddhism/dharma" that will be most relatable to and useful in the environments in which they teach. Such pedagogical pragmatism, however, should not come at the expense of traditional Buddhism. As he explained, "I feel very strongly that we should not overtly or subtly demean the ancient practices of merit building, ritual, monastic hierarchy, traditional roles of the laity, and all the other things that I see as expressions of the Buddha's original teachings."[74]

A fourth trend emerging from American Buddhism is to clearly distinguish between secular mindfulness and Buddhist mindfulness. Secular Buddhist Ted Meissner, for example, has long argued that secular mindfulness and Buddhism are distinct entities and the former should not be measured against the latter. The view that mindfulness both can and ethically should be completely separated from Buddhism is common in people with Buddhist backgrounds who teach mindfulness in education. In some instances, it is used as a direct counter to "stealth Buddhism" and the "Trojan horse" approach. Megan Cowan, cofounder of Mindful Schools and a former Theravada Buddhist nun, spoke critically of this approach. As she put it, "I feel pretty strongly about not being a stealth Buddhist. Not only is it illegal, but it's unfair and dishonest. And so, when I first started, I had to really contemplate and consider for myself: what are we doing? I believe very firmly that we can offer a skillset to young people that doesn't have a religious or spiritual container."[75] A good example of the trend to fully separate Buddhism and secular mindfulness is Peace in Schools, a nonprofit organization that serves mostly public high schools in Portland, Oregon. Spanning more than seventy-five hours over one semester, its program is described as "a comprehensive contemplative curriculum that allows students to move beyond basic mindfulness skills to create an environment of CARE (confidentially, awareness, respect and empathy)." The organization was founded by Caverly Morgan, who spent eight years in a Zen monastery in North America and is a regular attendee of the Gen X Buddhist conferences. Aside from a reference to "the original spirit of Zen" on her website, however, Morgan jettisons the language of Buddhism altogether and does not seek to relate or legitimate her approach explicitly or implicitly to or through Buddhism.

Morgan explains that while she appreciates those who are concerned with preserving distinct religious forms, she is much more interested in innovating new forms that are based in "the recognition of a shared beingness" and "creating universal practices in a language that is available to everyone." She sees much desire across religious and secular lines to move beyond the culture of individualism and overcome the multiple divisions that mark modern life. Morgan emphasizes the lived experience of the teenage students in her program, who come from diverse racial, socioeconomic, and religious backgrounds, noting that they have all benefited from an immediate experience of connectedness. She feels it is important to highlight common human qualities—oneness, interconnection, love, and wholeness—that cut across religious and secular differences but do not erase them. As she put it: "My teens are not hungry for specific religious forms, they are hungry to find answers to questions such as how can I befriend myself? How can I know that I am good? How can I see myself in others and how can I move from isolation to love?"[76]

Mindfulness and Buddhist Modernism

The mindfulness movement should be located in the lineage of scientific rationalism, one of the three main discourses of modern Buddhism, and is clearly traceable from U Ba Khin's modernist reframing of mindfulness as a nonsectarian practice to Kabat-Zinn's scientific universal iteration.[77] Indeed, Buddhist scholars such as McMahan, Wilson, Sharf, and Braun are united in seeing secular mindfulness as an extension and expression of Buddhist modernism. Buddhist critiques of mindfulness, however, show considerable opposition to core modernist components: universalism, individualism, an emphasis on the experiential, and the scientific-rational lineage. While the "mindfulness wars," are often portrayed as a clash between traditional and modern Buddhists, many of the mindfulness critiques are themselves questionable from a traditional Buddhist perspective.[78] I suggest rather that such perspectives reflect an interrogation of Buddhist modernism from a postmodern and postcolonial rather than a traditional Buddhist perspective.

One example of this postmodern and postcolonial perspective is the critiques of the science of mindfulness, which reflect a general postmodern suspicion of science as a grand narrative of modernity. Linda Heuman's series of interviews for *Tricycle,* for example, all apply pressure to modernist framings of science as objective and free of cultural ideology as well as problematize its assumptions of epistemological superiority over religious discourse. Heuman calls on Western Buddhists to interrogate how scientific paradigms are shaping and restricting their understanding of Buddhism. She suggests that although Western practitioners are quick to discard elements of the premodern cultural context of Buddhism, they often fail to see how science functions as a comparative cultural ideology because the primary story science tells about itself is that it is objective and above cultural discourse. Modern Buddhists, however, need to be less naive about the relationship between Buddhism, science, and technology and recognize that we are living in what sociologist Theodor Adorno has called an "administered society," in which technological rationality and industrial organization deeply shape all areas of life.[79] In a related vein, Evan Thompson draws on Michel Foucault to draw attention to the sociopolitical interests at play in the science of mindfulness. He is wary of the legitimating role neuroscience is playing in creating new forms of subjectivity—"the mindful person"—that fit well with neoliberal regimes of instrumentalization, productivity, and efficiency.[80]

The shift from the modern to the postmodern in the Buddhist scientific-rational lineage can also be seen in contemplative neuroscientist Willoughby Britton's research. Britton problematizes the assimilative and epistemologically arrogant nature of the encounter between science and Buddhism in which science "has thrown out anything that is not congruent with the modern worldview." One of the "casualties" of "modern dharma cherry picking" has been the Buddhist soteriological goal of liberation, which has been discarded as "religious folklore." As Britton notes, however, if you ignore the aim of Buddhism, you might as well "throw out Buddhism, too." She delivers a multilevel critique of the reductive state of the science of mindfulness but ends on a positive note that there is an emerging "Contemplative Science 2.0: The Hybrid Revolution," which consists of researchers who have a depth of experience and understanding in both religious and scientific discourses and are endeavoring to replace these reductive approaches with more sophisticated and dialogical ones.[81]

Similarly, postmodern and postcolonial trends are on display in the emerging developments within mindfulness. The social justice turn, in particular, demonstrates a move away from an abstract universalism and a nuanced attention to the different sociocultural contexts of mindfulness. In fact, Bhikkhu Bodhi's own socially engaged approach is described as "a model aimed at articulating a postmodern integral understanding of Buddhism.[82] I conclude that the mindfulness critiques, emerging trajectories around mindfulness, and emic descriptions such as "second-generation mindfulness" and "Contemplative Science 2.0" are, taken together, indicative of a shift from Buddhist modernism to Buddhism in postmodernity.

Sex, Scandal, and the
Shadow of the Roshi

The striking grey cover of the 2014 winter issue of popular Buddhist quarterly *Buddhadharma* featured a woman's face staring behind bold green lettering that declared "Confronting Abuse of Power." Inside it featured various reflections on the sexual scandals that had inflicted a number of American Buddhist communities. Two of the three contributors were trained in specialized psychotherapeutic knowledge as well as being practicing Buddhists. One was Pamela Rubin, a women's trauma therapist, who stressed that despite holding "tremendous wisdom," Buddhist communities were as vulnerable to sexual abuse as any other institution and noted soberly that in the case of the recurring scandals, "ordinary worldly knowledge is valuable."[1] Another was Tibetan Buddhist teacher and Jungian psychotherapist Rob Preece, whose contribution "Our Teachers Are Not Gods" reminded his fellow practitioners of that fact and examined the dynamics of projection and transference that often distort the teacher-student relationship.[2] *Buddhadharma*'s coverage was closely followed by an open letter on the Internet signed by ninety-nine American Zen teachers who thanked the magazine for exposing the scandals and declared the signatories' commitment to ending the culture of silence and the idealization of the teacher that had enabled them.[3] In both the magazine and the letter, the sexual scandals were framed primarily in therapeutic language: these incidents were abuses of power, committed by narcissists and sociopaths, partly enabled by students' idealizations, and occurring in Buddhist sanghas that resembled dysfunctional families with poor interpersonal boundaries.

But not all American Zen practitioners have been enthusiastic about the use of psychotherapeutic discourse to interpret the scandals. A number of objections, ranging from the concerned to the caustic, have been raised in popular Buddhist magazines and on websites and blogs to what is seen as the American dilution of traditional Zen at work in such therapeutic responses.[4] Complaints have been directed at what is considered to be a misguided conflation of psychological and religious discourses, such as the comparison of the guru-disciple relationship to the therapist-client relationship. At the heart of these critiques is a concern that American Zen is being reduced to a form of psychotherapy geared toward healing the individual self rather than preserved as a religious tradition aimed at the radical realization of the emptiness of self and reality.

Debates around the American psychologization of Buddhism are not new. David McMahan has shown that depth psychology, as heir to Romanticism, is one of the three main Western discourses that has shaped Buddhist modernism.[5] Many Buddhist scholars and practitioners have critiqued what they see as the assimilation of Buddhism to psychotherapeutic narratives. Theravadin monk Thanissaro Bhikkhu, for example, has lamented what he calls "Buddhist Romanticism," the therapeutic dilution of Buddhism in the West.[6] Such critiques, however, have tended toward identifying general cultural patterns rather than providing any detailed analysis of why and how certain American Buddhist communities have adopted psychotherapy.

Through a focus on the Zen sex scandals, this chapter redirects attention to practice communities to provide a more nuanced consideration of intersections between American Buddhism and psychotherapy. The scandals provide a useful focus for a number of reasons. First, they reveal under what particular conditions psychotherapy has been incorporated into certain Zen communities. Second, they show which psychotherapeutic discourses have become dominant and the specific ways they have been adopted. Third, they illustrate how the introduction of psychotherapy has been legitimated within a wider Buddhist hermeneutic, which has produced new Buddhist discourses, practices, authorities, organizational structures, and even soteriological models.

Sex in the Sangha (Again): The Reoccurrence of American Buddhist Sex Scandals

Since the early 1980s, a number of Western Buddhist communities have been rocked by sexual abuse, sexual misconduct, and other related improprieties. These scandals have cut across Buddhist lineages but have been particularly predominant in Tibetan and Zen teacher-centric communities and have included both Asian and American teachers. While no means exhaustive, the following discussion details some of the most prominent cases. From the Tibetan Buddhist community, the openly promiscuous Chögyam Trungpa, founder of Shambhala, died at the age of forty-seven partly due to years of heavy alcohol use.[7] His American dharma heir, Osel Tendzin, had unprotected sex with several students and transmitted HIV to one of them; that student and his girlfriend later died of AIDS, as did Tendzin.[8] June Campbell, former translator for Kalu Rinpoche, revealed that she had been his secret tantric consort and lover for many years and had been intimidated into silence by threats of metaphysical retribution.[9] In 1994, Sogyal Rinpoche settled out of court a $10 million lawsuit on charges of sexual, physical, and mental abuse yet continued to face charges of sexual abuse by female students.[10] More recently, the first American to receive the Tibetan Buddhist Geshe degree, Michael Roach, has come under much critical scrutiny after the mental breakdown of his former wife and coteacher, Christie McNally, and death of her husband and senior student Ian Thorson.[11]

The American Zen community has been similarly shaken. The San Francisco Zen Center asked Richard Baker Roshi, the dharma heir of Shunryu Suzuki, to resign after it was discovered he had been having an affair with one of his married students.[12] Taizan Maezumi Roshi of the Zen Center of Los Angeles was revealed to have had multiple affairs with female students and publicly began treatment for alcoholism in 1983.[13] One of Maezumi's American lineage holders, Genpo Merzel, promised to disrobe as a Zen priest after confessing to a series of sexual affairs and charges of financial improprieties occurring over two decades.[14] Eido Shimano, founder of the first Rinzai Zen monastery in the United States, Dai Bosatsu, was forced to resign from his position after a series of allegations of sexual abuse and misconduct occurring over forty years.[15] Shortly after, Joshu Sasaki Roshi, the founder of Mount Baldy Zen Center, came under similar scrutiny after his longtime sexual improprieties with female students came to public attention.[16] Given the status of the offenders, the time scale of their offenses, the seeming complicity of their communities, and perhaps the media coverage received, the latter two cases in particular triggered a period of deep, public reflections within the Zen community.

The scandals have initiated the drafting of new ethical guidelines, grievance and conflict resolution procedures, institutional reshapings, and doctrinal discussion across North American Buddhist communities. At the forefront of this were the San Francisco Zen Center, Spirit Rock Meditation Center, and the Buddhist Peace Fellowship.[17] More recently, the Pittsburg Zen Center has developed "An Olive Branch," a Buddhist-inspired mediation organization to help Buddhist communities deal with sexual misconduct through a series of projects ranging from individual community work to public community webinars.[18] The scandals have also generated a considerable amount of literature from American Buddhists exploring them from a diversity of perspectives, including feminism, sociology, cultural anthropology, organizational psychology, psychoanalysis, cult studies, and Buddhist history and doctrine.[19] Without disregarding these insightful perspectives, I focus on psychotherapeutically informed responses, examining them through three case studies: Grace Schireson and the Shogaku Zen Institute, Barry Magid and Joko Beck's Ordinary Mind lineage, and Diane Hamilton's Integral Zen. I have chosen these cases because of the centrality of the sex scandals in the formation of their psychotherapeutically informed approaches and because these are well-known, respected teachers in the American Zen community.

Zen Zombies and Misbehaving Monks:
Grace Schireson and the Shogaku Zen Institute

On January 13, 2015, shortly after *Buddhadharma* explored abuses of power in American Buddhist communities, *Lion's Roar* published an open letter titled "A Pledge from the Next Generation of Teachers" signed by more than ninety Zen teachers. Cowritten by Grace Schireson and Genjo Marinello, the letter expressed gratitude for *Buddhadharma's* issue and journalist Mark Oppenheimer's *Zen Predator of the Lower East Side* for reporting on the power abuses of Eido Shimano and other teachers. It apologized for the "collective failure" of the wider Zen community to prevent the great harm caused to community members, especially women, and promised to "build more visible ethics codes, working toward consensus on national standards on behavior and oversight, and seeking outside consultation to educate and empower students to come forward if they have been abused." In particular, they challenged the idealization of the teacher that had enabled the scandals and would guard against "the scoundrels and sociopaths" who "walk among us— sometimes as teachers and priests."[20]

Schireson has been one of the main commentators within the American Zen community on the sex scandals. She has published a series of reflections on her Sweeping Zen blog and has contributed to a number of public letters penned to Eido Shimano and the Zen Studies Society and to Genpo Merzel and the Kanzeon community. Schireson is also president and cofounder of the Shogaku Zen Institute, which runs an annual training program for Zen priests and community leaders that aims to combat certain contributing factors to the scandals. As the following discussion demonstrates, the influence of Schireson's therapeutic training is evident in her interpretation of and response to the scandals.[21]

Myoan Grace Schireson began her training in the 1960s at the Berkeley Zen Center and received dharma transmission from Sojun Mel Weitsman Roshi of the Suzuki Roshi Soto Zen lineage in 2005. She has also trained in Japan and has been given permission to teach koans from Keido Fukushima Roshi of Tofukuji Monastery in Kyoto, Japan. After receiving a doctorate in clinical psychology, Schireson specialized in work with children and women before retiring to teach Zen full time. She currently runs the Empty Nest Zendo, a Soto Zen training facility in North Fork, California, with her husband and coteacher Peter Schireson, whom she married in 1968.[22]

Drawing from fifty years in the American Zen community and her clinical training, Schireson has devoted much attention to exploring the complex dynamics of the scandals. While she has not shied away from diagnosing repeated sexual offenders such as Shimano as "sociopathic," she has also shifted attention away from individual "bad apples" to structural patterns undergirding the scandals, which she has broken down into three central areas: the personal, the interpersonal, and the transpersonal.[23] The *personal* indicates the individual psychological issues of both student and teacher and the ways in which they can harmfully combine. Schireson claims that many students come to Zen practice with unconscious attachment needs, such as a desire to be connected to a powerful parental figure, which often fatally intersect with a teacher's unconscious psychological need to be seen as special and idealized.

The *interpersonal* refers to the ways that teachers who have not reached mature adult development and have many unresolved narcissistic needs have been enabled and shielded by their sanghas. Schireson specialized in the study of group dynamics as part of her clinical training and has done much to unpack what she sees as the various components of dysfunction in Buddhist communities.[24] To begin with, she notes that when Buddhism came to North America, there was a tremendous "idealization of the exotic practices" in large part because of the general idealism of the 1960s counterculture. This included a collective romanticization of the "mythical Zen teacher," who often has been mistakenly seen as existing beyond "relative" dualistic morality in the realm of the nondual Absolute. Unlike in Japan, where students see priests as much more human and ordinary, American students have tended to grant too much power to charismatic teachers. To combat this, Schireson calls on teachers to be transparent about their own flaws and difficulties and for students to create sanghas in which teachers are viewed as ordinary human beings rather than as perfect enlightened beings.

Similarly, Schireson draws on cultural psychology to identify different challenges Asian and American sanghas face and advises the latter not to unthinkingly imitate traditional Japanese Zen but to forge new American models that take cultural particularities into account. She notes, for example, that unlike Japanese Buddhists, who practice Buddhism within a wider cultural context that includes the emotional support of their families, most Americans came to Buddhism as an alternative to the religion of their parents. This predisposes Americans to see Buddhist communities as a substitute for family support, which risks replicating dysfunctional family dynamics in which "the teacher is the lost father" and "people with father issues are gravitating towards the teacher instead of supporting each other."[25] Schireson is particularly wary of ways in which Buddhist sanghas can discourage critical thinking, foster emotional immaturity, and hinder individuation under the guise of devotion to the ideal of enlightenment and the teacher.[26]

The *transpersonal* dimension signifies confusion between spiritual and psychological development and absolute and relative levels of reality. Schireson refers frequently to the work of John Welwood, who coined the term "spiritual bypassing," to describe the ways in which spiritual practice can be used to circumvent psychological developmental tasks.[27] She believes that both present and past Zen teachers have failed to integrate their meditative attainments with emotional and interpersonal development. She points to the work of the sixteenth-century Confucius scholar Ito Jinsai as evidence that "throughout history, people have noticed that the awesome power of Zen practice can be misused even by accomplished practitioners. Spiritual power does not automatically inform and transform emotional and social behaviors."[28] Further, new students are often unable to differentiate between an awakened state and charisma, a situation that has been compounded by Zen rhetoric on the absolute level of reality as being beyond conventional morality and by literary tales of the wild Zen master. This confusion, Schireson laments, is "an occupational hazard for Zen practitioners" and demonstrates the importance for sanghas to study psychological dynamics such as transference and idealization as well as Zen literature and philosophy.[29]

Another distinctive feature of Schireson's analysis is a consideration of the role of gender-specific psychology. She identifies a long-established female "addiction" or "cultural delusion" to seek power through sexual relations with powerful men. Another way females achieve status via powerful male proxy is by isolating and blaming other women who have come forth with abuse accounts. In large part, because of the monastic segregation of the sexes within traditional Zen, Schireson believes that Zen priests are not equipped to deal with their female students' sexual transferences. Now that Zen communities have become gender mixed, however, American Zen needs to develop new formal trainings to deal with these "specific gender delusions." Nonetheless, while identifying various ways that female cultural conditioning, biology, and early traumatic experiences have contributed to the scandals, Schireson is clear that ultimate responsibility lies with the teacher, who must "teach any woman seeking sex via enlightenment that seduction and ingratiation are not the route to Zen awakening."[30]

Schireson has called for the implementation of multiple new practices to prevent the reoccurrence of the scandals in American Zen. These include educating individual sanghas, adopting peer review processes, drafting clear ethical guidelines and grievance procedures, and promoting clergy misconduct laws.[31] My focus here is on the psychotherapeutic components of these suggestions. For example, Schireson notes that in thirteen US states, relationships between clergy and congregant as well as therapist and client are illegal. In arguing for the adoption of such laws in American Zen communities, Schireson legitimates her position through drawing on her expertise and authority in the psychology of unequal power relations, particularly the fields of sexual abuse and posttraumatic studies.[32] The main psychotherapeutic influence is via the introduction of additional Zen training programs that will educate Zen priests, lay teachers, and sangha members in the specific psychological dynamics and processes that have contributed to the scandals. As Schireson notes:

> It seems to me that one of the most urgent tasks facing the Western Zen community is establishing more wholesome and effective training programs that address both personal and sangha developmental needs. We need to lessen our reliance on imitating our Asian teachers, and we need to find ways to effectively integrate Zen's core teachings in our everyday life here in the West to become mature and well-balanced

Zen teachers. We need to introduce ministerial training, self-care, and sangha care into the Zen training curriculum.[33]

With Lewis Richmond, Schireson has codeveloped one such training program called the Shogaku Priest Ongoing Training (SPOT), which is offered through the Shogaku Zen Institute, a religious nonprofit organization.[34] SPOT takes place annually at Empty Nest Zendo and is designed for Zen priests, lay teachers, and community leaders. It was originally offered as a three-year training program but switched format to a three-week intensive to make it more available for teachers and students working in the world. SPOT can be traced back to 2006, when a group of about fifteen teachers in the Shunryu Suzuki Roshi lineage gathered to discuss how well they were following Suzuki's advice to "establish an American way of Zen life" rather than merely re-create the form of Japanese Zen. They discovered that their traditional Zen training had not prepared them sufficiently to address all of their own or their students' psychological, emotional, and physical needs and thus developed the SPOT curriculum to complete these "missing pieces." In 2006, the first program was run by six faculty—Schireson, Lewis Richmond, Darlene Cohen, Gary McNabb, Alan Senauke, and Steve Stücky—and had thirty trainees, mainly drawn from students in the Shunryu Suzuki lineage.

In planning their curriculum, SPOT faculty pinpointed three main areas to tackle: the idealization of the exotic, the imitation of Asian models, and emotional repression. The underlying premise of SPOT is that Zen meditation training and spiritual attainment do not automatically translate into emotional and relational maturity. Hence, "we have to reach the stage of a mature adult in the personal and interpersonal realm before we can fully internalize and integrate the transpersonal level of emptiness-awareness realization."[35]

To aid with this development, the SPOT faculty designed a comprehensive curriculum that includes training in a variety of areas such as group dynamics, conflict resolution and prevention, and building healthy sanghas. Chief among SPOT's aims is educating priests and sangha leaders in "issues of power, transference, projection, idealization, and conflict." One way that SPOT counters the dynamics of teacher idealization is through a model of coteaching, which serves to undercut a concentration of power in one person and presents a multitude of perspectives rather than one absolute view. As Schireson notes, having teachers side by side questioning each other on a subject "goes a long way to taking the teacher out of some idealized master realm."[36] Other activities include role playing and fishbowl and small group inquiries. Schireson describes how role playing illuminates how easily sexual dynamics can arise between a teacher and student:

> I'll give a woman a script that says "Okay, you've got a crush on your teacher and you're trying to angle yourself into an invitation to his birthday party that you heard about through your friends, and you go after him with all you've got, all your flirtation." Then I'll write a script for the person playing the teacher, saying "You're recently divorced, you're lonely, you're attracted to this woman, but you're trying to maintain your boundaries." But then they go after each other. She goes after him, and he tries to maintain his boundaries. But you can hear the audience gasp when he says "I really feel warmly about you" or something like that. He gives in. So, we show people how hard it is when you're attracted to someone or you're feeling vulnerable.[37]

In terms of trainee demographics, Schireson estimated that around fifteen participants attend the annual summer intensive with a gender makeup of roughly two-thirds men and one-third women. Most of the participants have regular jobs and lead small sanghas rather than being full-time priests. Geographically, the majority of participants have come from the East Coast and Midwest, although participants have also come from Europe and Australia. Students have come from a variety of Japanese Buddhist lineages, including those of Shunryu Suzuki, Dainin Katagiri, Shogaku Okumura, and Sasaki Roshi, as well as Vietnamese and Korean Rinzai Zen. This diversity, Schireson stresses, has considerably enriched the training program for faculty and attendees alike.[38]

One important thing to note about SPOT is that it is not seen as a replacement for traditional Zen training. Rather, it is advertised as its complement, and all participants are required to have their teacher's permission to attend. Similarly, although SPOT draws on psychological knowledge to fill gaps in traditional Zen training, particularly issues of an emotional and interpersonal nature, it is distinct from psychotherapy. As Schireson emphasizes, psychological dynamics within SPOT are explored within the wider context of Zen practice rather than a psychotherapeutic container.[39] She acknowledges that many within the American Zen community are concerned that "we will go too far with psychologizing Buddhism" and that devotional and religious aspects of the practice will be lost. While honoring this as a valid concern, Schireson believes that Western insights on transference, projection, and defense mechanisms can be adopted without Zen being assimilated into therapy. For Schireson, the integration of psychotherapeutic tools is part of what Buddhism has always done historically: adapt to and learn from local cultures while preserving its foundational, universal truths on the nature of self and reality. Further, Schireson emphasizes that psychological components are already inherent to Buddhism. As she puts it: "The Buddha was the first historically recognized psychologist. He emphasized the importance of the mind and all the activity that came from the mind."[40]

The concern to differentiate Zen from psychotherapy is also seen in the legitimation of SPOT through Buddhist rather than psychotherapeutic authority. The mission statement of the Shogaku Zen Institute draws frequently on Shunryu Suzuki, the historic Buddha, and Zen masters and teachings to frame and validate its approach. Similarly, Schireson believes that her approach to publicizing the scandals reflects Zen's imperative to "face reality as it is."[41]

"Enlightenment Isn't All That It's Cracked Up to Be": Barry Magid

In the wake of the sexual scandals, many American Zen teachers have acknowledged the need to incorporate more psychoanalytic insights into traditional Zen practice. New York–based Zen teacher and psychoanalyst Barry Magid has been at the forefront of putting the two disciplines into dialogue. Magid's first encounter with Zen occurred in 1975 when he was training in psychiatry and began sitting with Eido Shimano at the Zen Studies Society. Magid claims that Shimano's "own mixture of charisma, insight and sexual misconduct provided a whole generation of Zen students with their first true koan" and shares that his own development of a "psychologically-informed Zen" is an attempt to "keep working on that first koan: the relationship of realization to personal character and psychology."[42]

After training with Shimano and Bernie Glassman, Magid became a student of Charlotte Joko Beck, who had received dharma transmission in 1978 from Taizan Maezumi Roshi at the Los Angeles Zen Center before starting the Zen Center of San Diego in 1983. In 1996, Beck gave Magid permission to establish the nonresidential Ordinary Mind Zendo, and two years later he received dharma transmission from her. Ordinary Mind Zendo is part of the Ordinary Mind School, a loose network established by Beck and three of her dharma successors. Its website states that it is dedicated to Beck's vision of developing "a psychologically minded Zen adapted to the needs of American students practicing in the context of their everyday life."[43]

Beck fashioned her own distinctive approach to Zen in large part as a response to the first wave of scandals that involved many Buddhist teachers, including Maezumi Roshi, who was an alcoholic and engaged in sexual affairs with his students.[44] At the basis of her reshaping of Zen was disillusionment with the traditional koan system of practice, which she concluded had obviously failed to address Maezumi's psychologically damaged, addictive behavior patterns. She believed this was because much of koan practice was about suppression through sheer concentration, which dangerously bypassed rather than worked through emotional issues that would latter return in powerful, distorted forms such as addiction and sexual misconduct.[45] One of the great limitations of Zen, Beck believed, was its neglect of emotional life. As a corrective, she developed a transmutative method of working directly with emotional experience that involved fully experiencing the bodily tensions of whatever emotions arose and labeling but not engaging the thought narratives that accompanied them. This, she taught, enabled the stripping down of the conditioned egoic self and a shift from a self-centered, dualistic to a nonreactive, nondual experience of life.[46]

Another core feature of Beck's approach was to downplay the importance of kensho (enlightenment) and other dramatic meditative breakthrough experiences, which she perceived as often only strengthening the conditioned ego self. She stressed that it was more important how such experiences were translated into everyday behavior and functioning. Hence, she described enlightenment as an ongoing process rather than as a definitive grand experience and presented everyday life rather than the meditation cushion as the primary site of realization. Nonetheless, Beck was careful to distinguish between Zen and therapy, describing her own approach as "therapeutic but not therapy." She framed her emotionally inclusive approach within the wider Zen metaphysics of nonduality and the Mahayana Buddhist emphasis on the union of wisdom and compassion.[47]

Magid claims that Beck transformed the nature of Zen in North America and brought about "a sea-change in how our generation thinks about the nature of practice and its relationship to our personal psychological make-up."[48] He notes that when he first started practicing Zen in the 1970s, psychotherapy tended to be dismissed as superficial and less important than spiritual training. Because of the reoccurring and widespread sexual misconduct involving teachers with the most "impeccable credentials," however, he believes that the Zen community has become more willing to acknowledge the psychological issues at play in the scandals and engage psychotherapeutic discourse to address them. As he puts it, "The reoccurring inability of many teachers from a broad variety of spiritual disciplines to deal appropriately with the eroticized longings of their students—and with the emotional reactions and temptations that arise in the teachers themselves as a result—has been *one of the main sources* of a growing appreciation in Buddhist communities for psychoanalytic training and the experience it brings to meditation practice."[49]

According to Magid, the turn to psychoanalysis is essential because of inherent limitations within traditional Zen. By "traditional Zen," Magid means all of its core aspects—koan practice, kensho, monastic training, ethical precepts, and even certain models of enlightenment—which he sees as insufficient in and of themselves to uncover and transform the unconscious dynamics revealed by the scandals. To begin with, Magid points to the limits of meditation and the "enlightenment experiences" it produces. Like Beck, he describes how koan practice is often used in a dissociative manner to cultivate states of concentration, or samadhi, that prematurely transcend rather than work through emotional vicissitudes.[50] This is a classic example of Welwood's spiritual bypassing, and Magid laments that practitioners of his generation adopted the belief from Zen mythology that "enlightenment experiences would spontaneously dissolve all neurosis and that one would emerge from them cleansed of all past conditioning."[51] This view, he cautions, is not only false but dangerous. Magid points to the research done by American Buddhist teacher Jack Kornfield, who interviewed almost one hundred spiritual teachers and found they were still struggling with psychodynamic issues despite having had powerful enlightenment experiences. Magid argues that this, combined with the sexual scandals, is clear evidence that although Zen offers deep insights into the nature of reality, it does not resolve unconscious dynamics, particularly emotional and sexual issues, nor does it uncover the operation of unconscious cultural biases.[52]

For Magid, the main problem with traditional Zen is that it leaves a gap between ontological *insight* and the personal *integration* of that insight. Bluntly put: "The realization of emptiness and interconnectedness by human beings does not, it seems, reliably transform them into something more than human. (It doesn't, I'm sorry to say, even reliably turn them into good human beings.)"[53] Some participants have explained this lack of integration as being due to inadequate training, but for Magid the fact that the scandals included such highly regarded Zen teachers points to a much deeper problem. Hence, he warns against the idealization of Japanese Zen monasticism and suggests that such training can actually foster emotional dissociation and repression. He ascribes part of this to the Japanese cultural value of group harmony, which, while valuable in certain aspects, can become distorted and generate conformity and compliance. Further, trying to directly graft this culturally specific communal-collective Japanese model onto an individualized and highly therapeutic American culture is impossible.

Similarly, whereas other commentators have suggested that the problem lies with the modern overemphasis on nondual mystical experience and a lack of engagement with the traditional monastic and lay precepts that are central to Zen, Magid does not believe that a recovery of the latter is sufficient. Although ethical guidelines are valuable in providing basic safeguards for individuals and communities, he claims that the "boundary violations" occurring in the scandals are rooted in deeper psychodynamic issues, particularly unresolved narcissistic needs of teachers.[54] One of Magid's main psychoanalytic influences is Heinz Kohut's self-psychology, which revolutionized classical psychoanalytic understandings of narcissism. Kohut explored the essential role narcissism plays in psychological development and the analytic relationship. His work on archaic and mature "selfobjects" identified different narcissistic needs and transferences and the various ways in which they can be integrated or go astray. For Magid, neither ethical precepts nor legal boundaries provide sufficient protection against the acting out of narcissistic disturbances.[55]

Magid's questioning of traditional Zen extends all the way to its soteriological goal of enlightenment. He claims that models of final, complete, and perfect enlightenment are little more than hagiographical constructs. Awakening exists as the moment-by-moment realization of suffering, impermanence, and emptiness rather than the attainment of any final transcendental state of absolute freedom. In keeping with his humanistic orientation, Magid consistently undercuts normative textual claims and returns focus to the behavior of actual Zen teachers. Moreover, even if such enlightenment were attainable, it would be so rare as to be irrelevant to North American Zen populations.[56]

Given the limits in traditional Zen, Magid suggests that the answer lies not in transplanting the traditional monastic system to North America, but rather in developing a psychologically informed Zen lay practice as a corrective.[57] Central to this approach is an illumination of the multiple ways in which Zen practice can be appropriated and distorted by unconscious psychological defenses. One avenue is through "curative fantasies" or "secret practices," that is, the self-centered psychological defenses such as fantasies of absolute autonomy and perfection that often motivate and shape practice.[58] Another is through the powerful transferences and countertransferences that inevitably develop in the idealization of the teacher and the intimacy of the student-teacher relationship.[59]

Magid's latest work is informed by relational theorists such as Jessica Benjamin and Philip Bromberg and explores the intricacies of how early intersubjective developmental attachment patterns play out in Zen practice and the teacher-student relationship.[60] Magid warns that historically teachers have had little awareness of their own or their students' unconscious dynamics. His sees this slowly beginning to change, however, as many of the current generation of American teachers undergo and become trained in psychotherapy. Magid calls for a continuation of this trend and the development of an American Zen that acknowledges the emotional and relational needs of both teachers and students. Such an approach, he concludes, represents an "evolutionary advance" over traditional Zen.[61]

Despite its psychoanalytic additions, Magid's psychologically minded Zen should not be confused with the assimilation of Zen into psychotherapy. Like Beck, he is careful to distinguish between the two and emphasizes that Ordinary Mind Zen is a "religious practice," grounded in the larger Soto Buddhist tradition, and is not "any form of self-improvement."[62] He differentiates his psychoanalytic integrative approach from decontextualized therapeutic uses of Buddhist meditation that are at play, for example, in much of the mainstream medicalization and instrumentalization of mindfulness. Unlike this, his project is not concerned with the reduction of Zen to psychoanalysis but rather in fashioning a dialogue between the two as distinct systems that can each potentially correct the limitations of the other.[63]

Getting a Handle on Scandal:
Diane Hamilton and Integral Zen

In the wake of the mainstream media coverage of Eido Shimano and Joshu Sasaki, the 2013 Buddhist Geeks conference hosted a pointedly titled panel, "Getting a Handle on Scandal," with the stated aims of identifying factors that contributed to the scandals and illuminating ways to navigate "the complex territory of sexuality and spirituality."[64] Facilitating the discussion was Integral Zen teacher Diane Hamilton, who began with a sober reflection that all those in the American Buddhist world had been affected by the sexual misconduct, including her own Zen community, which had been shocked by revelations of repeated sexual improprieties by their teacher Genpo Merzel. Hamilton drew on psychology and evolutionary science to provide insights into the nature of the scandals and shared that she had adopted new ways to work with sexual energy in addition to following traditional Buddhist ethical precepts. Hamilton led the audience through one such method. In pairs, she invited each participant to take turns relating an occasion when they felt they had made a poor decision as regards their sexuality, and then copanelist and fellow Integralist Sophia Diaz guided them through a somatic meditative exercise that tracked the energetic impact of their sharing. While ethical guidelines were important, such embodied "shadow practices," Hamilton continued, were essential to developing a more mature, "integral" approach to Buddhism that addressed the blind spots of traditional Zen, many of which, she explained, reflected its premodern cultural origins.

As indicated by its name, Integral Zen is shaped by the integral theory of Ken Wilber and the Soto Zen lineage of Maezumi Roshi. From the former, it has incorporated psychological discourse not only to make sense of the scandals but also to generate novel Zen practices and to refashion the soteriological goal of Zen Buddhism. Diane Musho Hamilton Sensei and her husband Michael Mugako Zimmerman Sensei co-lead the Two Arrows Zen community, which is part of the White Plum Asanga, in southern Utah.[65] Hamilton and Zimmerman are both dharma heirs of Dennis Paul Merzel, better known as Genpo Roshi, who is the second of Maezumi Roshi's twelve American dharma heirs. Merzel established the Kanzeon International Sangha in 1982 and originally taught in Bar Harbor, Maine, before relocating under controversial circumstances to Salt Lake City. Merzel is also known in the wider American Buddhist community for his creation of the Big Mind/Big Heart Process, a psychospiritual methodology that integrates Zen with Hal and Sidra Stone's Voice Dialogue work in order to reclaim disowned aspects of the self.[66]

Merzel has been the subject of much controversy in the American Zen world, mainly because of his engaging in sexual affairs with his female students over a period of thirty years. He has also been critiqued for financial improprieties, particularly regarding the high fees charged for the Big Mind teaching. In protest of his behavior, some members of the wider American Zen community undertook a series of actions in an attempt to suspend his teaching authority. The first of these, in 1992, was an unsuccessful attempt to persuade Maezumi Roshi to revoke Merzel's teaching permission.[67] The next, occurring nearly twenty years later between February and April 2011, were the publishing of two open letters on a number of Buddhist websites and a local newspaper. The first letter identified a thirty-year pattern of sexual misconduct with students, called on Merzel to make a public apology, and required that he take an indefinite leave from teaching while seeking intensive therapeutic treatment for sex addiction.[68] The second protested the fact that despite publishing his own apology in which he declared that he would "continue to work on my own shadows and deeply rooted patterns that have led me to miss the mark of being a moral and ethical person and a decent human being," Merzel did not disrobe as a Soto Zen priest, as he had promised.[69] The situation was also somewhat exacerbated by the public unraveling of events and tensions between the Kanzeon sangha and the wider American Soto community on the most appropriate ways to deal with Merzel and the community breakdown that followed his confession.

Merzel's sexual misconduct had a deep impact on Hamilton and Zimmerman's approach to Zen and led them to rethink the organizational form, ethical guidelines, and practice modalities of their community. Here I focus on the psychological dimensions of this refashioning. In a series of blog posts, Zimmerman has documented some of the ways in which the larger Kanzeon sangha came to terms with the Merzel issues.[70] One main area of concern is how to create healthy teacher-student relationships. Zimmerman suggests that both teacher and student need to be educated in psychological understandings of transference and countertransference, as many of the ethical problems between them can be traced to a lack of awareness of these dynamics. To this end, he provides a booklet addressing psychological dynamics in the teacher-student relationship that was written by Nicolee Jikyo McMahon, a therapist and member of the White Plum Asanga, and was distributed among teachers at the 2011 annual Kanzeon community meeting.[71] On a more personal note, Zimmerman also shares how painful it had been for him to work through his idealization of Merzel and see him as a human peer.[72]

Another main area highlighted is the ways in which a community can create a healthy sangha. Here Zimmerman calls on individuals to extend their meditative awareness to the relational and structural dynamics that make up a spiritual community. He proposes the creation of a more transparent, democratic structure, in contrast to the hierarchical top-down model of traditional monastic Zen.[73] In conclusion, Zimmerman notes: "If this Zen lineage is to continue to grow and prosper, it must accommodate the political and psychological insights of the soil in which it has been planted. A consequence should be the development of a sangha culture and correlative governance structure that will be premised on a more sophisticated understanding of the psychological dynamics that tend to develop between teacher and student and sangha and the perils of those dynamics."[74]

Hamilton and Zimmerman's approach to spiritual practice and psychological dynamics and the ways in which they manifest in communal and governance structures is heavily indebted to Ken Wilber, with whom Hamilton has worked since 2004. Wilber's "integral map" draws from what he considers the best of premodern contemplative traditions, modern science, and postmodern epistemology to present an all-inclusive model of individual and cultural development. He presents this as a "post-metaphysical spirituality" that preserves the contemplative wisdom of liberation traditions such as Buddhism while discarding their archaic cultural baggage.[75]

Wilber's theoretical signature is the integration of Western developmental structural models with the different cartographies of consciousness charted by Asian religious traditions presented within a wider evolutionary framework. A core feature of the integral approach is its distinction between "states" and "stages" of consciousness. Premodern contemplative traditions such as Buddhism have produced detailed cartographies of states of consciousness, from the conventional "waking-gross" to the liberative nondual states, as well as an array of sophistical meditative techniques to access them. Western developmental structural theory, such as Spiral Dynamics, has mapped out cultural developmental stages of consciousness that emerge sequentially along an evolutionary path from the most primitive "mythic-ethnocentric" to the most advanced "kosmocentric." According to Wilber, states of consciousness are always unconsciously interpreted via the cultural stage of development in which they are experienced; thus traditional Buddhism, which originated in premodernity, translates profound contemplative experiences though a mythic and ethnocentric lens.[76] In general, the aim of integral theory is to create a total spiritual matrix in which higher states and stages of consciousness cohere and are enacted on multiple levels: individual, interpersonal, institutional, and cultural.

Hamilton and Zimmerman have adopted a number of features of Wilber's paradigm to craft Integral Zen, "a post-modern Buddhist practice" that reframes enlightenment through a developmental framework. Hamilton defines enlightenment as "an evolutionary process in which awareness unfolds into greater and greater identification with reality."[77] A key component of this process is to reclaim what Carl Jung identified as the "shadow," namely, those aspects of the self that are unacceptable to consciousness so are repressed, disowned, and projected onto other people. Wilber views knowledge of the shadow as one of Western psychology's greatest contributions to spirituality, and shadow work is a core aspect of integral practice.[78] Following Wilber, Hamilton believes that Buddhist meditation alone cannot resolve the psychological issue of the shadow and so teaches it as a central practice of the Two Arrows sangha alongside traditional zazen.

One main way that Hamilton works with the shadow is through the "3-2-1 Shadow Process," which is a guided exercise between two participants during which they are each alternatively instructed to identify a quality that they find irritating in another person and then sequentially move through a third-person, second-person, and first-person perspective in an attempt to understand and ultimately claim ownership of the shadow quality.[79] As well as acknowledging the influence of Wilber and Jung, Hamilton also legitimates shadow work through a Buddhist nondual, tantric hermeneutic. She distinguishes between renunciate and transmutative strands within Buddhism and draws a parallel between shadow work and the transmutative work with the wrathful deities that one finds within Tibetan Buddhism. Similarly, she points out that the nondual approach of Zen embraces both sides of polarities rather than solely guarding against the negative, as found within the earlier renunciate tradition of Theravada Buddhism.[80]

Common Patterns in Psychotherapeutically Informed Zen

A number of shared themes can be seen in these three case studies, as well as the influential work of Buddhist teachers and therapists such as Jack Kornfield, John Welwood, and Rob Preece, from which they significantly draw. First is the common background of the authors. Labeled by William B. Parsons as "cultural insiders," these are the first generation of Western Buddhists who are familiar professionally with depth psychology and have significant experiential knowledge of Buddhist practice and thought.[81] Second is the shared conviction that "traditional" Buddhist practice—with a particular emphasis on meditation—does not heal and can even compound certain psychodynamic issues. In some instances, teachers draw on cultural psychology and attribute this to differences between premodern Asian constructions of the self and modern Western ones rather than to an inherent limitation of traditional Buddhism. Others, however, believe that modern psychoanalytic knowledge has brought new insights that were unknown in premodernity and that essentially improve traditional Buddhism. Both positions emphasize how the shift from monastic to lay practice in American Buddhism has brought up emotional and interpersonal issues that might not have arisen in monastic settings.

Third, the scandals have had a profoundly humanizing effect on Buddhism. The transcendental and metaphysical aspects of Buddhism are not entirely dismissed but certainly are played down, and there is much emphasis on the humanness of Buddhist students and teachers alike. Closely related is the fourth theme—that participants advocate for Western Buddhists to supplement their Buddhist practice with psychotherapy. This can take a range of forms, from individual treatment to incorporating therapeutic modalities into Zen training programs. In some cases, this is seen as an adjunct to Buddhism that does not affect its "traditional" goal; in others, however, the goal of Buddhism seems to have been expanded. Common to both is a call for a more "mature" approach to Buddhism, which favors a more immanent rather than transcendental soteriology, often framed within a tantric hermeneutic of embracing both relative and absolute reality.

Fifth, the scandals have had a generative effect in producing new practice terminology and modalities. Terms such as "spiritual bypassing," "the shadow," "individuation," and "maturity," which were originally psychodynamic, have now become commonplace within American Buddhist discourse. Similarly, an approach to Buddhist meditation has developed that emphasizes a nondual inclusion of emotional-somatic experience. Further, entirely new practices such as relational meditative exercises, interpersonal inquiry, and shadow work have been incorporated alongside traditional Zen practices. These are framed within a larger Buddhist hermeneutic but draw from non-Buddhist psychotherapeutic sources.

Sixth, psychotherapeutic perspectives are often gendered as gentler, feminine approaches to practice in contrast to what is seen as the hypermasculine striving approach of traditional Zen.[82] This gendered aspect is highly significant, given the role that feminist analysis has played in the scandals.[83] Critiques of psychological approaches often reproduce but reverse the value of this gendered rhetoric so that such a feminine approach is delegitimated through gender stereotypes and sexist and misogynist language.[84]

Reservations About and Resistance to the Psychologization of American Zen

Despite the widespread adoption of psychotherapeutic concepts such as "spiritual bypassing" and "the shadow" within American Buddhism, psychologically informed approaches to Zen such as those detailed above have not been unequivocally embraced. Some practitioners have raised concerns, ranging from the hesitant to the vitriolic, about what they fear is the American psychotherapeutic takeover of traditional Zen. Both Schireson and Magid, for example, have come under heavy fire on the Sweeping Zen website. Adam Tebbe, editor of Sweeping Zen, reports that reflections on the scandals have generated more traffic than any other posts and that he has been attacked for hosting them.[85] Although they are often interlinked, for clarity I look at the main objections individually:

1. *The sufficiency of traditional Zen:* This perspective states that Zen has successfully existed without the intervention of psychotherapeutic discourse since the sixth century and should not be adapted to accommodate the needs of Americans. Within this position, the sex scandals are generally attributed to the fault of individual character failings or an inadequate engagement with traditional Zen, whether as insufficient monastic training, not attaining profound meditative insights, or neglecting the ethical precepts. This perspective often seems to express tensions between monastic and lay forms of Zen, with the latter being delegitimated and a place from which to critique the former.

2. *An emphasis on Buddhist ethics rather than psychotherapy:* Closely overlapping with the above but worthy of its own mention is the view that the scandals are generally attributable to a lack of engagement with the Buddhist ethical precepts and an overemphasis on meditative experience and charismatic teachers. Proponents of this criticism point out that the antinomian Zen lineage is only one strand in Zen and emphasize that Zen monasteries adhere to a strict set of ethical precepts and regulations.

3. *The therapeutic domestication of Zen:* This perspective is concerned with what is seen as psychotherapeutic attempts to regulate the very antinomian figures on which Zen rests: the lineage of iconoclastic Zen masters who have transcended all dualities, including the conventional morality of good and bad. It insists on the irreducible difference of the Zen master-student relationship and rejects comparisons to the therapist-client relationship and attempts to democratize Zen. It celebrates the legitimacy of Zen masters to utilize whatever tools, however con-

troversial, they want in order to bring about awakening. While acknowledging the potential dangerous nature of awakening, this position stresses that it is the choice of individuals whether to engage the relationship or not.

4. *The imposition of puritanical American sexual morality:* Overlapping significantly with the above, this line of argument specifically critiques the imposition of American sexual norms and emphasizes differences across and within cultural constructions of sexuality. Shinge Roko Sherry Chayat, new abbot of Dai Bosatsu Zendo, claimed that Japanese and European students of Shimano, for example, believed that it was "ridiculously puritanical" of Americans to force Shimano to resign.[86] Jay Michaelson also questions whether terms like "sex addict" fit Shimano and warned against the projection of "our own Western sex negativity onto non-Western teachers."[87] There is also evidence of tensions between second-wave and third-wave feminist analyses around issues such as female sexual agency and sexual practices outside of hetero-monogamous norms.[88]

5. *An attack on psychotherapeutic authority:* This perspective ranges from ad hominine attacks on individuals to concerns about the creation of governing bodies to regulate individual sanghas. The former includes Zen teacher-psychologists being labeled as "arrogant" and "sanctimonious" and their perspectives as "pseudo-scientific" and "puritanical." There is also a significant discrediting of or outright misogynistic attacks on female victims and critics of the scandals.[89] The latter includes a more serious consideration of authority and governance in American Zen and what might be at stake in forming national transectarian regulatory bodies.[90]

At first glance, critiques of psychotherapeutic approaches suggest that the dominant struggle is between a religious/transgressive ethic and a psychological/normative one. The situation, however, is more complex.

First, some of those who privilege a Buddhist rather than a psychotherapeutic response stress the ethical precepts of Zen rather than its more
transgressive elements. Second, many of those arguing for a psychotherapeutically informed approach suggest it as a supplement to rather
than a replacement for Buddhist ethics. It is generally agreed, though,
that psychodynamic work provides a deeper internal transformation of
character than the external regulatory approach of Buddhist precepts.
And third, it is misleading to equate psychotherapeutic responses with
sex negativity, as a range of attitudes toward sexuality actually exists
within these approaches.[91] What is common, however, is a tendency to
support their position on sexuality with reference to scientific data and
the unequivocal promotion of transparency as an essential part of modern Buddhist sexual ethics.

From Reductive to Dialogical Approaches in the Buddhist-Psychotherapy Encounter

The incorporation of psychodynamic insights into Zen in the wake of
sexual scandals reveals two new patterns in the development of Buddhist modernism in North America. The first is the emergence of reductive and dialogical approaches in the Buddhist-psychotherapy interface.
A reductive approach is one in which psychology is privileged as the
meta-discourse and religious phenomena are assimilated and reduced
to psychological language. A dialogical approach puts religion and psychology into conversation with each other as two distinct systems and
generally employs psychology as a tool to extend, through dialogue, the
aims of religion.[92]

Most analyses of the psychologization of Buddhist modernism focus on reductive approaches. McMahan, for example, offers a brief history
of the Western psychological reconfiguration of Buddhism showing how
cosmological realms have been translated into psychological forces and
how Buddhist practices such as meditation have been rendered as psychotherapeutic techniques.[93] Similarly, Buddhist scholar Richard Payne
decries the common assimilation of Buddhism into the Jungian narrative of individuation.[94] From a related angle, Thanissaro Bhikkhu argues
that although Buddhist Romanticism offers therapeutic benefits such as

a sense of connection and wholeness, it is severely limited in comparison to the full awakening available in traditional Theravada Buddhism.[95]

There are undoubtedly many examples of the reduction of Buddhism to psychological discourses. Much of the secular mindfulness movement has repackaged Buddhist meditation in strictly therapeutic techniques. The growing Buddhist recovery movement also provides numerous instances of the direct translation of Buddhist terms into psychological concepts.[96] However, the case studies here illustrate dialogical approaches rather than reductive approaches. Magid has repeatedly warned of the dangers of reducing Zen to psychotherapy and distinguishes his approach from the psychologization occurring in the mindfulness movement. Schireson believes that therapeutic insights can be incorporated without compromising the integrity of the tradition, and the Shogaku Zen Institute markets itself as a complement to rather than substitute for traditional Zen training. Similarly, Hamilton uses shadow work as an important supplement to traditional Zen practice. Perhaps the one area of assimilation is through the comparison of the teacher-student relationship with the therapist-client relationship and the call for an adoption of the same laws that govern the latter to apply to the former.

Further, such dialogical trends are not limited to Zen but can be seen across convert Buddhist communities. In earlier research on a strand within the Insight community, which I labeled as West Coast Vipassana, I argued that attempts to integrate psychotherapy were more dialogical than reductive in nature.[97] This provides further evidence for William Parsons's claim that the Buddhist-psychoanalytic encounter is marked by three distinct models: negative/reductive, idealistic/Romantic, and dialogical.[98] Dialogical approaches are more sophisticated than their predecessors because they do not assimilate Buddhism into psychological paradigms but attempt rather to put the two distinct worldviews into critical conversation. One example of this is Zen Buddhist and psychoanalyst Jeffrey Rubin's book *Psychotherapy and Buddhism: Towards an Integration,* which argues for the need to move beyond both Orientalism, that is, the romanticization of Asian religions, and Eurocentrism, that is, the privileging of Western values. Another is Tibetan Buddhist teacher and therapist Harvey Aronson's *Buddhist Practice on Western Ground,* which offers a careful consideration of how differences between

Western and Asian subjectivities shape Buddhist practice for Western practitioners.[99] Buddhist teacher David Loy has come to a similar conclusion about the maturation of the Buddhist-psychotherapy encounter. He echoes the case studies above by noting the insufficiency of meditation practice to resolve psychological problems and how knowledge of transference and projection can guard against Buddhist practice going wrong. For Loy, the main challenge is for Buddhism and psychotherapy to resist "the temptation to swallow one another." He ends on a positive note about the future of the dialogue, however, because "it is anchored empirically in what really works to reduce the *dukkha* of therapeutic patients and Buddhist practitioners."[100]

The second pattern revealed is that although therapeutic incorporations are often dismissed as forms of modern Buddhism that have distorted traditional Buddhism, the dialogical approaches emerging act as *correctives to* as much as *continuations of* Buddhist modernism. Each of the three case studies rejects the privileging of individual meditation experience that definitively marks Buddhist modernism and stresses the need for a wider context to support meditation practice.[101] There is recognition that the meditation training that the first generation of Americans received from their Japanese teachers was unmoored from its traditional cultural and religious matrices. The mission statement of the Shogaku Zen Institute, for example, notes that compared with Japanese Zen priests, the first generation of American teachers did not "get the whole package." As well as extending Buddhist modernist trends, therefore, such teachers are attempting to correct the decontextualization of Buddhist meditation that defines earlier forms of Buddhist modernism. Rather than simply call for a return to tradition, however, these dialogical projects attempt to forge new contexts that draw from both premodern Buddhist and modern Western cultures, particularly psychotherapeutic strands. In this sense, dialogical approaches should be seen as distinct from both traditional Buddhism and Buddhist modernism. As more self-reflexivity around the historic emergence and distinctive features of Buddhist modernism grows, one can reasonably predict the emergence of more dialogical enterprises as well as the proliferation of the reductive approaches characteristic of early Buddhist modernism.

F • O • U • R

Meditation and Awakening in the American Vipassana Network

A shaved-headed man covered in bright tattoos and dressed casually in a green T-shirt and black sweat pants sat comfortably, one leg over the other, in a chair at the front of a room. With the ease that his informal attire suggested, Josh Korda said that he was feeling excited and nervous. This was because, he continued, although he had taught many silent mindfulness retreats, the goal of this particular one would be to cultivate relational mindfulness with others. It was quite scandalous, he continued with a giggle, that so many Buddhists could cultivate a real depth of meditation practice on retreat but not function well interpersonally in the world. Thus began the annual 2015 Dharma Punx NYC + Brooklyn retreat, cotaught by Korda and Jessica Morey, which legitimated the practice of relational mindfulness as much through psychoanalytic attachment theory as through the Pali Canon. Drawing on affective neuroscience to advocate for *kalyana mittas* (spiritual friendships) as a corrective to inadequate parenting, Korda's opening dharma talk was as distinctive as his appearance.

Over on the Dharma Overground website, another distinct but quite different approach to Buddhist meditation practice has developed. Calling for a systematic and technical approach to meditation, the site offers detailed and precise information on various meditative practices. Under subsections such as "Concentration" and "Claims to

Attainments," participants share their experiences traversing Buddhist developmental paths to awakening. One user, for example, reveals that he has reached the stage of "stream entry" through sustained application of Mahasi Sayadaw's method of noting; another records passing waves of terror and anxiety that accompanied the dissolution of self through the same technique.[1] Hosted by self-proclaimed "arahat" Daniel Ingram, Dharma Overground continues the path he laid down in his provocative book *Mastering the Core Teachings of the Buddha: An Unusually Hardcore Dharma Book,* which declares his own "unrestrained voice" as coming from "one whose practice has been dedicated to complete and unexcelled mastery of the traditional and hardcore stages of the path rather than some sort of vapid New Age fluff or pop psychological head-trip."[2]

These two distinct snapshots of contemporary Buddhist meditation practice illustrate certain patterns that have developed around meditation and enlightenment, or awakening, as many prefer to call it, in the American Insight network. I define that network here as a loose affiliation of individuals and communities that prioritize Vipassana meditation as their central practice and trace their immediate Buddhist roots to Burmese and Thai Theravadin lineages. One current emphasizes a more relational and integrative orientation to meditation and draws significantly on psychotherapeutic discourse. The other stresses a more systematic and goal-oriented approach to awakening and relies heavily on traditional Buddhist canonical and commentarial literature. Although there are places of mutual influence and overlap, these two currents—the relational/integrative and the textual/technical—are distinct and at times position and legitimate themselves as alternatives to the other. In this chapter I trace these currents, across both first- and second-generation convert teachers, highlighting the orientation toward meditation, the preferred style of practice, the gendering of meditation, the understanding of enlightenment, and the strategies of legitimation advanced within each before reflecting on their significance for the unfolding of Buddhist modernism in the United States.[3]

"Even the Best Meditators Have Wounds to Heal": The Relational/Integrative Current

The Insight Meditation Society (IMS) was established on May 19, 1975, in order to "provide a secluded retreat environment for the practice of meditation in the Theravada Buddhism tradition."[4] The four American cofounders of IMS, Joseph Goldstein, Jack Kornfield, Sharon Salzberg, and Jacqueline Schwartz, had all recently returned to North America after spending several years in Asia being trained by Theravadin monastic and lay teachers from both Burmese and Thai Theravadin lineages. In January 1976, IMS acquired a mansion on seventy-five acres of rural farmland in Barre, Massachusetts. Shortly after, it began to offer teacher-led intensive meditation retreats, which typically ran for ten days, during which time participants maintained complete silence and followed a daily schedule of around ten hours of sitting and walking meditation. IMS's main practice is Vipassana, or Insight, meditation. There are different forms of Vipassana, but IMS adopted the style of the Burmese monk Mahasi Sayadaw (1904–1982), who taught a Vipassana technique of mental "noting" and emphasized intensive meditation practice under silent retreat conditions. Mahasi had written an extensive commentary called *Manual of Insight* with a detailed exposition of the Progress of Insight, the four stages of the path of awakening detailed in Theravadin canonical and commentarial literature. He taught that following this path systematically would result in the attainment of Nirvana and even gave out certificates to mark the attainment of each stage.

Although IMS adopted the Mahasi method, it decided not to promote the Progress of Insight as he had done. According to senior Insight teacher Steve Armstrong, teachers felt such an approach would be counterproductive for American students, partly because, as he explained, "many of us who were coming to practice in the 1970s were enthusiastic, diligent and spiritually ambitious. For us Western seekers, there was a danger that the Progress of Insight could have led to excessive striving and imbalanced effort as well as misevaluation of one's practice."[5] IMS also departed from Mahasi in creating a team teaching structure and having multiple Theravadin lineages represented by inviting teachers who had trained in Thailand as well as Burma.[6]

Nonetheless, following the Mahasi lineage, the focus at IMS was on intensive silent retreat practice, with little attention to community building. In the 1980s, however, a group of IMS teachers, most notably Kornfield, James Baraz, Sylvia Boorstein, Howard Cohen, Julie Wester, and Anna Douglas, decided they wanted to create a "wider dharma stream" that focused more on integrating meditation practice with daily life. Some of these teachers were members of a Californian Vipassana sitting group named Insight Meditation West that had begun in 1974, and they began to search for property to develop a West Coast Insight center. In 1988, they bought 410 acres of land in Woodacre, California, and began building a meditation hall and community center. It was named Spirit Rock in 1996, and a residential retreat center was added to it in 1998.

As James William Coleman notes, although IMS and Spirit Rock share similar organizational structures, they have taken distinctively different directions. Under the leadership of Goldstein and Salzberg, IMS has remained close to the Burmese model, whereas Spirit Rock, strongly influenced by Kornfield, has incorporated the insights of other spiritual traditions and Western psychology.[7] In earlier research I delineated these differences through the signifiers "East Coast Vipassana" and "West Coast Vipassana" and noted that while IMS has remained faithful to the intensive retreat model, Spirit Rock has prioritized the integration of meditation with daily householder life.[8]

Spirit Rock's integrative vision is expressed on multiple levels: organizational structure, general ethos, and teaching format. The responsibility for the spiritual direction of the center falls to the Spirit Rock Teachers Council. This is a collective of twenty-nine lay teachers and two Western monastics, Ajahn Amaro and Ayya Anandabodhi, both of whom trained in Ajahn Chah's Thai forest tradition. A few of the senior lay teachers have trained and been ordained in monasteries in Asia; other lay teachers have received teacher training from them. One of the most striking characteristics of the Teachers Council is the considerable percentage of teachers who are also practicing psychotherapists. Another notable feature is that many teachers declare that they are influenced by the nondual teachings of Zen and Tibetan Buddhism and the Hindu school Advaita Vedanta. Also, many of the teachers are married with children, a situation that has greatly influenced the general ethos of the center.

Spirit Rock declares that its "teachings are grounded in the essence of the Buddha's teaching in the Pali discourse," but it also significantly departs from Theravada Buddhism in drawing from a number of other spiritual and psychological traditions and offering a range of innovative programs. For example, one can find classes called "Sexuality as Spiritual Practice" alongside "Vipassana Meditation," and "Working with Judgments" next to "Core Buddhist Teachings." This reflects what Kornfield describes as Spirit Rock's dual commitment to preserving its Theravadin lineages and expressing a willingness to be innovative.[9]

A central characteristic of West Coast Vipassana is its distinctive relational and integrative approach to meditation and enlightenment. At the core of Kornfield's project is his belief that meditation is not sufficient for full awakening. On the first page of his *Bringing Home the Dharma,* a book he heralds as containing the wisdom of forty years of teaching Buddhism in North America, Kornfield laments, "Mistakenly, people associate Buddhist teachings exclusively with sitting quietly in meditation." As a corrective to this misperception, he says, "The wholeness of awakening is the message of this book."[10] Since the 1980s, Kornfield's teachings have been littered with reflections such as, "For most people meditation practice does not do it all. At best, it's one important piece of a complex path of opening and awakening."[11]

Kornfield supports these statements with reference to his own personal experience, sharing the problems he faced as he made the transition from monastic to householder life:

> Although I had arrived back from the monastery clear, spacious, and high, in short order I discovered, through my relationship, in the communal household where I lived, and in my graduate work, that my meditation had helped me very little with my human relationships. I was still emotionally immature, acting out the same painful patterns of blame and fear, acceptance and rejection that I had before my Buddhist training; only the horror was that I was beginning to see these patterns more clearly.... The roots of my unhappiness

in relationships had not been examined. I had very few skills for dealing with my feelings or engaging on an emotional level or for living wisely with my friends or loved ones.[12]

Kornfield claims that many of his peers began Buddhist practice with the fantasy that they could transcend their individual painful psychodynamic histories. However, addressing personal emotional issues is essential because whatever meditative heights are reached, one can never fully transcend the personal self. This point was repeated in my interviews with Spirit Rock teachers: all stressed that profound moments of awakening were inevitably followed by a return to the self. Similarly, they referred to students who had deep spiritual experiences but remained unhealthy and neurotic in their personal lives.[13]

Kornfield also reports that at least half of the Western students on the annual three-month retreats at IMS are unable to continue with Vipassana practice because they encounter so many unresolved emotional and psychological issues.[14] This confirmed the earlier findings of Jack Engler and Dan Brown, who conducted a Rorschach study of Vipassana meditators before and after a three-month retreat and found that about half were unable to sustain Vipassana practice because they became overwhelmed by unresolved developmental conflicts. As Engler explains: "Trying to get them to redirect their attention to note simple arising and passing away is usually unsuccessful. The press of personal issues is just too great."[15]

Kornfield and Engler also draw attention to accounts by Asian Buddhist teachers who have confessed to being bewildered at the psychological problems they encounter in their Western students. On his first visit to the United States, Mahasi Sayadaw revealed that many students seemed to be suffering from problems that were unfamiliar to him and said he discovered a new form of dukkha, called "psychological suffering."[16] Similarly, the Dalai Lama was astonished to hear that many Westerners suffer from self-hatred and pointed out that there was no equivalent Tibetan word for this psychological issue.[17] For Kornfield and Engler, these observations signify that freedom from personal emotional issues cannot be achieved simply by prescribing more meditation practice. Engler believes this is particularly true for relational issues such as trust and intimacy: "These issues can't be resolved simply by watching the moment-to-moment flow of thoughts, feelings, and sensations in the mind. These problems arise in relationships; they have to be healed in relationships."[18]

The inability of meditation to act as a total cure for all has led Kornfield and others to advocate for the integration of meditation with other healing practices. This "meditation-plus" approach has led to a number of innovations, such as incorporating trauma theory into retreat settings. The Insight teacher training program started at Spirit Rock, for example, requires that trainees complete one year of psychotherapeutic training, and Peter Levine's "somatic experiencing," a psychosomatic approach to healing trauma, is one of three optional therapeutic modalities. Kornfield also calls for a more general integrative approach toward meditation. In reflections such as "Daily Life as Meditation," "Moving into the World," and "Honoring Family Karma," Kornfield cautions against limiting Buddhist practice to meditation retreats and describes parenting as a "sacred act" and the home as "a wonderful temple."[19] This approach is promoted at Spirit Rock with events such as the family program, which seeks to make Insight teachings and practices relevant to the daily lives of families, teens, and children.

While retreats at Spirit Rock include Mahasi Sayadaw's noting practice, West Coast Vipassana also favors a distinctive style of Vipassana drawn from Ajahn Chah's Thai forest tradition and heavily influenced by nondual Mahayana and tantric Buddhist approaches. Rather than the Mahasi method, for instance, Kornfield teaches Vipassana as a nonresistant awareness of whatever is arising in one's experience. He links this back to Ajahn Chah's teacher Ajahn Mun, who taught an approach to Vipassana that was rooted in a "nondual, unconditioned awareness."[20] Ajahn Amaro, the sole male monastic on the Spirit Rock Teachers Council, draws similarities between Ajahn Chah's style of Vipassana practice and *rigpa*, the tantric nondual awareness practice taught by Tsoknyi Rinpoche, with whom many of the Spirit Rock teachers have trained. Amaro sees a number of similarities between Chah's approach and Dzogchen, such as the understanding of the mind as nondual awareness and a focus on resting in this awareness in daily activity. He concludes that in some ways the Thai forest tradition has more in common with the Dzogchen than the Burmese Theravada tradition.[21]

Another distinctive characteristic of West Coast Vipassana is the promotion of a gentler and heart-centered orientation to meditation practice rather than the rigorous and demanding approach associated with the Burmese tradition. Kornfield discusses how his approach to meditation has relaxed over the course of his teaching career: "In the first years we put an emphasis on great striving and effort, just as we were taught in Asia. But we learned that, in this culture, when people use great striving, they tend to judge themselves or tie themselves in knots. Feelings of unworthiness and self-criticism create huge problems so we learned to integrate a lot of metta or loving-kindness."[22]

Kornfield genders this striving approach to meditation as masculine: it is practicing like "a samurai warrior," "the warrior fighting a battle mode of practice," and it revolves around "having to defeat the enemy in battle."[23] Correspondingly, he frames his alternative as an expression of a wider feminization of Buddhist practice that has occurred in the West. Kornfield states that Asian Buddhism has been largely a masculine and patriarchal affair. Men have had sole authority over the tradition and have presented enlightenment as a condition to be attained through renunciation and self-mastery. American Buddhism, however, has developed a more feminine style of practice. As he explains, "Not only is there a clear movement to abandon the superficial structures of sexism and patriarchy, there is also a more profound movement to develop the dharma as a practice of relationship with the body, the community, the earth, and to stress interdependence and healing rather than conquering or abandoning."[24]

This reorientation toward meditation takes place within a wider revisioning of the Buddhist goal of enlightenment. Kornfield promotes a pluralistic perspective, noting that there are many valid Buddhist and non-Buddhist paths to awakening, and he rejects the concept of a linear, hierarchical path in favor of a more circular process.[25] He also rejects the Buddhist soteriological concept of a complete and perfect enlightenment in which all afflictions have been permanently uprooted. Although the latter appears in Buddhist texts, Kornfield explains it as an archetypal ideal and inspirational guide rather than a concrete reality.

In place of a transcendent, final liberation, Kornfield advances what he calls "an embodied enlightenment" or "mature spirituality."[26]

The revisioning of meditation and enlightenment seen within West Coast Vipassana is supported by three legitimation strategies: Buddhist, experiential, and pragmatic. Kornfield explains differences between Spirit Rock and IMS as reflecting differences between the Thai and Burmese Theravadin lineages. He notes that Ajahn Chah and Mahasi Sayadaw had very different approaches to meditation and enlightenment. Describing Chah, Kornfield confesses: "While he was a fantastic dharma teacher, he was not a very precise or detailed meditation teacher. The reason was simple: he wasn't that interested in meditation experiences." Chah rarely taught about different stages of enlightenment because he believed students would become attached to them. His approach, rather, was to focus on "the embodiment of practice" in the wider monastic community. By contrast, with Mahasi, "There was no community practice—it was all about silent meditation practice."[27]

Another main way that Kornfield legitimates his approach as Buddhist is to align it with Mahayana and tantric nondual Buddhist lineages. Although Spirit Rock officially states that it is "based upon the dharma, the teachings of the Buddha, as expressed in the suttas of the Pali Canon," teachers commonly qualify this with the statement "we do Theravada with a Mahayana attitude."[28] Kornfield also frames the integrative current in American Buddhism as part of the evolution of Asian Buddhism. He argues that earlier forms of Buddhism were primarily renunciatory and rejected the body, sexuality, and the world as obstacles to liberation. As later schools of Buddhism developed, however, a nondualistic perspective that celebrated "liberation in this very life and on this very earth" developed. It is this nondual perspective, Kornfield claims, that is spreading throughout American Buddhism.[29]

The second main source of legitimation Kornfield draws on is the experiential, referring frequently to his own experiences and those of his peers and students to illustrate the limits of meditation. He reinforces this experiential thread by pointing to the gap between textual ideals of a perfect enlightenment and the behavior of actual Buddhist teachers. For example, he observes that many Buddhist teachers have been involved in sexual scandals and other forms of impropriety.[30] Closely related to the experiential thread is the pragmatic. Kornfield says that because convert American Buddhism is predominantly a lay phenomenon, questions of integration and relationship have naturally come to the forefront: "The most frequently asked question (from retreatants) in that first decade of retreats and thereafter was some version of, 'How do I live this? How do I integrate it? How do I have support for embodying this year-round?'"[31]

Secure Attachment and External Mindfulness: The Relational/Integrative Current in Gen X

While Kornfield has done much to legitimate the integration of psychotherapeutic discourse into Buddhism, his writings contain little specific information on what types of therapeutic thought and methods he draws from. Dharma Punx NYC + Brooklyn teacher Josh Korda, however, explicitly integrates the two fields and is a useful example of how the relational/integrative current in the Insight network has been further developed by Gen X teachers. Describing itself as "an alternative Buddhist community in the Insight/Vipassana tradition," Dharma Punx NYC + Brooklyn runs autonomously but is informally affiliated with the Against the Stream Buddhist Meditation Society, a growing network started by Noah Levine. Levine became well-known in American Buddhist convert circles through his memoir *Dharma Punx,* which details his journey to sobriety through Buddhist practice and his crafting of an alternative form of American Buddhism that draws its inspiration from the punk/hardcore scene rather than the hippie counterculture that shaped the first wave of American convert teachers.[32]

In 2003, Levine began Dharma Punx NYC but passed over the main teacher role to Korda when he returned to the East Coast two years later. Alongside training under Levine, Korda has trained primarily with Ajahn Sucitto, Ajahn Amaro, and Thanissaro Bhikkhu, Western monastics from the Thai forest tradition, and Tara Brach, a popular Insight teacher and psychotherapist. Although Brach is situated on the East Coast in Washington, DC, her approach, which stresses self-acceptance, emotional maturity, and an embodied rather than transcendent practice, places her firmly in the "West Coast" camp. Korda has developed

a distinctive approach to Buddhism that draws heavily on psychoanalytic developmental narratives, particularly attachment theory. Drawing from theorists such as D. W. Winnicott, John Bowlby, and Mary
Ainsworth, many of Korda's dharma talks present a narrative of a basic
universal trajectory of human development—what is needed for its successful navigation, and the ways in which it can go awry. Taking this
developmental narrative as his starting point, Korda focuses on how aspects of Buddhism can be utilized to promote emotional and relational
health for American students and how these developmental insights can
be incorporated to make Buddhist practice safer and more effective in
the West.

Korda promotes Vipassana meditation as a tool for emotional,
particularly relational health, but also sees it as a potential danger to
that health. To understand this, it is necessary to grasp his distinction
between different forms of Vipassana, or mindfulness: one form is focused on observing inner phenomena, specifically to develop awareness of the three marks of existence—*dukkha* (suffering), *anicca* (impermanence), and *anatta* (no-self); another form is rooted in *sati,* the
cultivation of awareness of whatever is arising in the four foundations of
experience rather than a strict focus on the three marks of experience.
When Korda promotes Vipassana practice as contributing to emotional
regulation and relational healing, he is referring to *sati sampujanna,*
which he translates as "a non-judgmental, inquisitive, somatic awareness" and "a fully receptive present time awareness."[33] When Korda criti-
cizes Vipassana practice as psychologically counterproductive or even
injurious for certain people, such as those struggling with depression
or depersonalization, he is most often referring to the cultivation of a
detached observation of the three marks of existence as articulated in
the Progress of Insight model. For this reason, Korda says he teaches
only open-awareness forms of Vipassana and mindfulness. He typically
describes the function of *sati sampujanna* in the following way:

> Vipassana is about creating a space in which these feelings
> can be felt and welcomed. It allows a space for messy and
> spontaneous and authentic feelings to unfold. Resistance is
> what makes these feelings so powerful. Meditation is giving

our feelings the mothering that we have been craving so long.
We give ourselves the parenting we never had and begin the
process of healing: opening and reintegration, softening and
healing, we own all our experience, which is the most emotionally healthy state we can be in.[34]

Vipassana, in other words, becomes the means to establish that
which was not developed in childhood: the internalization of a secure
basis that allows for emotional self-regulation and attuned relationships
with others. Although Korda does not explicitly gender his approach as
feminine, his emphasis on the mothering function and maternal aspects
of mindfulness echoes the feminization of Buddhist practice explored
above regarding Kornfield, who describes his approach through maternal metaphors, switching from describing his practice as being like "a
samurai warrior" to one of "a devoted mother of a newborn child."[35]

Although Korda promotes Vipassana as a tool for developing emotional self-regulation and secure attachment, he also warns that it has
limits and can be used in psychologically damaging ways. One such way
is when the practice is employed as a dissociative technique for "spiritual bypassing," or the use of spiritual practice for developmentally defensive purposes.[36] Korda stresses the limits of Vipassana for individuals
with disorganized attachment patterns. As he notes: "Painful emotions,
born of early childhood abandonments and poor attachment schemes,
do not go away on their own. They require reliable relational support to
override."[37]

For such people, individual meditation practice is limited, and they
would benefit more from community support. Korda, however, laments
that the sangha, used here in a loose sense of "Buddhist community," has
been all too often neglected in American Buddhism. As a corrective, he
frequently refers to the importance of *kalyana mitta*, or spiritual friendship, and the centrality of the sangha in the Pali Canon. He supports this
canonical perspective through psychoanalytic and neuroscientific evidence on the inherently social nature of humans and reframes the purpose of sangha through the lens of secure attachment. His dharma talks
are littered with claims such as, "Secure connection via wise friendships
are the whole of the path, the foundation of understanding the dharma,

the security of the third refuge."[38] Similarly, he champions the sangha as providing a "safe container," which can collectively contain emotions that individuals cannot tolerate alone and thereby help heal past relational wounds.[39]

Another population vulnerable to the misuse of Vipassana are people who have suffered from trauma. For these individuals, Korda explains, Vipassana can trigger a "flooding" of overwhelming sensations. In such cases, he recommends switching to concentration meditations in order to lessen the impact. Similarly, Korda has questioned the centrality of intensive silent retreat practice in the Insight community. He laments "a fetishization, if not outright idealization of long-term silent retreats as a solution for all forms of suffering and despair."[40] This view is problematic because such retreats can actually be psychically damaging for certain people. For example, for those who have insecure, ambivalent, or disorganized attachment patterns, the silent, no-eye-contact format of these retreats can retrigger attachment breakdowns. Further, for some participants, the dissolution of self experienced through the Progress of Insight path can lead to intense states of psychic regression. For such students, the allotted fifteen-minute interview with the teacher is insufficient, and teachers must strive to provide reassuring emotional exchanges. This was one of the reasons Korda incorporates periods of interpersonal inquiry and relational mindfulness practices into his retreats. Moreover, he believes that Vipassana retreat teachers should be trained to recognize and respond appropriately to practitioners showing signs of retraumatization. He believes it is crucial that teachers are able to discern between someone who is contemplating impermanence versus someone who is experiencing a dissociative episode or experiencing depersonalization.[41]

In addition to using relational psychoanalytic insights to temper classical Buddhist meditation practice, Korda has also begun to develop a number of relational and external mindfulness practices that aim to bring the focused awareness cultivated in individual meditation to interpersonal interactions.[42] Although Korda draws from non-Buddhist sources, such as "conscious interaction," in developing these practices, he also legitimates them as Buddhist via Bhikkhu Analayo's commentary on the *Satipatthana Sutta*. Analayo discusses the refrain on internal and external mindfulness within the sutta, noting that the presence of the latter has been put aside in modern translations. After considering various interpretations, Analayo concludes that external mindfulness means being mindful of other people and discusses several ways to practice this. His recovery of "external mindfulness" in the *Satipatthana Sutta* has made a strong impact on the Insight community and is one of the required texts in Spirit Rock's Community Dharma Leaders program.[43]

Jessica Morey, who is founder of Inward Bound Mindfulness Education and coteaches an annual retreat with Korda, has also developed external mindfulness practices, which she says she developed out of personal and pedagogical necessity. Despite her own extensive meditation training at both the IMS and Theravadin monasteries in Burma, she found that she was still struggling with interpersonal dynamics in her life. She also found in her work with teenagers that they were unable to exclusively focus on silent individual meditation practice. These two experiences prompted her to foster a more relational approach with her Buddhist and secular mindfulness practice.[44]

Korda and Morey's employment of relational mindfulness practices reflects emerging patterns within both the wider Insight and Dharma Punx communities. One example of this is Gregory Kramer's Insight Dialogue, which he developed after discovering that Insight practice was not sufficiently addressing the suffering generated by interpersonal dynamics. Kramer, who trained with Theravadin monastics, believes that even in Buddhist traditions in which community life is a transformative practice, meditation is largely an internal individual practice. He developed the practice of Insight Dialogue, or interpersonal meditation, to attend to a part of the Buddhist path—the relational—that he believes has been historically neglected. While it is grounded in Theravada Buddhism, it utilizes psychotherapeutic insights and is presented as particularly relevant for the needs of Western students.[45] Another example is the work of George Haas, who has developed two Buddhist and attachment theory courses delivered in either a ten-month or eight-week intensive format—The Meaningful Life for general audiences, and Meditation Interventions for the Addiction Process for the recovery community—as well as a mentoring training and certification program for Against the Stream. Haas is responsible for the circulation and systematization of attachment theory in the Against the Stream network. Morey notes that her work on relational mindfulness is indebted to the mentorship she received from Haas.[46]

As with Kornfield's approach, Korda's distinctive relational approach is situated in a wider framework that reconfigures classic Buddhist soteriology. Korda rarely mentions Nirvana, and when he does it is always in naturalistic rather than metaphysical terms. Liberation is "the capacity to be with whatever arises in life" rather than a "mystical state." His descriptions of Nirvana fall into two main categories: one defines it as the absence of the three poisons, generally rendered in psychotherapeutic terms such as the relinquishing of "unskillful defense mechanisms and addictive behaviors"; and the other is an unconditioned state, "a true stillness that is deep and unassailable." He sees both as impermanent experiences rather than the permanent uprooting of afflictions that are detailed canonically.[47] Korda has little interest in teaching a classical Progress of Insight practice and instead focuses on the cultivation of "an awareness without agenda," which he believes is inherently healing and transformative. He recognizes that this is a departure from, but not necessarily at odds with, canonical Theravada. Korda believes that the difference between his approach and the canonical is that he sees therapeutic goals like secure attachment not only as necessary preconditions for higher stages of practice, but as legitimate Buddhist goals in themselves.[48]

Korda legitimates his relational revisioning through three main strategies: Buddhist, pragmatic, and cultural. He validates his approach as Buddhist through referring frequently to the Pali Canon, which he sees as offering "the first profound and complete set of psychological insights."[49] As is common to the Against the Stream network, Korda presents the Buddha as an early radical psychologist. The pragmatic strategy refers to the fact that his approach responds to the specific emotional needs of his students. The cultural strategy is when Korda legitimates his innovations by situating them as continuous with the assimilations that Buddhism undertook as it traveled across Asia. Korda feels "every entitlement to import insights from modern neuroscience, schools of western philosophy and clinical psychology into my teaching and personal practice because the Buddha insisted, in the *Kalama Sutta,* to constantly examine our beliefs in terms of usefulness in real, daily life."[50]

"Liberation in This Very Life": The Textual/Technical Current

Whereas both Kornfield and Korda promote a form of Vipassana meditation that is associated with the non–goal-orientated awareness practice of Ajahn Chah, practitioners within the textual/technical current have focused on the systematic and progressive Progress of Insight practice as taught by Mahasi Sayadaw. One of the earliest iterations of this approach came from U Pandita Sayadaw (1921–2016), the successor of Mahasi, whose emphasis on "heroic effort" in meditation practice was motivated by his belief that Nirvana was attainable for monastic and lay practitioners in "this very life."[51] U Pandita is described by his IMS students as a "spiritual warrior," and it was his rigorous approach to meditation and enlightenment that Kornfield rejected in favor of a more heart-centered and gentler approach.[52] However, senior Insight teacher Steve Armstrong, who is the cofounder of the Vipassana Metta Foundation on Maui, has refocused attention on the approach of U Pandita, under whom he trained for five years as a monastic in Burma. Armstrong was the managing editor of a fifteen-year project that resulted in the 2016 publication of the first English translation of Mahasi's two-volume book *Manuel of Insight,* which offers a detailed explanation of how to attain liberation through Insight practice. Whereas the first generation of Western Vipassana teachers avoided speaking about the attainment of liberation through Insight because they feared their students would become obsessed with spiritual attainment, Armstrong asserts the importance of this "roadmap" in order to fully uproot suffering and aims to introduce it to a wide audience.[53]

 In addition to the Progress of Insight, practitioners in the textual/technical current have also turned their attention to concentration, or *jhana,* meditation. There are two main types of meditation in canonical Theravada Buddhism: concentration meditation (*samathabhavana*), which aims toward the achievement of states of deep concentration, and Insight meditation (*vipassanabhavana*), which aims at the liberatory realization of the three marks of existence.[54] Traditionally, *jhana* practice was undertaken as preparation for Insight meditation. Mahasi, however, taught Insight without prior cultivation of concentration, and because the IMS adopted his method, *jhana* practice was not taught in the Insight network until recently. According to Kornfield, the founders of IMS made a "trade-off" and decided to teach Insight rather than concentration practice because "attainments of concentration won't really serve you to live as a liberated being in the world."[55]

Although initially neglected in the Insight movement, as Natalie Quli traces, around 2007, the *jhanas,* or the eight states of consciousness brought on by concentration, started to become "kind of a buzzword" in Insight circles, and teachers began to offer retreats based on them. Quli has examined the work of the most popular monastic and lay *jhana* teachers whose work is accessible for an English-speaking audience and has delineated a number of shared characteristics. One is that all of the teachers emphasize meditation practice and a firm belief that Nirvana is available in this lifetime for both lay and monastic populations. Another is that teachers draw heavily on the early suttas or commentaries or both. Some accept both the suttas and the later commentaries, particularly the *Visuddhimagga,* and others privilege the suttas and reject the later commentaries.[56]

Erik Braun has also examined the increasing popularity of *jhana* practice within the Insight network. He has identified the common characteristics of *jhana* practice as taught within the network as well as highlighting the factors he believes are responsible for its popularity. To begin with, all *jhana* teachers believe that enlightenment is possible and available to both monastic and lay practitioners. They claim that cultivating the *jhanas* before Insight practice is vital to attaining enlightenment. For example, Ajahn Brahm reflects: "Many Buddhists, monastics and lay have completed many meditation retreats lasting longer than seven days and remain unenlightened. Please do not blame the Buddha!"[57] Brahm goes on to explain that the problem is that many practitioners do not undertake Vipassana practice with the purified and focused mind that results from *jhana* practice. Not only are the *jhanas* crucial to reaching enlightenment, they are also very useful in making speedier progress along the path of Insight. Leigh Brasington, for example, calls them "techniques" that offer a "turbo-charge" toward enlightenment.[58]

Another core characteristic of *jhana* practice is a commitment and fidelity to traditional Buddhist teachings and practices. As Braun notes, although there is a strong trend of Western practitioners secularizing and psychologizing Buddhism, the interest in the *jhanas* illustrates a countercurrent: "The *jhanas* tend to promote a vision of practice that actually demands a greater commitment to Buddhist teachings and modes of practice."[59] Brasington, for instance, requires students who come to his *jhana* retreats to have completed at least two seven-day retreats, and his retreats last from two weeks to a month. Similarly, interest in the *jhanas* demonstrates an appreciation for canonical and commentarial Buddhist literature. There is, as Brasington states, "a desire to adhere more closely to what is perceived as the much more pronounced valuation of the *jhanas* in the canonical texts than previously acknowledged."[60]

In a 2016 interview titled "Mastering the Jhanas," Shaila Catherine, founder of Insight Meditation South Bay in California, detailed the practice of *jhana* meditation with close reference to Theravadin canonical and commentarial literature. Describing the *jhanas* as a "precise technology" that is indispensable to the attainment of enlightenment, Catherine first began concentration practices on a yearlong retreat in 2003–2004. She says that this was a time when very little reading material on the *jhanas* was available in English, and very few Westerners practiced them.[61] Since then, however, Catherine has written two influential books on *jhana* practice and is now renowned as an expert on it.[62] Santikaro Bhikkhu, for example, endorses her as part of a movement "to restore a well-rounded understanding of Buddha-Dhamma," extolling this over "the trendy promises of pop Buddhism—better relationships and the like."[63]

Armstrong and Catherine illustrate that in addition to the relational/integrative current, another distinct trend to emerge from the Insight network is an interest in more textual- and technical-based forms of Buddhist meditation practice that are specifically geared toward the soteriological goal of enlightenment. Shinzen Young, another figure who has designed a systematic, technical approach to Vipassana, describes himself as "one of those teachers who is comfortable with the

E-word."[64] Further, as the comments by Santikaro Bhikkhu indicate, this approach is often presented as more legitimately Buddhist and superior to the relational, therapeutic approach of figures like Kornfield and Korda. Pragmatic Dharma, a loose network of practitioners who promote intensive meditation practice and enlightenment as an attainable goal, provides a useful case study of the textual/technical lineage because they incorporate U Pandita's rigorous approach to meditation, draw heavily on *jhana* practice, and explicitly position themselves as an alternative to the relational lineage.

"Enlightenment Is Not a Dirty Word": Pragmatic Dharma

Pragmatic Dharma, also dubbed Hardcore Dharma, refers to a developmental, goal-oriented approach to meditation associated with two American teachers, Kenneth Folk and Daniel Ingram, and the loose international virtual community committed to this "hardcore" form of practice. Ingram describes Pragmatic Dharma as a "reformist meditation movement" that is marked by a pragmatic, experiential, and transparent approach to awakening. The community is nonsectarian and draws from a number of Buddhist and non-Buddhist models of awakening. However, both Ingram and Folk trained intensively in the Mahasi lineage, and the Progress of Insight map occupies a privileged position in the network. Much of Pragmatic Dharma occurs online; on websites such as Dharma Overground, the Hamilton Project, and the Awake Network, practitioners from across the world discuss their meditative attainments within a pragmatic framework.

As is characteristic of the movement, Folk discusses his meditation accomplishments frankly and frequently.[65] His interest in awakening began with a profound experience of "unity consciousness" after taking LSD, an experience that, he claims, cured him of a cocaine addiction with which he had been struggling as a "suicidal and depressed" musician. After this, Folk began to explore a range of spiritual approaches before meeting his primary teacher, Bill Hamilton, in 1982. Hamilton taught the Mahasi method of Vipassana and, like Mahasi, talked openly about attaining the four paths of enlightenment as described in the

Visuddhimagga. Inspired by this systematic and transparent approach to awakening, Folk trained in the Mahasi lineage and completed more than three years of intensive retreat in the United States and Burma.

Folk has extended Hamilton's transparent and systematic approach to meditation and awakening, which he offers as an alternative to the "culture of secrecy" that characterizes the Insight community. Folk laments that although the IMS is faithful to the Progress of Insight model, it discourages any talk of attaining enlightenment. As he puts it: "Even the head teacher there, Joseph Goldstein, does not claim to have reached enlightenment. I think this is discouraging for practitioners. I found it very disempowering and feel there is a false modesty in the culture. Enlightenment is almost a dirty thing to talk about."

When Folk attended the annual three-month retreat at IMS in 1991, he received only vague responses from teachers when he described his meditation progress; and when he worked there as a staff member almost a decade later, he was considered "something of a renegade" for talking openly about his meditation accomplishments. He attributes this "culture of silence" to Goldstein's own "modest nature" as well as IMS's respect for monastic Vinaya culture in which monks are forbidden to share their meditative attainments for fear of causing disharmony in the sangha. Folk feels strongly that the lack of transparency regarding meditation progress is unhelpful and harmful to students as it leaves them unmotivated and confused about their meditation practice. As well as stressing the pedagogical value of a transparent, goal-oriented approach to meditation, Folk believes it is "useful for shaking up and galvanizing the Buddhist mainstream culture."

In privileging enlightenment, Folk both draws on and disrupts Buddhist narratives. On one hand, he follows the Progress of Insight model to define awakening as the liberatory realization of the three marks of existence: *dukkha, anicca,* and *anatta.* He also frequently references early canonical Buddhism and Buddhist teachers such as Mahasi Sayadaw to legitimate his approach. On the other hand, he does not hesitate to reject elements of Buddhism that do not align with his personal meditative experience. For example, he discards the metaphysical/cosmological and institutional dimensions of the tradition and sidesteps ethics, noting that they are important but not what he teaches.

Folk presents himself as a secular Buddhist teacher or "meditation coach" who has "stripped the dogma away" from awakening. He values Buddhism for providing conceptual maps and techniques for awakening but distinguishes between "technologies of awakening" and the vehicle for those technologies. While Buddhism has served as a traditional vehicle for awakening, it "may not be the best container for us anymore and we are seeing other vehicles emerge for these technologies of awakening." Folk offers one of these new vehicles by reframing awakening through a secular and naturalistic lens. He proposes a model of "contemplative fitness" in which meditative progress is seen as analogous to sport and health development. Naturalizing enlightenment also has the effect of democratizing it. In Buddhist Geek talks such as "Enlightenment for the Rest of Us" and "Ordinary People Can Get Enlightened," Folk stresses that enlightenment is accessible to a much larger population than acknowledged in traditional Buddhism.

Daniel Ingram, another leader in the Pragmatic Dharma community, is a longstanding friend of Folk, whom he first met in 1998 when Ingram was a sound assistant for a rock band that Folk joined. Folk introduced Ingram to Hamilton, and Ingram also began practicing in Mahasi's Burmese lineage. However, he dates his interest in the contemplative life to much earlier, to experiences he had as a child and teenager, which he recognizes in retrospect as *jhana* states.[66] He made an impact in Western Buddhist circles with the publication of his book *Mastering the Core Teachings of the Buddha,* in which he claimed the title of "arahat" and offered an alternative approach to awakening than that found in the mainstream "boomer" Buddhist world. In a provocative tone, Ingram argues that mainstream Western dharma has become overpsychologized and has replaced the soteriological goal of Buddhism—attaining enlightenment through intensive meditation practice—with a therapeutic focus on emotional health. It has substituted the classical Buddhist focus on the *processes* of experience with attention to the *contents* of experience and in doing so has transformed meditation retreats into therapeutic sessions.[67]

Ingram believes that the boomer teachers have promoted a more relaxed "just staying with your experience" approach over the rigorous goal-oriented model of Mahasi because the latter is difficult to practice and is also hard to sell to a mainstream audience. American students, he feels, have been "shortchanged" in being given only vague medita- tion instructions and actively discouraged to strive too much in their practice. For Ingram, the fact that practitioners do not realize that linear meditation progress can be made is nothing short of a "tragedy." Like Folk, he attributes this to a culture of silence that prevails in the Insight mainstream, which, borrowing from Hamilton, he dubs "mushroom culture" because just as "mushrooms are fed manure and kept in the dark," so Western practitioners are not receiving proper meditation in- structions nor being sufficiently educated on the stages of awakening.[68]

Ingram's aim is to transition from the overpsychologized dharma of the boomer generation to focus on the specific attainments detailed in the Pali Canon and commentaries. To this end, *Mastering the Core Teachings of the Buddha* offers a detailed first-person account of travers- ing the Progress of Insight path, with careful attention to the hindrances, or the "dark night," met along the way. By following the Mahasi method rigorously, Ingram claims that meditators can attain "stream entry" in two or three months, an achievement that will result in a considerable diminishing of suffering in their lives.

In presenting his pragmatic and goal-oriented approach, Ingram alternates between claiming Buddhist authority and disrupting it. On one hand, he defines enlightenment as the realization of the three marks of existence and legitimates his approach through recourse to the Bud- dhist canon and Buddhist teachers such as Mahasi. Similarly, he calls himself a "Buddhist traditionalist," one "who really tries to plunge the depths of the heart, mind and body as the Buddha so clearly admonished his followers to do."[69] On the other hand, Ingram does not limit himself to Buddhism and states that one of his goals is to develop a nonsectarian meta-map of human contemplative experience. As he enthuses, "I imag- ine that one day there will be training on the maps and basic spiritual development in some generic, non-sectarian way in elementary school, just as we learn about biology and mathematics, and so this would be- come just another ordinary, accepted, standard part of human educa- tion, and so everyone would know about these things as if they were the ordinary, natural things they are."[70]

Ingram was the subject of a *New York Times* article, which notes that although his arahat claims are "audacious," they are being corroborated by an increasing number of practitioners in online forums.[71] The most popular of these is the Dharma Overground, which Ingram started with technological assistance from Buddhist Geeks founder and fellow Pragmatic Dharma teacher Vincent Horn. As Ingram explains, the function of the site was to provide a virtual equivalent to the early Buddhist community, in which "the novices would be listening to the anagamis and arahats debating stuff and it was all just this sort of open thing back in the day."[72] The main principles of Dharma Overground are set out on its homepage: pragmatism over dogmatism, practice over faith, personal responsibility, transparency, collectivity and mutual support rather than hierarchical teacher-student models, and inclusion. Dharma Overground features an extensive "Dharma Wiki," which offers detailed information regarding various meditation techniques ranging from the Mahasi noting technique to choiceless awareness practice and Buddhist and non-Buddhist maps of awakening. All of these are situated within a wider pragmatic and experiential frame in which contributors are reminded, "adding an entry to the wiki is explicitly a claim to direct, personal understanding and attainment of whatever you are saying."[73] Another feature of Dharma Overground is its lively and often combative discussion boards on which users debate their meditative attainments under categories such as "Insight and Wisdom," "Concentration," "Dharma Diagnostic Clinic," and "Claims to Attainments."[74]

Aloha Dharma, which is run by Ron Crouch, a well-known teacher in the community, is another popular Pragmatic Dharma website.[75] After a few years of meditation practice, Crouch began to have powerful experiences but struggled to understand them until he stumbled upon a book about the *jhanas*. It was not until he became Folk's student in late 2009, however, that he started making real spiritual progress. Crouch was astonished but inspired by Folk's claim that ordinary people could become enlightened, and after meeting with Folk once a week to receive personalized meditation instructions, he claims to have reached the fourth state of Insight himself in about a year and a half. After being empowered by Folk in 2011, he began teaching and reports having had around three hundred students since then.[76] He says that typically his students have received vague meditation instructions and are discouraged in their local sanghas from going deeper in meditation, so they come to him looking for precise and pragmatic guidance. His student testimonies confirm this with comments such as, "He guided me out of the Dark Night, through Stream Entry, and past 2nd Path in about 2.5 years' time" and, "He's very upfront with everything he teaches, which is refreshing in the meditation world."

Crouch reaches a wider audience through Aloha Dharma, which had 60,000 visitors and more than 170,000 page views between 2011, when the site went live, and 2016. The site contains a number of posts written by Crouch, such as "What Is Pragmatic Dharma?," which defines it by five key characteristics: pragmatism, transparency, a digital community, secularism, and a focus on awakening in ordinary life. Under the Common Questions section, Crouch states, "the purpose of meditation is not to become a better person or to become more relaxed but to attain enlightenment." He explains that the "path" is not a metaphor but "a clear and richly detailed description of what happens to a meditator from their first sit all the way to enlightenment." The signposts on the path are "universal, automatic and impersonal" and occur naturally if the technique is followed correctly regardless of "individual needs."[77]

Another distinct characteristic of Pragmatic Dharma is its overwhelmingly high demographic of male participants and the common use of hypermasculine imagery and terms such as "cowboy," "wild-west dharma," "ninja," and "testosterone-fueled" to describe its approach. No exact figures are available, but the community consensus is that more males than females participate. Both Ingram and Horn have acknowledged that Pragmatic Dharma attracts a particularly white and male audience, saying, "We're just a bunch of dudes hanging out" and, "We're mostly a white, geeky men's club."[78] There has been much commentary from both inside and outside the community on its hypermasculine rhetoric and imagery. Popular blogger Nella Lou at Smiling Buddha Cabaret, for example, noted that Pragmatic Dharma's "masculine approach to dharma" contained "lots of sports, video game and barroom metaphors" and "combative and abrasive" commentary.[79]

Gender and diversity have also been provocative Dharma Overground topics. One thread titled "DhO Male Gender Skew," which ran for more than a month, raised the question of why the number of women participating was so low. A male participant suggested it was due to the fact that women were "nicer" and less likely to participate in aggressive online debates. A female respondent noted that female absence on the site was "no mystery" when the majority of contributors were male and masculine imagery and a combative debating style predominated. Recognizing that women and minorities may be alienated by such things, Ingram has introduced speech guidelines to promote a more inclusive and welcoming online space. Similarly, the original Dharma Overground logo was replaced after it was deemed to be "too militaristic." A tension remains in the community, however, between balancing the need to "encourage gender diversity while not losing the spirit of the place."[80] Although Ingram and others show a sincere interest in increasing female participation and diversity, there is also a clear commitment to retaining Pragmatic Dharma's foundational "hardcore" stance. Much of this is due to the fact that Pragmatic Dharma explicitly positions itself as an alternative to the "softer" feminine approach of mainstream dharma. The masculine rhetoric of Pragmatic Dharma is explicitly claimed as resistance to the "feminization" of North American Buddhism, which is seen as resembling psychotherapy more than Buddhism. As Crouch puts it, Pragmatic Dharma is a "reaction against this new westernized style. It is a move to focus on what matters in the dharma—awakening and what leads to it—rather than the things that seem to be more lifestyle or therapy oriented."[81]

From Meditation Experience to Embodied Enlightenment and Back Again

One of the defining features of Buddhist modernism is an emphasis on meditation experience. Robert Sharf attributes this not to canonical Buddhism but to the influence of Romanticism on Buddhism during colonialism. He traces the modern understanding of individual experience as the core of religion to Friedrich Schleiermacher's attempt to protect religion from Enlightenment critiques. According to Sharf, the interior experiential model was adopted by influential twentieth-century Asian Buddhists from Zen and Theravadin lineages. The Burmese lineage of Mahasi Sayadaw, for example, combines an emphasis on interior meditative experience with the commentarial literature of traditional Theravada. Sharf, however, questions the assumption that meditation experience is central to traditional Asian religious practice. He points out that while meditation might have been esteemed in theory, it did not historically occupy the dominant role in monastic life that is sometimes supposed. Taking the Vipassana movement as an example, he notes that the meditation techniques promoted within it cannot be traced back to before the late nineteenth century and thus are an unreliable source for the reconstruction of premodern Theravada Buddhism. For Sharf, the privileging of meditation seen in the Vipassana movement is problematic because it has unmoored meditation from its traditional Theravadin context of ethics, cosmology, and community.[82]

How are we to situate the two currents explored here in relation to Buddhist modernism and meditation? At first glance, the relational/ therapeutic current appears to be a clear continuation of the modernization of Buddhism. Theravadin monk Thanissaro Bhikkhu, for example, has convincingly argued that many of its themes—wholeness, integration, and interconnectedness—reflect not Buddhism, but Romanticism and its contemporary heir, depth psychology. Hence, he labels it "Buddhist Romanticism" and maintains that although it brings therapeutic benefits to practitioners, it is severely limited compared with the full awakening and freedom from suffering available within Theravada Buddhism.[83]

As with the psychotherapeutic dialogical approaches emerging in the wake of the Zen sexual scandals, however, this current should be seen as both a continuation of and corrective to Buddhist modernism. The relational current questions the privileging of individual meditation experience and stresses the need for a wider communal context to support it. In prioritizing integration over experience, it essentially attempts to reembed the decontextualization of Buddhist meditation that marks Buddhist modernism. Rather than call for a return to Buddhism's traditional ethical and monastic matrix, however, the relational current attempts to forge new foundational contexts that draw heavily from contemporary Western culture, particularly psychotherapeutic discourses. In short, it has replaced traditional ethics with psychotherapy and the monastic context with the lay community.

In calling for a renewed focus on meditation and awakening, the textual/technical current presents itself as a return to traditional Buddhism. Take, for example, Ron Crouch's claim that Pragmatic Dharma is "a return to traditional Buddhism," which "strongly emphasizes attaining specific outcomes, like insight knowledges or stream entry, which are viewed as imminently practical."[84] However, scholars would identify this privileging of meditation and awakening as characteristic of Buddhist modernism rather than traditional Buddhism, in which, as Sharf notes, the practice of meditation did not play a central role. Indeed, Pragmatic Dharma displays many of the features associated with Buddhist modernism: a desire to return to the original teachings of the Buddha in the Pali Canon, an emphasis on meditation, the conviction that Nirvana can be attained in this life, a rejection of superstition and ritual, a belief in the compatibility of Buddhism and modern science, the embrace of democratization and laicization, and an ecumenical attitude toward other Buddhist sects.[85]

Yet, just as with the relational/integrative strand, the textual/technical narrative is more complicated than it appears at first glance. Both Quli and Braun have argued that the popularity of *jhana* meditation complicates the Buddhist modernist narrative. Braun, for instance, tracks the presence of elements more associated with traditional Buddhism, such as a greater commitment to Buddhist teachings, and the acceptance of more supernatural elements, such as meditative powers. Hence, he concludes that interest in the *jhanas* counters the secularization process under way in Buddhist modernism. As he states, "the growing popularity of *jhāna* meditation suggests that radical secularization is only one of a number of possibilities, for the *jhānas* tend to promote a vision of practice that actually demands a greater commitment to Buddhist teachings and modes of practice."[86] A similar observation can be made for the Pragmatic Dharma movement. Ingram, for example, has begun to engage more with the Buddhist *siddhis,* or supernatural powers, associated with certain forms of meditation.[87] Both the relational/integrative and textual/technical currents of meditation and awakening, therefore, simultaneously display patterns of modernization and the renewal of tradition, and neither fits neatly into a Buddhist modernist model. The relational/integrative continues certain Romantic trends, but it also disrupts the privileging of meditative experience and shifts focus to issues of reembedding meditation in a wider cultural container. The textual/technical extends the modernist emphasis on meditation and awakening, but it also reintroduces elements that were initially discarded in the modernist process.

Another notable meditation development that disrupts certain modern sensibilities is the appearance of more contextually aware and population-specific approaches to meditation. As discussed, Buddhist modernism has been marked by the historically unprecedented appearance of large lay meditation retreat centers in both Asia and North America. Underlying this mass-scale practice phenomenon is the modern assumption that meditation is a universally accessible and beneficial practice. The dhamma, as S. N. Goenka put it, "is a universal remedy for universal ills."[88] Such assumptions, however, are increasingly being questioned across the Insight network. As early as the 1980s, Kornfield raised concerns about the psychological suitability of the intensive retreat model for certain populations, and Korda has continued this by calling for Vipassana teachers to be trained to recognize trauma symptoms in retreatants. Motivated by his own experience of "contemplative dissociation," Insight practitioner David Treleaven researched Vipassana through the lens of trauma theory and concluded that the assumption that awareness of the body yields universal beneficial results is misguided.[89] Willoughby Britton's Varieties of Contemplative Experience research project has brought wider attention to the potential deleterious cognitive, affective, perceptual, and psychological effects of meditation practice, much of which she attributes to the lack of wider communal context and support systems for practitioners.[90] One emerging response to these issues is the development of trauma-sensitive approaches to meditation that consider the specific contexts and populations of practice rather than following a one-method-for-all approach.[91] Taken together, the two currents—and an increasing contextual sensibility around Vipassana meditation, which cuts across them—reveal further complexities in the unfolding of Buddhist modernism in North America.

The Dukkha of Racism

Racial Diversity, Inclusion, and Justice Work

On July 1, 2015, a group called Buddhists for Racial Justice started circulating an open letter across Buddhist social media that spoke of the deep sadness at the murders of the nine members of the Emanuel African Methodist Episcopal Church in Charleston, South Carolina, on June 17, 2015. These murders were not only the result of an individual deluded by racial hatred and a desire to start a race war, it stated, but also reflected the legacy of slavery and white supremacy that persisted in the collective consciousness and institutional structures of the United States. As Buddhists, it continued, we are obliged to realize the interconnectedness of experience, to recognize the causes and conditions that perpetuate this collective suffering, and to respond compassionately by uniting the precept of nonharm to tangible actions. Alongside this open letter were two "Calls to Engage": one for white practitioners to awaken to white privilege, and one for practitioners of color to "investigate their own unconscious patterning that perpetuates the suffering of racism." By the next day more than five hundred people from a wide variety of Buddhist lineages had endorsed this letter, and two weeks later that number had risen to fourteen hundred.[1]

The immediate origins of Buddhists for Racial Justice can be traced to May 14, 2015, when a delegation of 125 Buddhists from sixty-three organizations gathered for the first White House–U.S. Buddhist Leadership Conference. At the conference they presented two letters: one on climate change and one titled "Buddhist Statement on Racial Justice." The latter opened with the declaration that as Buddhist teachers they were distressed by the killings of unarmed African Americans brought to attention by the cases of Michael Brown in Ferguson, Missouri, and Eric Garner in New York City. As with the open letter, it intertwined the language of Buddhism—suffering, interdependence, nonharm, and compassion—with that of racial justice.[2]

The impetus for this letter was attributed to the courage of the people of Ferguson and the Black Lives Matter movement, which had brought urgency to Buddhist racial justice work. Both letters, however, should be seen as part of efforts to challenge racism and white privilege in American Buddhist convert communities spanning over two decades. Many of the themes expressed on the website of Buddhists for Racial Justice, for instance, were articulated in *Making the Invisible Visible: Healing Racism in Our Buddhist Communities,* a booklet compiled by a small group of Buddhist practitioners of color and their white allies distributed to the Buddhist Teachers in the West conference at Spirit Rock Meditation Center in June 2000. It declared that for many years the Euro-American middle-class sangha had been resistant to the efforts of people of color and their white allies to raise awareness of the reproduction of oppressive racial and socioeconomic conditions within Western Buddhist sanghas, and unless this was addressed, the dharma risked becoming "irrelevant to vast parts of our society." Interweaving personal experiences of racism with Buddhist teachings and critical race theory, the comprehensive collection also offered a number of resources for combating racism in Western sanghas, ranging from providing institutional diversity trainings to addressing racism in dharma talks.[3]

Many of the contributors to this collection and others have continued to address the lack of diversity and presence of racism and white hegemony within American convert sanghas through a variety of strategies, from hosting forums to creating exclusive meditation groups and retreats for people of color. Some of this work is described in the 2004 anthology *Dharma, Color, and Culture: New Voices in Western Buddhism,* edited by Hilda Gutíerrez Baldoquín, a lineage holder in the Soto Zen tradition, which was the first collection to bring together the voices of Western Buddhist practitioners of color across a broad spectrum of lineages.[4] For much of this time, however, such efforts have been marginalized and ignored in mainstream American Buddhism. For example, the January 2009 issue of *Shambhala Sun* titled "Celebrating 30 Years of Buddhism in America" does not mention inclusion and diversity work. Nonetheless, because of the persistent efforts of a small but deeply committed network of American Buddhists of color and the wider cultural critical mass around racial justice in the United States, such work is now coming to the forefront of American Buddhist convert communities. This is reflected in the increased coverage of racial diversity and justice issues in Buddhist media. Take, for example, *Buddhadharma*'s summer 2016 issue, with the unequivocal title on the front cover, "Free the Dharma: Race, Power, and White Privilege in American Buddhism."[5]

Diversity and inclusion work is transectarian and has occurred across meditation-based Buddhist lineages; it is also a transgenerational phenomenon, with boomer pioneers such as Tibetan Buddhist Jan Willis, Insight teacher Ralph Steele, and Zen Buddhist Mushim Patricia Ikeda working alongside Gen X leaders such as angel Kyodo williams and Viveka Chen. In recent years, a few communities and teachers have been particularly active and influential.[6] From the Insight network, the East Bay Meditation Center, in Oakland, California, has been at the forefront of diversity and inclusion work on the West Coast, with New York Insight, the Insight Meditation Community of Washington (DC) (IMCW), and Flowering Lotus Meditation and Retreat Center in Mississippi important hubs to the east.[7] Of particular note from American Zen lineages are Zenju Earthlyn Manuel, whose groundbreaking 2015 book *The Way of Tenderness: Awakening Through Race, Sexuality and Gender* explores the relationship between marginal identities and Buddhist awakening and the Brooklyn Zen Center.[8] From the Tibetan Buddhist community, Lama Rod Owens, who co-wrote *Radical Dharma: Talking Race, Love, and Liberation* with williams and Jasmine Syedullah, has emerged as a leader on racial justice issues.[9]

For brevity, in this chapter I examine some of the main features of diversity and inclusion work through a case study of IMCW. I consider the main pragmatic and hermeneutic strategies by which diversity and inclusion initiatives are legitimated within Buddhist thought and practices at IMCW as well as the opposition such work has faced from many of its overwhelmingly white, middle-class and upper-middle-class members. Then I consider how the work at IMCW reflects shifts around racial diversity and white privilege in the wider Insight community. In conclusion, I explore the significance of racial justice and diversity work in terms of the status and unfolding of Buddhist modernism in the United States.

Before turning to this case study, a note on terminology. I use the umbrella term "racial diversity and inclusion work" as shorthand for a variety of initiatives, from promoting diversity to challenging white privilege. As I discuss later, communities are increasingly adopting the terms "inclusion" and "equity" rather than "diversity" in recognition of the fact that a deeper reconfiguration of power is needed within overwhelmingly white sanghas than merely adding more people of color to preexisting structures. On a related note, although diversity and inclusion work includes multiple categories of diversity, such as race, class, gender, sexuality, and disability, my focus in this chapter is specifically on race, and I adopt the acronym POC (person/people of color) as the emic self-identifier of participants. It should be noted that within this broad term different minorities—African Americans, Latinos/as, Asian Americans, and Native Americans—report distinct as well as common experiences, which future research should attend to more. Given the specific historic oppression and ongoing discrimination and racism faced by African Americans in the United States, I focus particularly on the experiences of African American convert Buddhists.

From the "Empty Seat" to the "Beloved Community": Inclusion and Equity at IMCW

In 2010, Travis Spencer, an African American, visited Tara Brach's popular Wednesday night class at IMCW. Although Spencer had been practicing meditation alone for more than two years, he was looking for a community with which to practice. He had visited Brach's class only once before, a week earlier, and had been excited to return after having a positive experience with her teaching and connecting well with some

THE DUKKHA OF RACISM

people in the community. When he arrived, he sat down in the second row and waited for the class to begin. Brach's class is the most popular at IMCW, with a regular audience of between 275 and 300 people, and the room steadily began to fill to capacity until every seat was taken—except the one next to Spencer. As the meditation began, his thoughts started to race as he began to speculate on this empty seat. In his words, he was visited by "the Ghost of Racist Past," who taunted him with questions such as, "Why am I the only person to sit next to you? Do they think you will rob them?" Wanting to flee, but not wishing to disturb his fellow meditators, Spencer sat through the meditation in inner turmoil. As soon as the class was over, however, he bolted for the door rather than stay to help pack up, as he had originally planned.[10]

Later in the week, Spencer wrote a blog about his experience. In "The Color of the Buddha Heart," he wrote that the teachings of the Buddha challenged any form of racist ideology and that IMCW was filled with wonderful people who were not intentionally racist. Yet he also recognized that dominant white culture is permeated with racial stereotypes and conditioning and that his own past experiences of racism had amplified his feeling of separation from the predominantly white practitioners in the room. Interweaving the various aspects of his experience—the cultural and political, the emotional and spiritual—Spencer ended, "When we do not bring issues of race, racism and prejudice into mindfulness, we give way to or deepen the trance that holds us in fear of one another and our differences." Spencer decided to send the blog to Brach, an action that initiated a longstanding commitment to IMCW, and a personal friendship with Brach. Just a couple of weeks after his encounter with the "empty seat," he attended his first daylong event with IMCW's POC affinity sangha, an experience he blogged about under the title "It Felt like Home," and since then he has practiced regularly with the POC group and now serves on IMCW's board of directors.[11]

Spencer's empty seat reappears in a dharma talk Brach delivered in June 2015. In "The Beloved Community," she shares his experience and acknowledges that although in this particular case there was "an unusual and beautiful end to the story," in most cases, after having such an experience, a person of color would not want to return. This is understandable, she continues, because despite its good intentions, IMCW, as an overwhelmingly white organization, is often unaware of the white privilege and racism that it carries as part of its collective conditioning as a dominant culture group. Interweaving reflections on the ongoing legacy of slavery in the United States with Buddhist thought, Brach explains that racism is the collective manifestation of an existential sense of separation that creates an illusion of an individual self that is based in fear of the "unreal other." In order to wake up to the truth of our interconnectedness, we must shine a light on the dukkha of racism. Through utilizing the teachings of the dharma and the practice of mindfulness, it is possible to break free of "the collective white spacesuit" of white privilege and create truly inclusive sanghas, or beloved communities. For Brach, such work is at the very heart of Buddhist practice: "It's become a central part of spiritual awakening. I can't be whole without including those I've excluded in my heart."[12]

Brach received more feedback about her "Beloved Community" dharma talk than any other she had given in more than thirty years teaching at IMCW. Much of this was positive: a number of African American students, for example, thanked her for the unusual move of discussing racism in the context of Buddhism. Some feedback, however, was not positive: a few members walked out as she was giving the talk, and others questioned why she was bringing up politics when they had come to meditate and hear the dharma. Following the trajectory of the empty seat to the beloved community brings into focus some of the many challenges IMCW has faced in relation to racial inclusion and equity work. Here I explore the history of this work and draw attention to its central features. In particular, I focus on the diversity initiatives IMCW has undertaken and the ways in which teachers have framed and legitimated such work as an extension and expression of Buddhist practice, and I consider the main obstacles and resistance to this work. The bulk of the material comes from eight interviews with members of IMCW, most of whom have been heavily involved in this work since its inception: two white senior teachers, one senior African American teacher, one racial awareness consultant, one POC teacher and retreat manager, one POC affinity sangha member, and two white members who have served on the IMCW board. Interviews typically lasted sixty minutes and took place over Skype or cell phone, with follow-up questions in certain cases. Interviewees were given the choice of being named or remaining anonymous. Additionally, I analyzed material on IMCW's website and two IMCW dharma podcasts that explicitly addressed racism.

Inclusion and Diversity Work at IMCW

IMCW developed out of a small sitting group begun in 1988 by Tara Brach, a senior teacher in the Insight community who is well-known in American Buddhism largely because of her best-selling book *Radical Acceptance: Embracing Your Life with the Heart of a Buddha,* which bridges Buddhism and psychotherapy. In 1992, Brach moved to Bethesda, Maryland, a wealthy middle-class suburb of Washington, DC, and began a Wednesday evening group at the Unitarian Universalist congregation there. Two years later the group relocated to the main sanctuary of the church, where it has functioned for more than a decade. During that time, IMCW has grown into a large, flourishing organization that offers a number of programs across the DC area. These range from daylong events to nine-day retreats, from affinity groups for specific populations to secular mindfulness classes. In 1998, IMCW was recognized as a non-profit religious organization and granted tax-exempt status. It employs four part-time administrative staff but relies heavily on a team of volunteers for most of its operations. A governing board of eight members, including senior teachers, meets bimonthly to discuss the organization's resources and programs and makes major decisions. IMCW has a large teaching body, with twenty-seven teachers and thirty-one affiliate teachers as well as nearly fifty guest teachers listed on its website.[13]

IMCW is more established and larger than many Insight groups in the United States, but its overwhelming majority white, middle-class to upper-middle-class demographic is typical of most American meditation-based convert sanghas. La Sarmiento, who identifies as a genderqueer POC and has been at the forefront of inclusion and equity work at IMCW, recalls that on the first visit to IMCW, "When I walked into the room, other than the Buddha sitting next to Tara, I was the only person of color in the room."[14] Similarly, in explaining what had prompted IMCW's diversity initiatives, Hugh Byrne, one of the senior teachers, said, "As we looked around our community and saw that about

90 percent were white, well-educated, middle-class and upwards, and [there was] not a lot of visibility around LGBT identity and issues, it was clear that we needed to address this."[15]

As Insight teacher and pioneering diversity and inclusion leader Larry Yang notes, "For organizations that are already in place, the challenge is to retrofit a multicultural pattern into a cultural pattern that has long been geared toward a white, middle-class sensibility."[16] IMCW's first efforts at meeting this challenge began in 2005 when a small group of teachers and practitioners that was racially diverse and of mixed gender and sexual orientations formed a diversity committee. Three members of this group agreed that despite their "good intentions," white participants did not have the experience to create a safe enough space for POC, and the group dissolved after about a year and a half. One positive outcome of the committee, however, was the formation of two "affinity sanghas"—one for POC and one for LGBTQI practitioners. Wider interest in the two groups was drummed up with the help of guest teachers Yang and Mushim Patricia Ikeda from the East Bay Meditation Center, and Insight teacher Arinna Weisman, who visited and held daylong events for POC and/or LGBTQI populations as well as gave advice on identity-based groups. Sarmiento formed both of these groups and has been their teacher since their inception in April 2006. The groups initially met in Sarmiento's home but have since moved to commercial spaces with the POC group, renting space at a yoga studio in the Woodley Park neighborhood of DC.[17]

The POC affinity sangha meets monthly and is open to anyone who self-identifies as a POC. On the IMCW website, its aspirations are listed as:

> To explore our identity as People of Color in the light of the Buddhist dharma, across multiple and intersecting lines of difference that include, but are not limited to: race, ethnicity, sexuality, gender, socio-economic class, age, and dis/abilities.
>
> To provide a safe and intimate space where People of Color can deepen the practice of meditation and mindful dialogue.

To study the dharma from diverse perspectives and to inspire insightful discussions.

To cultivate a sense of belonging and community both within the People of Color sangha and the larger IMCW sangha.[18]

Sarmiento says that the POC affinity sangha has an email subscription list of 292 people but tends to draw between ten to thirty participants, of which about 85 percent to 90 percent are African American and the rest are a mix of Asian Americans and Latinos/as. Gender wise, the group consists of about 85 percent to 90 percent women, with Sarmiento the only transgender-identified member, although there are a number of LGBTQI-identified members. The group has a wide age range, with members in their early twenties up to those in their seventies.

The group follows a general format of meditation, dharma talk, and mindful dialogue, which is aided by the use of mindful sharing guidelines based on the *kalyana mitta* guidelines, which many Insight meditation communities use. Mindful dialogues often explore the impact of racism on the daily lives of sangha members. Given the centrality of teachings on suffering and the end of suffering in Buddhism, this is hardly surprising. As Sarmiento noted, "Some of these folks have this suffering historically and ancestrally, they have this deep suffering and pain of not being seen as worthy or human—it is in their DNA, this really deep suffering."[19] POC interviewees reported that the teachings and practices of Buddhism were of tremendous benefit to them. Sarmiento discussed how mindfulness had illuminated how embodied Sarmiento's conditioned defensives were: "Once I got this visceral sense of being this way in my body, I recognized that this is not the way that I want to move through the world and I can engage the practices and teachings in a way where I can still be open hearted and compassionate but at the same time protective and resilient."[20] Another interviewee said that he had found the practices of equanimity and metta particularly helpful: equanimity to balance the rage of being subject to a dominant cultural system that constructed certain groups of people as being less than others, and metta to help heal his pain of internalizing that systematic conditioning.

All three affinity sangha interviewees stressed how important and nourishing the safety of the group had been for their Buddhist practice. The affinity sangha clearly functions as what Sarmiento describes as a "great refuge" for participants and has been indispensable in nurturing POC taking up roles in IMCW's leadership and teaching body. The mainstream IMCW sangha, however, has been less successful in attracting POC members, and all interviewees acknowledged that there was a significant and problematic gap between the two. Although the POC group is under the organizational umbrella of IMCW, it is, by all counts, a self-contained unit, and the majority of its members do not identify with IMCW as a larger institution. Sarmiento revealed that most POC members consider the affinity group as their primary sangha, and some even belong to other Buddhist groups in the area in which they feel more reflected and accepted as POC.

Much of the present gap between the mainstream organization and the affinity sangha is rooted in a painful history between the two. An incident with a POC member and the IMCW board appears to have amplified POC feelings that the mainstream culture and leadership did not take their needs seriously enough and were not fully committed to supporting diversity and inclusion. This led to a period of conflict and breakdown, about which Hugh Byrne said, "There was a lot of animosity and a growing feeling of 'Us' versus 'Them.' Looking back, one of the main problems was that members of the board had not done enough of their own work on racial privilege and inner transformation. Because they were supporting POC financially, they felt resentful and defensive when they were critiqued."[21] Similarly, another interviewee noted, "We were well intentioned but hadn't done a lot of work, so any criticism or feedback given with a more direct approach was perceived as an injury or that people were being called racist."

Sarmiento felt that one of the problems was the lack of strong enough relationships between POC and white members to "hold" conflicts, and so with Brach, they formed a mixed POC and white "diversity friendship group." Consisting of about twelve people, including teachers, board members, and members of the POC sangha, the group began in 2011 and met quarterly until October 2015. The morning session was mostly devoted to "check-ins," with each member sharing what was going on in their life and practice; the afternoon was spent on an activity.[22]

The group did not have a formal role in developing IMCW policy, but it helped with what one senior teacher described as "clarifying future directions for IMCW." In my interviews with four members of this group, each said that it had helped overcome distrust that had developed between white and POC members and fostered a deeper capacity for people to be vulnerable with each other. All stressed the importance of developing personal relationships as the foundation of diversity and inclusion work. As Sarmiento explained: "We just felt that trying to address inclusivity and diversity from the top down was not working for us. . . . In order to have these difficult and challenging conversations around race and difference, it's really crucial to have relationships with other people you're having the conversations with. If you don't have these relationships, people aren't going to hang in there with you."[23]

The diversity friendship group was one of the two events that Byrne felt had enabled a shift from the painful impasse between the board and the POC sangha. The other was the formation of white awareness training for the board members and teaching body of IMCW. Although this was the first institutional white awareness training, it was not the first attempt of white IMCW members to explore their own unconscious conditioning around race. In 2009, about fifteen white IMCW members formed "White Awake," a small grassroots group organized to inquire into white privilege; it went through two six-month iterations, one led by an outside facilitator and the other peer-led. Klia Bassing, one of the original members and the only IMCW teacher in the group, said that two events were instrumental in her decision to join the group. One was her experience as a member of the third iteration of the Community Dharma Leader program (CDL3, from 2005 to 2007) at Spirit Rock, which included diversity awareness training, particularly with regards to race, but which many members of her cohort felt was insufficient. The other was her friendship with Sarmiento, which had "made me realize my perspective was pretty limited to my own experience and that those who didn't have the same dominant-culture identities were having a very different—often much more painful—experience."[24] When the first iteration of White Awake advertised itself at IMCW, Bassing was surprised at the lack of interest from the wider sangha and dismayed that it even provoked some suspicion and hostility from other white members. She was also somewhat frustrated at a lack of engagement from IMCW's board members regarding a challenge to the POC sangha's sanctity as exclusively for members who identify as POC.[25]

The first white awareness training for the leadership at IMCW also used the name White Awake but was distinct from, although influenced by, the earlier grassroots efforts. Eleanor Hancock developed the official White Awake training after meeting Kristin Barker, one of the founding members of the White Awake grassroots group at IMCW, at one of Joanna Macy's Work That Reconnects (WTR) workshops in South Carolina. Hancock drew on Barker's notes, her own experience in racial justice work, and the WTR workshop to create a body of resources for the WTR community, which has a demographic similar to that of the Insight network. Although she had some success in bringing the WTR workshop to a more diverse audience, Hancock realized that the project needed to be developed further and offered to a wider audience. She was given permission to use the name White Awake and expanded its resources into a website and workshop. In 2013, she taught an intensive workshop series for IMCW and was then invited to cofacilitate a yearlong process with its leadership body in 2014.[26]

Hancock believes that for racial awareness training to be truly effective, it needs to be grounded in an inner transformation, a process she believes is particularly well supported by the practice of mindfulness. The website for White Awake has a whole section devoted to the spiritual component of the program, which states it employs several aspects of mindfulness and Buddhist practice. Hancock explains that the main aim of White Awake is "to understand racial awareness, and [that] transformation around our own privilege and racial conditioning is a necessary part of our own liberation. Doing racial awareness work is part of reclaiming our full humanity as white people." Reflecting on the success of the program at IMCW, she concludes: "What is coming out of the White Awake process is more sophistication in how the IMCW leadership is thinking of themselves and the complaints and frustrations of POC over years. They are asking how IMCW can work with internal dynamics so that there is not a POC sangha, which is like a separate island."[27]

Byrne noted that this official training marked a significant development because it sent the signal to POC that the white leadership and teaching body was truly committed to inclusion work and had more than good intentions. Brach echoed this: "The White Awake program . . . is the number one thing really: having our senior teachers and board membership do the year-long program."[28] Similarly, Brach and Byrne emphasized that it was essential for white members of a sangha, particularly those in leadership roles, to examine their own conditioning around race. Without white members taking responsibility for their own racial biases, conversations with POC were likely to result in more harm. Put simply by Sarmiento: "Trying to have conversations with white people is pretty painful and exhausting. That's why white folks need to start doing their own work and not rely on folks of color to educate them."[29]

In addition to the white awareness training, IMCW has undertaken a number of organizational diversity initiatives. One early attempt was to try to have more POC on the board. As Byrne acknowledged, however, this had too often been "ad hoc and left the members of color in a difficult and isolated place."[30] Its website prefaces information on the board with the statement, "IMCW is committed to expanding the diversity of its board and committees, and especially encourages individuals from a diversity of race, sexual preferences and age to offer their services," and in early 2018 there were five POC serving on the board out of a total of fourteen members.

Another main area of focus has been the attempt to diversify the teaching body, through both external and internal strategies. One external strategy has been to invite guest POC teachers to run POC events at IMCW, and since 2007, when Yang co-led a retreat with her, Brach has endeavored to have a teacher of color coteach retreats with her. Internal strategies include nurturing and supporting teachers of color within the IMCW sangha to teach events at IMCW and to undertake trainings within the larger Insight community. Another is incorporating inclusivity and racial awareness trainings in IMCW's local teacher training program. Brach also added that IMCW teachers are now being "strongly encouraged" to address racial justice in the dharma talks they give to the still overwhelmingly white mainstream sangha. One example is senior teacher Jonathan Foust's talk "The World Is One Family: Healing the Wounds of Racism and Discrimination," given on June 8, 2015, which is posted on the IMCW website. However, a cursory search under "Talks" using the keywords "diversity," "race," "racism," and "inclusivity" found only five talks, so clearly this strategy is extremely embryonic.

In a 2014 pilot study on mindfulness, Western Buddhism, and equity work, Harrison Blum discusses the importance of "going out" as well as "inviting in" marginalized populations for effective inclusion and equity work. IMCW is involved in two such community-based projects: "Minds, Inc.: Mindfulness in DC-Area Schools" and "Insight on the Inside" (IOI), which takes mindfulness to incarcerated populations. Minds Inc. is making an effort to teach in low-income areas so as to meet underserved populations where they are, while IOI teachers are trained in cultural sensitivity programs and utilize Ruth King's workshop on oppression.[31] IMCW has also played a central role in developing a national Buddhist response to the wave of killings of unarmed African Americans by police in the United States. One major component of this was taking an instrumental role in fundraising and launching Buddhists for Racial Justice, which has since become an initiative of the North American Buddhist Alliance.

IMCW's Buddhist Hermeneutics of Inclusion

In reflecting on the trajectory of IMCW's diversity and inclusion work, Brach concluded that it has moved from being one of the many projects or issues at IMCW to becoming "central to everything that we do."[32] Undergirding this shift is the framing of such work as an intrinsic and essential part of Buddhist practice. Brach continued: "To understand how we create separation is so integral to waking up; it is a lens that is part of every subject we touch on. So that is a shift, and a major shift."[33] How is such work integral to Buddhism? To begin with, all teachers stated that Buddhism is about suffering and the end of suffering, and racial conditioning and injustice is a major form of suffering. As one teacher put it:

I don't identify as an activist. I just want to be able to notice suffering when I see it and not perpetuate it, and alleviate it, if I can. It's all about suffering for me. Doing this diversity work is actually addressing suffering, addressing it in the ways that some people perpetuate it and some people have to live it. So, when some people say to me, "What does this have to do with our practice?," it's like, this *is* the practice. If you don't get that, well I don't know.

Once racial injustice has been established as a form of dukkha, the next move, following the Four Noble Truths, is to inquire into the causes and conditions of that suffering. Brach teaches that the root of racism is the existential tendency to create a false sense of self and "an unreal other" that we respond to with aversion and fear. In essence, therefore, racism is a cultural manifestation of this existential illusion of separateness. To wake up to the reality of interdependence requires an investigation of both the individual and the collective conditioning around race that keeps one ensnared in separateness. Certain Buddhist practices such as mindfulness offer potent tools for inquiring into and becoming free of this conditioning. Ruth King advances the practice of mindfulness as a way to develop the capacity to tolerate the discomfort of the complexity of afflictive emotions generated by conversations around race. She believes that through utilizing mindfulness, one can pierce through racial conditioning that distorts reality. Only then can practitioners create the third jewel of Buddhism: a truly inclusive sangha, or borrowing from Martin Luther King Jr., "the beloved community." Pushing against the individualism and separateness of much of American convert Buddhism, she emphasizes the centrality of sangha to awakening: "Our spiritual community becomes the fertile ground for our awakening. . . . So, belonging is a relative necessity for enlightenment. It's the soil in which we awaken."[34]

IMCW teachers also often referred to the Mahayana Buddhist doctrine of Buddha-nature. This was used both as a resource to help POC overcome feelings of inferiority that some have internalized as a result of living in a system that constantly devalues them and also as a way to

soften oppositions that can develop in racial justice work. As Sarmiento
put it, it's important to remember "that not only do I have but everyone
else has Buddha-nature, even the cops that are killing our young black
men. It's all there, it's just hidden and buried under so much ignorance
and so much delusion."[35] Finally, as with the teaching of dukkha, the
centrality of compassion in Buddhism was consistently referred to by
teachers. For them, responding directly to the suffering caused by a cultural worldview and institutional system based in delusion and aversion
was seen as an expression of compassion in action.

Central to IMCW's Buddhist hermeneutics of inclusion is a shift in
focus from the individual to the collective, the internal to the external.
This happens in a wider spiritual framework in which the emphasis is
on an embodied and engaged rather than a transcendent approach to
Buddhist practice. In one dharma talk, Foust, for example, delineates
between two approaches to awakening: seclusion from the world, in
which one purifies through strict abstinence, and engagement with the
world, "where you actually use the events that show up in your life as the
guru, as the teacher."[36] This moves IMCW out of a traditional Theravadin model but keeps it fully congruent with a certain stream within the
Insight community, which I have argued elsewhere has a distinctively
tantric flavor.[37]

It should be noted that just as IMCW teachers use Buddhism to
spiritually validate diversity and inclusion work, some practitioners
have drawn on Buddhist doctrines to delegitimate this work. One
way this occurs is through an apolitical hermeneutics of Buddhism in
which racial justice work is deemed as political and therefore irrelevant
to Buddhist practice. As noted earlier, for example, when racial issues
are brought up in dharma talks, some practitioners point out that they
come to the sangha to meditate, not to engage in political discussion.
Both Brach and Byrne reported that white practitioners have walked out
of the group when racial justice issues were addressed in dharma talks.
Another way opposition manifests is when practitioners claim that diversity and inclusion work is actually in opposition to Buddhism. One
common objection is that such work emphasizes difference and causes
separation, which is at odds with Buddhist teachings of interdependence. This is often supported with reference to the Buddha's rejection

of caste with the charge that POC and LGBTQI groups create a quasi-caste system. As Brach explained: "People say, If the Buddha taught that we are all the same, no difference between male or female, black or white, if there's really no difference between different castes and classes, why would we create these separate pathways, why would we give special scholarships, why would we create these distinctions?"[38] Another common accusation is that inclusion and equity work produces more anger, which should be dealt with internally rather than directed at others. Closely related to this is the view that the aim of Buddhism is to cultivate calm and peaceful states, and conversations about racial justice are disruptive to this goal.

In response to Buddhist-based objections about separation, three interviewees pointed out the difference between ontological interdependence and a naive sociocultural universalism, in which claims that "we are all the same" effectively function to assert white experience as the universal standard and to dismiss the actual lived experience of POC. As one member observed: "One of the things that happens out of ignorance and a commitment to Buddhism is to try and equalize everyone. People say, 'Aren't we here to liberate all of us?'" Sarmiento made a similar point: "When I started the affinity sanghas, my straight white friends were all like, 'Why do you need to separate yourself out. We are all one.' My response to that was 'Yes, but who's "one" are we being?'"[39]

Four interviewees also expressed frustration at how some sangha members used Buddhist teachings on anger as a poison to "shut down" important conversations around the harm of racism. "There are some interpretations of Buddhism that say that you should not feel or show anger," Brach explained. "Whereas when there is wounding and trauma, anger is a natural expression of it, anger is an intelligent emotion, and if we say that you aren't supposed to feel angry, we are telling those who have been wounded, those who are part of the legacy of slavery, that they should not have a feeling about [that wounding and legacy]."[40]

Another interviewee noted that there was a place in Buddhism for "fierce compassion" and that such a teaching was an effective and necessary tool in relationship to white mainstream objections to diversity and inclusion work. In her words: "One of the things that doesn't happened enough is a direct challenge, some fierce compassion that really targets what we are talking about and allows us to say, 'You will be attended to but now is not your time; you need to take a back-seat. POC suffering is so great and so profound that that's what we need to attend to now.'" In short, IMCW teachers attribute Buddhist-rooted objections to inclusion and justice work as resulting from a lack of understanding or cultural misinterpretation of Buddhist teachings rather than anything inherent to Buddhism itself. For them, inclusion and equity is an inherent expression of Buddhism rather than an external concern brought into conversation with it.

From the Margins to the Mainstream: Ongoing Challenges

One of the biggest challenges facing IMCW is to bring its inclusion and equity work into the mainstream culture of the organization. This is an ongoing process that faces a number of significant obstacles. As discussed above, one of these is an apolitical Buddhist hermeneutics; the others can be divided into the following four intersecting categories: the mainstream sangha demographic, the POC affinity sangha's lack of interest, IMCW's organizational and structural limitations, and the focus on individual meditation practice at IMCW and the Insight community at large.

One major obstacle facing IMCW is the specific sociocultural location and emotional-psychic makeup of its mainstream sangha population. In short, the majority demographic of IMCW is a highly privileged group: they are white, middle-class to upper-middle class, well educated, and affluent. Three of my interviewees who located themselves within this demographic felt that the majority of their peers were unaware of the depth of their privilege and had no idea of the type of suffering that came from living in poverty day by day. One interviewee was pessimistic about the possibility of bringing the inclusion work from the margins to the center because she felt that the mainstream sangha would resist giving up its privileges since "power is set up to keep itself in power." From a related angle, Bassing said that she had been thinking a lot about white fragility and how "hard it is for white people to self-identify as oppressor," particularly for those who are politically liberal, as the majority at IMCW are.[41] Brach made the same point: "They assume that they are liberal, and that they want equality, but don't realize the privilege they are living from and they don't realize the amount of violence and oppression towards POC."[42]

On an emotional-psychic level, interviewees felt that many members of the mainstream sangha were too preoccupied with their own personal suffering to address suffering generated by racism. As one interviewee said: "Many people are drawn to spiritual communities out of their suffering and it comes from a deep and dark place of childhood trauma. So just in terms of the psychological and interpersonal piece, there are often not enough adults in the room." Brach feels that many members misunderstand the relationship between personal and social suffering, seeing them as distinct rather than intricately related: "People are so caught in their own suffering that they don't feel it will serve them [to attend to the suffering of others]. They say, 'Let me heal myself and then I will pay attention to the social suffering.' What people don't get is that it is only when we realize we are part of something bigger, that [we can be] part of the healing."[43] This misunderstanding was seen as reflecting a deep-seated individualism that permeated the majority culture of the wider Insight community.

A second major area of resistance comes from POC themselves. As already noted, many POC have little interest in IMCW as a larger organization and are content to practice solely with the POC affinity sangha. Whereas white teachers unequivocally agreed that historically the POC sangha "did not have a reason to trust the dominant white sangha," there was also a hope for more future engagement from the larger POC sangha. Although tensions between the mainstream culture and the POC sangha seem to have considerably abated, a significant distance remains between the two. Much work from the mainstream sangha is needed to bridge this gap, but POC members are also called on to play a role and examine their own unconscious conditioning that holds them back from fully participating. Sarmiento felt that the lack of interest in participating in mainstream sangha events had a limiting effect on the practice of some members of the POC affinity group, who "very seldom if at all participate in any other IMCW classes or retreats. It's pretty insular in that way, as much as I try to invite folks to get that the POC sangha is a really powerful place but it is not reality."[44]

A third considerable obstacle relates to IMCW's organizational and structural format. One major aspect pertains to having a clear enough division between the board, teaching body, and specific committees, such as an inclusion and equity committee, so that each group is clear about its roles and responsibilities and there is a transparent system of power checks between them. Another dimension involves the decentralized nature of IMCW, in which many different subsanghas operate autonomously. One interviewee felt that this made it difficult to communicate effectively and establish a unified front on inclusion and equity initiatives. These organizational issues particularly influence inclusion and equity work because, as one interviewee said: "Structure creates safety. . . . Because there hasn't been that kind of structure, some of the pain has been compounded because there hasn't been a clear path or clear communication about what needed to happen. A big part of this was really basic stuff and the need to understand organizational culture, but it never got addressed."

Another senior teacher echoed this and pointed out that POC are rendered vulnerable by a lack of institutional structure and community. For example, if there is no clear institutional accountability process, POC members feel invisible and unsafe. A closely related structural issue is the geographical location of Brach's Wednesday night class in Bethesda, which is affluent and difficult to reach via public transportation. For those low-income practitioners who do not own a car, many of whom are POC, getting to the Wednesday night class poses a significant challenge. Travis Spencer, for example, had attended Wednesday nights regularly until his car broke down. In contrast, the POC affinity sangha is held in an accessible and racially diverse area so there is little pragmatic incentive for many POC members to attend mainstream programs in Bethesda.

Another obstacle mentioned was the individual meditation–orientated nature of IMCW and the Insight community in general. IMCW classes and events were typically centered around silent meditation practice and a dharma talk with little structured interactive time. This format was seen as hindering the building of relationships and the creation of a diverse and inclusive sangha. As Sarmiento joked: "With

Vipassana groups, you go and pray that no one talks to you. There is a benefit in silent practices, but it has stunted the evolution of a relational dharma."[45]

Reflecting on IMCW's diversity and inclusion trajectory, Byrne said: "First we thought, 'What can we do to make IMCW a more welcoming and accessible place?' Looking back, it was a somewhat simplistic approach."[46] One of the main shifts that has occurred since IMCW started diversity work more than a decade ago is that the leadership board has slowly come to realize that for real and sustainable change to occur, a decentering of white hegemony has to occur on multiple levels of the organization. Rather than just inviting more POC to attend mainstream events, a radical reconfiguration of the mainstream culture is necessary that includes a distribution of power and authority. As Sarmiento put it:

> I often use this analogy about dominant culture sanghas or organizations having a dinner party, and they want to invite these new guests to the dinner party, and the new guests are like, "Oh, we want to share our food, and we also want to listen to music, and to dance," etc. But the dinner party hosts are saying, "No, we already have the menu, we just want you to sit at the table." So, it's like this dynamic where it's more about, can we just have more diversity visually, but it's not really interested in looking at the different contexts of privilege or consciousness around difference. But if you really want to become a more integrated sangha, it requires a level of sharing the power, creating space in a way where you are actually bringing in what other people have to offer and how they offer it.[47]

One way this shift in IMCW's approach has been expressed is in its recent adoption of the language of "inclusion and equity" rather than "diversity." The employment of "inclusion" rather than "diversity" has been influenced by angel Kyodo williams, who has been at the forefront of Buddhist and racial justice work and with whom IMCW has developed strong ties. In June 2015, she appeared on a panel titled "Beloved Community: Healing What Separates Us" with Brach and Hancock, which was advertised using her quotation, "It's the community's job to figure out how we can stretch into the so-called margins to broaden our understanding and the ability to be inclusive. Inclusivity is not 'how do we make you a part of what we are?' but 'how do we become more of what you are?'"[48]

The language of equity comes from Gretchen Rohr, an IMCW member, who forwarded "equity" as a term that focuses on results rather than intention and process. This is important because, although a process might appear to be fair in the abstract, other strategies such as affirmative action are often needed to produce actual equitable outcomes because of historical racial disparity and contemporary racial bias. This perspective also applies pressure to rhetorical ideals of universalism and sameness that have no basis in sociocultural and economic realities. Having developed a more sophisticated understanding of racial disparity, Brach concludes that IMCW is now fully committed to significantly changing the mainstream "consciousness and culture" with a shift of focus from inviting in to expanding out. One practical way this will occur, for example, is by holding more classes in areas that are accessible and racially diverse and showing solidarity with regard to issues of concern for POC and minority populations. As noted above, however, much work is still needed for this aspiration to be actualized. Byrne stresses that it is crucial to maintain a critical mass around inclusion and equity aims and for white teachers and leaders to consistently keep such aims in the forefront as a central goal. Similarly, much emphasis is now being placed on the importance of white sangha members doing their own racial awareness work. In short, after a long and painful process, IMCW has arrived at what williams declared in 2011, namely, the understanding that inclusion work is not just for minority sangha members for also for mainstream white members:

> In American Buddhism, these kinds of changes don't need to come because we need to do people of color a favor, or we need to make space for the gender variant people. We have to get clear that an essential aspect of our practice is to shift

these things internally for ourselves, because our personal liberation, the very thing we come to the dharma for, is completely bound up in making these kinds of changes. It's not a superficial concern.[49]

Diversity, Inclusion, and Equity in the Wider Insight World

One way to gauge how IMCW is reflective of larger patterns in meditation-based convert Buddhism is to consider the status of diversity, inclusion, and equity work at the two main US Insight centers: IMS and Spirit Rock. In a 2001 article titled "Something Has to Change: Blacks in American Buddhism," Insight teacher Ralph Steele recalls teaching a metta retreat at IMS with its cofounder Joseph Goldstein in 1991. On realizing he was one of only two POC at the retreat, Steele said, "Joseph, something has to change," to which Goldstein replied, "Yes, but for now just do the practice." Steele also remembers the resistance among white teachers at Spirit Rock about proactively seeking out Buddhists of color: "They got the message that their sangha wouldn't be the same and they got scared. . . . The reaction was: 'I don't know if I could handle that kind of shift.'"[50]

Sixteen years later, however, something does appear to have changed, with both Spirit Rock and IMS emphasizing diversity and inclusion as central to their mission. IMS's website features a substantial section on "Diversity, Equity and Inclusion," which includes an inspiring vision statement, information on the organization's multiple diversity initiatives, and a range of resources, from academic books on race and racial justice in the United States to dharma talks addressing diversity and white privilege within American Buddhism.[51] It also includes updates in the categories of organizational learning, systemic change, teacher training, and community engagement and is accompanied by a detailed "Diversity, Equity, and Inclusion Plan," which unequivocally states that "diversity practice and dharma practice are not separate."[52]

Here I document certain major shifts that have occurred at these two centers and some of the key figures responsible for them, as well as highlight ongoing challenges to dismantling white privilege in the

Insight network. The history of racial justice initiatives within the Insight world has been both made and documented by a small group of practitioners of color and their white allies. Many of these figures feature in *Making the Invisible Visible: Healing Racism in Our Buddhist Communities* (2000), including Larry Yang, who provides an indispensable timeline and autobiographical account of diversity events in the Insight community in his 2017 book *Awakening Together: The Spiritual Practice of Inclusivity and Community*.[53]

As examined earlier, some practitioners have denounced POC Buddhist events as divisive and counter to Buddhist concepts such as no-self.[54] There is no doubt, however, that such events have been instrumental in fostering community between POC Buddhists, introducing meditation-based convert Buddhism to a much wider multicultural audience and catalyzing transformation in mainstream white sanghas. The first Insight meditation daylong retreats for POC began in the early 1990s, and the first POC retreat at Spirit Rock was in 1999, with the center reporting that the retreat has been full or nearly full since 2006.[55] In August 2002, Spirit Rock hosted the first ever African American Dharma Retreat and Conference, and this was followed in 2004 by an Asian American & Pacific Islander Dharma Retreat and Conference.[56] In the same year, Evan Kavanagh, then the executive director of Spirit Rock, announced that the board of directors had set diversity as one of its main goals and was in the process of forming a diversity council, hiring a diversity coordinator, and offering teachings for diverse populations.[57] Marlene Jones was one of the driving forces behind these initiatives, founding the first Diversity Council at Spirit Rock, the first daylong and residential retreats for POC, and the first diversity trainings for Spirit Rock staff between the late 1990s and 2005.[58]

Three teachers of color at Spirit Rock—Charlie Johnson, Spring Washam, and Larry Yang—were founding members of the East Bay Meditation Center (EBMC), which has undoubtedly had the biggest impact on diversity and inclusion work at Spirit Rock. EBMC's origins can be traced back to discussions in the 1990s between a number of teachers, predominantly from the Insight community and associated with Spirit Rock, to develop a meditation center tailored specifically for the diverse, multicultural populations of the East Bay. In 2001, the group incorporated as a nonprofit organization under the name "East Bay Dharma Center" and would undergo several shifts in membership until the summer of 2006 when only four people were left on the committee: Johnson, Yang, Washam, and David Foecke. In March 2007, Mushim Patricia Ikeda, a Zen-trained Buddhist teacher and professional diversity facilitator, and Kitsy Schoen, an Insight teacher, joined this committee. According to Yang, two things were essential in ensuring that EBMC did not reproduce the same demographics that marked the wider Insight network: one was that four of the six "core teachers" were POC, and another was that rather than impose the standard Insight group structure, thereby reproducing the same culture and demographics, these teachers asked local communities what they wanted from the center. In response to community feedback, EBMC held its first POC meditation class in October 2006 and its first POC sitting group for communities of color in December of the same year.[59]

EBMC's mission is "to foster liberation, personal and interpersonal healing, social action, and inclusive community building," and it draws its inspiration from the liberatory social justice teachings of figures such as Martin Luther King Jr. and Audre Lorde as much as the liberatory teachings of Buddhism. To symbolize its primary pledge to diversity, EBMC intentionally put up an LGBTQI flag even before it assembled its altar, and its commitment to diversity is expressed on multiple levels, from organizational and leadership structures to teaching policies and practices. In addition to holding regular events for POC, for example, a core requirement of EBMC teachers is that they have a sufficient understanding of diversity and can demonstrate how their classes will be relevant to a multicultural audience. EBMC has also developed various strategies such as tracking demographics and reserving space in events for POC. Further, the center employs a model of "gift economics," with teaching programs offered on an all-dana (generosity) policy. Input from the wider EBMC sangha is also regularly invited through evaluation forms, community meetings, and interactive social media forums.[60]

Celebrated by Kornfield as "one of the most diverse sanghas in the world," EBMC has steadily grown in size and influence. Core EBMC teachers Yang and Washam are members of Spirit Rock's Teachers Council, and Yang and Ikeda have advised on diversity and inclusion initiatives at other Insight centers, including Spirit Rock and IMCW. Rachel Uris, director of development and marketing communications at Spirit Rock, shared some of their recent implementations, many of which have been adopted from EBMC, in the areas of registration policies, financial accessibility, diversity trainings for staff, and diversity teaching policies. To increase POC participation, for instance, Spirit Rock now tracks demographics more specifically and reserves 15 percent of residential retreat spaces for POC practitioners, 20 percent for month-long retreats, and twenty spaces for nonresidential daylongs. Spirit Rock has also "greatly enhanced" its scholarship commitment, including pricing affinity daylongs at 45 percent of the standard rate, adding scholarships for nonresidential retreats, and prioritizing POC in the scholarship award process. The board, teachers, staff, and community members at Spirit Rock have all completed Undoing Racism training led by the People's Institute for Survival and Beyond, and it has hired staff members to support diversity, equity, and inclusion work such as a human resources inclusion project manager.[61]

Similar to Spirit Rock, diversity and inclusion work at IMS can be credited to the pioneering work of individual POC teachers and their white allies. The first POC retreat on the East Coast was held at the Garrison Institute in 2003 and was cosponsored by IMS and New York Insight. As with EBMC, New York Insight was founded as an urban-based Insight center with a commitment to diversity. It runs a number of programs, including POC sitting groups at its main location and in Brooklyn and Harlem, and leadership trainings for POC.[62] Gina Sharpe, one of the cofounders of New York Insight, has been particularly influential in shaping diversity and inclusion work at IMS. Upon joining the board in 2000, she proposed a Diversity Committee, for which she and Goldstein where the only two volunteers. Their discussions led to a donor-sponsored IMS POC retreat in 2003, which was held for the first two years at the Garrison Institute before moving to IMS in 2005 where it has run annually with full attendance and a high return rate since. Sharpe and Goldstein invited Ralph Steele to plan and lead the first POC retreat, and Steele asked Sharpe to coteach it with him. She has since led eleven subsequent POC retreats, inviting Goldstein and later Sharon Salzberg to coteach with her.

Sharpe and Yang, who have co-led many of these retreats, note that attendees consistently report that the feeling of safety at POC retreats enables them "to access the teachings in a way they have not been able to in the mainstream, and as they have deepened their practice they can bring that level of safety so they can enter the mainstream."[63] Sharpe says she includes a wide range of cultural references, from Maya Angelou to Martin Luther King Jr., in order to render the teachings more relevant to diverse populations. Yang adds that while Insight teachers are pedagogically encouraged to teach from their personal experiences, this might need to change if the dharma is to be made accessible to a wider multicultural audience. As he explains, "In order to be able to reach people who are different than me, I actually have to do a slightly different practice of exchanging self for other, of putting myself in their shoes, of putting my community in their community's shoes, and invoking that *Satipatthana* practice of internal and external in order to reach people who have different life experiences."[64]

Yang's reference here is to Bhikkhu Analayo's commentary on the *Satipatthana Sutta*. Analayo discusses the refrain on internal and external mindfulness within the sutta, noting that the presence of the latter has been put aside in modern translations. After considering different interpretations, he concludes that external mindfulness means being mindful of other people and discusses several ways to practice this.[65] Following Analayo, Yang argues that while the Insight community has historically focused exclusively on mindfulness in the internal realm of the individual meditator, diversity awareness is the application of mindfulness to the external realm of the community.[66] Another way Yang has canonically legitimated diversity and inclusion work is through reference to a story in the Pali Canon in which the Buddha is approached by two Brahmin monastics who are concerned that the teachings of the dharma are being corrupted because others are putting the teachings into their own dialect. They suggest that the teachings should be rendered into a classical dialect. The Buddha, however, rebukes them and states: "Monastics, the words of the Buddha is not to be rendered into classical metre. Whoever does so commits an offense of wrongdoing. I allow the words of the Buddha to be learned in one's own language." Pointing out that in oral cultures, language is determinative of culture,

Yang argues that in effect the Buddha was saying that the dharma should be taught in different cultural forms.[67]

Yang also points out that this was exactly what the white founders of the Insight movement did when they brought the dharma back from Asia: they discarded what they saw as the "cultural trappings" of Asian Buddhism and presented the teachings in ways that were more relevant to their own communities. Goldstein acknowledges that "when we came back from Asia and started teaching, we kind of infused the teachings with our white, educated, middle-class perspectives."[68] Further, as Goldstein explains, this whiteness was so normative to the IMS community that it did not even occur to them that it was a problem. Mostly through feedback from POC participants, however, the center slowly realized that it was far from a welcoming or even neutral space for POC. While the POC retreats have been indispensable in creating a safe space, Goldstein recognizes that for real change to occur, a transformation of IMS's mainstream culture is necessary.[69]

The first public acknowledgment of the need for deeper structural work at IMS came in the 2008 *Sangha News* when Bob Agoglia, the executive director, noted that despite the popularity of POC retreats, IMS "has been and continues to be a predominantly white community and, as such, contributes unwittingly to a sense of separation and disconnection felt by people from different racial, ethnic and religious heritages."[70] A useful historical overview of IMS's diversity efforts is available in a four-page document published in August 2016 which acknowledges that racism has been structurally woven into institutions in the United States, including IMS, and notes some of its key initiatives, beginning with its adoption of its first diversity vision statement in 2007. It also gives detailed information on its current diversity action plan, which is structured around three key areas. The first of these is "deepening awareness," which is centered around cultivating an understanding of the multiple levels of racism and is being addressed through actions such as running regular diversity and inclusion trainings for staff members. The second is "building competency," which is focused on fostering skills to support POC and LGBTQI retreatants and includes role-play trainings based on case studies of micro-aggression. The third is "removing barriers," which is aimed at creating POC leadership, eliminating financial burdens for POC participation, and increasing racial awareness throughout the community.[71]

IMS's current diversity action plan also identifies training its teachers, particularly its guiding teachers, in diversity awareness and multicultural fluency as "vital." Much of this is because practitioners of color at IMS have reported that Buddhist teachings such as no-self, anger, and equanimity have been harmful for them when presented through the filter of a white dominant cultural lens and that they have been dismissed and further injured when they have attempted to discuss instances of racism with retreat teachers. As IMS teachers are internationally located, it is difficult to provide onsite trainings, so the center has recently distributed relevant literature and training manuals. This includes a booklet titled *On Understanding Race and Racism: Essential Information for White Dharma Teachers at IMS*, compiled by Sebene Selassie, a teacher and former executive director at New York Insight, and former IMS staffer Eric McCord. The booklet discusses how race and racism play out at IMS and is based on conversations with POC and white IMS staff and retreatants. It was emailed to teachers in July 2017 with an acknowledgment that "as more people of color yogis attend IMS retreats, instances of concern and undue suffering have arisen because of ignorance on the part of white teachers. In many of these cases, our teaching teams have not been prepared or skillful enough in responding to our people of color yogis."[72]

While training white Insight teachers is essential, even more vital is increasing the number of teachers of color. The diversity trajectories of all three centers under analysis—IMCW, Spirit Rock, and IMS—show that for real, lasting transformation to occur, POC must be fully represented in leadership and authority roles. As early as 2000, Kornfield acknowledged that the lack of teachers of color in the Insight community was a barrier to participation for POC.[73] This was confirmed in my interviews with numerous practitioners of color who shared the unique sense of safety and psychosomatic relaxation they experienced working with teachers who looked like them and shared life experiences with them.[74] Insight teacher demographics, however, are sobering. Yang estimates that there are currently between 350 and 375 certified Western Insight teachers, and only 10 to 11 of these self-identify as teachers of color.[75]

From these numbers it is evident that prioritizing the training of teachers of color is essential for the success of diversity and inclusion work. Teaching authority in the Insight community is established through three programs: the Kalyana Mitta, or Spiritual Friendship program; the Community Dharma Leaders (CDL) program; and the more advanced Teacher Training program.[76] The Kalyana Mitta is the most basic of the three and enables experienced practitioners to co-lead discussion groups. In 1997, Spirit Rock established the two-year CDL program in order to train and empower long-term practitioners to begin and lead Insight groups in their local communities with a focus on underserved communities. Yang engineered the first attempts to consciously include POC participation in CDL. He and Sharpe personally identified, contacted, and encouraged potential leaders among practitioners of color to apply. The demographic shift was stunning. In CDL4 (2010–2012), 37 percent of participants were POC, and this increased to 40 percent for CDL5 (2013–2015), as compared with an average of 6 percent in the three previous CDL iterations.[77] In addition, many trainees of color in the current Teacher Training programs are graduates from the previous two CDL cohorts, and the program appears to have generated a strong sense of community and solidarity among teachers of color and their white CDL "siblings."

The four-year Teacher Training is the most prestigious program in the Insight community. Kornfield started it at Spirit Rock, which ran the first six iterations alone, before joining together with IMS for the last two. Until the 2017 training, senior teachers nominated individuals who are then subject to a vote by a larger teaching body. Only graduates from this program are certified to teach residential retreats, which means that in addition to being vested with public authority in the community, they are better positioned to support themselves financially through retreat dana. Yang, Sharpe, Washam, and Anushka Fernandopulle, who co-leads an LGBTQI weekly group in San Francisco, were the four POC trainees in the 2002–2006 cohort of twenty-two.

In 2012, Yang and Kornfield began discussing how to increase participation of trainees of color in the Teacher Training program.[78] The three main parties involved were the proposed guiding teachers Yang and Sharpe, who were later joined by Kate Lila Wheeler, a fellow graduate

from the 2002–2006 cohort, and the two cosponsoring centers of Spirit
Rock and IMS. It was not until 2015, however, that IMS and Spirit Rock
announced that Yang and Sharpe would be leading the next Teacher
Training starting in January 2017 with the goal of having 75 percent of
the twenty trainees be POC.[79] Drawing on their extensive experience in
diversity work, Yang and Sharpe requested that, in order for the four-
year program to be sustainable for POC trainees, new structural components be implemented, particularly regarding financial support and
mentorship between trainees and retreat teachers. When IMS and Spirit
Rock declined to meet these conditions, Yang, Sharpe, and Wheeler resigned. The official public responses from both IMS and Spirit Rock accepted responsibility for the situation. A letter from Spirit Rock's board
of directors in March 2016, for instance, acknowledged the "unconscious
racism" present at the center, declared that they "hold ourselves responsible," and identified structural accountability and transparency as essential if their diversity goals were to "match our intentions."[80] Similarly,
IMS's February 2016 *Sangha News* contained a statement that heralded
Yang and Sharpe for providing "vital leadership," acknowledged that
much organizational work was necessary at IMS in order for its diversity
aspirations to be successful, and announced that the center was committed to transformation through dialogue with Yang and Sharpe.[81]

Given the tone of IMS's statement, it was quite surprising when
Ed Hong, the board president, stated that in July 2016 IMS had voted
unanimously not to accept Yang and Sharpe's most recent proposal. He
said that negotiations between the parties had been emotionally fraught
but did not specify exactly why IMS found the proposal unacceptable
or what had changed since the February statement. It did, however, an-
nounce that IMS remained committed to offering a training program
for teachers of color, although "the specifics are not yet clear."[82] In December 2016, IMS announced that it would run its own Teacher Training program led by senior teachers Goldstein, Kamala Masters, and Gil
Fronsdal; guiding teacher Rebecca Bradshaw; and DaRa Williams and
Bonnie Duran, who were two of the five POC graduates of the 2016 IMS/
Spirit Rock Teacher Training.[83] This was followed by an introduction
to the twenty trainees, 75 percent of whom were POC, and details of a
fundraising initiative to complete the program in 2021.[84]

It was not until two months after IMS's withdrawal that Spirit Rock announced that it would also run its own training led by Yang, Sharpe, and Wheeler.[85] René Rivera, a member of Spirit Rock's board of directors who was instrumental in developing its current Diversity, Equity, and Inclusion Plan, said that there had been a coordinated attempt by the wider POC sangha and their allies at Spirit Rock to express their unequivocal support for Yang, Sharpe, and Wheeler. He saw this as being a decisive factor in moving the process forward as it demonstrated a collective determination for change that could not be dismissed or reduced to individuals.[86] After unanimous approval by the board, the training began in July 2017 with twenty trainees, 90 percent of whom identify as POC. It has two interrelated focuses: a deep understanding of the dharma and an awareness of how context has shaped all historical expressions of the dharma. As the teachers explained: "We want our trainees to understand the underpinnings of how Dharma has developed and been taught in Western society, inflected by complexities of culture and identity in the West as well as those inherited/adopted/adapted from Asia—and how these can inter-relate beneficially or not." In line with their commitment to internal and external practice and individual and collective awakening, Yang, Sharpe, and Wheeler's aim is to help their trainees to be able to skillfully guide individual meditators in retreat settings and to be spiritual leaders across diverse communities. As they put it, "We understand Dharma as liberation internally and externally; we endeavor to have them [the trainees] explore deeply how these inter-relate."[87]

Reflecting on the process, Development Director Uris said that as painful as it had been, Yang, Sharpe, and Wheeler's "boundary drawing" had ultimately functioned as a "wake up call" and "catalyst" for real change at the center.[88] Similarly, Executive Director Michelle Latvala identified it as a "major shift" that had provided an opportunity to develop *karuna,* or compassion, in "understanding racial suffering on a systemic level at Spirit Rock."[89] Although I was unable to get any direct feedback from IMS, its current diversity plan, which emphasizes the need for a deeper analysis of power and privilege on a structural level, suggests a similar impact.[90] Moreover, combined together, the two programs will produce thirty-three teachers of color, which will mean an extraordinary increase of 330 percent in the number of teachers of color in the Insight community.

In many ways, therefore, the final outcome of the teacher training process has been a positive one. Nonetheless, it is important not to underemphasize the turmoil and trauma of the process, which has left deep fractures in the Insight teaching community, as it raised many crucial questions for the future of diversity work in meditation-based convert Buddhism. One major question is, What type of organizational structures best support or hinder diversity and inclusion work? While all figures involved have sustained emotional pain and fatigue, it is important to recognize that the three main parties were not on an equal playing field. IMS and Spirit Rock are dominant organizations invested with power and authority and significant resources, whereas Yang, Sharpe, and Wheeler are individuals with limited resources attempting to bring about radical transformation in the culture of these organizations. In addition, there are also power differentials between the senior teachers of IMS and Spirit Rock and Yang, Sharpe, and Wheeler, who were partially trained by those teachers.

To best ameliorate such glaring power disparities, it is essential to have established, transparent structures and communication processes. From all accounts, however, these were strikingly absent in the teacher training proposal process. It is still unclear, for instance, why IMS moved from seeing Yang, Sharpe, and Wheeler's proposal as a "call to action" to being "unsustainable." Spirit Rock also made no official statement on why it took two months to approve the proposal. Without such information, it is difficult to ascertain exactly why the two centers arrived at such different responses. Similarly, the mechanics of communication and the sheer duration of the process both reflected and reproduced unconscious structures of white privilege. When I asked Yang why a process involving people and organizations who had all previously collaborated took more than four years, he said that there had been a "constant revisiting and recension of minutiae" and that none of the negotiations was face to face until three and a half years into the process, and even at that meeting many of the major decision-makers were absent. This might be attributed to the bureaucratic mundanities of large organizations, but such delays place a disproportionate burden, however unintentionally, on individual agents and work against change. As Yang and Sharpe observe, "the organizational and corporate structure of the meditation center itself becomes an oppressive instrument."[91]

Another major area of inquiry for meditation-based communities is how the particular historical and cultural formations of Buddhism that they have adopted and developed intersect with diversity and inclusion goals. Put simply, what Buddhist practice modalities, canonical teachings, and community formations best align with progressive diversity and inclusion commitments and what formations reinforce dominant cultural worldviews and hierarchies such as white privilege?[92] As examined in chapter 3, IMS has preserved the Burmese Buddhist modernist retreat model, with a focus on intensive individual meditation practice, whereas Spirit Rock has forged a more relational/integrative approach that focuses on awakening in daily life. Given the centrality of community to diversity work, the individual retreat model might pose some boundaries on the type of transformation that can be done. Goldstein offers one indication of how fundamental differences in orientation toward practice between the two centers have played out in diversity work: "They [Spirit Rock] incorporated a little bit more of the political dimension in the retreats. They would have discussion groups about racism. They would be addressing those issues very specifically. At IMS, it was basically a straight dharma retreat, but . . . we wanted to make available to people of color the same experience that white people had when they came to retreats."[93]

One way to situate the comments from Goldstein, which point to the preservation of the modernist retreat model IMS inherited from its Burmese lineage, and the contextual as well as meditative emphasis of Spirit Rock's teacher training is to see them as the latest expression of a longstanding difference in orientation between IMS and Spirit Rock, or what I identified in earlier research as "East Coast" and "West Coast" Vipassana.[94] Although this distinction captures much of what is at play, it should be applied cautiously, with some important qualifications. First, these categories risk misrepresenting individual trainees in suggesting that Spirit Rock trainees are less accomplished meditators and that IMS trainees are less committed to collective awakening. Second, given the privileged status of meditation in the mainstream Insight community,

such a framing also implicitly bestows more spiritual power and authority to IMS. Third, using the language of a "straight" versus "political" retreat approach risks fetishizing IMS's model as culture-free rather than
what it actually is: a specific cultural and religious product of Buddhist
modernism. Hence, the approaches of *both* IMS and Spirit Rock are best
understood as reflecting specific cultural iterations of Buddhism—the
former a more assimilative modernist approach, and the latter a more
radical postmodern, postcolonial approach. I explore this distinction in
more detail below.

"Whose 'One' Are We Being?"

In earlier research on the LGBTQI Alphabet Sangha at EBMC, I argued
that its embrace of diversity and intersectionality reflected the wider
cultural shift from the modern to postmodern in which modern liberal goals of assimilation were displaced in favor of a postmodern and
postcolonial affirmation of difference.[95] I come to a similar conclusion
here, seeing racial diversity and inclusion initiatives as applying pressure
to a number of core Buddhist modernist characteristics—universalism,
the "essential" versus "cultural" Buddhist distinction, liberalism, and
individualism—and displaying perspectives more associated with the
postmodern and postcolonial than the modern.

Racial diversity and inclusion work replaces a modernist narrative
of universalism with a postmodern one of cultural particularity. Proponents argue that the universal truth of the dharma needs to be rendered
universally accessible through attention to cultural difference. It should
be noted, however, that this is not so much a question of bringing more
cultural sensitivity to a universal "culture-free" teaching but rather
of recognizing that Buddhist teachings have *always* been presented
through a cultural lens, which historically in the Insight community has
been that of the dominant white, middle-class mainstream. Hence, what
is rhetorically claimed as a "universal," or "classical," approach is, in ac-
tuality, a culturally distinct modernist rendering of Buddhism. Rather
than reproducing a false universalism, advocates aim to both render
the historic, sociocultural particularity of American Buddhist modernism visible and expose its exclusionary operations. For teachers such as

Yang, Ikeda, and Zenju Earthlyn Manuel, it is impossible to transcend culture, so embracing multicultural difference is the only real way to foster a sense of interdependence.[96]

The recognition that all forms of Buddhism are cultural undermines the common modernist distinction between "essential" and "cultural" Buddhism, which has often been mapped onto the distinction between Euro-American converts and Asian American immigrants. As Natalie Quli points out, Euro-American convert Buddhism is as culturally embedded as any form of Asian Buddhism. In response to Helen Tworkov's claim that convert American Buddhists were developing an essential Buddhism, Quli replies:

> For Tworkov, a truly American Buddhism is free of culture—as are real Americans. But do we really believe that Euro-American whites are culture-free? Or is it that white American culture is simply transparent to those on the inside? We need to consider the implications of such an attitude. Rosaldo asks: "What are the cultural implications of making 'our' cultural selves invisible? What cultural politics erase the 'self' only to highlight the 'other'? What ideological conflicts inform the play of visibility and invisibility?"[97]

Advocates of Buddhist diversity and inclusion work are sensitive to the ways in which Asian immigrant communities have been historically dismissed by mainstream convert Buddhism. Many of my interviewees, for instance, were literate in postcolonial perspectives and were critical of white convert claims to be teaching "real" Buddhism.

The liberalism of Buddhist modernism has also come under interrogation. Although American convert Buddhism is often celebrated for gender equality, this has been forwarded through a second-wave liberal feminist agenda that has given insufficient attention to race and class differences. More than one IMCW interviewee commented that the liberal base of IMCW was an obstacle to diversity and inclusion work. Bassing, for example, noted that it was particularly hard for white liberals at IMCW to "self-identify as oppressor." Similarly, IMCW realized that for real change to occur, it had to move from its earlier naive liberal approach to diversity, which relied on assimilating POC to its preexisting culture and structures, to a much more radical decentering of white hegemony on multiple levels of the organization.

Finally, diversity and inclusion work has mounted a significant challenge to the privileging of the individual meditator and the general individualism of Buddhist modernism. A repeated theme in such initiatives is the recovery of the sangha, or "beloved community," and the need to move from individual to the collective aspects of Buddhist practice. Yang, for example, has argued that in large part because of the liberal Protestant and Western psychological influence on Buddhist modernism, the Insight community has focused on mindfulness as an inner experience for the individual meditator whereas diversity awareness is the application of mindfulness in the collective realm. He sees the consolidation of sangha within POC Buddhist spaces as offering a valuable gift to the American Insight community.[98] Another way that community features is through the development of relationships between sanghas and the local communities in which centers are situated. EBMC, for example, credits much of its success to its close relationship with local communities. Similarly, Greg Snyder, cofounder of the Brooklyn Zen Center, said that from the inception his vision was to create a community-based Zen center, and Brooklyn Zen Center has cohosted events with local groups on topics such as gun violence.[99]

Diversity, inclusion, and equity advocates see Buddhism as a potent remedy for collective American suffering—the dukkha of racism—and racial diversity and inclusion work as a potent remedy for certain limitations of modern Buddhism. Whereas members of the first generation of American convert teachers have focused on using Buddhism to address individual psychological suffering, Buddhist principles are now being applied to the sociocultural dimensions of that individual self and the collective suffering of racial injustice in the United States. Demonstrating a postmodern and postcolonial sensibility, racial inclusion and justice work therefore should be seen as both a corrective to earlier Euro-American Buddhist modernist trends and a continuation of the modernist application of Buddhist teachings to contemporary Western forms of suffering.

S • I • X

Buddhism Unbundled

From Buddhist Geeks to Meditate.io

At the 2014 Buddhist Geeks conference, Triratna teacher Bodhipaksa delivered a talk called "Debugging the Source Code of the Dharma," which he contextualized as being centered on the convergence of the Buddhist tradition, personal meditation practice, and academic scholarship. Bodhipaksa's main argument was that the Buddhist commentarial literature did not faithfully represent the Buddha's teachings as recorded in the suttas. As he explained, the monastics who wrote commentaries, such as Buddhaghosa, did not meditate and this led them to depart from the original teachings and introduce "bugs in the source code." Bodhipaksa wanted to "debug" the dharma by returning to the suttas to clarify what the Buddha actually taught. Offering a close reading of differences between the suttas and the commentaries, Bodhipaksa's lecture was littered with quotations from the Buddha, extracts from the *Visuddhimagga,* and Pali terms such as *sankhara, skandhas,* and *vedana;* and it was supported by scholarship from Buddhist monks such as Bhikkhu Analayo and academics such as Sue Hamilton. He concluded with a plea for the audience to engage academic scholarship to find a "cleaner, leaner source code" of the dharma in order to liberate self and others from suffering.[1]

At first glance, Bodhipaksa's presentation appears to be the perfect illustration of the mix of tradition and innovation, Buddhism and technology, that was the signature of the Buddhist Geeks project. An online Buddhist media platform launched in 2007 by Vince Horn and Ryan Oelke, two self-identified millennials who wanted to combine their passion for Buddhism with their "geeky skills," it quickly gained a wide audience for its pioneering explorations into the convergence of Buddhism, technology, and global culture. "Debugging the Source Code of the Dharma" stood out to me at the 2014 conference, however, not because it was representative of the event but rather because it was distinctive. Bodhipaksa was one of the few Buddhist teachers at the conference and the only speaker who engaged Buddhist canonical literature to any significant degree. While his technological metaphors resonated well with the event theme, the explicit Buddhist content distinguished it, along with a couple of others, from the majority of presentations and the general "vibe" of the event.

The 2014 conference was my third successive year undertaking participant observation at the Buddhist Geeks annual conference. While there were some familiar faces, such as Pragmatic Dharma teacher Daniel Ingram and posttraditionalist Buddhist Hokai Sobol, I recognized fewer people than before. This was confirmed when Horn informally counted raised hands and estimated that around 80 percent of participants were attending the conference for the first time. As well as the demographics, I also noticed a discernable shift in discourse, with the emphasis much more firmly on the "Geek" part of Buddhist Geeks rather than the "Buddhist" part. Much of the attention and energy centered on "contemplative technologies," some of which, including an Oculus Rift virtual reality headset designed to immerse the user in a three-dimensional digital landscape, were on display in stalls set up inside the main conference room. Previous conferences had also featured topics such as "gaming as spiritual practice," but, unlike earlier presenters, the 2014 speakers seemed much less interested in relating, let alone legitimating, their tech innovations to Buddhism. In his promotion of contemplative technologies, for example, Mikey Siegel, the founder of the "consciousness hacking movement," mentioned the words "Buddhism" and "dharma" only once each.[2] Similarly, innovative game designer Robin Arnott described technologically reproducing an LSD "trance experience," with no reflection at all on how either cutting-edge "technodelics" or old-school psychedelics might (or might not) align with the tradition.[3]

On the basis of my experience at the 2014 conference, I would have been much less likely to have drawn the conclusion of my earlier research that alongside their considerable innovations, Buddhist Geeks were committed to preserving Buddhism.[4] Here it was clear that the encounter between Buddhism and technology was more about assimilation than conversation and that the particularity of Buddhism was being displaced by perennial signifiers such as "contemplation," "consciousness," and "awakening." It was less of a surprise to me, therefore, when I received an email two years later from Vince and Emily Horn which told me that they were closing their decade-long Buddhist Geeks platform and turning attention to Meditate.io, a new teaching project that they described as "mind training for the digital age." As they explained, "We're excited to step out of the explicitly Buddhist space and work with folks who are interested in the practice of meditation as a tool for living in the 21st century."[5]

Through an analysis of the Buddhist Geeks project and a consideration of its replacement, Meditate.io., I explore in this chapter the impact of technology and digital culture on American convert Buddhism. I draw on discourse analysis, formal interviews with some of the main players of the Buddhist Geeks project, informal interaction with multiple Buddhist Geeks participants, and participant observation at three annual Buddhist Geeks conferences from 2012 to 2015.

"Buddhist Geeks Is Dead. Long Live Buddhist Geeks!": Buddhist Geeks, 2006–2016

> Unbundled and reconstituted
> in new and different forms,
> Buddhism is merely a name for that
> Which is constantly being reborn.[6]

Buddhist Geeks was an online Buddhist media company that launched in 2007 and originally consisted of a weekly audio podcast and a digital magazine; it later expanded to include a series of annual conferences and a virtual training and practice community. Rather than having a mission statement, Vince Horn, one of its cofounders, framed and explained Buddhist Geeks as a contemporary koan, or ongoing question. At first, he explained that Buddhist Geeks was "a podcast where we interview geeky Buddhists about things we don't see being talked about anywhere else." As the project developed, however, it became a lived inquiry into the question "How can we serve the convergence of the time-tested practices and models of Buddhism with rapidly evolving technology and a global culture?" or "How can we help bring Buddhism into the 21st century?"[7]

The beginning of the project can be traced to the summer of 2006, when Horn and Ryan Oelke, who at that time were both students at the Buddhist-inspired Naropa University in Boulder, Colorado, began working on a podcast. They planned to use it as a platform to explore issues that were particularly relevant to them as young Buddhist practitioners in the twenty-first century but that were rarely addressed in prevailing Western Buddhist circles. They were joined later by a third member, Gwen Bell, and the three wanted to provide a public forum for the kind of discussions they were having among themselves, such as what was actually happening in their meditation practice and how to think more positively about the way "practice is changing to meet the culture."[8]

Their original idea was to interview a different person every week and then post it as a podcast on the Buddhist Geeks website where it would be available for free download. The innovative and interdisciplinary nature of the podcast was emphasized in its advertisement as "an ongoing conversation with the individuals and communities who are experimenting with new ways of practicing Buddhism, as well as new ways of bringing Buddhist and contemplative insights into other disciplines."[9] Horn explained that there was no specific criterion for whom he interviewed and that he tended to choose people, both Buddhist and non-Buddhist, he was personally interested in learning more about; he also confessed that he increasingly moved toward the latter group.[10] The result was the production of nearly four hundred podcasts, which included more than two hundred interviews with a range of people from across Buddhist traditions and lineages but also from fields as diverse as neuroscience, technology, business, social justice, and the creative arts. The last set of interviews, for example, explored the topic of ethics from multiple angles through interviews with David Chapman, a popular Buddhist blogger; Emma Seppälä, the scientific director of Stanford University's Center for Compassion and Altruism Research and Education; James Hughes, the executive director of the Institute for Ethics and Emerging Technologies; angel Kyodo williams, an ordained Zen priest who founded the nonsectarian Center for Transformative Change; and Stephen Batchelor, a secular Buddhist teacher and author.[11]

One indicator of the popularity of a podcast topic is the number of times the podcast is downloaded. Horn shared the downloaded statistics on their top twenty episodes from 2013 to 2017, when the podcast was hosted on SoundCloud. The top ten podcasts, which had been downloaded between approximately 20,000 and 44,000 times, featured interviews on mindfulness, psychedelics, meditation, and neuroscience and critiques of Western Buddhism by popular blogger David Chapman. More surprising, perhaps, given the white male techie demographic of the Buddhist Geeks community, was the interview with angel Kyodo williams, "Talking Race, Love and Liberation," which had been downloaded 44,123 times by April 2017. The following nine were "Psilocybin: A Crash Course in Mindfulness" (downloaded 39,941 times), "Mindfulness ++" (27,724), "Meditating on Mushrooms" (23,603), "The Science of Compassion" (22,238), "Secularizing Buddhist Ethics" (21,738), "The Mind Illuminated" (21,638), "The Progress of Insight" (20,669), "Western Buddhism Is Dead" (20,333), and "Buddhist Ethics Is a Fraud" (19,202).[12]

Horn and Oelke reported that after a few years, and more than a million downloads of their weekly podcasts, "it became clear that Buddhist Geeks was something closer to a movement or community, rather than just a podcast."[13] The desire to bring this community together in person inspired the 2011 Buddhist Geeks conference at the University of the West in Los Angeles, which was to be the first of four successive annual conferences. Given the size of the conference—just 165 participants—the international media coverage it received was quite extraordinary. In large part because of Horn's media savviness, the conference received positive attention in both the national and international press. Mitchell Landsberg of the *Los Angeles Times,* for instance, reported that the conference brought together "bloggers, tweeters, scholars, teachers and just plain old Buddhist practitioners for two and a half days to talk about such topics as 'the science of enlightenment,' 'the emerging face of Buddhism,' and 'the Dharma and the Internet.'" In the British *Guardian* Ed Halliwell validated the Buddhist legitimacy of the conference and enthused that "Geekery could bring a radical heart and soul to 21st century Buddhism."[14] Equally enthusiastic were reports from attendees. David Chapman exclaimed: "It's extraordinary. There's a level of enthusiasm, engagement, excitement here far beyond what I've experienced at any large Buddhist gathering. It totally rocks. . . . It's making me feel more optimistic about Buddhism than that I have in many years—perhaps ever. It's not so much the intellectual content (although some of that has been remarkable) as the vibe of 'we can do things differently, and create an unexpected future for our religion.'"[15]

Inspired by the positive reception of the first conference, Horn and Oelke planned a larger one for the following year. In August 2012, the second conference was nearly twice the size of the first, with 260 attendees; it was followed by the 2013 conference, with 276 attendees, and the 2014 conference, with 242. As with the podcasts, these conferences featured a mix of Buddhist and non-Buddhist speakers with the main areas of focus including scientific research on mindfulness, developmental maps of meditation, contemplative technological innovations, spiritual entrepreneurship, meditation and the creative arts, and contemplative-based social justice activism. Key representatives of these fields included researchers such as Willoughby Britton, David Vago, and Rick Hanson; meditation teachers such as Shinzen Young, Daniel Ingram, and Kenneth Folk; game designer Jane McGonigal and cyber anthropologist Amber Case; entrepreneurs such as Tami Simon of Sound True and Buddhify app designer Rohan Gunatillake; multimedia artist John. F Simon; and Engaged Buddhists such as David Loy and Michael Stone. The conference format consisted of keynote addresses with question-and-answer periods; twenty-minute TED-style talks; "roundtable sessions," with five or six panelists discussing a set topic; and "community-led unplugged sessions," that is, small group discussions on audience-chosen topics. There was also morning practice, including guided meditation and yoga sessions, and evening social entertainment.

At the 2012 conference I sat alongside young hipsters in thick-rimmed glasses, silver-haired ladies in shawls, and techies of all ages armed with glowing iPads and listened to the opening keynote speech, "Does Buddhism Have to Die to Be Reborn in the West?," by American Tibetan Buddhist popularizer Lama Surya Das. Das warned that Buddhist communities risked becoming stagnant unless they engaged with technology, but he emphasized the importance of bringing awareness and compassion to the emerging digital culture. The next morning, I and about thirty others attended one of several practice sessions: a guided meditation on "inclusive awareness" led by "posttraditional" Buddhist Hokai Sobol. Among the punchy, entertaining, and seemingly well-received TED talks, two in particular stood out: Willoughby Britton's "Mindful Binge Drinking and Blobology" and Daniel Ingram's "It's a Jungle in There." Britton, an assistant professor of psychiatry at Brown University Medical School and a Buddhist practitioner, took aim at the state of scientific research on mindfulness, lamenting the decontextualization of the practice from its larger soteriological framework and deflating many of its hyperbolic claims. She ended her talk, which received a standing ovation, on a note of reassurance that a new, more sophisticated generation of contemplative neuroscientists was emerging. Pragmatic Dharma teacher Ingram, who is also a medical doctor, had the crowd howling with laughter with his slightly manic delivery. Dressed in khaki, he called on meditators to apply the "spirit of openness" and meticulous exploration that he admired in nineteenth-century naturalists to catalogue contemplative experience across different developmental scales.

Breaking up the formal presentations were the community-led unplugged sessions. On offer were audience-proposed themes such as "the pros and cons of speaking openly about enlightenment," "how to speak skillfully about enlightenment," "what is the difference between being a Buddhist and being a Buddha?," "contemplative art," and "how do we begin to occupy dharma?" I opted for a session facilitated by Pragmatic Dharma teachers Kenneth Folk and Beth Resnick Folk in which fourteen participants, mostly young men in their twenties, related their meditation practice to the stages outlined in the Progress of Insight. Later in the afternoon, I watched a roundtable session on "DIY Buddhism: What's New Now?" in which first-generation Western Buddhists

Ken McLeod and Stephen Batchelor and Gen X teachers Hokai Sobol and Kelly Sosan Bearer discussed the pros and cons of a nonhierarchical "ground-up approach" to Buddhism. On one hand, they legitimated such an approach via the Pali Canon's Parable of the Raft, in which the Buddha compares the dharma to assembling a raft to cross a body of water and then discarding it when one has reached the other shore. On the other hand, they admitted that such a do-it-yourself (DIY) sensibility risked descending into a superficial type of "IKEA Buddhism."

In reflecting on the trajectory of the conferences, Horn said: "In the beginning, they felt really significant to us because they brought all of these people together for the first time. I saw connections and relationships be built and have seen them continue." However, the labor involved in producing the conference began to outweigh the benefits: "The amount of energy it takes to organize an event like that, the amount of overhead and the amount of risk you take in doing so, it's really out of proportion with, at least for us and our organization, the returns and sustainability." He also acknowledged a shift in the energy of the conferences: "I think that the freshness and the novelty, once you start doing it, becomes rarified. It was time to let it go and do something new."[16] Similarly, Hokai Sobol, who helped plan the conferences, agreed with my observation about the general tenor of the 2014 conference and felt that the conferences "were less and less 'Buddhist' and increasingly 'Geeky.'"[17]

"Awakening Is a Team Sport":
Buddhist Geeks Virtual Community

According to both Vince and Emily Horn, the conferences were instrumental in building community, with many attendees forging ongoing friendships and professional relationships. The desire to build on the community initiated at the conferences led to three different attempts to create a virtual practice community: the Life Retreat, the Buddhist Geeks Community, and the Buddhist Geeks Dojo. Another motivating factor behind these efforts was that Vince and Emily had both started teaching in 2010—Vince through the Pragmatic Dharma lineage of Kenneth Folk, and Emily thought the Insight lineage under the guidance of

Jack Kornfield and Trudy Goodman—and they wanted to start offering online training.

Emily, who also attended Naropa and had gotten involved with Buddhist Geeks when they began planning the 2011 conference, was the main driving force behind their first virtual teaching program, the Life Retreat. Described as a "new delivery model," which included weekly one-to-one personalized instruction and feedback with a teacher as well as small peer group meetings, it launched in June 2012. In a short video, which would be the format adopted for future advertisements of programs, the Horns explain that it is designed for two main groups: people who cannot attend traditional retreats because of family or work commitments and people who want more continuity between traditional retreats, with "traditional" here referring to the Buddhist modernist format of intensive silent retreats common in the Insight community of between seven days and three months. The two main themes of the Life Retreat were daily life as the site of practice and the importance of community support, or as Vince said, borrowing from Folk, "awakening is a team sport." In keeping with Buddhist Geeks' signature rhetoric, the program also recast Buddhist practice using language from tech, business, and well-being culture: "The Life Retreat is aimed at optimizing your meditation practice in daily life. Think of it [as] like being on a meditation team with a personal coach."[18]

Vince felt that "the natural next step from the immersive Life Retreats and conference was to continue this training and the peer-to-peer contact that was unique to Buddhist Geeks through a new program."[19] This resulted in the formation of the Buddhist Geeks Community (BGC), which drew inspiration from bitcoin, the Occupy Wall Street movement, and the Burning Man gatherings. Influenced by Daniel Thorson, who had lived at the Occupy camp for six months before officially joining the Buddhist Geeks team in 2012, the BGC's aim was to create a decentralized and self-organized network of practitioners that would be entirely peer-led and centered around the concept of "conversation as practice."[20] The BGC ran between 2012 and 2014 and had between one hundred and three hundred regular members, although Vince confessed that "since things were constantly changing, we didn't keep very close metrics on this project."[21]

The radical decentralization of the BGC was one attempt at enacting DIY Buddhism on a community level. The experiment, however, soon ran into some serious problems. As Vince bluntly put it, "We had a totally decentralized system and it totally decentralized out into space." One of the main problems was that in a well-intentioned attempt to empower all community members, the BGC actually ended up disempowering many participants, including Vince and Emily. They had created something of a power vacuum, Vince explained, and in lieu of any formal authority, some participants began to take on teaching roles without Vince and Emily's knowledge or permission, a situation that brought up all kinds of safety and liability issues. For instance, he asked, "What do you do when a conversation goes off the rails or someone shares something inappropriate in a Google hangout? Who's supposed to be responsible for that?" Emily added that it was a big lesson for them both in learning about power, authority, and taking the teacher's seat. Another problem was that they had not structurally connected the Life Retreat and the BGC, and this was disconcerting for some of the members. "Emily and I were teaching through the retreats," Vince said, "and a lot of people we were working with were also in the community, but they were in totally different spaces. There was no real connection there for us in terms of our goals or relationships with people. So, people started dropping out."[22]

In reflecting on what went wrong with the BGC, Vince and Emily borrowed the concept of "natural hierarchy" from Naropa and Shambhala Buddhist founder Chögyam Trungpa. Trungpa used this term to signify that people have unique and different skill sets that should be utilized and not ignored in the building of spiritual communities, and the Horns felt they had disrupted this natural hierarchy. Another way Vince expressed much of the challenge with the BGC was through differentiating between "decentralized authority" and the "distribution of authority." As he explained:

> I've really been thinking a lot more in terms of distribution of authority as opposed to decentralized authority. Because it's part of what failed at the last iteration of the community. . . . We were the architects of the structure of the design and all

that, but we really didn't do much in terms of actual leadership inside the community outside of being the architects
of it, so we really opted for the decentralized self-organizing
model, and it totally, from our point of view, failed.[23]

Thorson, who was one of the architects of the BGC, came to a similar conclusion. Overall, he felt it had been a stressful but valuable learning experience for everyone involved and that it illuminated one of the
core tensions in the Buddhist Geeks approach: getting the right balance
between structure and freedom. The problem with BGC, he explained,
was that "we went too heavy on decentralized authority and gave people
too much autonomy and responsibility. We needed to make the power
dynamics more explicit but were unwilling to do that."[24]

After almost a year of "soul-searching" and reflecting on what
went wrong, the Horns launched their third and final Buddhist Geeks
teaching and community platform: the Buddhist Geeks Dojo. Vince describes it as "the phoenix that arose out of the ashes" of their previous
projects and says that he had something of an epiphany after hearing
a comment by John Maeda, a fellow panelist at PopTech, that "when
rebels mature, they build institutions." It was a moment, he explains,
in which he recognized that "with Buddhist Geeks, we have an opportunity to build something that can last, that can serve people. We can
build something that can be more than just a bright flash in this interesting emergence of digital Buddhism and can be something that actually
serves an ongoing role."[25]

The Horns had realized that the most important thing for them
was teaching and practice or, as Vince put it, "not just having ideas but
enacting those ideas, making them part of our lives and creating a training ground." Whereas the podcast would still serve as a "portal of perspectives," the Dojo would be the place to put their "multiperspectival"
and "metaperspectival" approach into practice. Unlike the decentralized
BGC, the Dojo would follow a distributed authority model in which the
Horns would "take more strong leadership roles and work more closely
with people" in order to create a virtual training space "where people
feel safe, where people feel they can go deep into the material, and know

who they can talk to—the kind of things that we started to hear about after the BGC was over."[26]

In terms of structure, the Dojo, or "cloud-based sangha," had three main components. One of these—"just sitting"—was an updated version of the BGC's successful "open practice" sessions in which a small group of people, usually around ten, would get together in Google hangouts at various scheduled times and meditate, with one person ringing the bell to start and end the virtual session. Another feature was teacher-led events, which included regular guided meditations and "Ask Me Anything" (AMA) sessions with Vince and Emily or guest teachers speaking on particular topics of interest and offering one-to-one personalized instructions. In describing their particular teaching approach, the Horns said they had developed a modular approach to meditation that consisted of five main styles of meditation that had been "reverse engineered" from the Buddhist traditions they were most familiar with. The third feature was peer groups, which were geared toward practice and book study. Their aim was to help develop facilitators for these groups who in turn could support the emergence of a more structured and "deeper collectivism."[27] Another distinctive feature of the Dojo was a "Fall Training Period" (FTP), an intensive practice period inspired by the rain retreats in Theravada Buddhism. Alongside their virtual retreats, the Horns offered two in-person retreats held in Ashville, North Carolina, where they had relocated in 2013. The first was between March 29 and April 4, 2015, and had twelve participants; the second was from July 11 to 18, 2016, with fifteen participants.

Participation levels at the Dojo ranged from between 150 and 200 regular members. As Vince and Emily did not collect specific demographic data, Vince could offer only anecdotal information in terms of participants, although he could confirm that they came from all over the world: North America, South America, Western and Eastern Europe, India, and Australia. When I interviewed him in 2015, while the Dojo was still operating, he said, "A lot of people are coming in [to the Dojo] having only a brief introduction [to Buddhism], but almost no one coming in is totally new to practice or to Buddhism." While different Buddhist lineages were represented, he identified the majority as being from

"Insight, Vajrayana, or mindfulness" and noted that a "decent number" of people were from local and virtual hybrid sanghas, and some were "involved in multiple virtual communities."[28]

The Emerging Faces of Buddhism in the Modern World: Common Themes

According to Ken McLeod, the 2011 Buddhist Geeks conference was a "pivotal game changing moment in the development of Buddhism in the West." The "genius" of Buddhist Geeks was that it was able to provide a platform for unprecedented conversations about the future of Buddhism. This, he explained, was because of the diversity of people it interviewed for its podcast, its attraction of a much wider audience than that of typical Western Buddhist sanghas, and its freedom from traditional Buddhist institutional structures.[29] What were the main themes of this conversation? First and foremost, there was a fundamental optimism about the impact of technology on Buddhist practice in the twenty-first century. Although the dangers of technology—such as the fragmentation of attention or the sense of disembodiment it can produce—were acknowledged, the main emphasis was on its benefits and potential for Buddhist or contemplative practice. Much of Buddhist Geeks was devoted to celebrating how technology and social media were being used to both aid traditional Buddhist practices and enable the emergence of radically innovative forms of Buddhism. At one end of the technology spectrum was the promotion of common technologies such as Skype and Twitter to aid classical Buddhist practices. Horn, for example, pointed out how Skype had enabled him to have "real interaction" with geographically distant teachers and Twitter had socially reinforced his practice commitments through connecting him with other practitioners. At the other end was an enthusiasm for radical future technological potential such as an "enlightenment machine" or a "Buddha Helmet" that could accelerate the process of awakening. In between ordinary and extraordinary technologies was the designing of new technological aids to meditation such as Rohan Gunatillake's meditation app Buddhify, which enabled "meditation on the go" in four settings—traveling, walking, working out at the gym, and being at home—as well as an array of contemplative-based games from designers such as Jane McGonigal, Jonathan Blow, and Robin Arnott that reconfigured "practice as play."[30] This affirmation and embrace of technology signified a discernable shift in the dialogue between Buddhism and technology. As Horn noted, Buddhist communities have started to utilize technology as a spiritually transformative tool rather than dismiss it as a hindrance to practice or reluctantly accept it as a necessary evil of modern life.[31]

A second theme was the advancement of an integrative and world-affirming approach to Buddhism in which all aspects of contemporary daily life—technology, business, relationships, social justice, and creativity—were legitimated as potential sites for awakening. One example of this integration were discussions about the relationship between Buddhism and business at the 2012 Buddhist Geeks conference. Reflecting on how spirituality and economics might be brought together in more productive and transparent ways, participants explored both how Buddhist principles could be applied to business practices and how business models might help reform Buddhist communities. Further, speakers questioned the dualism between "the sacred and the profane" and advocated a more holistic approach that sacralizes worldly practices often excluded or seen as "un-Buddhist."[32] Another example was the framing of daily life as practice site. On the Life Retreat video, Emily Horn says that much of her motivation for developing the program was so people who could not attend traditional retreats could use daily life as "the sacred ground" of practice.[33] Gunatillake's Buddhify similarly establishes urban space and "practice on the go" as equally valid as the "quiet, controlled and supportive" space of the retreat center.[34]

A third theme was the advancement of a pragmatic and experiential approach to Buddhism that utilizes whatever teachings and practices are helpful to end suffering. This type of orientation, commonly referred to as "DIY Buddhism," was the topic of one of the roundtable discussions at the 2012 conference. Gunatillake used the analogy of computer "hacking" to describe the expedient attitude toward Buddhism that characterized many of the Buddhist Geeks participants. As he explained: "Everyone here is a hacker of the dharma. We take methodologies, systems, techniques, teachings and we make them personal to ourselves. We sort of cobble together teachings with bits of string and tape and we sort of make it all work and we get results and progress and what we're looking for. And that's the experience of hacking."[35]

Another example of this pragmatism was seen in the impact Kenneth Folk and Daniel Ingram's Pragmatic Dharma had on Buddhist Geeks. Horn's bio notes that in 2016 he received "dharma transmission from his core teacher Kenneth Folk," and both Folk and Ingram were regularly featured on the podcast and at conferences. As explored in chapter 4, Pragmatic Dharma is a goal-oriented, developmental approach to awakening focused on attaining the highest stages of Buddhist insight and concentration meditation.[36]

A fourth theme was a disruption of traditional Buddhist forms of hierarchy and authority and an emphasis on the democratization of practice. This democratization occurred on multiple levels, from the recasting of enlightenment as a natural human developmental capacity to the emergence of more collective and participatory models of Buddhist communities. As Folk stated, the goal was "enlightenment for everyone," not just for a few privileged monks and nuns.[37] Technology has played a fundamental role in this trend through enabling unprecedented direct access to and mass availability of Buddhist teachings without the mediation of a teacher or community. Similarly, with the rise of the cyber-sangha, the traditional teacher-student model has often been replaced or supplemented by a peer-to-peer approach. One iteration of this at Buddhist Geeks was seen in the idea of "conversation as practice," which was a guiding principle of the Buddhist Geeks Community. Institutionally, McLeod observed that a defining feature of the 2012 Buddhist Geeks conference was its nonadherence to traditional hierarchical Buddhist structures; for example, teachers and students mixed freely, and there were no formal markers of authority, such as special seating for teachers. However, as examined above, through their experiment with the BGC, the Horns came to realize that there were limits to this radical decentralization of authority and moved from a position of "decentralized authority" to democratization to "distributed authority" and respecting rather than disrupting "natural hierarchies."

According to Horn, one limit of the DIY approach is that "it can become a solitary and arrogant endeavor."[38] Such an approach is at clear odds with another defining theme of Buddhist Geeks: developing relational and collective aspects of practice. One example was the promotion of technology as a means to foster community from the cybersangha to new interpersonal practice modes. Horn, for example, pointed out that the Internet had enabled people to "gather in this sort of virtual collective or virtual pods that are geared around particular styles of practice or shared aims" and described Facebook as the virtual equivalent of small villages where relationships were a central part of the development of spirituality. In addition to celebrating the relational components of prevailing technologies, Buddhist Geeks members also developed new relational practices. Horn designed a practice called "Two Player Meditation," which added an interpersonal dimension to individual sitting practice, and Buddhify has a two-person-plus option that allows interaction with friends, partners, or colleagues.[39] Another expression was rhetorical, with the frequent use of terms such as "network," "collectivity," and "community." The Buddhist Geeks conferences were advertised as "interactive events" that included "community-led sessions." The Life Retreat declared that "awakening is a team sport." Similarly, in the promotion of the Dojo, Vince described practitioners as "nodes in the network of consciousness" and suggested that "our awakening is tied to the awakening of all." His main wish in setting up the Dojo was to connect more practitioners to "the awesome community of people" that constituted Buddhist Geeks.[40]

A fifth theme was a pluralistic and nonsectarian approach to exploring not only multiple Buddhist lineages and traditions, but also other contemplative traditions and systems and discourses of knowledge. While meditation-based lineages were certainly privileged, no one approach dominated or was advocated over another. Similarly, themes such as ethics were explored from multiple angles—Buddhist, Western philosophical, scientific, and social justice—without one seemingly advanced over another. Vince described the podcast as providing a "multiperspectival" or "metaperspectival" platform. Posttraditional Buddhist teacher Hokai Sobol, who was involved in all of the conferences, also highlighted this pluralistic aspect in his reflections on what the distinguishing features of Buddhist Geeks were, noting that alongside it being "tech-savvy," it was "open-minded and nonideological." In fact, Sobol said that he stopped participating in the Buddhist Geeks community partly because he "didn't resonate with a pluralistic practice-context."[41]

From Dharma Bums to Dharma Brats

From its inception, Buddhist Geeks was marked by a self-reflexivity about how generational differences among practitioners were affecting American Buddhism. Horn and Oelke started the podcast to provide a platform for interests and concerns they had as millennials that were not reflected in the "boomer Buddhism" of their teachers. Indeed, one of the common emic or "insider" sentiments of the Buddhist Geeks network is that they represent a new generation of Buddhist practitioners, a generation that is creating Buddhist models that are distinct from both traditional Buddhism and their Western Buddhist predecessors. In fact, Buddhist Geeks participants particularly sought to distinguish themselves from those Buddhist forms associated with the baby boomer generation. Within the Buddhist Geeks network, there was considerable reflection on differences between the boomer generation and Gen X and millennials and on how this "generation divide" had produced and shaped the Buddhist Geeks project.[42]

One of the major differences identified between the generations was that Gen X and the millennials were much more comfortable with and fluent in digital culture than the boomers. Much emphasis was placed on the shift from a counterculture hippie mentality to an urban technologically savvy subculture mindset. For instance, Lodro Rinzler, a millennial teacher from the Shambhala Buddhist tradition who appeared on the Buddhist Geeks podcast and at the 2013 conference, explained that he wrote his books, such as *The Buddha Walks into a Bar . . . : A Guide to Life for a New Generation,* because many of the Western Buddhist texts, written by boomer authors such as Pema Chodron and Jack Kornfield, were not relevant to him as a younger practitioner. He noted that meditation had become much more mainstream and is considered a pragmatic tool rather than "an eastern other worldly hippie-dippy thing."[43] Similarly, Rohan Gunatillake situated many of the technological innovations featured on Buddhist Geeks as reflecting a shift from a "hippie" to a contemporary design aesthetic. He explains that he designed Buddhify after having conversations with millennial peers who were interested in Buddhist meditation but felt alienated from its association with "hippie or new age culture." He saw this as an indication that the "aesthetic of meditation is broken" and an opportunity to repackage Buddhist medi-tation to attract a young urban demographic.[44]

Generational differences between the boomers and Gen X are also stressed in the Pragmatic Dharma community, which formed a large crossover with the Buddhist Geeks network. As explored in chapter 4, Ingram, who was a big presence on the podcast and the conferences, has explicitly presented the Pragmatic Dharma movement as an alternative to the type of Buddhism taught by the "hippie" baby boomer generation, particularly the American Insight movement. In his book *Mastering the Core Teachings of the Buddha: An Unusually Hardcore Dharma Book,* he identifies his perspective as "the unrestrained voice of one from a gen-eration whose radicals wore spikes and combat boots rather than beads and sandals, listened to the Sex Pistols rather than the Moody Blues, wouldn't know a beat poet or early sixties dharma bum from a hole in the ground and thought that hippies were pretty friggin' naive."[45]

Generational differences were a topic at the 2011 Buddhist Geeks conference, and attendees at the 2012 conference echoed the points made by representatives such as Gunatillake, Rinzler, and Ingram. In a lengthy 2012 preconference discussion thread on generational differ-ences in Buddhism, for example, participants who identified as belong-ing to Gen X or Y distinguished themselves from the boomer generation of Western Buddhists in the following ways: (1) they were more comfort-able with technology and social media, which have made the dharma more accessible and democratized teaching structures; (2) they wanted to combine traditional Buddhism and contemporary culture in more spiritually transformative ways; (3) they were concerned with evolving spiritual practices as householders and translating spiritual experience into meaningful everyday activity; and (4) they considered themselves as less naive and more savvy, critical spiritual consumers than their pre-decessors. As Horn, who self-identifies as a member of Gen Y or a mil-lennial, put it:

> I observed many things from older "spiritual" boomers who
> seemed really deep and profound in many ways, and then just
> [didn't have] a clue in many other ways (like relationships, or
> work, or whatever). These were members of my immediate

family, as well as family friends. This definitely shaped my
approach to Buddhist practice, and my overall skepticism of
Buddhism, or any other general system, that tries to explain
all aspects of human life. Actually, that's what gave rise to
the Buddhist Geeks project—a questioning of what this stuff
actually means, and where its limits are. Far from thinking
that the Buddha, or any other person in history, has figured
it all out, I very much see these as shifts in generations, now
as in the past, as an evolution and development of greater
awareness.[46]

Tempering the divide between generations, however, Daniel Thorson, who held both voluntary and paid positions with Buddhist Geeks,
noted that there was also a sizable presence of "older white men" both
as mentors and as community members. Certainly, the Horns' teaching
and business mentors are boomers: Folk, Kornfield, McLeod, and Silicon
Valley entrepreneur Jerry Colonna.[47] The technological innovations and
self-representation of Buddhist Geeks, nonetheless, very much marked
it as a millennial project.

There are various ways to measure the impact and appeal of the
Buddhist Geeks project. In earlier research, I suggested that the network
signaled a more positive embrace of technology than previously seen in
Buddhist communities. When I explored this with Hokai Sobol, Daniel
Thorson, and Kelly Sosan Bearer, all three mentioned starting conversations around Buddhism, technology, and digital culture that were not
happening before. Vince Horn also identified this as the main contribution of Buddhist Geeks to Western Buddhism. As he reflected:

One of the things that maybe Buddhist Geeks did that was
unique was to take a tech-positive approach and kind of
open up that conversation or that perspective. Whereas before with the boomers, it's not even that they took a tech-
negative approach, they just hadn't grown up with technology so they just took a curmudgeonly approach in general
or just a mostly uninformed approach, which is in itself an

approach. So, I think we kind of started that kind of tech-positive conversation and opened that up in some way.[48]

Another indicator is the size of the Buddhist Geeks audience: the website recorded between seventy-five thousand and one million downloads each month, and as of April 2017, Buddhist Geeks had more than sixty-six thousand "likes" on Facebook and more than sixty thousand followers on Twitter. The majority of its website traffic came from the United States (between 60 percent and 70 percent), but there were also sizable percentages from the United Kingdom, France, Canada, and India. By April 2017, Horn said that one of their metric services had recorded 7.3 million unique downloads, but they had not started using that service until a few years into the program, so he estimated that the number of unique downloads was around 10 million.[49]

"Love It or Hate It, Mindfulness Is Where It's At": Meditate.io and Mindfulness++

The official ending of the decade-long Buddhist Geeks project was declared in an email of September 20, 2016, which gave details on the wrapping up of the Dojo training periods and concluded that Buddhist Geeks had "substantially impacted the development of both the Western Buddhist and the Mindfulness movements, while also becoming part of a larger cultural conversation about the role of technology in contemporary times." The email also signaled what was to take the place of Buddhist Geeks: Meditate.io, a new teaching project that would take a "modular approach to meditation" for practicing in the digital age.[50] Clues to the demise of Buddhist Geeks, however, could be detected as early as the 2014 conference. In "Buddhism Unbundled," Horn's opening keynote speech, he acknowledged that although Buddhist Geeks was committed to serving the convergence of Buddhism, technology, and global culture, there was a possibility that "Buddhism as we know it may not survive this convergence." He framed this process through the concept of unbundling, which he described by reading the Wikipedia definition: "Unbundling is a neologism to describe how the ubiquity of mobile devices, Internet connectivity, consumer web technologies, social media and information access in the 21st century—so basically technology—is affecting older institutions (education, broadcasting, newspapers, games, shopping, etc.)—*I'd add Buddhism to this list*—by breaking up the packages they once offered (possibly even for free), providing particular parts of them at a scale and cost unmatchable by the old order."[51]

Just like the media and social institutions such as education, Buddhism was being unbundled and rebundled in the digital age, that is, broken down into its composite parts, which were then combined with new discourses such as psychology, art, science, and technology and re-embedded in multiple contexts. The mindfulness movement, Horn continued, was a perfect illustration of such an unbundling. Referencing Erik Braun's book *The Birth of Insight*, he traced the beginning of the unbundling of meditation from Buddhism that occurred in Burma during colonialism to a current Wikipedia definition of mindfulness and psychology that contained no reference to Buddhism at all—a definition in which mindfulness had become "completely unbundled." Moreover, Horn suggested, the unbundling of Buddhism had only just begun, with many other aspects of its three trainings of ethics, meditation, and wisdom, or what he called the "core operating system" of Buddhism, undergoing similar processes of decontextualization and recontextualization. While many Buddhists were lamenting this, for Horn, as long as such reconfigurations drew from the "same deep operating code," it did not matter whether they were called "Buddhist" or not. He felt that there would always be people who would preserve Buddhism, but he was more interested in what came next.[52]

The end of Buddhist Geeks and the beginning of Meditate.io.—a new teaching platform and community offering two courses under the mindfulness signifier "Mapping the Mindful Path" and Mindfulness++— was no surprise to me. The Horns had been working on Meditate.io for most of 2016. They had set up a Meditate.io Facebook page on December 1, 2015, and shortly after, Meditate.io posts began to appear both on that page and on the Buddhist Geeks Facebook page. On March 11, 2016, they announced that they had recorded their first Meditate.io project, and posts advertising in-person Meditate.io "pop-ups" in Ashville followed, as well as short articles such as "Making Meditation Modular" and "A New Spiritual Immune System." The former unpacks the modular approach to meditation at the heart of Meditate.io. Rather than trying to preserve Buddhism, Vince explains, he and Emily had decided to embrace the wider cultural processes and "unbundle" five core styles of meditation across Buddhist traditions: concentration, mindfulness, heartfulness, inquiry, and awareness. Through such a "modular design approach," individuals can identify the practices most helpful to them and reconfigure a system or "meditative path of their choosing."[53]

As part of the launch of Meditate.io, the Horns offered a free online course called "Mapping the Mindful Path." Drawn from both "ancient Buddhist maps & more modern understandings of the path," it broke the path into five stages—seeking, breakthrough, disillusionment, resilience, and completion—with short videos outlining the characteristics and challenges of each. As of April 2017, 2,047 people had signed up for this course. A more comprehensive ten-week program with a fee, called "Mindfulness++: Reprogram Reality from the Inside Out," shortly followed. It began on February 13, 2017, with 115 participants from North and South America, Europe, Asia, South Africa, and Australia. (A detailed description of the Mindfulness++ training is available on the Meditate.io website.) The course is fully interactive and contains a number of YouTube videos led by either Vince or Emily as well as sessions with guest teachers Jack Kornfield, Trudy Goodman, and Oren J. Sofer from the Insight community; Michael W. Taft, a science-based meditation teacher; and author Caroline Contillo, who trained at the social justice–oriented Interdependence Project and teaches at Lodro Rinzler's secular center MNDFL in New York City. It is organized into three main sections, with numerous subdivisions. The first, "Meditations: Designed for the Digital Age," contains guided meditations organized into four categories; the second, "Teachings: Clearly Seeing the Path Beneath," includes a variety of conceptual and practical teachings for specific stages of practice; and the third, "Circles: Human Powered Support," are small practice circles facilitated by Vince and Emily that meet regularly in real time.[54]

One distinctive feature of the program is its emphasis on social meditation. In a video on the website, the Horns claim that individual practice is no longer sufficient for the challenges of the contemporary world, and so they have focused on designing relational or social forms of practice. They model one such form—a social noting practice—that is essentially an interpersonal adaptation of the noting practice of Mahasi Sayadaw discussed in chapter 4. Such relational practices, they continue, counter some of the problems associated with individualistic forms of mindfulness. Borrowing from Alexander Bard, a Swedish cyber philosopher, they explain this as a move away from a "theology of individualism" to a "theology of the network," which recognizes that the fundamental reality of the universe is relational.[55]

The reconfiguration of mindfulness from an individual to relational practice is one of the main characteristic of what Horn calls "the second generation of mindfulness." While recognizing many of the mindfulness critiques as valid, Horn said that "he was over the critiquing of mindfulness and feeling like I have to hold up the Buddhist institution. It just doesn't square with how I think of organizations and creative projects anymore." He wanted rather "to serve some of the needs that Buddhism has served, but to do it in new ways that are more accessible. I think the superpower of mindfulness right now is that it can reach into so many more contexts and be more applicable."[56]

Horn's "second generation of mindfulness" directly borrows from a model called the "general hype cycle for technology," which was developed by the information technology research firm Gartner and says that the social maturation of technologies has occurred over five distinct stages. Horn adopts this framework to plot what he sees as the different stages mindfulness has gone through over the past decade. The first stage, "the technology trigger," was the acceptance of mindfulness as a valid field of scientific research largely through the efforts of Jon Kabat-Zinn. The second stage, "the peak of inflated expectations," denotes the idealistic and marketed narrative that "mindfulness cures all problems." The third stage, "the trough of disillusionment," signifies the many mindfulness critiques that have deflated this idealism. Horn believes, however, that "a second generation of mindfulness" is moving out of this disillusionment into the fourth stage, "the slope of enlightenment," which learns from the critiques and reimagines mindfulness as "an imperfect tradition."

Horn sees the second generation of mindfulness—of which he is a part and Mindfulness++ is an expression—as driven by technological innovations, deeply connected to social concerns, and increasingly focused on the underlying ethical contexts of mindfulness.[57] As he explained: "There's an increasing disillusion with the idea that mindfulness is ethically neutral. It's like mindfulness as a practice might be able to be adapted into different frameworks, but the choices and intentions to adapt it into those frameworks are very ethically driven."[58] Moreover, he insists that the rebundling of Buddhism into mindfulness does not necessarily signify a dilution of the practice.

In reflecting on the transition from Buddhist Geeks to Meditate.io, Vince said that he had begun to lose interest in Buddhism around 2013.[59] Although the Dojo had built up a core community and was financially stable, both he and Emily had begun to feel that the Buddhist Geeks framework was not a good fit—pragmatically or theoretically—for their creative vision and teaching ambitions. One issue was a disjuncture that existed between Buddhist Geeks as a media project and Buddhist Geeks as practice community. As he put it, "There was a mismatch between our emerging aspirations as teachers and Buddhist Geeks, which was designed as a media project and never designed or meant to be a teaching platform." It was a lot of physical and emotional labor for two people with a young child trying to manage both media and teaching components of the organization. Another, more existential, aspect was that both he and Emily had been increasingly wrestling with the tension between the "Buddhist" and "non-Buddhist" components of their project. Although they had initially been committed to both, Vince started to feel that the Buddhist frame was "restrictive": "It started to feel like we were running this really progressive organization in an increasingly conservative space. And I saw mindfulness was a much more progressive movement in a lot of ways. And we're too young to be conservative!"[60]

Another determinative factor in making the transition was Vince and Emily's experience with their students. Vince explained that it was clear to both of them that "people weren't there to become Buddhist. And they weren't into the Buddhist identity. They were really looking for practical tools that they could implement in their lives."[61]

Unsurprisingly, then, most of the students were supportive of the transition and have continued working with the Horns at Meditate.io. Vince continued:

> Some of them were just like "totally no big deal, makes total sense, glad you're doing it." Some people were a little sad and disappointed because of the connection with Buddhism that they had. A couple of people dropped off, but I don't know that it had to do with Buddhism per se—more just like this is an opportunity to clarify how we want to continue working together or not. I didn't really hear any feedback of people being upset, which doesn't surprise me, because these people already had a very spacious attitude toward Buddhism.[62]

Conversations with two long-term "core members" of the Dojo who had made the transition to Meditate.io substantiated Vince's reflections. J. Carl Gregg, a thirty-nine-year-old white male who is a Unitarian Universalist minister in Maryland, felt that the transition to Meditate.io "made absolute sense" and was particularly enthusiastic about the Horns decision to "take on a more explicit and directive teaching role." He had been a member of both the BGC and the Dojo and had gotten very frustrated with the peer-to-peer format, which he felt left members without expert guidance. When I asked whether he was sad to see the "Buddhist" signifier dropped, he replied: "Not at all, if anything it was the Geeky side [that attracted me]. I liked the upfront embrace of nerdy culture." Gregg had initially been drawn to Buddhist Geeks via the podcast and said that he was particularly drawn to the pragmatic and transparent approach of Horn, Pragmatic Dharma, secular Buddhism, and Shinzen Young. In particular, he appreciated how they "drew from the full depth of Buddhist traditions but are also fully engaged with technology and neuroscience" as well as how "they will use tradition to the extent it is skillful and let it go when it is not." For Gregg, Meditate.io was about putting the emphasis on the practice rather than the Buddhist teachings. "This was not to say that Buddhism is not welcomed," he said. "It is just not centered—the practice is centered—and that to me is what it should be."[63]

Similarly, Francis Lacoste, a Canadian "techy" white male in his late thirties who started listening to the podcast in 2013 and had also been a core member of the BGC and Dojo, explained that what was most important to him was practice and the focus on "meditation as a technique." Lacoste, who has more than a decade of experience in various contemplative traditions, reported that he had been attracted to Buddhist Geeks because of its "ecumenical" approach in which multiple spiritual perspectives were explored in conversation with modern technology. For him, the most influential part of the Dojo, what had been a "turning point" and "game-changer" in his own practice, was the monthly contact he had with Vince and Emily, who were both his teachers. He had also greatly benefited from the peer-to-peer groups and said that his Dojo group continued to meet after the Dojo was officially closed. Although there had been a mourning period for the loss of the Buddhist Geeks network, none of the core members he knew were upset by the loss of the explicit Buddhist side, and the ones who hadn't made the transition based their decision on financial rather than ideological considerations. Several times in our conversation, Lacoste noted that he was not interested in the religious aspects of Buddhism and differentiated between the Buddhist Geeks network and "religious Buddhists."[64]

Perhaps another reason participants have found the transition from Buddhist Geeks to Meditate.io smooth is because there is much continuity between the projects in terms of both presentation and content. Granted, the language on the Meditate.io site is more generic, with "Buddhism" being replaced by "age-old wisdom" and terms such as "transformation," "learning," "growth," and "empowerment" taking the place of Buddhist concepts such "koan," "dojo," and "enlightenment," but the Geeks had also made much use of modern terms such as "meditation coach" and "optimizing practice." Practice-wise, the Horns were already teaching a modular approach to practice in the teaching section of the Dojo, and the social and community aspect that was emphasized in all three Buddhist Geeks teaching projects is emphasized with the social meditations. As with Buddhist Geeks, Vince Horn has also framed Meditate.io as a millennial project: the "About Us" section on the Meditate.io website, for instance, was emblazoned with the words "Made with [heart symbol] by Millennials," and Vince's bio opened by identifying him as "part of a new generation of meditation teachers translating age-old wisdom into 21st century code."[65]

There is little direct mention of Buddhism on the site, but the backdrop for the Mindfulness++ program on the Meditate.io website—an outline of a faded Buddha statue sitting among a universe of stars—is a good visual expression of the implicit Buddhist influences. The influences are not as much in the forefront as they were for Buddhist Geeks, but they can be discerned by those familiar with the tradition. For example, Zen Buddhists would likely hear echoes of the Zen teaching of "great faith, great doubt, and great determination" in the headline to the Mindfulness++ introductory video, "Great Uncertainty Calls for Great Practice." Similar traces are found in the guest teachers' biographies: Contillo, for instance, "trained in the Buddhist tradition" but teaches in "meditation centers" and wants to "create a space where people can learn to be with whatever is coming up in their lives in an open and engaged way." An engagement with Buddhism has not disappeared, but it has faded into the background, like the outline of the Buddha.[66]

From Buddhist Hippies to Buddhist Geeks to Meditate.io: Post(Modern) Buddhism

In many ways, Buddhist Geeks can be seen as continuing the reformation of traditional Buddhism initiated within earlier Asian and Western forms of Buddhist modernism.[67] First, it continues the scientific interpretation of Buddhism that is a defining characteristic of Buddhist modernism. Since the nineteenth century, Asian and Western Buddhists have commonly presented the Buddha as a rational empiricist and Buddhism as a religion that is compatible with science.[68] Buddhist Geeks extended and updated this scientific lineage through the translation of classical Buddhist teachings and practices into contemporary language and concepts associated with technology. For example, many of the popular speakers on the Buddhist Geeks podcasts and/or conferences were committed to integrating science and Buddhism and used scientific language to interpret and/or reframe classical Buddhism. These included former Buddhist monk and Vipassana teacher Shinzen Young, who has collaborated with neuroscientists from UCLA and the Harvard

Medical School in order to chart how meditation affects the brain. In his 2011 Buddhist Geeks Conference keynote speech "Towards a Science of Enlightenment," Young called the Buddha "the first and greatest scientist of human happiness" and claimed that Buddhism can be improved by incorporating the insights of science.[69] The updating of the scientific lineage is also seen in the adoption of technological language and concepts that are likely to speak to a younger, technologically savvy demographic. One example of this is Horn's refashioning of the Buddhist doctrine of *anatta,* or no-self, and Vipassana meditation through the lens of hacking, the culture of repurposing technological systems. Horn compares the target of *anatta*—an illusory sense of a permanent, unchanging self—to "windowsME," a human operating system that is preprogrammed to have a mistaken but persistent sense of a solid, essential self and world. He then envisions meditation as a form of "mind-hacking," which is used to hack into and rewrite this illusory "windowsME" so that self and reality are experienced as they actually are: fluid, changing, and impermanent.[70]

A second key feature shared with Buddhist modernism is a major emphasis on and privileging of meditative experience. A clear articulation of this is found in Folk and Ingram's Pragmatic Dharma, which Ingram describes as a particularly goal-oriented approach to awakening that draws from various meditative techniques across the Buddhist spectrum. One of the main claims of the Pragmatic Dharma movement is that Western Buddhist communities such as the Insight community do not focus enough on meditative experience. As explored in detail in chapters 1 and 4, this emphasis on experience is a major characteristic of Buddhist modernism.

While continuing major trends within Buddhist modernism, however, Buddhist Geeks in other ways could be more usefully understood as responding to certain limitations of Buddhist modernism and displaying characteristics more associated with the postmodern than modern. Buddhist Geeks displayed traits that are characteristic of postmodern culture in general and also characteristic of the distinct sociological category "postmodern religion." In terms of the former, Jean-François Lyotard advanced the seminal definition of the postmodern as an "incredulity towards metanarratives," claiming that the defining, absolute beliefs

of the modern age, such as the Enlightenment understanding of continual human progress through reason and science, had been replaced by
the emergence of a plurality of small and local competing frameworks
of meaning.[71] I argue that the Buddhist Geeks network demonstrated
a postmodern sensibility in destabilizing Buddhism as a metanarrative
or absolute system. This occurred on multiple levels, from its pluralistic
embrace of other discourses to its reluctance to exclusively identify with
the signifiers "Buddhism" or "Buddhist." To begin with, Horn explains
that the Buddhist Geeks project developed out of his conviction that
neither Buddhism nor any other single system or discourse had all of
the answers needed for the human predicament in the twenty-first century, and, in multiple places, he relativized Buddhism as just one way
among many to perceive or point to a much larger reality.[72] Indeed, both
Horn and Gunatillake cautioned against holding a Buddhist identity too
tightly and noted that at times it can be "unskillful" to identify as a Buddhist. Furthermore, many 2012 Buddhist Geeks conference participants
preferred to label themselves as "hybrid" rather than Buddhist, and others wondered whether the term "Buddhist" had become superfluous and
even an obstacle to disseminating the pragmatic tools of the tradition to
a wider audience.

The commitment of Buddhist Geeks to the pluralism characteristic of postmodernity is also clearly demonstrated by both its provision
of a nonsectarian platform for exploring Buddhism and its production
of nearly four hundred podcasts featuring a range of figures from fields
as diverse as neuroscience, technology, business, social justice, and the
creative arts as well as many of the major Buddhist lineages. Similarly,
the eclectic DIY or hacking approach to Buddhism found within the
community illustrates the creative bricolage approach that has marked
much cultural and artistic production in postmodernity.

Yet, at the same time as undercutting Buddhism as an absolute
system, a main concern of Buddhist Geeks was to preserve the depths
of Buddhist wisdom and to avoid the dilution of Buddhism to "stress-
reduction tools."[73] Popular speakers such as Willoughby Britton and
David Vago bemoaned the "McMindfulness" approach that characterizes the dialogue between Buddhism and science and were presented as

being part of a new generation of scientists who are willing, unlike their predecessors, to talk openly about the wider ethical and soteriological context of Vipassana meditation.[74] In calling for a serious engagement with classical elements of Buddhism, Buddhist Geeks appeared to have resisted the linear process of secularization seen in various Western assimilations of Buddhism, such as the secular mindfulness movement. David McMahan and Jeff Wilson have noted similar trends in their studies, which show that Western adaptations of Buddhism increasingly demonstrate an interest in more traditional elements of the religion that were neglected during the modernization process. McMahan has further observed that within contemporary Buddhist modernism a reclaiming of tradition and the appearance of various combinations of tradition and innovation have occurred alongside the existence of an increasingly detraditionalized Buddhism. As he points out, these various combinations of the traditional and modern, innovative and reconstructive are more characteristic of late or postmodern than modern conditions.[75]

Finally, in addition to displaying postmodern cultural characteristic, Buddhist Geeks also fits well into the more specific sociological category of "postmodern religion." According to Paul Heelas, postmodern religion is characterized by an intermingling of the religious and the secular, a consumer approach, and a willingness to combine high and low culture and draw from disparate frameworks of meaning and is associated with postmodern forms of pragmatism and relativity.[76] Similarly, in their exploration of different forms of postmodern spirituality, Lynne Hume and Kathleen McPhillips describe postmodern religion as being marked by fluid parameters, spiritual bricolage and inventiveness, the discovery of the sacred in unlikely places, and a sense of playfulness.[77]

One might also reasonably argue that Buddhist Geeks was just too firmly grounded in modernist narratives of science and technology to be considered postmodern. A clear example of this is Young's aim to develop a "science of enlightenment," which will improve, if not replace, the meditative maps found within Buddhism. While it is indeed indisputable that Buddhist Geeks reiterates the modernist narrative of progress through science, there are other discourses of technology in addition to the modernist one, and these alternatives are also glimpsed in Buddhist Geeks. In her landmark essay "A Cyborg Manifesto," Donna Haraway both critiques and celebrates the potentialities of technology in postmodernity. Although she condemns the exploitative and exclusory nature of modern scientific discourses, she refuses "an anti-science metaphysics and demonology of technology." Rather, Haraway calls for a democratization of science, which will serve historically disenfranchised populations such as women and racial minorities, and advances the model of the cyborg as a new decentered postmodern subjectivity that disrupts the boundaries on which modernity depends.[78] As Vincent B. Leitch notes, following Haraway, a number of cultural theorists have distinguished between modernist science and postmodern technoscience. Leitch attributes the postmodern eruption to the breakdown of boundaries between once distinct fields, or what he calls "a moment of mixed disciplines," and he characterizes technoscience as being rooted in "a pragmatic, positive, yet wary engagement with science and technology à la Haraway, emphasizing micropolitics and creative life-enhancing alternatives."[79] Certainly, Buddhist Geeks, with its both/ and commitment to Buddhist and technological narratives, qualifies for this mixing of discourses; and a number of common features of postmodern technoscience—the hybrid, the cyborg, the democratization of technology, and a questioning of the assumptions and boundaries of mainstream, hegemonic science—populate the Buddhist Geeks network, alongside the modernist narratives.

This mix of modernist and postmodernist characteristics provides a strong argument for framing Buddhist Geeks as displaying features more associated with the postmodern than the modern, but how does the shift from Buddhist Geeks to Meditate.io affect such a thesis?[80] As should be evident from the discussion above, Meditate.io continues and radicalizes many of the modern and postmodern traits of Buddhist Geeks: it utilizes terms and models common to digital culture and technoscience, and it offers a developmental path of meditative experience undergirded with scientific evidence. Meditate.io also shares much of the creative playfulness, bricolage, and consumer approach associated with postmodern religion: its own meditation app, the use of YouTube videos, aesthetics such as rocket ships and Facebook icons, and marketing strategies such as pop-ups and free introductory courses.

For Horn, chief architect of both projects, the most important consideration has always been to maintain a pragmatic "multiparadigm" perspective and not be limited to any one system of knowledge— Buddhist or otherwise. He determines the value of any paradigm by how useful it is in serving specific needs or purposes. In reflecting on the clash between Buddhism and mindfulness, for example, he noted: "What is the purpose of these different paradigms? They serve different people and different purposes. Clearly, they're all still alive and we're still using them, otherwise, they would be dead."[81] In Buddhist Geeks, this pragmatic multiperspectival approach played out as a dialogue between Buddhism and other discourses, but in Meditate.io, such an approach has rendered the particularity of Buddhism redundant. Buddhism, for Horn, no longer serves the goal he has become most interested in: having a large-scale effect on contemporary culture. Similarly, Thorson agreed that the most exciting and unique part of Buddhist Geeks was being exposed to so many different practice traditions, but he agreed with Horn that maintaining Buddhism as a distinct tradition was no longer necessary. "Buddhism is largely a dying tradition," he explained. "It is not relevant, and this is a reason why young people don't want to associate with traditions. I think we should save what needs to be saved, but make it more available and accessible."[82]

In dropping the signifier "Buddhism," Meditate.io parallels what David McMahan identified as the emergence of "post-Zen" in the work of Toni Packer, whom he describes as the "most striking example of a Western Zen that has virtually ceased to be Zen." Packer was Philip Kapleau's successor at the Rochester Zen Center, but she left Rochester to establish the Springwater Center for meditative inquiry and retreats, which had no overt affiliation with Zen or the tradition's standard formalities. McMahan notes that Packer was "not typical of Zen in the West" in admitting that she was "no longer really practicing Buddhism, while still emphasizing meditative inquiry."[83] McMahan returns to Packer and the signifiers of "post-Zen" and "post-Buddhism" in his concluding chapter of *The Making of Buddhist Modernism,* suggesting that a postmodern Buddhism is emerging from the strains of Buddhist modernism.[84] Extending McMahan, I conclude that the trajectory of the Buddhist Geeks and Meditate.io projects is best understood as signaling a shift from Buddhist modernism to Buddhism in post-modernity, with each denoting distinct but related strands in the heterogeneous postmodern landscape—the former, a hybrid combination of tradition and innovation, and the latter, a detraditionalized form of "post-Buddhism."

From the Boomers to Generation X

O
n the morning of June 10, 2011, at the Garrison Institute, a former Catholic monastery that now functions as an ecumenical contemplative center, two groups of Western Buddhist teachers—the self-identified "pioneers" or first-generation of teachers and what they called the "NextGen" of younger teachers—gathered together to recognize and to facilitate continuity between the two distinct generations. Each group presented the other with a set of declarations and requests. The "Three Statements" of the younger group opened by expressing deep gratitude to their elders for translating the Buddhist teachings from Asia and bestowing mentorship and support, continued by acknowledging their responsibility to maintain the dharma and carry forth the transmission they had received, and ended by declaring that they would transform the dharma in their own unique way—being called, in particular, "to bring the Dharma more fully to the needs of our diverse world, serving the Buddhist community more equally, and answering the call of injustice and inequality everywhere in our world."[1]

This ceremony took place on the day before the 2011 Maha Teacher Council, the most recent in a series of international Buddhist teachers conferences.[2] The first of these, co-organized by the Dalai Lama and Lama Surya Das, took place in 1993 in Dharamsala, India, and brought together twenty-two teachers to forge connections across lineages and discuss the challenges of bringing Buddhism to the West. A second major gathering occurred in 2001 at Spirit Rock, in California, with the Dalai Lama and other notable Asian Buddhist teachers in attendance.[3] Ten years later, at the 2011 conference, 230 mostly American teachers met to discuss three main issues: "the promise and the pitfalls" of the wide dissemination of the dharma into secular Western culture, the challenges of adapting the dharma to these new contexts without sacrificing its depth, and "passing the torch as it were from elders to the next generation."[4]

It was the last of these—the informal transmission to the next generation—that marked the 2011 conference as particularly distinct. As Surya Das noted, for the first time the conference organizers had "consciously" included forty-five to fifty "young" (younger than forty-five) dharma teachers in order to explore how the elders could best "help the younger generation empower themselves" and "genuinely serve as midwifes at their delivery." Similarly, co-organizer Jack Kornfield asked, "How can those of us who were pioneers in the '60s and '70s, support them without getting in their way and let them know that they have our blessings and support?"[5]

While the reflections of Surya Das and Kornfield suggest an intentional and smooth generational transition, Rachel Zoll, one of only two reporters invited to the event, presented a tenser and more dramatic situation: it was a meeting of "elders versus young people," or "the preservers of spiritual depth versus the alleged purveyors of 'Buddhism-lite'" to "tackle their differences" on issues that had been "percolating for years" in Buddhist circles with nothing less than the "future of Buddhism at stake." According to Zoll, on one side, younger teachers were "pushing in new directions, shaped by the do-it-yourself ethos of the Internet age and a desire to make Buddhism more accessible." On the other, the aging boomers, approaching retirement and death, were concerned that such rapid changes and experiments risked descending into superficiality and losing touch with the tradition. Further, while the pioneers had spent decades training in Asia, they were now passing over leadership to "the first Buddhist convert generation trained almost entirely in the West" for whom "spending several years cloistered abroad, absorbing the cultural traditions of another country, seems not only unnecessary but counterproductive for reaching Westerners."[6]

Zoll, in short, framed the event as a clash between tradition and secularization, preservation and innovation, depth and accessibility. Characterizing the boomers' approach as "traditional," however, is inaccurate and misleading. As I explore thoroughly in this book, the boomers represent an influential iteration of Buddhist modernism in the West. How, then, should the NextGen of teachers be positioned and understood in relationship to them? Do they, as Zoll suggests, extend and further radicalize modernization processes? Or do they show signs of disruption and complication of Buddhist modernist narratives? Similarly, has the transition between generations been fluid and beneficent, as boomer reports have suggested? Or has it been marked by conflict and struggle, as Zoll claimed?

In this chapter I attempt to answer these questions through an in-depth exploration of the experience of Gen X teachers. Drawing primarily on thirty-three interviews with Gen X teachers, I identify what they see as the main characteristics and concerns of their generation. I consider how they locate themselves in relationship to the boomer generation as well as Asian Buddhism and how they are simultaneously continuing and countering the modernization process. Rather than present their perspectives as facts, I offer them as "ideal types" that indicate the main directions Buddhist modernism is headed in a shifting American cultural landscape.

From the NextGen to Gen X: Interviewee Population

Before I explore the Gen X gatherings and the interview data, some explanatory context on the interviewee population is necessary. First, a few words on terminology: at the Garrison conference the boomers had labeled the younger teacher as the NextGen. However, Insight teacher Martin Aylward, one of the most seasoned teachers of the group, had suggested that they refer to themselves as Gen X because "'Next Gen' sounds like it's about people who haven't arrived yet but might do sometime. I remember us being focused more on being 'Gen X,' born

1960–80, and therefore a group that would evolve together. If we are not already, then we certainly will increasingly become "This Gen."[7] I have adopted this emic self-identifier, and when locating Gen X in reference to the boomer or first generation of teachers, I identify them as the "second" generation or "younger" generation.

In order to generate a thick description of Gen X teachers, my aim was to interview as diverse a population as possible in terms of personal demographics and Buddhist lineages. To recruit interviewees, I posted a research request on the Gen X Dharma Teachers Facebook page. I also drew on Buddhist contacts from previous research projects and elicited recommendations and contacts from interviewees. Out of my thirty-three interviewees, twenty-eight had attended at least one of the three Gen X gatherings (2011, 2013, 2015), and seven had been conference organizers. Six of seven who had not attended had close friends who had either organized or attended the conferences. There were no notable differences in responses from those who had attended a conference and those who had not.

Demographically, twenty-seven interviewees identified as white, five identified as people of color (POC; three as black and two as Asian American), and one identified as biracial. Only two defined themselves as coming from a working-class background; the majority said they had experienced financial hardship as adults but had grown up in middle-class to upper-middle-class families. In terms of gender and sexual orientation, twenty-one identified as male, twelve identified as female, twenty-five identified as heterosexual, and eight identified as LGBTQI. Seven had children, and three of these said parenthood had significantly affected their practice. The following traditions were represented: the Insight community, Against the Stream Buddhist Meditation Society, the Thich Nhat Hanh Community of Interbeing, the Japanese Soto and Rinzai lineages, Korean Zen, Korean Taego Zen, Tibetan Buddhist Kagyu lineages, the Triratna Buddhist Community, Fo Guang Shan, and secular Buddhism. Another significant feature was that twenty-eight of the thirty-three interviewees had trained in more than one Buddhist lineage or non-Buddhist lineages, ranging from nondual approaches to shamanism.[8]

As relevant as who is included is who was underrepresented and excluded. Within my interviewee population, one extremely underrepresented group was monastics: only two of the thirty-three interviewees were currently monastics, although a high number had experienced monastic life for periods between two months and fourteen years. Hence, this chapter has a heavy lay slant, which somewhat reflects the Gen X conference participant demographic thus far. For example, Tenku Ruff, a Soto Zen teacher who served on the committee for the 2017 Gen X conference, noted that monastics were underrepresented at Gen X teacher gatherings, estimating monastic participation at around 25 percent at the 2013 conference and just 5 percent at the 2015 conference.

Perhaps the most glaringly absent voices are of those of the first-generation teachers. For brevity, I have chosen to focus solely on Gen X voices. A comparative consideration of how the two groups view themselves and each other would enrich the data considerably. Similarly, Sumi Loundon Kim, one of the 2011 Gen X conference organizers, also pointed out that an unintentional consequence of the dates they used to define the boomers and Gen X was that a number of "in-between" teachers between the ages of forty-five and sixty were left out of the conference. This included influential figures such as Lila Kate Wheeler, Greg Scharf, and Gil Fronsdal, who she sees as "more clearly inheriting teaching roles and centers" and whose approaches might bridge some of the differences between the boomers and Gen X teachers presented here.[9] Finally, because this project is focused on the transformation of convert lineages, also absent are Gen X teachers primarily serving Asian American Buddhist communities. A comparative study of the two groups, however, would significantly enhance the understanding of changes within the broader landscape of American Buddhism.

Naming the Gen X Teacher Community

The emergence of a self-reflexive and collaborative Gen X teacher community has come primarily from a series of gatherings beginning with the Garrison conference. These gatherings have also produced social media spaces such as the Gen X Dharma Teachers Facebook Group and created informal support networks among Gen X teachers. As Zen teacher Eshu Martin said: "I was able to connect with people from all over, and I'm still connected to them through social media, and I can contact them regularly. I feel like I can serve students better because of that."[10] Before turning to interview data, some consideration of these conferences is useful. The idea for the first gathering of "Next Generation Dharma Teachers" appears to have come from Jack Kornfield and Noah Levine. The two of them put together a "Next Generation Planning Team," which consisted of six well-known American teachers: Levine, the founder of Dharma Punx and Against the Stream networks; Willa Baker, a lama authorized in the Kagyu lineage; Spring Washam, an Insight teacher and POC community leader; Sumi Loundon Kim, an Insight teacher and author; and Josh Bartok, a Soto Zen teacher and editor at Wisdom Publications. Regarding the invitation process, Loundon Kim explains, "In assembling a group of Generation X teachers, those born between 1960 and 1980, we focused on ensuring diversity across lineage, ethnicity, and sexual orientation, as well as balance between genders and monastic-lay status."[11]

Loundon Kim describes the process for assembling Gen X teachers as a long and well-researched one, aided by her and Bartok's familiarity with the broader landscape of Buddhism in North America. For example, they intentionally reached out to lineages not normally included in these types of Western Buddhist conferences, such as Soka Gakkai and the Buddhist Churches of America. As she describes it, "There was a massive push to find Asian and Asian American young teachers, as well as monastics." However, Loundon Kim also acknowledges that the invitation list "was more diverse than who actually accepted or was able to come."[12] The final result was a group of about forty teachers younger than forty-five, which one participant described as fairly diverse but "inevitably Vipassana slanted." Before the official Garrison conference began, this group and a smaller group of twenty-two boomer teachers met separately for two days and then came together on the third day. Martin Aylward, a British Insight teacher who has run his own residential retreat center in France since 1995, reported that the first Gen X gathering was marked by an intimacy and identification between participants. As he put it: "There was a recognition. These are my dharma buddies. This is my sangha."[13]

One activity that many participants described as particularly powerful, and which appears as symbolic of Gen X orientations, was a sociometric exercise called "Crossing the Line," which was led by Vinnie Ferraro, an Against the Stream teacher, who uses the activity in his work with disenfranchised youth. Ferraro would read a statement such as "Cross the line if you identify as being gay, lesbian, bisexual, or queer" or "Cross the line if you have ever attempted or seriously considered suicide," and participants would silently cross a line marked on the floor if the statement applied to them. The purpose of the exercise is to allow participants to explore their own and other identities and to raise awareness of diversity and inclusivity. Aylward interpreted it through a Buddhist hermeneutic of dukkha: "It's really about pain, about suffering. Seeing each other crossing the line and crossing back as an expression of the different kinds of suffering: social, racial, historical, personal, religious as well in terms of traditions." He felt that the personal nature of the exercise enabled new ways of understanding and communication: "Many of us were in tears, and being able to look in others' eyes across the line and just meet the suffering went much deeper towards an acknowledgment and a commitment to working with the pain of those issues than a lot of talking could have done."[14]

The exercise was so meaningful and effective for the Gen X group that they decided to invite the boomer group to participate. Aylward reports an initial wave of resistance from them, saying that it took "twenty-four hours of serious negotiations" for a final list of questions to be approved. He believes that the boomers were afraid that the exercise was going to be used to challenge and attack them.[15] While confidentiality rules restricted what could be shared, all the Gen X interviewees said that the cross-generational exercise was so powerful that the two small groups decided to incorporate it into the official conference. According to Aylward, "What happened there will probably be the most enduring sense of what was beautiful about the meeting."[16]

But one participant, David Brazier, a British first-generation Pure Land Buddhist teacher, was critical of the exercise: "It was essentially an ideological exercise in which large group pressure was mobilized to get one to identify with a liberal American agenda only distantly related to Buddhism. That this was what will probably prove to have been the centre-piece of this conference tells us, I think, that the values that this community coheres around—and this will have been an effective exercise in generating cohesion—are those of 'progressive America.'"[17]

Brazier was not the only one to level critiques at the Garrison meeting. A number of Buddhists took to the Internet to raise concerns over the "closed door" nature and exclusiveness of the event. Provocative Gen X teacher Brad Warner, for example, complained (incorrectly as it later transpired) that he had been "uninvited to the Buddhist Party," and popular Gen X blogger David Chapman depicted the event as a "select group of Buddhists consolidating their power interest and pushing their agenda on what Buddhism in America should look like."[18]

Gen X attendees partially substantiated critiques. While co-organizer Loundon Kim reported an appreciation of "the richness of different styles and teachings" at the Garrison conference, she also acknowledged the presence of "lineage snobbery" and "unconscious racism."[19] Hence, when plans were made for Gen X teachers to meet again as a separate group in two years, they wanted to build on the 2011 objective of putting diversity and inclusion at the top of the agenda: "How could the gathering be inclusive of more cultural diversity, teachers from and working with groups historically marginalized in mainstream western society (ethnic minorities; lesbian, gay, bi-sexual, transgender, queer), Asian immigrant Buddhist groups and churches, those teaching in new forms (such as primarily via the internet), and increasing the relatively low proportions of teachers in attendance with monastic and deep retreat experience."[20]

The following Gen X conference took place at Deer Park Monastery, in Escondido, California, June 5–9, 2013. The organizing committee consisted of Jay Rinsen Weik, a Soto Zen teacher; Anushka Fernandopulle, an Insight teacher; Brother Phap Hai, a monastic in the hosting Thich Nhat Hanh community; and Viveka Chen, a senior teacher in the Triratna tradition. Registration for this conference was "open to Buddhist teachers who are actively teaching and who were born between 1960 and 1980" and was advertised on Buddhist media. The aim of the conference was to "build relationships between teachers in different traditions and explore the challenges facing them as next-generation teachers."[21] The gathering was attended by fifty-seven teachers who represented various lineages. Interviewees who attended this conference commonly remarked on the high standard of facilitation by Fernandopulle and Chen, who are both professional facilitators. Another observation was that the absence of senior teachers allowed for more intimate peer-to-peer contact.

The third Gen X Dharma Teachers Gathering took place June 6–10, 2015, at Dharma Drum Retreat Center in New York State. Drawn from attendees at the 2013 conference, the planning committee consisted of Rebecca Li, a Chan Buddhist teacher; two Tibetan Buddhist teachers, Andrew Merz and Lama Rod Owens; Dave Smith from Against the Stream; and Deborah Eden Tull, who teaches Zen and mindfulness. The challenge of inclusion continued to be a central issue as the number of applicants increased. Alongside the open application invitation, the committee posted a "letter of transparency," which shared that the 2013 attendees had agreed to keep the gathering "as intimate as possible (around 75 participants)," and hence their focus was on "committed and active Buddhist dharma teachers" who had "made practicing and serving the dharma a central priority in their life."[22] These qualifications were in response to two groups—secular mindfulness teachers and younger, less experienced Buddhist teachers—who had expressed interest in attending. They indicate that Gen X teachers feel it is important to distinguish Buddhism from and prioritize it over secularized practice forms and recognize the importance of the length and depth of Buddhist training. The final group consisted of fifty-five teachers from a variety of lineages who discussed a wide range of issues, from how to develop practice communities to the role of ritual in modern practice.[23]

A fourth Gen X Dharma Teacher Sangha meeting took place at Dharma Ocean's Blazing Mountain Retreat Center in Crestone, Colorado, June 6–11, 2017. The steering committee members were Tenku Ruff, a Soto Zen Buddhist; Doyeon Park, a teacher in the Won Buddhist tradition; Nina La Rosa, a teacher in Shinzen Young's community; Kaira Jewel Lingo, a former nun and lay teacher in the Thich Nhat Hanh community; and Tibetan Buddhists David Iozzi and Lama Justin von Bujdoss. Continuing the focus on diversity, one of the aims of the 2017 conference was to increase the participation of monastics and teachers from nondominant social locations. Organizers also limited attendee criteria to those who had an active and primary commitment to teaching the dharma for at least five years as well as noting that "Dharma teachers must be accountable to an organization other than themselves, remain in good standing with their organization and have no pending ethics complaints."[24] One notable change was redefining the demographic age range for those born between 1963 and 1982 rather than 1960 and 1980, although previous attendees who fell outside of these new dates were still welcome. Another was the creation of a more formal and sophisticated online forum for conference attendees hosted by the Hemera Foundation.[25] All of these changes suggest the continued growth and institutionalization of the Gen X network.

Loundon Kim, who has written two books on young Buddhists and been a longstanding insider cataloguer of their trajectories, offers a reflection on the Gen X gatherings in which she identifies their main concerns as peership, cross-lineage learning, ongoing education around racial justice, struggles around supporting oneself financially, and creating a system of ethical accountability.[26] My interview data collaborate and flesh out Loundon Kim's claims as well as showing Gen X interest in developing teaching modalities that are more personal and collective, as well as balancing innovations with interest in aspects of Buddhism neglected by the first generation.

"I Felt Like I Found My Tribe!": Gen X Teachers in Their Own Words

All of my interviewees except one who had trained mostly in Asia expressed a sense of recognition and belonging with their peers. Describing the Deer Park conference, Heather Sundberg said, "It was amazing, and especially for someone like me where most of my time in the dharma communities has been with people twice my age, it was just, I felt like I found my tribe!"[27] While a few interviewees cautioned against reifying Gen X as a homogenous body, all agreed that they shared generational issues. As Aylward put it, "One of the things that was clear to us is that our generation has different challenges in all kinds of ways."[28]

Nearly all of the interviewees began their reflections on the boomers by expressing a deep sense of gratitude toward them, frequently using words such as "respect," "appreciation," and "grateful." Sundberg, who worked as the manager and teacher of the Spirit Rock family and teen program for more than a decade, said: "I really have a direct sense of the passion that they had, the courage that they had to take the risks that they made, and the sacrifices that they made. Huge sacrifices for the love of the dharma and for seeing whether this concept of the dharma in the West was actually viable. Really, I stand on their shoulders with so much appreciation and respect." Echoing this indebtedness, an interviewee who teaches at Against the Stream acknowledged, "All of these conversations are only possible because the first generation went into the deep end and just started to try to do things."[29]

Nonetheless, interviewees agreed that whether it was due to cultural generational shifts, pragmatic limitations, or individual karma, there was a limit to what the first generation could establish. As a former Theravadin nun reflected: "The first generation had a very particular role to play. In some ways, I don't know if this is karmic, but I feel like there was a ceiling on what they could do. There's just a certain seeing that our generation has that I think is new and unique and evolving."[30] This new perspective was seen as less a radical break from the founders and more an extension of processes they started. Secular Buddhist teacher Michael Stone illustrates this with an anecdote about an Engaged Buddhist meeting with Bernie Glassman that he had attended a couple of years before the Gen X meeting. The conversation at that meeting had been focused on starting a program to feed people, but when Glassman discussed the program at the Gen X conference, one of the first questions he received was, "What kind of food would we serve people who are hungry?" Stone shared this story to illustrate that the Gen X group was refining and developing practices that the boomers had pioneered.[31] Other interviewees emphasized that Gen X teachers were able to learn from the mistakes of the founders' generation. As Chen puts it:

> We are freer to, perhaps, look at the history of our particular practice tradition, and the leadership and influential people in it and hopefully with an eye of gratitude and appreciation for the gifts we've been given, and also with the eye of some distance being able to get curious and interested in the

limitations, or what I call the "not so gifts." I think there can be a healing and a deeper learning and that later generations are freer to just not repeat certain behaviors.[32]

On the Boomers: Mavericks, Lone Wolves, and Dharma Rock Stars

Gen X interviewees depicted the boomers as a very individualistic generation, frequently describing them as "strong," "driven," and "powerful" personalities and referring to them as "mavericks" and "charismatics." Jay Rinsen Weik articulates several dimensions of this individualism:

> Most of the first generation of American teachers were certain types of people. They were more maverick individuals, breaking free of 1950s normative culture. The same is true of the first wave of Zen teachers to the US. They were not typical representatives of your average Zen priest in Japan. Most Japanese, for a start, don't want to leave Japan because they think they will lose some of their "Japanese-ness." So, the Zen teachers who did come were maverick and singular. And it was a case of "mavericks meet mavericks!" This generation was individualistically oriented: teachers received transmission and went off as lone wolves to teach. They had no accountability or checks on their power.[33]

Interviewees appreciated that this type of strong individualism had been necessary in order to set up dharma centers from scratch, but they also identified a number of drawbacks: lack of accountability, poor interpersonal skills, and a performative and hierarchical approach to teaching. "Lone wolf" teachers, for example, were seen as lacking peer feedback and not being interested in sharing power. One teacher said, "There's a lot of sense with the boomer teachers that people never called each other out." Similarly, Eshu Martin felt "there is no delegation for the boomers."

Another consequence of this individualism was a lack of interpersonal and communication skills between the boomers. Jessica Morey shared her experience as part of a cohort of young practitioners at IMS:

I understood that many of the first generation of Insight teachers hadn't developed strong personal friendships, they didn't have conflict resolution mechanisms, and there was no ground of support to navigate relationships. Our teachers from that generation wanted a different experience for us, which is why they created a mentoring program for about twenty or so practitioners. They didn't want us all to be teachers, but they wanted us to be friends, to support each other in the dharma, no matter what.[34]

Morey put these relational challenges into the context of the first generation's focus on intensive silent retreat. As she continued, "The practice they were doing was so internal, there was no emphasis on relationship, and they had none of these other skills about how to communicate."

A third consequence of the individualism that flavored the boomer generation was the production of the "dharma rock star." Four interviewees used this term to describe the phenomenon of "big name" American Buddhist teachers who had "expensive book contracts" and went on "dharma tours." Related to this was a sense that boomers were more performative in their teaching roles and lacked the interest or ability, or both, to be more intimate and vulnerable. As one interviewee mused, "A lot of the teachers, either they're not interested in that level of intimacy or they don't have access to it or it's just they think they're doing something different."

"Communication Is Oxygen for Us": Feedback, Friendship, and Vulnerability

Gen X teachers saw themselves in many ways as the opposite of the boomers: they were committed to maintaining peer accountability, developing friendships, and being more pedagogically vulnerable. While interviewees acknowledged that some Gen X teachers were more famous than others—with the names Noah Levine, Michael Stone, and Brad Warner coming up—they all felt that their generation was warier of the type of "celebrity" teacher model that had emerged among the boomers. As Ji Hyang Padma enthused: "Part of the beauty of the Gen X coming together is having peers coming together and there being no one who puts themselves on a pedestal. There are a few folks who have more charisma, but there is less need to have that star quality. We are happy to sit together as colleagues."[35] Stone said that while the experience was a new one, it had been very powerful: "I was always the star at the front of the room or I was the student. And I never really had an experience being in a room full of peers and really feeling them as peers. I didn't know that we didn't know that we needed each other."

Similarly, Gen X interviewees saw themselves as much more open and committed to peer feedback. "That is a distinguishing feature of Gen X," one teacher stated. "There is something about our generation where everyone is teaching each other, they're giving each other feedback. I think that is enormous—it's almost more important than certain aspects of having formal teachers." Interviewees also felt that their generation was much less performative as teachers and much more comfortable with personal disclosure. In describing their teaching pedagogy, they frequently used words such as "authenticity," "honesty," "vulnerability," and "transparency." As Morey put it, "One thread for the Gen X feels like a kind of radical authenticity—so much less of a needing to be the wise person on the pedestal." Similarly, Lama Rod Owens, who trained in the Tibetan Kagyu lineage, said: "For me, I find myself suspicious of teachers who don't believe in personal narratives. I just feel like it's a vulnerability issue, and that makes it easier to hide behind the teachings and not actually admit where we struggle."[36] Lama Karma Justin Wall, who teaches in the same lineage, contrasted this with the boomer generation: "The difference between the younger crowd and the older crowd is that we are very interested in relationship and dialogical interactions, sharing a space of vulnerability and disclosure. We wanted to level whatever kind of power dynamics there were."[37] A more critical edge was voiced by angel Kyodo williams:

> The boomers are very smug. It's softened with some people, but this "looking down" haughtiness of many people of the boomer generation definitely exists. I think in that generation that is what accomplishment was—to climb that mountain and be one of "those." And so, if you're sitting up there,

and you're looking at the younger dharma teachers as they unfold, it's sort of like, "Wow, you're not as pulled together. You're too loose." But they don't understand that that is our cultural proclivity: to be more at ease, and not to create pretentious presentations of ourselves.[38]

There was also a sense that Gen X had been more intentional in creating more opportunities to connect and communicate than the boomers had. As one teacher put it: "My sense is that overall, even outside of the conference, the way people are kind of talking and knowing each other—the word that comes up is 'common language.' There is something generational about people's ability to communicate and understand. That is getting increasingly noticeable." Similarly, williams explained: "We are just coming into contact with each other differently, and so we can communicate differently. You know, it's really the sense of sangha. We're rubbing up against each other and softening a lot of the edges that a lot of the boomers didn't get the chance to soften."

After "Founder-itis": Leadership Styles

Gen X teachers attributed many of the differences between themselves and the first generation to the psychology of leadership and the institutionalization of charisma. Insight teacher Tempel Smith, for example, reflected on the different characteristics and experiences of leadership for the two generations:

> It's psychologically very difficult to find yourself a leader of a big movement, without a lot of experience. It's gentler on us, in a way. Not being thrown into fierce leadership early on allows you more time to grow within your community. We have to be more delicate as to how we rise up in leadership in an already formed community. We can't just lead by rash charisma. We have to be much more institutionalized. The founders didn't have to do that. But we are coming to a point where all these communities need to start being more functional and organized.[39]

Similarly, Martin reflected on how the Zen teachers from the founding generation were "basically made of steel," showing incredible power and perseverance in building centers and organizations from scratch. He also felt, however, that some of the same qualities were obstacles to moving into the next stage of development, and "the skills needed to actually carry it forward are missing." Indeed, a central theme among interviewees was how to carry forward the centers established by first-generation teachers. They discussed the need to develop and remodel retreat/teaching centers, teacher training programs, and teacher gatherings along more transparent, relational, and collective lines. One area of focus was the need to build upon the intensive silent retreat model in order to break down dichotomies between retreat and real life practice, establish stronger relationships between teachers and students, and provide ongoing support for students outside of intensive practice periods. As Aylward noted:

> I think silent retreats were the great innovation of the first generation of Western dharma teachers, at least in the Vipassana world. And I really appreciate that they put so much attention there, establishing the deep heart of dharma practice as serious, intensive meditation practice. But the challenge of the second generation, without in any way dismissing the value of silent retreat, is to build on that foundation to give more support to people in the rest of their lives, so that all aspects of their lives feel like practice, and to dissolve the unnecessary and unhelpful dichotomy between their spiritual practice, which happens on retreat, and the rest of their so-called normal lives.[40]

Echoing Aylward, other interviewees noted that because the boomers had been so focused on retreats and because of the size of retreats, not enough people had gotten the type of individual and consistent contact that was needed outside of a retreat to help them fully develop. Whereas some people could navigate this alone, one interviewee felt that the majority of students need more personal mirroring and feedback and want to see more of an emphasis on one-on-one work as teachers.

Similarly, another highlighted a lack of teacher-student contact that he felt cut across traditions: "Even with the Tibetans, it's perhaps worse because the teacher lands from the airplane, comes out and gives the transmission, and then gets back on the airplane." Lama Rod Owens shared his struggles with the traditional three-year Tibetan Buddhist retreat at Kagyu Thubten Choling Monastery in New York State and discussed how they were making the model more sustainable for a contemporary Western context:

> I think coming out of the retreat and not having any support is difficult—having this retreat experience and then trying to make a meaning out of the experience, in the world, as someone who is expected to support themselves, and at the same time having to represent dharma but not really getting support for that. Not just financially supported, but emotionally supported, having people relate to you in a way that's healthy. For us, we need to add a few more pieces, which is what we are doing in KTC [Kagyu Thubten Choling] right now. We are having that dialogue of, What do we need to make this more beneficial for Westerners? We have therapists that go in and out of the retreat to work with people. There's a year of support where graduates are required to stay put and be supported and receive mentorship from senior lamas. We are adding teacher training and mental support.

Another distinct theme was the development of smaller, more personable, and localized centers. Reflecting on the Insight tradition, one interviewee felt there was going to be a shift from "big, expensive centers, which produce big, expensive teachers" to community dharma centers. On a related note, Aylward expressed frustration at what he felt was the "oppressive" structures of the main Insight centers. "The teachers live far away," he said, "and they just come in, run the retreat, and then go away again. It's the administrators that tend to live in, and that gives a very different feel to the place." From the Soto Zen tradition, Ryushin Hart also expressed the benefits of moving toward more collective-oriented models:

There is this bottleneck of power given to the teacher that is to the detriment of the sangha. Meaning, you have a teacher that's holding all of the power, and all of the expectation is on that one person to solve the sangha's problems. And, it's actually not healthy because no one person is going to have all of the answers. A sangha is going to be much stronger if there's a way to hear from members at the middle level, the people who have been practicing for several years, whether they are lay or ordained. And then, even the people that are just coming in the door bring all of their life experience, even if its non-Zen related. They've got other fresh ideas that are worth hearing, too. So, my encouragement was to figure out how to widen the base of power, and to create space for all the wisdom in the community to be heard.[41]

Similar limitations were brought up with respect to teacher training programs. One interviewee attributed many of the organizational problems within the Insight community to the fact that it was straddling two teaching models: the traditional mode of dharma transmission and a modern training certification program. As he put it, "What you're getting now in the dharma community is an in-between those two." However, he continued, "If all of these dharma centers are moving away from the kind of Asian 'I whisper the mantra in your ear' model, and they're teaching facilitation and diversity, then they really have to do it properly."

The sense that it was not being done properly was the dominant reflection on boomer-organized teacher gatherings. Many interviewees expressed frustration at their "top-down," "talking heads," and "hierarchical" facilitation approaches. Chen, for example, said that at the larger Garrison conference, "there was a bit of whispering about there being a lot of talking heads pontificating and not a great quality of conversations. Engagement outside of sessions was wonderful, but somehow in-session it just felt like, 'Oh, so much more could happen here!'" Interviewees identified a number of problematic areas: insufficient preplanning, an overreliance on keynote speakers, lack of peer-to-peer conversation, an absence of group facilitators, and no feedback/evaluative procedures.

When organizing the Deer Park gathering, Fernandopulle explained: "We took a systems approach. Gen X is less likely to tolerate a top-down approach. We are more participatory. Our philosophy is to approach it like we are all colleagues and peers, and not privilege one person to talk for forty minutes and others listen."[42] This approach was certainly successful. Every interviewee who attended the conference highlighted the facilitation, such as Sundberg: "The facilitation was top-notch. I've been to so many different and various dharma events and trainings led by various founding or boomer generation teachers. There's just no comparison. Anushka and Viveka are professional facilitators, and that was part of what made it so incredible." Similarly, Aylward compared his experience of attending a teacher meeting at Spirit Rock directly after the 2013 Deer Park gathering:

> The difference was night and day! Because they're dharma teachers, everyone is used to running things and being in charge. But there wasn't really the sense that just because you're a teacher, that doesn't mean you've the skill set of how to facilitate a group of peers. So, I actually spoke a lot at that meeting of how good the Gen X meeting had been and begged and pleaded that the next time we do this, let's hire someone to facilitate the meeting for us. And there was actually a lot of resistance, surprising resistance, but eventually, we did manage to get to that part so we'll have proper facilitation the next time and feedback and evaluative procedures offered at events.

The importance of strong organization and facilitation skills was in large part due to the recognition that, as Sundberg said, such skills enabled "this real openness to connect and learn from each other" and "allowed these conversations to happen that could have never happened in another environment." The conversation topics identified most frequently by interviewees were teacher transmission, racial diversity and inclusion, power and ethical accountability, and the relationship between teaching dharma and supporting oneself.

Passing on the Baton, Transmission, and Taking the Teacher Seat

Lama Karma identified lineage transmission as a central topic for the Gen X teachers: "We are still struggling with what lineage is, how we represent it, how lineage is transmitted, how do we keep it intact as we move forward with Buddhism in the West, and what kind of authentic transmission there is in America." These issues differed between interviewees, as each lineage has distinct avenues by which teaching authority is granted. One clear and striking difference, for example, was between interviewees from traditions that were more hierarchical and had more singular models of authority, such as Zen and Tibetan Buddhism, and interviewees from traditions where models of spiritual friendship predominated, such as the Insight tradition and Triratna.

Nonetheless some common themes emerged from the interviews: (1) differences between lineages in establishing teaching authority, particularly how it is easier to become a teacher in some traditions than in others; (2) transmission struggles, which included reluctance from boomers to give transmission to Gen X teachers, the authority granted by transmission, and teaching without transmission; (3) standardization and professionalization of teachers; (4) the importance of distinguishing between teachers and instructors; and (5) the subjective experience of taking the teacher's seat.

Many interviewees commented on the "notable differences" across traditions in what was required to become a teacher. Ruff, who has trained extensively in Soto Zen in Japan and the United States, pointed out that in Zen, gaining the authority to teach was an arduous process that could take twenty years or more, but in other communities one could teach after only a few years. It is of little surprise, therefore, that Gen X teachers reported differences in how their teachers had supported them in their taking of the teacher's seat. Almost all interviewees from the Vipassana community felt that the founders had supported and nurtured them. The only complaint raised was that more formal and structured personal mentorship would have been useful.

Interviewees from the Zen tradition, however, painted a very different and much more fraught and conflicted picture. One teacher felt there was an overall deep sense of mistrust from the boomer teachers toward the Gen X teacher network and said that some teachers had gone as far as "to demand" the names of Zen priests who had attended Gen X conferences. Similarly, interviewees frequently described the "resistance" and "reluctance" of the first generation to give dharma transmission, and there was a common sentiment of being "held back" by their teachers. Four of the Zen interviewees, two males and two females, also reported difficult and painful struggles with their primary teachers that in some cases had led to an acrimonious breakdown of the relationship. As Ruff observed: "The Gen X conference did draw some people who were having difficulties with their teachers—people from a long teaching background who were having trouble handing over the reins. That was a big theme."[43] Explaining this in reference to the San Francisco Zen Center, Kokyo Henkel felt that "there's some feeling of, it's their baby; some people have been there since the beginning, and it's hard to make that transition, that leadership transition is sometimes a struggle." He shared his own personal experience:

> I went through that struggle a little bit at Santa Cruz Zen Center because it was the teacher in her eighties who had practiced with Suzuki Roshi, who really wanted to retire, who really wanted to pass it on, but it was like her baby and it was like she really didn't want me to change anything, but I'm going to be a new person with a new style. It was a little unusual because I wasn't even her student. I mean, a little bit I was, but I hadn't practiced with her so much. So, I think it's hard, and I think that the previous generation really has to let it go and trust that it will evolve in some beneficial way.[44]

In some cases, this had led students to leave teachers and centers after long periods. One interviewee, for example, had come to a painful realization that he had to leave the monastery in which he had trained for fifteen years because of a "lack of leadership opportunities" and his need to "fully grow up." For Koshin Paley Ellison, who is trained in the Zen tradition and is the cofounder of the New York Zen Center for

Contemplative Care, struggles with a teacher had made him rethink the nature of the teacher-student model as presented in American Zen:

> I saw what was happening with me personally was also part of a larger pattern, and this wider context was really healing for me. I realized that I needed a change, a different type of teacher-student relationship that was more about mutuality and thinking through things together. One that was still a teacher-student relationship but in which there was more of a sense of working through challenges together. I want to be with a teacher who is curious to talk about changes in relationship. I wanted to talk about the struggle of difference more openly. This was possible with the Gen X group but not always so much with the older generation of teachers. They seemed to me to be more comfortable with a hierarchical model, whereas I wanted more of a horizontal "spiritual friend" model.[45]

The perceived reluctance of boomers to authorize dharma heirs had a number of other consequences. One was concern around "aging sanghas." Hart said that the majority of the American Soto Zen Buddhist Association members were in their sixties and seventies, and Ruff pointed out that within the same organization, only eleven teachers, 7 percent of full members, were younger than fifty. Koun Franz also noted that he "was always the youngest person in my community or group" and warned, "The average age of Zen teachers in America is sixty-eight, so there will be a large contraction soon."[46] Indeed, Ruff pointed out that temples were already closing because of a lack of dharma heirs:

> At the first meeting [of the Soto Zen Buddhist Association] I went to, a discussion topic was succession of temples. I was the only person in my age group present. I listened to people talk about how difficult it was going to be to pass temples down to the next generation. After listening for over an hour without speaking, I then asked the teachers present if they had talked to anyone in the next generation about what we

thought was important in inheriting a temple and our perspective on temple leadership. No one had. They were surprised that I even asked. One teacher I respect greatly had a
disciple about three years younger than me, but he left, so she
had to sell her temple. As for the others, I don't know. Others
don't have anyone to take over their temple, but they're not
willing to let go of enough control for that to happen.

Both Zen and Tibetan interviewees also talked reflexively about
the power and politics of transmission. On one hand, they acknowledged the important and useful ways in which transmission legitimized
them. For example, williams, who has received transmission in the Zen
tradition, observed that because of that, people listened to her and took
her more seriously. Similarly, Tibetan teachers Owens and von Bujdoss
said that they had been able to do more innovative and radical work
because they had the authority and blessings of lineage transmission.
On the other hand, interviewees were wary about the ways in which
the authority of transmission could be manipulated and mishandled.
One expressed concern that teachers had given transmission to their
spouses; another reflected on the validity of transmission with teachers
who had been caught up in sexual scandals.

Another topic to emerge was people who were teaching without
formal transmission. Weik noted that historically dharma transmission
was "the recognition of both awakening and the ability to teach others."
He claimed, however, that in American Zen, it was becoming increasingly accepted that people could be awakened but not have the specific
skills required for teaching, and that some people may have charisma
or aptitude for leadership but are not deeply realized. Weik pointed to
the model developed by Boundless Way Zen that formally recognized
progressive levels of teaching ability and authority—practice leader,
dharma teacher, senior dharma teacher, transmitted teacher—as one
emerging alternative to the singular transmission model of authority.
Similarly, Hart said that the Soto Zen Buddhist Association had been
wrestling with this somewhat "weird category" of people teaching without transmission. Whereas priests in Japan would receive transmission
after a few years of monastic training, in the United States, "you have

some priests whose teachers require a really long maturation process for their students. So, these priests have been ordained for ten, twelve, or fifteen years, they are functioning in many teaching roles, possibly even leading a sangha, but they haven't received transmission."

On a related note, Hart also advocated for what can be thought of as the professionalization or "standardization" of Zen teaching. He felt there was real value in having a professional association that established some clear professional and ethical standards, although he acknowledged that there would always be teachers who would operate outside of these. From the Insight tradition, Matthew Brensilver reflected on how organizational structures that were more transparent and demanded ethical accountability of the leadership had resulted in a "demystification of the dharma seat." While such measures were necessary to mitigate the "unskillful use of power," he also recognized that

> there are adverse effects because, in certain ways, if a teacher can use power carefully, it's very effective, and in a certain way, we are undercutting some of the power of the dharma seat. And I think if used altruistically, it can be quite beneficial, and it's sort of like, yeah, it's an aspect of one's teaching that is quite, can be quite, powerful. And it's not just we're losing some of the strength of the placebo response, because I think that is happening. But we're also losing some of the strength of just the transmission power when somebody holds a seat like that. I'm willing to tolerate that loss, and I think many other teachers are too, in part because of their own hesitancy to take that seat, but it is a loss.[47]

However, williams, cautioned against Zen going too far in the direction of certification. Taking the Community Dharma Leader program at Spirit Rock as an example, she mused, "Spirit Rock has ending up re-creating, unfortunately, some class dynamics around the idea of 'I graduated, and so I know something.'" Without dismissing the value of programs like the Community Dharma Leader program, she also felt that certification trainings could lead to an erasure of significant practice and teaching differences: "Someone has spent twenty years training, right? They do something like deeply cultivating practice. Someone else goes through two years [of] training, and we equate them because they're both Buddhists—I'm not belittling at all the intention of the dharma leaders, but because of the commodification of Buddhism, I think there's a lot of grasping at positionality. And so, completing the Community Dharma Leader's program becomes this sort of anointing certificate."

Another adverse effect of certification-based programs identified by williams was that some of the graduates "end up lacking confidence when they are up against the traditions that have a more seasoned feel to them." Deborah Eden Tull echoed these concerns: "We have this world, especially with mindfulness, where people are eager to teach, and that's not what serves deepening their own practice and just allowing the teaching process to happen organically."[48] In fact, Insight interviewees themselves expressed concerns about taking on the teaching role too prematurely. For example, two teachers, one male and one female, said that they had declined their first invitation to participate in the Teacher Training program because they had wanted more practice time as students. Considering lineage differences in becoming a teacher, williams felt it was necessary to "make some distinction between instructors and teachers." And it was important to recognize that awakening was not something that could be easily measured and regulated. "I don't care how many retreats you've been on," she said. "We ripen at different times. And not on the same tree." On one hand, then, interviewees expressed the value of clear, systematic teacher trainings; on the other, they raised concerns around trying to measure realization and the premature production of teachers.

Diversity and Inclusion, Power and Privilege

When asked what they saw as the main concerns of their generation, the first response of nearly three-quarters of interviewees echoed what Sundberg said: "Issues around diversity and inclusivity come to the foreground immediately. As a group, we seemed to be much more oriented to inclusivity, to diversity." In particular, interviewees emphasized the need for racial diversity, inclusion, and justice but also talked of class, gender, sexual orientation, and disability issues. Interviewees affirmed the pioneering work of older teachers, but they unequivocally agreed that their generation had more consciousness of and concern for diversity and inclusion than the founders. Several interviewees talked of the greater awareness around diversity and issues of power and privilege among Gen X populations. Fernandopulle, for example, said: "My impression is that the younger population has had a different experience— of growing up in a different time where they were more used to the potentials of more diversity. Even people who are white and straight in the US are more likely to have had more exposure to diversity than older generations."

Similarly, Tempel Smith noted: "We care about it [diversity] more at our stage of teaching than they did when they were at the same stage of development. I think anyone who has been privileged and not had to worry about certain things of society, won't consider it as much as members of minority communities." Sundberg also said that when the founders and NextGen groups had come together at the Garrison Institute, it was apparent that diversity was much higher on the agenda for the latter than the former.

Interviewees talked of how much American boomer Buddhism was white, middle-class, and heteronormative. Further, williams pointed out how difficult it was for boomers to see the operations of white privilege because of the homogeneity of their sanghas: "It's unreflective, the positionality of their own condition. I mean, we've all got it, and it's hard to see it when you're around people who are exactly the same. And to me the challenge is of encountering difference that makes you realize that 'Wow—this is actually a position, it's not reality.'" Ji Hyang Padma felt that Gen X teachers, unlike the boomers, were aware of the limits of this homogeneity: "One of the characteristics of this generation is that we are more culturally aware, more aware of how the cultural lens of white Anglo-Saxon Protestant culture has shaped and influenced our sanghas. We know that our sanghas end up mirroring the dominant culture in terms of class, race, and gender." Interviewees also discussed the ways in which they were personally committed to diversity and inclusion work in their sanghas. Three white interviewees said that they had undergone racial justice training and were committed to bringing that awareness to their sanghas. Oren J. Sofer, an Insight teacher, for example, said that as a "straight white male, I feel a responsibility to use my privileged position to raise awareness of white privilege. If not, I am complicit."[49] Moreover, Owens and williams have had a significant impact on the racial justice perspectives of Gen X. They pioneered a series of "Radical Dharma" talks across the United States in which they put Buddhism and the black prophetic tradition into dialogue, and with Jasmine Syedullah they have recently published *Radical Dharma: Talking Race, Love, and Liberation.*

In terms of sexual orientation, eight interviewees identified themselves under the spectrum of LGBTQI (as either queer, gay, or bisexual), and those who identified themselves as "straight" or "heterosexual" expressed support for the LGBTQI community. In terms of gender, five identified themselves as cisgendered male or female rather than just male or female, showing awareness of gender inclusivity. Both male and female interviewees expressed appreciation for gender equality at the Gen X gatherings. Ruff, for example, pointed out that "one of the rules was about gender equality. If someone noticed that a man had spoken the last few times, we agreed as a group to speak up. Someone would say 'Excuse me, but a man has spoken the last three times; let's hear from a women's perspective.' It was so refreshing."

One notable feature, however, was that none of the interviewees talked about gender dynamics with as much urgency and passion as racial diversity. This appears to be due to the fact that racial diversity is considered an area in which first-generation female teachers made great progress. Sundberg, for instance, expressed deep gratitude for "the women teachers because they were dealing with gender dynamics coming out of the Asian traditions that I cannot hardly even imagine. I'm such a beneficiary of all of their work and everything they went through." Similarly, Ruff observed: "We have women in the baby boomer generation who have put a lot of effort into gender equality. But at the Gen X meeting, there was a lot more diversity: there were queer people, brown people, black people, laypeople, and ordained people."

Another area of concern was age. With the exception of the Insight interviewees, particularly the Dharma Punx community, which attracts a younger crowd, many teachers expressed concerns about the lack of age diversity in their traditions. As already noted, many Zen teachers are concerned about their "aging sanghas" and American Zen facing a "die-off." Speaking of Triratna, Vimalasara Mason-John said that in the UK, attempts at diversifying were focusing on "attracting younger people into the movement. That's where the edge is at the moment because it is an aging community. I'd say the average age of the people in our order is about fifty-five. So, there's a real push to bring younger people into our sangha."[50]

Diversity and inclusion issues, particularly racial justice, appeared at the top of Gen X concerns; and their reflections, on the whole, demonstrated a fairly sophisticated sociopolitical understanding of the challenges minorities face in and out of Buddhist sanghas, intersectionality, and power and privilege. Some of this awareness appears to have come from the Gen X gatherings themselves, where ongoing conversations around racism have led to concrete actions. One was the production of a *Buddhadharma* issue dedicated to investigating power and privilege.[51] Koun Franz, the editor, said that "discussions from the Gen X meeting came up over and over again in putting this [issue] together. That meeting was/is a touchstone."[52] Another was the founding of a Spanish-speaking sangha at the Dharma Bum Temple in San Diego, which founder Jeffrey Zlotnik said had "come about in many ways from our most recent Gen X gathering at Dharma Drum Retreat Center."[53]

Sex and Power, Transparency and Accountability

Another main focus for Gen X teachers was the sexual scandals that have afflicted a number of Buddhist communities since the 1980s and their underlying issues of the abuse of power and the ethical accountability of teachers (see chapter 3). As Paley Ellison put it, "There is more willingness and desire among the Gen X teachers to be more open and discuss the types of problems around teacher-student relationships and other factors, including abuses of power and sexual misconduct." The sexual scandals were a "huge topic" particularly for Zen interviewees, given that American Zen had been marred by the exposure of Joshu Sasaki Roshi and Eido Shimano. Two of my interviewees had been students of Sasaki Roshi and had firsthand experience of a community in the throes of sexual scandal. In discussing the scandals, four themes particularly stood out: psychological integration, transparency, greater awareness of power dynamics, and accountability.

Interviewees pointed to a combination of individual psychological issues, a lack of institutional or peer accountability, and religious rhetoric within Zen that legitimated unconventional behavior as causing the scandals. Echoing the conclusions of chapter 3, most teachers, however, particularly emphasized a "lack of psychological integration" in teachers. Weik, for instance, talked of the importance of recognizing the "shadow" and guarding against spiritual bypassing. Another interviewee referenced work by John Welwood and Harvey Aronson that explored how Buddhist practice could be distorted by unconscious psychodynamic patterns and suggested that it was helpful for Zen practitioners to have some basic understanding of psychological ideas "to be able to see things that traditional dharma practice doesn't pick up." Similarly, Paley Ellison thought that Zen would benefit from adopting the psychologically inclusive Insight approach: "Jack Kornfield requires a minimum of one year psychotherapy training, and he also requires the teachers to be in therapy. This is incredibly important: to be teachers we have to look at and deal with our own stuff."

These voices reflected a clear consensus among Gen X teachers that psychological insights and trainings were a useful and often necessary supplement to Buddhist practice. Although a couple of interviewees expressed concerns about the "overpsychologization" of Buddhism and emphasized the importance of not conflating the two, the psychologically integrative approach to practice introduced by the boomers seems to have been adopted more or less wholesale and noncontentiously among Gen X teachers. As Sofer put it: "There is no debate over the usefulness of psychotherapy. It is more a question of distinction and how much they [Buddhism and psychology] should be mixed. In the early years, it was felt that dharma practice would solve everything, but now people understand other modalities are necessary." Similarly, Loundon Kim felt there was a much more nuanced understanding of the relationship between Buddhism and psychology that was less assimilative and more dialogical. Rather than seeing psychotherapy as diluting Buddhist practice, she felt they worked hand in hand.[54]

Expanding the topic of psychological integration, a second theme to emerge was that Gen X populations were more savvy and educated about how power operates. Three of my interviewees, for instance, talked about the psychology of leadership. Chen said: "There's a book called *Mistakes Were Made but Not By Me,* which explains about people in power and the whole area of ethical breaches and how cognitive dissonance obstructs the recognition of and responsibility for harmful impacts of actions." Closely related was the theme of responsibility and accountability. Chen continued: "I think that the younger generation has a responsibility to basically just create a new reality, new norms, given what we know, given the evolution around consciousness, around power and sex and teacher-student relationships." One way to take responsibility was through developing structures of peer accountability. This, as Ruff said, was a "huge topic" and already under way:

> There is a group of people who want a Buddhist Ethics Council. When that group was meeting at the conference, a lot of people wanted to be a part of it. One idea was to voluntarily sign an agreement that if we did something [unethical], our peers would hold us accountable. We all want that—we want to be held accountable. We want to agree to be held accountable before we are in a place of power, so we can work to prevent abuses of power and ethical misconduct.

The final theme to emerge was the importance of transparency. Owens, for instance, said that in his Tibetan community, teacher-student relationships were permitted, but they were subject to a transparency procedure:

> We believe that authentic relationships can develop between a teacher and a student; however, there is etiquette to work with that. It's a transparent process. The transparencies are different for different traditions or sanghas, but basically, if you recognize that a relationship is starting, you have to clarify that and disclose that to the leadership team or board, and you have to break that student-teacher relationship, so

the student would study with someone else in the sangha, but then that relationship can proceed in an open and transparent way for the sangha.

He compared this open process with the secrecy of traditional Tibetan Buddhism, in which, he claimed, "The abuse of male monks is almost normalized. It's just an unspoken part of the community." Similarly, von Bujdoss pointed to the difficulties within the tradition of speaking out about abuse. "Take the story of Kalu Rinpoche, the Tibetan lama who reported being sexually abused," he mused. "He was accused of denigrating the tradition."[55]

Transparency was also crucial for Triratna teachers Chen and Mason-John. Explaining how she had dealt with the sexual accusations leveled at Sangharakshita, the founder of Triratna, Chen said "the fact that it was all coming out and there was a lot of internal debate about it" was crucial to her decision to remain in the community. Similarly, Mason-John explained: "Whenever anybody wants to get more involved with our tradition, we ask them to read the [book] *Triratna Story*, and it's in there. . . . So, we're upfront about it and people make the decision."

Dharma, Dana, and Making a Living

A third topic identified by interviewees as "impactful" and "heated" was how teachers were financially supporting themselves and the appropriate relationship between dharma and money. A few interviewees referred to an exercise at the Deer Park gathering in which teachers were invited to reveal their financial situations as being particularly meaningful. Hart said that it was "interesting to see the variety" of financial situations, "From the people that earn nothing because their salary pays for the rent for their sangha, to the monastics who earn nothing and live off the generosity of the sangha, to people who earn a little bit and then people who earn what people were considered exorbitant amounts." He added that "there was also a lot of heat in the room when it got to that topic."

The main theme around dharma and money was the viability of the Asian model of dana, or the practice of giving, in the United States. On one end of the spectrum were teachers who were fully committed to living solely from dana. Sundberg, for example, felt that the Insight meditation dana system, in which retreat centers typically charge a fee for living expenses but leave teacher reimbursement to dana, was a "work in progress" and a "creative solution" to the difficult task of adopting dana to a very different cultural context. Sundberg lives completely off of dana and is fully committed to a system of teachers being financially supported by dana "remaining alive and strong in the West," but she admitted that she was "more on the traditional side" than many of her peers. Indeed, the most common pattern among interviewees was to teach Buddhism on a dana basis but to mostly live off a separate primary income job. The most popular secondary jobs reported were working as a Buddhist chaplain and teaching secular mindfulness. Lama Karma, for example, said that some of his motivation for training in secular mindfulness was because he needed to make more money after living in poverty for more than a decade.

On the other end of the spectrum were teachers who felt that the dana model was not sustainable for individual teachers or centers in the West. Stone, for example, said that at the Deer Park gathering when teachers were invited to locate themselves along a range from "I am completely broke and I cannot support myself or my family" to "I am doing fine and I have a comfortable lifestyle," only four teachers, all white males, were in the latter category. As he said, "I looked around the room and I saw that most of the Buddhist teachers of my generation were unable to support themselves through the dana model." Stone attributed part of the problem to a misperception of the traditional dana system: "In the West, we're asked to give freely and give dana without having any regret. But that is actually a new practice. People didn't give freely; they gave because of the benefit to their family or merit for a future life or what have you."

Although he had originally taught under the dana system, after consultation with a business coach, a charitable lawyer, and a leadership coach, Stone adopted a sliding scale model and remodeled his charitable organization after a standard business organization. This switch, he reported, had been a great success: "In terms of running a retreat, we now have more people attending retreats at a lower cost than we've ever had. We also can afford things on retreats that we've never been able to afford, including having more learning practice positions for people who were unable to attend retreats before because of costs. Second, we are able to have better administration, and third, we have proper insurance, which is something we've never had before."

While charging for retreats is often criticized as being an unethical commodification of the dharma in the West, Stone felt that his model was both more pragmatically effective and healthier for Western lay teachers. His teachers had always taught him to "just trust that you will be taken care of"; and although he agreed that "some people can live like that, especially if you don't have a family to take care of or a mortgage to pay," he did not feel this was as viable for lay teachers with a family like himself. Further, he concluded: "I wanted to see if a proper business model could serve a different value system than the value system we're told business models serve, which is profit. And lastly, we all know that everybody that works for charities gets burned out."

Insight teacher Fernandopulle also pointed out some pragmatic and ethical limitations with the dana model in her community, with particular attention to the value of equity. One of these was that because there was a standard registration fee for retreats that goes to the institution, but the teachers receive only donations from participants at the end of a retreat, individual teachers rather than the institution were financially vulnerable. "The way the dana system works," she explained, "is that the individual teachers bear the risk of variability of income 100 percent. It is a complete roll of the dice for individual teachers whether they can make their monthly expenses. The purpose of institutions is to aggregate and bear risk for individuals, so it makes more sense for it to be the other way around." Another was that the system worked well only for a certain teacher demographic—that is, teachers who were independently wealthy or who had wealthy benefactors or partners—and thus reproduced a privileged, homogenous teacher body. Part of this was due to the ways in which racial and gender prejudices shaped how the dana model operated on the ground in the Insight tradition. "When you ask people to subjectively value what to offer different teachers as a donation," Fernandopulle continued, "the same unconscious (or conscious) bias plays out as it does in the labor market, where men are given more than women, white people more than people of color, etc. But there is no labor law to even theoretically balance this. So, the system is not set up with equity in mind and is blind to these societal dynamics." As a result of these problems, many good teachers had to teach secular mindfulness rather than teach at Buddhist retreats in order to secure a stable income. Hence, for her, rethinking financial systems was key to enabling a more diverse population of teachers, ensuring a better quality of teachers, and sustaining Buddhist centers. As she mused: "I think it is a systemic problem for our tradition. You want people to master the teachings and teach a lot so they get better at it. Otherwise, it is like someone is trained to be a surgeon but is changing bedpans because it pays better. It is a problem for the continuity of the teaching in our tradition that it is not being addressed."

Jeffrey Zlotnik, who since 2006 has run a nonsectarian Buddhist center now called the Dharma Bum Temple in San Diego, had the most critical perspective on Buddhism and money. He identified the conversation about money and dharma at the 2015 conference as a "low point" for him. As he put it, "I was the new kid on the block, but I was saddened by how much money changes hands around Buddhism in this country; we manipulate and take advantage of the word 'dana.'" Zlotnik felt that there was not sufficient focus on the teachings of generosity within American Buddhism, and he was wary about the framing of the word "dana" as "donation." He specifically instructs people who lead classes at the Dharma Bum Temple not to finish with a dana talk because he feels this puts pressure on students to give and undercuts the practice of generosity. Zlotnik felt strongly that "Buddhism is not a career" and advocated for teachers to live off secondary jobs to mitigate the commodification of dharma in the West. He felt teaching the dharma was an honor, and lay teachers "should be willing to make sacrifices in their personal lives." Although his perspective in the discussion was a minority one, he reported that after the session many people expressed appreciation for his "courage" in voicing it. Zlotnik was the only interviewee who legitimated his perspective with reference to the Buddha, who, he pointed out, "had only seven items and did fine."

The diversity of perspectives confirmed Hart's conclusion that "money is a hot topic, and money in relationship to Buddhism and being ordained, being a teacher, is not settled." One thing that interviewees did agree on, however, was the desire for more open conversations about how teachers were making a living. "As a whole group, we are more interested in being transparent about this aspect of the dharma," Sundberg said. "Whether our generation is choosing to have a formal sliding scale or to charge or to not charge, there is more interest in transparency and communication and growth and less awkwardness. That's what I would say more generally of my group."

Approaches to Traditional Buddhism

Initiatives of Gen X such as the development of new economic models and the embrace of progressive equity values might easily lead one to conclude that they have fully embraced the secularization of Buddhism begun in Buddhist modernism. However, I found that Gen X interviewees demonstrated a complex relationship to traditional Buddhism, showing both a critique of cultural/institutional aspects that they saw as rigid and oppressive and a renewed appreciation for aspects such as metaphysics, ritual, and devotion that had been neglected or discarded in the modernization process. Thus, they should be seen as both continuing and correcting modernization trends established by the first generation. Moreover, some Gen X teachers revealed an historical and sociocultural awareness about how the boomers had filtered Buddhism through a modernist, Protestant cultural lens and expressed a desire for a "fuller picture" of the tradition.

A common framing of American convert Buddhism is that it is forging a more essential form of Buddhism that is free from the cultural accretions of traditional Asian Buddhism and its oppressive institutional practices. An example of this is the Against the Stream community. While identifying its primary inspiration as the Pali Canon, Against the Stream sharply differentiates itself from Theravada Buddhism in Southeast Asia, which it believes has become distorted by mythical overlays and corrupted by "sexist, classist and racist politics."[56] The American convert distinction between "essential" and "cultural" Buddhism maps on to the key Buddhist modernist distinction between dharma as universal truth and Buddhism as religio-cultural product and has greatly facilitated the secularization of Buddhism. Consider, for example, Jon

Kabat-Zinn's framing of mindfulness as "universal dharma" uncoupled from Buddhism.

Gen X interviewees both reproduced and rethought the distinction between dharma and traditional Buddhism. Unsurprisingly, nearly all of the interviewees teaching in the Against the Stream and Insight communities identified themselves as dharma teachers rather than Buddhist teachers. This did not necessarily mean, however, that they rejected the "metaphysical" aspects of Buddhism. Many of the interviewees, for example, attributed their attraction to Buddhism as being due to karma. Brensilver said, "The fact that I was having what felt like a disproportionate emotional response to the class [on Buddhism] signified to me, okay, there's something going on here, some karma." Others also expressed belief in the more "supernatural" aspects of the tradition. As one teacher put it: "I believe in nonphysical entities. I'm not a materialist. I'm not one of these people who have a weird secular chip on my shoulder who have to make everything secular."

Nor was the distinction between dharma and Buddhism always made in order to assert the superiority of a supposedly culture-free American Buddhism. Fernandopulle, for instance, said: "I don't really identify as Buddhist. Having grown up within a Sri Lankan community, I don't practice the ritual aspects that make it a religion. I have a different context, so I would say I am a dharma teacher or meditation teacher." However, she did not position the dharma as more essential than Buddhism, as has often been the case. "It's not because I think it's better not to identify as Buddhist," she said. "I just have a different picture of what Buddhism is than many white Americans have, and I don't practice in that way. But I'm also okay if someone wants to call me a Buddhist!"

The most common reason for distinguishing between dharma and Buddhism was to critique institutional power and what were seen as static, rigid, and oppressive elements of traditional Buddhism. Von Bujdoss, for instance, explained: "Tradition is a vehicle for the dharma but [it is] not the dharma [itself]; you can criticize it without criticizing dharma. I think Westerners who say 'I only practice dharma' are trying to extricate themselves from power structures." He shared his struggles with conservative aspects of Tibetan Buddhism: "We suffer from being too orthodox. I really think the Tibetan tradition is too based on Tibetan culture and cultural practices. They say diversity is only a Western problem, for example." Von Bujdoss legitimated his position by frequently referencing the radical lineage of Mahasiddhas, who were known for their tensions with Tibetan Buddhist orthodoxy. For him, the distinction between dharma and institutional Buddhism had historical precedence and was more a means to revive rather than reject tradition.

Many interviewees demonstrated an appreciation for aspects of traditional Buddhism that had been neglected in Western Buddhism, with its emphasis on individual meditation. Chen, for instance, explained that a big part of her attraction to Triratna was its emphasis on taking refuge and spiritual community. Similarly, Kenley Neufield, lay teacher in Thich Nhat Hanh's community, explained that it was the fact that "sangha is a cornerstone of [Thich Nhat Hanh's] teaching" that initially drew him to that lineage.[57] Others were dissatisfied with the dryness of secular Buddhism. Stone said:

> After spending so much time the past couple of years hanging out with neuroscientists and cognitive scientists, I'm actually starting to have more appreciation for the more religious ritual-based practices because when you're engaged in them, you have no idea what they're about and there's something about that that's really rich. So, every morning, my family wakes up, we light incense, and our two-year-old son rings the bell and we chant the Heart Sutra and the bodhisattva vows together.

Echoing Stone, Henkel explained his embrace of devotional practices: "I feel that had I discovered them at the beginning, maybe they wouldn't have resonated, but after years of practice I think of them as a beautiful expression of practice, especially in our Western culture that can get so analytic and dry and too scientific." On a related note, another interviewee lamented that American Zen had cut off its historic Japanese roots and that the traditional dimensions of faith were "missing or undernourished" within it.

Another interesting pattern to emerge among certain Gen X interviewees was the presence of an historical and sociocultural awareness of

Buddhist modernism. They explicitly stated their interest in the more metaphysical, ritualistic, and devotional aspects of traditional Buddhism as a corrective to the selective secularization process undertaken by the first generation. As Padma noted: "We are also curious about aspects of the dharma that the first generation of Western Buddhists weren't as curious about. The boomers made certain choices about what to offer, what teachings they would center on, and what would be put on the backburner, like energy and metaphysics. They smoothed things over to get the dharma centers started." Echoing her, Franz said: "I think younger people are more interested in traditional form and ritual. I think these younger people want to go back and learn some of the things their teachers thought didn't matter." Similarly, Sean Feit frequently referenced the term "Buddhist modernism" and said:

> None of these traditions that I inherited came to me whole cloth. Like, when I got Zen, I got a particular version of macho Rinzai meditation. I didn't get long years of cleaning temples and memorizing sutras and going to births and funerals, and life cycle rituals. And when I learned Theravada, I didn't really get Theravada, I got Insight meditation. I didn't learn the monastic chants or learn how to bow to Buddhist statues; I didn't learn *sila* and the whole culture of it.[58]

Some of the awareness of these "missing pieces" had come from the interviewees' experience of training in Asia. Padma explained: "A turning point for me was recognizing that eclecticism was deeply in the tradition. When I went to Korea I saw the building at Buddhist temples devoted to the Mountain Spirit, an Earth altar. But the earth element was not held up or continued in this country. Why? What is lost when we look for respectability? When hegemonic Protestant culture takes over?" Similarly, Paley Ellison said that when he lived in Japan, he saw much more of an emphasis on community and service rather than just meditation practice.

Franz stated that as a result of his immersion in traditional Japanese monastic culture, he felt "a responsibility to value the traditional because there aren't that many people who do, and there aren't that many people who have seen it, so I want to take that seriously." Aylward picked up on the theme, noting that although he had cut out aspects of Buddhism because he was afraid to alienate or frighten students, he realized that he had a responsibility to the tradition:

> In the three retreats I've taught since the conference, I've been chanting the homage and refuges with people each evening, and closing the retreats with a thread ceremony, which is common in Thailand. And I've really noticed the fruits of that in how people have responded. I reflected that if I don't introduce any of those cultural and historical elements, then I'm partly responsible for them getting lost in my generation. So, I've been reconnecting with the sense of an unbroken tradition of women and men looking deeply into life in the Buddha's dispensation, and refreshing my own heart about what I'm teaching being not just dharma, but Buddhadharma."[59]

"We're Just More Fluid"

"There's a social shift in America in general," williams said, "a shift from the hyperindividualized to a more collective network. That's happening across the board in 'energized spaces'—that's what I call them, politically energized spaces." Gen X conferences, forums, and interview findings reflect this wider cultural shift: the unifying thread running across their multiple concerns is an embrace of the relational and collective. This is expressed on multiple levels: preferred teaching models, the desire for peer accountability, a more pluralistic nonsectarian approach to Buddhism, a focus on social conditioning and structures that produce individual and community suffering, and increased sociocultural awareness of the adaptions of Buddhism in the West. Much of this can be attributed to a shift in teacher demographics from a largely homogenous white, heterosexual, upper-middle-class population to a more racially, sexually, and socioeconomically diverse one. As williams observed, "Many white boomer teachers are from the owning class, and that's not as true for Gen Xers. There are those who have white-skin privilege but don't necessarily come from money. As a result, the whole

orientation shifts for them. . . . Gen X teachers are actually in real contact and authentic relationship with different people of color . . . they're
much more receptive and open around LGBT and trans people even if
they're straight."

Whereas the boomer generation is liberal and therapeutically
oriented, Gen X is more progressive and politically oriented. However,
they do not reject but rather radicalize key components of the boomer
generation: nuancing gender equality with intersectionalities of race,
class, and sexuality; expanding individual psychological integration to
include internalized social oppressions; and moving beyond the liberal emphasis on individual equality and assimilation to a postmodern
analysis of the multiple operations of power and privilege. In terms of
future developments, more attention is likely to be devoted to overcom-
ing divides between heritage and convert Buddhist communities and
monastic/lay teachers. Similarly, the identity marker of class is likely
to receive more attention and the relationship of Buddhism to capitalism and neo-liberalism to be increasingly interrogated. Gen X should
be seen as expanding the first generation's application of Buddhism to
contemporary forms of suffering: from the individual to the collective,
or, as one interviewee put it, from "the 'me,' to the 'we.'"

Critical, Collective, and Contextual Turns

Dressed in a mix of Tibetan robes, Zen rakusu, silk scarves, and bright tattoos, seven teachers of color and seven white teachers, seven females and seven males, were gathered together under the title "The New Face of Buddhism" on the March 2016 cover of *Lion's Roar*. On one end, Kate Johnson of the Interdependence Project stood above Insight pioneer Sharon Salzberg, who leaned into Dharma Punx's Josh Korda. On the other, angel Kyodo williams of the Center for Transformative Change sat below Soto Zen teacher Zoketsu Norman Fischer and touched knees with Tibetan Buddhist Anam Thubten Rinpoche. Inside the magazine, this mix of boomer, Gen X, and millennial teachers, carefully chosen, one assumes, to represent demographic as well as lineage diversity, responded to the question: "What is the most important truth to proclaim in today's troubled world?" A clear message, from the younger teachers in particular, was the need to *awaken collectively:* Johnson emphasized that the Buddha's liberation teachings were desperately needed, not only for individuals but also for communities, institutions, and the global political landscape. Lama Rod Owens interpreted the iconography of Green Tara through the revolutionary lens of black feminist Maya Angelou, calling on practitioners to "confront the ways in which we reproduce violence when we stay on our comfortable seats."[1]

Given that this edition of *Lion's Roar* represented a significant step forward in promoting diversity and advocating for the sociopolitical deployment of American Buddhist practice, it is not surprising that one of the first responses to it was a critique. More surprising, however, was that this critique was directed at the magazine's continuation of rather than challenge to Buddhist modernism. On the website of the Buddhist Peace Fellowship, five practitioners of color discussed what they described as the "awkwardly titled 'New Face of Buddhism.'" While expressing appreciation for the sincerity of the magazine's efforts to present a more inclusive representation of Buddhism, they forwarded three main concerns. First, they questioned what was "new" about the face and lamented the continued exclusion of Asian and Asian American Buddhists whose practices had long been dismissed as "superstitious" within convert circles. Second, they pointed out that the *Lion's Roar* "facelift" was only cosmetic and that deeper structural changes were needed to produce true inclusion. Third, they argued that the universal and "transcendent" teachings of Buddhism erased the cultural contexts in which Buddhism was always enacted as well as the particularity of practitioners of color and thereby reproduced the systematic exclusion and violence against black and brown bodies in the United States.[2]

The response of both *Lion's Roar* and the Buddhist Peace Fellowship display many of the emerging patterns explored in this book: "insider" critiques of meditation-based Buddhism, an emphasis on collective forms of practice, and an illumination and interrogation of the sociocultural contexts of American Buddhist lineages. In this chapter I focus on the appearance of these sensibilities—what I identify and will later expand on as critical, collective, and contextual turns—across communities with strong online platforms as well as the lively Buddhist blogosphere.

Decolonizing the Dharma: The "Radical Rebirth" of the Buddhist Peace Fellowship

The Buddhist Peace Fellowship (BPF) has emerged as a powerful emic force in challenging certain aspects of American Buddhist modernism, particularly its individualism, white privilege, and perpetuation of the "cultural" versus "essential" racialized Buddhist rhetoric. Founded in 1978 to serve as a catalyst for socially engaged Buddhism, BPF has been revitalized by its current codirectors Dawn Haney and Katie Loncke, who relaunched it on an entirely digital platform after it nearly collapsed because of recession-related financial problems. The BPF's quarterly newsletter *Turning Wheel* has been revisioned as the social media platform Turning Wheel Media, and BPF staff worked without a physical headquarters for three years, although BPF now has a modest office in Oakland, California. Loncke, who started working for BPF and Turning Wheel Media as a blogger a few months earlier, took over as a codirector in 2012 with Haney, who had started writing for BPF in 2011. In a 2013 article, Loncke articulated the ten principles around which BPF's "radical rebirth" was centered. The first, "Let's Go Beyond the Personal," urges readers to "THINK BIGGER" than their personal practice and "organize collective expressions of compassion and awakening" and then unpacks how such a collective liberation would challenge structural systems of oppression such as racism, capitalism, the prison-industrial complex, and US militarism. In response to whether BPF's rebirth represented a "kind of contentious political split that happened between the young radicals on one side and the middle-aged liberals on the other side," Loncke replied that it was more of "an extension and continuation," which built on the previous work that BPF had done but added the perspective of a younger generation.[3] Haney echoed this sentiment, explaining that the organization wanted to continue the Engaged Buddhism of the BPF by connecting with the sociopolitical issues and movements that were most pressing in this cultural moment, particularly Black Lives Matter and climate change justice.[4]

Between August 29 and 31, 2014, Loncke and Haney hosted BPF's first national gathering since 2006. The conference began with a public keynote event, an "intergenerational dialogue," between BPF elder Joanna Macy, Thai Buddhist activist Sulak Sivaraksa, Loncke, and Haney in front of an audience of nearly four hundred at the First Congregational Church of Oakland. This was followed by two days of workshops and activities on topics such as working toward climate change justice, healing racism, building beloved communities, and working with conflict at the East Bay Meditation Center. Since space was limited to 120 people,

Haney and Loncke utilized an intentional application process to ensure that participants were diverse in terms of race, age, geographical location, and Buddhist lineage, with POC, people younger than twenty-four and older than eighty, and people outside the Bay Area particularly encouraged to apply. The online application was presented as a "mandala form," with an accompanying explanation that "a mandala is a traditional Buddhist symbol representing the universe and its diverse components."[5] The end result was 120 participants from more than seventeen states, with 40 percent of participants identifying as POC and more than one-third being thirty-five years old or younger. Haney observed that the gathering was "historic for its diversity and intergenerational makeup," although both she and Loncke reported that they had received some pushback for their application process.[6]

The main aim of the gathering was to bring together a diverse group of people who, as Loncke put it, "don't just want to use Buddhism in a self-help personal context." Haney felt that there was a limit to what could be done through online programs and that getting people together in the same room was essential to fostering intimacy and strengthening bonds between participants.[7] In reflecting on the conference, the codirectors named two panels they felt had been particularly meaningful and successful, both of which were centered on community building between POC. One of these was "Black Rage, Black Healing," which included a dialogue between African American Zen teacher Zenju Earthlyn Manuel and author Mia McKenzie, who runs the website Black Girl Dangerous, which features the voices of queer and trans POC. This was facilitated by Loncke using "progressive stack," a discussion method designed to protect and privilege the voices of minorities, with POC being invited to speak first and those who do not identify as POC asked to hold their questions. The other was titled "The Invisible Majority: Will the Real Asian American Buddhists Please Stand Up," led by Chenxing Han, who is writing an academic book on the experiences of young adult Asian American Buddhists. "So many people raved about this session," Loncke enthused. "They were completely blown away and loved it so much." She felt this was because when attention is given "to that which deserves our attention—including race and racism—it actually helps people to open up and become alive and connect with each other in new ways." She added that she has "so much sympathetic joy" to see community building happen between people who identify as Asian and Asian American.[8]

The gathering ended with an improvised social justice action in which some participants performed a sitting blockade on the steps of the Oakland Marriott Hotel to protest its hosting of Urban Shield, a weapons expo and SWAT training for police to practice militarized techniques. For Haney, this blockade exemplified one of the core goals of BPF, which is to move beyond individual meditation practice. "As we develop mindfulness on the cushion," she said, "it's not just so we can have better and longer and clearer sitting practice, but for me at least, it's so we can have greater stability of mind and an openness of heart as we go about everything we do in the world, which for me is the activism I'm doing around Ferguson [Missouri] and other issues." She also linked the Urban Shield protest to the history of BPF, noting that the organization had largely grown out of the anti–Vietnam war movement and for many years had been focused on antiwar organizing. She reflected, "What does it mean to be working towards peace and doing antiwar movement building today when war isn't just only happening in Iraq and Afghanistan but is also happening here on US streets every day?"[9]

Many of the themes explored at the conference have been further developed in a series of in-person and online programs that BPF has since hosted. One of these was "Dharma and Direct Action," a 2015 workshop focused on "Buddhist infused creative non-violent organizing," which Loncke and Haney ran in Oakland, New York City, New Orleans, and Santa Fe. Haney described these as "in-depth, in-person workshops that combine spiritual practice with practical social justice skills, from nonviolent blockades and civil disobedience to messaging for spiritual and political audiences." The workshops were offered in various formats from half-day to three-month trainings.[10] I attended the "Dharma and Direct Action" weekend program held at the New York Insight Meditation Society in November 2015, and the first thing I noticed was how extraordinarily racially diverse it was for an event at an American Buddhist convert center. Another distinctive feature was that participants wore name badges that included their preferred gender pronouns. The emphasis of the workshop was more on direct action than dharma teachings. The morning opened with a meditative practice followed by a focus on learning about and designing creative, nonviolent, "Buddhist-informed" direct social justice actions. One such action was designing a blockade made up of meditators linking arms. A topic that came up repeatedly over the weekend was the relationship between Buddhist teachings on anger and equanimity and social justice activism. Rather than refer to canonical Buddhist approaches to anger, Loncke and Haney took a first-person approach, sharing their own experiences negotiating "righteous anger" as Engaged Buddhists and inviting participants to do the same. It became quickly clear that it was much easier to denounce anger as "non-Buddhist" when one was not part of a minority community that faced daily police harassment and violence.

Most of the attendees I talked to at the retreat practiced at sanghas in New York that are known for their commitment to diversity and social justice—Insight New York, the Brooklyn Zen Center, and the Interdependence Project—although a few had also traveled from out of state to attend. I also recognized four people from a workshop I had attended at the Brooklyn Zen Center a few months earlier on undoing racism.[11] Two of these were members of Trans Buddhism, a small collective of Buddhist practitioners from different lineages across the United States who have produced the guide "Developing Trans* Competence in Buddhism" to address the systematic exclusion of transgender and gender-nonconforming people from Buddhist spaces.[12] Another was Danielle Saint Louis, who is the cofounder and facilitator of a number of Zen and Insight groups that support the practice of mindfulness and meditation in POC, LGBTQI, and marginalized communities. Also present was Kate Johnson, who teaches at the Interdependence Project, Insight New York, and BPF and is emerging as an influential millennial teacher of color in American Buddhism.[13]

BPF has also launched a leadership development program, "Block, Build, Be" ("block harm and oppression, build inspiring alternatives, and be in alignment with dharma") that is aimed at developing a new generation of Buddhist activists. A nine-person facilitation team from across the US—Houston, New York, Oakland, Santa Fe, and Seattle—met online over a period of several months to plan the opening event, a weekend retreat in 2016. This brought together thirty-four participants in Petaluma, California, and provided a "welcoming space for emergent Buddhist activist leaders to connect, learn new skills, and strengthen their commitment to spiritually-informed action."[14] As with the national gathering, there was an intentional application process to secure diversity, with Haney reporting that more than 70 percent (twenty-five) of participants identified as POC and 88 percent (thirty) were younger than fifty. Haney said of the retreat:

> With a racially diverse crowd, our conversations about race dug especially deep—exploring the impacts of Japanese internment on US Buddhism, anti-blackness in Asian Buddhist temples and mostly white meditation centers, and how conversations about racism shift when white people are present but not at the center [of the conversation]. Despite these conversations getting heated and vulnerable, participants used their meditation practice to stay present, connected, and listening.[15]

As might be evident from the description of its programs, one characteristic feature of BPF is an emphasis on community building. One way this is achieved is through intentional pre- and post-event activities. After the "Dharma and Direct Action" workshop, for instance, I received an email with questions about my experience and photographs of the event as well as a personal check-in phone call from Haney. Similarly, in a conference call zoom session that followed the "Block, Build, and Be" retreat, participants were invited to share how the retreat had affected them and how their practice had since unfolded. One participant commented that she was excited to have made new friends and discussed how positive her experience had been of working as part of a team that articulated and embodied shared values. Another way this community spirit is demonstrated is through BPF's focus on coalition building among various social justice groups. Haney, for example, discussed the coalitions that had been forged between different revolutionary movements under colonialism and how individuals within such groups had become "lifelong friends." A similar community emphasis is evident in BPF emails and its website, which feature photographs and descriptions of its members. Taken together, these multiple expressions of community and emphasis on collective liberation mark a clear departure from the individualism that has often characterized convert Buddhism in North America.

Another main concern of BPF is to bring attention to and challenge the racism faced by Asian American Buddhists, who have long been marginalized in meditation-based convert Buddhism and patronized and dismissed for practicing "cultural" rather than "essential" Buddhism. Funie Hsu and Dedunu Sylvia, two of the contributors to BPF's response to the "awkwardly titled 'New Face of Buddhism'" issue of *Lion's Roar*, are Asian American Buddhists who have spoken out against the racism they and their communities have faced from white Buddhists. Haney said that Hsu, who is on the BPF board and is an assistant professor of American Studies at the University of San Jose, had taught the BPF community a lot about the exclusion of Asian Americans and the difficult work that Japanese Buddhist communities had done to keep the tradition alive in internment camps during World War II.

BPF members also reflected on the intersections between Asian Americans and African Americans both inside and outside of Buddhist communities. Loncke said that she was interested in the ways in which the Asian "model minority myth" was used as a weapon against black Americans by emphasizing the success of certain Asian Americans and thereby dismissing the reality of structural racism. "I am really curious," she said, "about how Buddhism is invoked in similar ways of, if we are mindful enough, if we are calm enough, if we are hardworking and disciplined enough through Buddhism we can be happy regardless of what the reality of suffering and oppression is showing us about life in the Americas."[16] One participant of the "Block, Build, Be" follow-up call shared how affected he had been by the acknowledgment of how antiblackness within East Asian Buddhist sanghas had harmed black practitioners and prevented them from participating in those communities. He experienced the naming and acknowledgment of this harm as having enabled a compassionate healing between the groups.[17]

While both Haney and Loncke are keen to stress continuities between past and present BPF formations, there are two new significant characteristics. One is the impact that the new media and technology format has had on the organization. In discussing the relaunching of BPF as the digital platform Turning Wheel Media, co-editors Loncke, Everett Wilson, and Jacks McNamara explained:

> Multimedia offerings like videos and podcasts bring a different kind of dynamism and can literally help amplify newer voices in engaged Buddhism. Cyber-connectivity and hyperlinks can guide inspired readers to groups already taking action, in their area or elsewhere. The faster pace of online life, and the ease of sharing articles, may help with a "regroupment" process for engaged Buddhism, allowing younger generations of dharma-informed activists (many raised on multimedia web culture) to more easily find one another, and hopefully collaborate on political work.[18]

Loncke, who describes herself as an "unlikely candidate" to be at the head of a Buddhist organization, got involved with BPF after the organization discovered her online blog, in which she took a "gloves-off" approach to describing her struggles to reconcile her Buddhist and social justice leanings. As with Vince Horn and the Buddhist Geeks/Meditate.io networks, Loncke has employed her technological skills and savviness to full effect—using formats such as Vimeo and Google Hangouts to build community and offer online trainings and teaching programs.

Another new characteristic is the shift in demographics of BPF practitioners. As noted above, BPF has been very successful in fostering racial and age diversity among its community, and Loncke and Haney are very much representative of this new demographic. Loncke is the granddaughter, on the side of her mother, of a Holocaust survivor, and her father's mother is a descendant of Afro-Caribbeans who survived the Middle Passage. She identifies as a black biracial queer cisgender female who has been influenced by a pop cultural critical analysis perspective. She lists Insight and Zen teachers of color as her main Buddhist influences. Haney is a white cisgender queer female who grew up in rural Indiana and has a long history in social justice and nonprofit work. She is a graduate of Spirit Rock's CDL 5 training program and currently serves on the leadership and teaching team of East Bay Meditation Center's Alphabet sangha. Reflecting on demographics at BPF, Loncke noted that BPF has been a place for people "who are trying to Venn diagram their different selves, their different lives"—for instance, "the political self, the activist self, or the self who really feels inexorably drawn to social justice movements." She says it can be a "confusing calling" because there is also "this dharma self, which can sometimes really pull us in what feels like an opposite direction towards more introspection, towards withdrawing ourselves from society." She says, "We haven't solved the problem but we are a scrappy and heartfelt group of people who are in love with these questions and this Venn diagram."[19]

The membership numbers of BPF are difficult to gauge, given that participation occurs on multiple levels and also because, as Haney explained, they have veered away from "member" language because membership had been tied to receiving *Turning Wheel* magazine in the mail, and that ended in 2010. Hence, they have shifted to thinking about their base in two ways: more than thirteen hundred people had given money to BPF in the previous year, either through a donation or registering for an event or program; and more than seventy-four hundred people received their e-newsletter two to four times per month to stay engaged in BPF's work.[20]

In a closing activity of the "Dharma and Direct Action" training weekend at the New York Insight Meditation Society, participants were invited to name out loud their spiritual influences and inspirations. This brought a panoply of spiritual ancestors into the room—beloved grandmothers and great-grandmothers, Engaged Asian Buddhists such as Sulak Sivaraksa and Thich Nhat Hanh, the black prophetic voices of Martin Luther King Jr. and Cornel West, and black feminist authors and visionaries such as Octavia Butler and Maya Angelou—as well as a palpable intimacy between members of the group. This ending seemed very much representative of the "radical rebirth" of BPF, which is fostering a new demographic that is familiar with, if not fluent in, critical race theory, postcolonial thought, and queer theory and bringing new concerns to American meditation-based convert communities.

The Critical Turn Online

Much of BPF's historical and critical consciousness around the formation of Buddhist modernism has been facilitated by its members with
academic backgrounds. This points to the fact that much of the critical
and contextual turns have been produced through an increased contact, fluidity, and overlap between Buddhist academic and practice communities. Buddhist magazines such as *Tricycle* have featured interviews
with Buddhist scholars such as David McMahan and Erik Braun, who
have discussed the historical and cultural formation of Buddhist modernism. Similarly, researchers such as Willoughby Britton and myself
have presented research findings at Buddhist conferences, and others
have been interviewed on popular Buddhist podcasts, such as those of
the Secular Buddhist Association. The Internet and social media have
greatly facilitated this contact between academics and practitioners as
well as providing a platform for the critical perspectives of those who
draw in a variety of ways from both worlds. Across the lively Buddhist
blogosphere, practitioners, scholar-practitioners, and scholars who are
former practitioners are producing critiques of contemporary Western
Buddhism. These critiques differ, and in some cases, are in tension with
each other, but they have two main things in common: all target various
dimensions of Buddhist modernism, and all draw on academic scholarship to do so.

DAVID CHAPMAN AND THE CRITIQUE
OF CONSENSUS BUDDHISM

Buddhist author and blogger David Chapman has developed a sustained
critique of the type of Buddhism produced by the boomer generation,
which he has alternatively labeled as "nice Buddhism" and "consensus
Buddhism" and which he has recently declared is "dead."[21] Drawing on
the scholarship of Robert Sharf and David McMahan, Chapman dates
consensus Buddhism to the Western counterculture encounter with
Asian "modernized export Buddhism," particularly the early-twentieth-
century Theravada Buddhist reform movement of Thailand and Burma
in the 1960s and 1970s. It is based on the premise that there is a "core

essence"—namely, meditative experience—to Buddhism and that disagreements among Asian Buddhist traditions should be dismissed as
merely superficial cultural differences. This core essence is fleshed out
and framed with the values of late-twentieth-century North America—
such as inclusivity, individualism, and egalitarianism. Hence, consensus
Buddhism, which is promoted mainly by Western Insight and Zen teachers, essentially consists of "meditation and liberal Western ethics" and
promotes a therapeutic ethos over traditional Buddhist soteriological
goals, or, as Chapman puts it, "emotional safety over enlightenment."

Chapman acknowledges that consensus Buddhism had value for
the baby boomers but problematizes it on the following counts. First, it
does not recognize its historic and cultural specificity and seeks rather
to universalize its own values in promoting a "single shared universal
vision" of Buddhism. This has produced, somewhat ironically, given its
stress on inclusivity, an exclusive form of Buddhism that has limited appeal outside of its Western middle-class to upper-class boomer participants. Second, in addition to consensus Buddhism being "an approach
to Buddhism that has its own values, beliefs and methods," Chapman
more contentiously characterizes it as an "informal alliance or political movement that promotes this approach." He dates the beginning of
consensus Buddhism as a political movement to the 1993 conference
of Western Buddhist teachers at Dharamsala during which, he claims,
the boundaries of what was to be included in and deemed acceptable as
Western Buddhism were erected by a select gathering of teachers. This,
he laments, then led to a "hegemonic rule and deliberate suppression of
alternative approaches."

For Chapman, the main problem with consensus Buddhism is that
it has eradicated fundamental differences between traditional forms of
Buddhism and has actively marginalized alternative forms of modern
Buddhism. In 2011, however, Chapman began to see signs that the he-
gemony of consensus Buddhism was beginning to crack. He interpreted
discussions about generational differences at the 2011 Maha Buddhist
Teachers Conference at the Garrison Institute as evidence that Gen X
Buddhist teachers were forming their own distinct approach to Bud-
dhism. He also pointed to the emergence of new forms of Western
Buddhism—such as Brad Warner's Hardcore Zen, Daniel Ingram and

Kenneth Folk's Pragmatic Dharma, Buddhist Geeks, and his own re-visioning of Vajrayana Buddhism—that offer alternatives to consensus Buddhism and have more appeal to those from Gen X and Gen Y. In 2015, Chapman declared that although future iterations of American Buddhism would be influenced by it, consensus Buddhism was over, as it had not been able to maintain relevance and compete against the secular mindfulness movement, which had essentially replaced it as a cultural force. He reiterated this with his typically hyperbolic declaration that "Western Buddhism was dead," citing the transition of Buddhist Geeks to Meditate.io as his primary evidence.[22]

ANGRY ASIAN BUDDHIST AND THE CRITIQUE OF "WHITE BUDDHISM"

Arun (pen name of Aaron Lee), the Los Angeles–based author of the *Angry Asian Buddhist* blog, explained the blog's name as an homage to other "angry Asian" bloggers who explore issues of racism and privilege in American culture.[23] After previously contributing to the *Dharma Folk* blog, which reflected on racism in Western Buddhism, Arun launched *Angry Asian Buddhist* in 2011. The blog was dedicated to challenging the exclusion of Asian American Buddhists, the largest Buddhist population in the US, by white Buddhists as well as problematizing the promotion of stereotypical representations of Asian Buddhists, such as the "wise monk" or the "suspicious foreigner" within Western Buddhism. One post, for example, questions why a *Tricycle* forum on Buddhist women does not feature Asian American women; another lambasts the exclusion of Asian and Asian American Buddhists at the 2014 Buddhist Geeks conference and disputes the group's claim to represent the "emerging faces of Buddhism." Arun also took up the question of how to create refuge for Buddhists of color, rendered specifically as establishing Buddhist centers in which those who are marginalized can find true community and support. His site included references to and reflections on academic scholarship, such as Joseph Cheah's *Race and Religion in American Buddhism: White Supremacy and Immigrant Adaptation* and Jane Iwamura's *Virtual Orientalism: Asian Religions and American Popular Culture,* and his critique of white Buddhists is grounded in postcolonial theory.[24]

Fellow blogger Richard K. Payne has delivered a similar critique of the racialized dimensions of American Buddhism on his blog *Critical Reflections on Buddhist Thought: Contemporary and Classical.* Payne, a scholar of Buddhism and a Shingon priest, has been a longstanding critic of Western Buddhism, targeting its individualism and its assimilation to depth psychology. He critiques what he has alternatively referred to as "White Buddhism," and "White-Safe Buddhism," drawing on American Buddhist scholarship and critical race theory to highlight the ways in which white American practitioners have erased Asian Americans from the history of Buddhism in North America and promoted the idea that an "authentically American" Buddhism is one in which its Asian origins and features have been eliminated. This racist "white-washing" of Buddhism is predicated on the masking of white identity as universal and neutral and has been a common feature of the Western encounter with Buddhism since the nineteenth century.[25]

THE CRITIQUE OF "NEOLIBERAL BUDDHISM" AND "WHITE TRASH BUDDHIST"

Engage! is a relatively new online project started by Shaun Bartone, a self-identified transgender Engaged Buddhist who is a PhD candidate in sociology at Dalhousie University in Halifax, Canada. Drawing on his own experience in Shambhala and Insight communities and on cultural theorists such as Michel Foucault, Bartone has written a series of blog posts that castigate class divisions and wealth dynamics in North American Buddhism. He argues that the most dominant form of sangha in North America is the "neoliberal sangha," which is marked by an elite consumerist and individualist attitude to Buddhist practice and a lack of interest in helping poor and disadvantaged populations. These sanghas are composed of "neoliberal practitioners" or the "new Brahmins," who view their privilege as the sign of a fortunate rebirth rather than an unjust social system.[26] As Bartone explains:

> I call it Neo-liberal Buddhism . . . it's classist, it's racist, it's hypocritical, it's self-serving. . . . Many of the Buddhist sanghas I've encountered in [the] Eastern U.S. and Canada are

overwhelmingly white and upper class. In my experience, it's
Buddhism for the rich. They exclude a lot of people, people
of color, without realizing it, and when they are confronted
with their racism, they don't want to deal with it. It's not so
bad for gay people and women, but basically, they just cater
to the rich and they don't care if you don't have the money
for their programs.[27]

While Bartone is a newcomer to the Buddhist blogosphere, his
class critique is significant in adding theoretical weight to longstanding emic laments of the class and wealth dynamics in American convert
lineages. Brent R. Oliver's "White Trash Buddhist," which was one of
the most trafficked articles on *Tricycle* in 2014, captures the limitations
of the upper-class demographics of convert Buddhism or what is often
sardonically referred to as the "upper-Middle Way." Oliver notes his surprise at finding Shambhala Buddhist centers devoid of Asian Buddhists
but "infested with upper-middle-class white people" and shares his ongoing struggles in trying to afford "cost-prohibitive" Buddhist retreats
and programs as a blue-collar worker with no disposable income or paid
vacation time.[28] Oliver is a regular contributor on The Tattooed Buddha, a web-based community project that developed from the blog of
Ty Phillips, Buddhist minister and "big city bouncer turned Buddhist,"
who wanted to "remove the commercialization in modern American
Buddhism."[29] Echoing Chapman, Oliver suggests that consensus Buddhism is dying and being taken over by secular mindfulness, which he
feels, as a whole, is more accessible to working-class populations than
"upper-Middle Way" retreat-based communities.[30]

SPECULATIVE NON-BUDDHISM AND THE
CRITIQUE OF "X-BUDDHISM"

The most theoretically sophisticated and sustained interrogation of
Western Buddhism has come from the Speculative Non-Buddhists.
Founded in 2011 by Buddhist scholar Glenn Wallis, the website Speculative Non-Buddhism (SNB) has several contributors, but the majority of
pieces come from Wallis, English literature professor Tom Pepper, and

Matthias Steingass, who all co-wrote the book *Cruel Theory–Sublime Practice: Toward a Revaluation of Buddhism,* which unpacks the theoretical underpinnings of the site. All three report a progressive disillusionment with Buddhist practice and a corresponding shift from a modern reformist orientation to a radical deconstructive critique of Buddhism informed by various academic interlocutors, particularly François Laruelle's nonphilosophy and the critical theory of Alain Badiou, Louis Althusser, and Michel Foucault.[31]

SNB defines its project as "the critical analysis of the ideologically underpinnings of x-Buddhism," a term that refers to "virtually all forms of Buddhism from the historical to the contemporary—from *a* (atheist) through *m* (Mahayana) to *z* (Zen)." The aim is to uncover how all of the various strands of Buddhism—from the traditional to the contemporary—are culturally and historically specific and contingent upon certain unsustainable, problematic transcendental or "unconditioned" foundations. In particular, Speculative Non-Buddhists have been focused on illuminating the complicity of Western Buddhism and secular mindfulness with ideologies of individualism, neo-liberalism, and global capitalism. While claiming to have no interest in offering a modern reform of Buddhism and at constant pains to distinguish themselves from contemporary reformers, SNB contributors privilege the doctrine of *anatta,* both in their commitment to rooting out any form of ideological essentialism in Buddhism (often referred to as "slipping the atman in") and in their revisioning of the doctrines of *anatta* and dependent arising along social, collective, and political lines. SNB contributors translate their academic project to the lived world of North American Buddhism by interrogating people and perspectives across the entire spectrum of contemporary Buddhists on the Internet. From Theravadin monastics such as Thanissaro Bhikkhu to Pragmatic Dharma teachers such as Kenneth Folk, from the secular orientation of Stephen Batchelor to the postcolonial feminist sensibilities of BPF, all have come under what Wallis calls the "coruscating gaze of reason."[32]

The SNB pieces are linguistically dense, jargon heavy, and theoretically challenging—an intentional strategy to serve as an antidote to what the authors bemoan as the "anti-intellectualism" of Western Buddhism, but one that also rendered its analytic project inaccessible to many. Another intentional strategy was SNB's adoption of an aggressive and combative communicative style in which participants were more often than not ridiculed, humiliated, and bullied. Wallis theorized his communicative style as performative of its analytic content, but it led to the blog receiving more commentary about its methods than its analysis. Buddhist blogger Seth Segall noted, for example, that Wallis "brings an interesting and provocative mind to the online mix. It's his tone, however, that I find disquieting. He intends his gaze to be coruscating, but his voice tends toward the corrosive—arrogant, scornful, and dismissive of those holding differing beliefs and attitudes."[33] Patricia Ivan, one of the few female contributors on the site, reported that the aggressive interchanges left her feeling that "SNB was just another boy's club" with the "same dynamics as the Buddhists they were critiquing."[34]

THE IMPERFECT BUDDHA AND THE THIRD SPACE

In his book *Buddhism in America,* Scott A. Mitchell observes that online communities have become increasingly relevant in the development of Buddhism in North America. As he points out, there are thousands of US-based Buddhist bloggers and website owners, and these spaces often function as a platform for Buddhist "discourses of dissent," with David Chapman, *Angry Asian Buddhist,* and Glenn Wallis among his examples.[35] The Imperfect Buddha Podcast is another significant online space for dissenting voices in Western Buddhism. Hosted by Matthew O'Connell, an Englishman who lives in Italy, the podcast has featured interviews with Wallis, Chapman, and Daniel Ingram, as well as academics such as anthropologist Ben Joffe and ecologist Adrian Ivakhiv. O'Connell advocates a critical approach to Buddhism, what he calls "post-traditional Buddhism," which views Buddhism as a thoroughly human cultural product and ideology to be deconstructed and strategically mined to contribute to the goal of human flourishing and ethical well-being. He aligns his project with Wallis's SNB and sees it as appealing to those "long-term practitioners who have ceased to be enamoured with Buddhism's exotic symbology, or disappointed by their lack of progress in practice."[36] One of the significant aspects of the Imperfect Buddha is that it brings together dissenting voices and shows that although they differ, many see them as forming a critical turn in Western Buddhism.

Anna Halafoff, Emma Tomalin, and Caroline Starkey offer the theoretical lens of the "third space" to interpret forms of virtual dissent seen in online Buddhist activity. They discuss how shifting authority has been a key theme in the intersection of religion, technology, and social media. They draw from the work of Stuart Hoover and Nabil Echchaibi, who have argued that the Internet acts as a third space in which traditional authority can be challenged. As Hoover and Echchaibi explain, "Third space arguably unsettles the singularity of dominant power narratives and opens up new avenues of identification and enunciation."[37] In their research on digital Buddhist female activism, which draws on both traditional and modern narratives, Halafoff, Tomalin, and Starkey conclude that the Buddhist cyberspace, or web sphere, is a location of both traditional expressions of religious authority and a third space where a hybridized and fluid context requires new logic and evokes unique forms of making meaning.

Buddhism 2.0: Secular Buddhisms

While much of the critical turn has been focused on problematizing the modernization of Buddhism, another emic or insider critique is that it has not been modernized enough. Australian scholar and practitioner Winton Higgins argues that Buddhist modernism draws on too many disparate elements to be coherent and that its traditional-modernist compromise is unsustainable. He reached such a conclusion after teaching Vipassana at a meditation center linked to a Theravada monastery where growing tensions around the nonmodern aspects or "relics" of Theravada, such as the marginalization of women and the monastic hierarchical power structure, eventually led to an acrimonious breakdown between modernist and traditionalist populations. Higgins and others broke away and began teaching Insight meditation at independent but similar urban-based groups. As he explains:

> These sanghas are all self-generated and have no organizational links to each other but they all march to the same

drum. They are self-evidently secular, free of ritual, inclusive, egalitarian and democratic. . . . Their members study the Pali Canon (the earliest teachings of the Buddha) in their historic context, in order to deepen their dharma practice in their own intellectual free-ranging way. They trade tips on books, journals, blogs and websites and Stephen Batchelor's work enjoys a certain prominence. Ethically speaking, their conception of dharma practice extends beyond the traditional five lay precepts to tackling the big issues of today's globalized world, and many are active in progressive social movements or community work.[38]

After some initial reluctance, Higgins adopted the term "secular Buddhism" to describe these emergent dharma communities. For Higgins, secular Buddhism represents a new stage in the translation of the dharma in the West, one that resolves "certain incoherences in Buddhist modernism (the 'push' factor) while responding to secularizing impulses in contemporary Western society (the 'pull' factor)."[39]

Buddhist teacher and author Stephen Batchelor makes a similar argument in his secular recasting of Buddhism. Using a technological metaphor, Batchelor claims that rather than designing new secular Buddhist software to run on the traditional Buddhist operating system (Buddhism 1.0), a fundamental secular upgrading of the Buddhist operating system is needed (Buddhism 2.0). By "traditional" Buddhism, he means "any school or doctrinal system that operates within the soteriological worldview of ancient India," arguing that the disjuncture between this framework and modernity is so vast that simply modifying traditional Buddhism to meet the needs of contemporary practitioners is insufficient.[40]

Batchelor has long been a controversial figure in Western Buddhism for claiming that belief in reincarnation is not a necessary component of Buddhist practice or identity. Alan Wallace, for example, accused him of promoting a "distorted vision of Buddhism," and the public exchange between the two exemplified the significant tension and, in certain cases, hostility between traditionalist and secular currents within Western Buddhism.[41] Perhaps reflecting some of these tensions, in a

2012 *Tricycle* article, Batchelor wrote that it had taken him years to "fully come out" as a secular Buddhist. He adopts the term "secular" in three overlapping ways: (1) in the popular sense, to denote that which is in contrast or opposition to the "religious"; (2) in the etymological sense, referring to its roots in the Latin word *saeculum,* meaning "this age," to emphasize the concern with how to live best in this world; and (3) in the Western historical-political sense, to refer to the transference of authority from the church to the state. His work is concerned with presenting a new form of Buddhism or the dharma that has encountered and been refracted through these three dimensions of the secular.[42]

Batchelor's version of a secular Buddhism is grounded in his primary reading of early canonical texts and replaces the soteriological ideal of Nirvana with the goal of human flourishing in this world within the context of the Noble Eightfold Path. He sees this as more than a contemporary secular revisioning of the Buddha, however, claiming that he is recovering the historical Buddha who, he argues, was not concerned with metaphysics and truth claims but rather with presenting a therapeutic and pragmatic path for individual and communal well-being. Batchelor concludes that the "Dhamma was gradually transformed from a liberative praxis of awakening into the religious belief system called Buddhism," and his project essentially aims to recover that original praxis and apply it to the context of contemporary Western modernity. At the core of this recovery is his translation of the "Four Noble Truths" as the "Four Great Tasks": namely, to embrace dukkha, or whatever situation life presents; to let go of the grasping that arises in reaction to it; and to stop reacting so you can act unconditioned by the reactivity. He frames this as a shift, or "unlearning," from a Buddhism based in soteriological "truth" or belief claims to a Buddhism based in praxis. As he puts it, it is a shift in orientation from Buddhist teachings that ask "Is it true?" to those that ask "Does it work?" Although such an approach challenges the soteriological and institutional frameworks of Buddhism, Batchelor prefers to look at it as the beginning of Buddhism 2.0 rather than the death of Buddhism 1.0—the emergence of a "culture of awakening" as equally accessible to laity as monastics, women as to men.[43]

Batchelor's vision for a secular Buddhism appeared in *Tricycle* and the academic publication *Journal of Global Buddhism,* but it also circulated around the Internet and found a home on various Buddhist community websites. For example, a quick Internet search came up with a copy of "Buddhism 2.0: A Secular Manifesto" posted on the Nashville Dharma Punx website.[44] Batchelor has been teaching secular Buddhism across the "retreat circuit" in Europe and the United States. For instance, he cotaught a four-day retreat, "Being Completely Human: A Retreat on Secular Buddhism and Beyond," with Joan Halifax at the Upaya Zen Center in Santa Fe in 2015.[45] Another major avenue in which Batchelor is developing secular Buddhism is at the recently established Bodhi College in the UK, of which Batchelor is one of the founders and core faculty members. Bodhi College describes itself as a nonsectarian college that offers "a contemplative education that seeks to inspire students to realise the values of the Dharma in the context of this secular age and culture."[46] It runs three two-year extended courses, one of which explicitly advocates a secular Buddhist approach. This is the Secular Dharma course, which Batchelor coteaches with Martine Batchelor, Letizia Baglioni, and Jenny Wilks. Beginning in 2016, and in its second year, twenty-one attended the course, which, as far as Batchelor is aware, "is the first time that such a long-term program formally advocating Secular Buddhism has been offered." He said that he had gotten a little wary of offering the teachings in a short retreat format and wanted to ground people in a longer program so they could explore together how a secular approach to Buddhism could be enriched and developed.[47]

Although Batchelor's 2018 book is called *Secular Buddhism: Imagining the Dharma in an Uncertain World*, he said that he prefers the term "secular dharma" because he feels that the term "Buddhism" brings a lot of "ideological baggage" that is an obstacle to revisioning the core tenets or the dharma from which the religion Buddhism developed. Nonetheless, he describes being "gratified" to see how the term "secular Buddhism" has entered Buddhist currency, noting its recent usage in an article by Bhikkhu Bodhi in which Bodhi distinguishes between "classical Buddhism," which "continues the heritage of Asian Buddhism, with minor adaptations made to meet the challenges of modernity," and "secular Buddhism," which "marks a rupture with Buddhist tradition, a re-visioning of the ancient teachings intended to fit the secular culture of the West."[48] In a similar view, Batchelor distinguishes between the more radical reconstruction of the dharma seen in secular Buddhism and modernist reformist configurations of Buddhism such as the Vipassana movement or Shambhala Buddhism, as well as new hybrid traditions such as the Triratna Order. As he explains:

> If you accept David McMahan's understanding of Buddhist Modernism to include all "forms of Buddhism that have emerged out of an engagement with the dominant cultural and intellectual forces of modernity," then I suppose that the way I think of "Secular Buddhism" would render it a form of "Buddhist Modernism." However, I am not entirely comfortable with this term since, to me and Winton Higgins, Secular Buddhism is not an adaptation of an existing form of Buddhism to modernity, but an attempt to rethink the Dharma from the ground up in order to address the contemporary world that speaks to its suffering and needs.[49]

SECULAR BUDDHISM IN THE UNITED STATES

An influential iteration of secular Buddhism in the US is the Secular Buddhist Association (SBA), whose founder and executive director is Ted Meissner. The SBA originated from a podcast, "The Secular Buddhist," which Meissner started in May 2009. Meissner, who coined the term, explained that he considered the name "naturalist Buddhism" but decided against it because "it sounds like we have a thing for being naked," so he settled on "secular" as the "most appropriate description for what this is." He also noted "it echoes a certain alignment with secular humanism, though that was more a happy accident."[50] Although the term "secular Buddhism" was "uncommon, if not virtually unknown" at that time, it clearly appealed, as podcast listeners were keen for more engagement and volunteered their time and skills to develop a platform that had more capacity for interaction and community building.[51]

The result was the SBA, subtitled "A natural, pragmatic approach to early Buddhist teachings and practice," which currently has more than five thousand subscribers to its website, more than twelve thousand members on its Facebook page, and about two thousand Twitter followers. It has produced more than 270 podcasts, which have been downloaded more than a million and half times, and the term has gained increasing currency from supporters and critics alike, with many people now identifying as secular Buddhists. The wide appeal of a secular approach is indicated by the fact that the three SBA guided meditations on the meditation timer app Insight Timer have gotten more than twenty thousand listens from when they were introduced in March 2015 to late 2017.

In October 2012, SBA started a Practice Circle, an online practice group that meets twice a month via videoconference. Mark Knickelbine, the practice director, models the format of the University of Wisconsin Health mindfulness group with which he practices. The circle opens and closes with a meditative practice, drawn from a variety of traditions, including MBSR and Theravada, Zen, and Tibetan Buddhism, and includes small and large group discussion. There are currently 130 members on the mailing list, although Knickelbine says that they generally have about a dozen participants a week. The main benefit of the Practice Circle, according to Meissner, is that it provides an opportunity for "those who are geographically or ideologically isolated to practice and engage with others who also have a secular approach."[52] This was the case for Jennifer Hawkins, SBA's diversity and inclusion director, who lives in a rural area and reports being isolated because of a disability before finding the SBA. She has been a regular member of the Practice Circle and Social Circle events for a few years and says that one of the benefits of SBA's "very supportive" online community is that she "can be connected to like-minded people anywhere in the world."[53]

The SBA website offers a number of articles and resources on secular Buddhism, an approach that it acknowledges is "not cut and dried" and "is still taking shape." Many of the descriptions on the site stress heterogeneity among secular Buddhists, and my five interviewees, four of whom have leadership roles at SBA and one who has recently joined the board of directors, also emphasized that they are "a very diverse bunch." Nonetheless, a review of the articles shows that two features appear most foundational: secular Buddhists either "find no evidence for" or "consider irrelevant" the concepts of rebirth or supernatural elements such as devas, and they have a this-worldly orientation and focus for their practice. My interviewees revealed many similarities between their approaches, particularly Meissner, Knickelbine and study director Doug Smith.[54] All three have been influenced by Batchelor's work, although Smith, who has a PhD in philosophy, does not agree with Batchelor's reading of the Buddha as an early secularist. Smith believes such a hermeneutic inserts present secular concerns "back into" the premodern Pali Canon, although he does believe that the early teachings of the Buddha portray him as an ethical pragmatist with views that are in basic alignment with secular humanism and require no metaphysical commitment to traditional views of rebirth to follow. Hawkins did not mention Batchelor but talked about how influential an online class with Buddhist scholar Rupert Gethin had been in helping her appreciate the diversity of Buddhist schools and make sense of conflicting presentations of the tradition as essentially philosophical or metaphysical in nature.

All three report various types of "cognitive dissonance" or "philosophical disagreement" with metaphysical beliefs such as rebirth and karma that made "no rational sense" or "conflicted with a contemporary Western scientific worldview." For Knickelbine, the SBA project was about providing a space where people felt no pressure to conform "to supernatural beliefs which are no longer acceptable to people who have been educated in the basics of what we know of the human organism and the universe." All three identify as atheists and humanists and see secular Buddhism as congruent with and a particular iteration of a humanistic orientation. While not explicitly identifying as an atheist, Hawkins has a background in biological sciences and said that she had been alienated by traditional Buddhists who insisted that she accept "the supernatural beings and cosmology as literal and unquestionable." For her, secular Buddhism was attractive not because it rejected these metaphysical aspects, but because it did not demand a "rigid" acceptance of them. A similar perspective was advanced by Amy Balentine, an SBA board member. She felt that secular Buddhism was "less reified and open to a variety of influences" than other forms of Buddhism and that this fitted well with her own shifting identity as someone who is "somedays agnostic, somedays nontheistic, other days theistic."[55]

As noted, the relationship between "traditional" or "religious" Buddhism and secular Buddhism has been tense and conflicted. One common narrative among secular Buddhists has been to explain metaphysical aspects of Buddhism as nonessential cultural accretions. As Balentine said: "I don't have to wade through religious and cultural customs and beliefs that have been a part of other groups. That baggage has often distanced and sometimes repelled me from other groups. Part of my spiritual journey has been dumping the baggage of religious ideology that has been constricting and spiritually stunting. The last thing I desire is to take on more of that."

The language of "baggage" and "religious ideology" should be understood in the context of Balentine's "deconversion" from a prescriptive, oppressive form of Christianity. As discussed earlier, however, the dismissal of cultural Buddhism has played out in harmful, racialized ways for Asian and Asian American Buddhists. Hence, one of the main critiques leveled at secular Buddhism is that it is Orientalist, ethnocentric, and racist. SBA's diversity and inclusion director, Jennifer Hawkins, who is an African American female in her thirties, addressed this issue in detail. She acknowledged that the use of language such as "cultural baggage" and "superstitious beliefs" common in secular Buddhist narratives was problematic and had unintended harmful effects on Asian and Asian American Buddhists. However, she also felt that unreflexively embracing such aspects could itself be a form of cultural appropriation. "When I first encountered Buddhism," she explained, "I had left Christianity and did not want to trade blind faith in things that probably weren't real for blind faith in different things that probably weren't real and weren't even of my own culture. As in, I didn't know the term for it at the time, but I had no interest in cultural appropriation."

For Hawkins, it is important to distinguish between secular Buddhism and the "dominant-biased white culture" in which it is situated as she felt that the two were often inaccurately and unfairly conflated by other Buddhists. She shared, for instance, that on an online Buddhist course "I had someone so deeply cling to the belief that I must be racist because I was a secular Buddhist that he went so far as to actually swear at me and troll me online" and that her experience had been that secular Buddhists "weren't welcome in many Buddhist spaces because the chant that SB equals racist has seeped into many minds." This was particularly jarring for Hawkins because it was the inclusivity of SBA that had drawn her to the community:

> I don't encounter the race-based biases at SBA that I encounter in so many other communities. There's no expectations, positive or negative, placed on me just because of how much melanin my skin likes to retain. At the same time, there's an understanding that race conditions, in the Buddhist sense of that term, a lot of my experience. Sometimes I need refuge when I encounter bias somewhere else. . . . I have become a leader with responsibilities that I can handle. No other community has accepted where I am and given me what I needed to be able to regain some of my strength—to allow me to become a real leader.[56]

Nonetheless, she recognized that despite SBA's intentions, the fact that it operates within a cultural context of white privilege means that concerns around harmful racialized effects of secular Buddhist rhetoric were understandable and legitimate. Hence, the SBA has been recently focusing on initiatives such as fostering diversity in leadership and teaching, discussing cultural appropriation, changing the wording on its website, and reaching out to organizations like BPF and Buddhists for Racial Justice.

Perhaps reflecting some of this work, unlike Batchelor, who has not shied away from taking aim at traditional Buddhism, SBA interviewees were keen to minimize any sense of conflict been a traditional religious perspective and a secular one. Meissner talked appreciatively of his experiences with Theravadin monastics and stressed continuity rather than discontinuity, situating secular Buddhism as "the fourth main branch of the Buddhist tree, on the same level as Theravada, Mahayana, and Vajrayana." Smith shared that he practiced at New York Insight Meditation Center, where people with various religious and secular orientations practiced in the same space with no conflict and that he had enjoyed the visits of religious monastics as much as those of secular teachers. Knickelbine added that SBA was not "trying to talk anyone out of their beliefs. Nor are we trying to overturn or supplant traditional

Buddhist lineages. . . . While many of us might reject aspects of traditional Buddhist doctrines, we have great respect for those whose efforts
and dedication throughout the centuries have made Buddhist teachings
accessible to us." In a similar vein, Dana Nourie, the SBA technical director, noted that "secular Buddhists do not feel the need to erase the
colorful, rich history of Buddhism, nor do we want to destroy traditions,
their practices, their rituals, or their beliefs. Most secular Buddhists do
not consider traditional Buddhism as 'wrong' and secular Buddhism
as 'right.'"[57]

More research would be required to see whether the efforts and
more careful rhetoric of SBA leaders align with the viewpoints of a
wider range of SBA participants. The heated debates on the SBA website,
some of which run to more than two hundred comments, undermine
claims that among secular Buddhists there is no sense of certain traditional Buddhist claims as "wrong," although secular Buddhist claims
are as equally passionately disputed. The main point to note here is that
the leaders and prominent representatives of SBA are concerned with
minimizing conflicts between traditional and secular communities and
stress continuity as much as discontinuity between the two. Balentine,
for example, talked of balancing relevance to new Western contexts with
respect for Buddhist Asian roots. As she put it: "I think it's actually important for traditional and Western forms of Buddhism to engage each
other on these issues. . . . [Secular Buddhism] hopefully provides Buddhist wisdom to modern Westerners in a way that is both relevant and
connected to its roots."

Nonetheless, secular Buddhists do see themselves as offering an
historically distinct and new form of Buddhism. In terms of the relationship of that new form to Buddhist modernism, although Higgins and
Batchelor see secular Buddhism as pointing beyond the Buddhist modernism of the Asian meditation reforms as well as their immediate Western successors such as the Insight community or Shambhala, it is harder
to draw lines between the two in the SBA community. Referencing the
scholarship of David McMahan and Jeff Wilson, Knickelbine sees secular Buddhism as the continuation of Buddhist modernism: "It began as a
project of Asian teachers from traditional Buddhist lineages attempting
first to reposition Buddhism vis-à-vis colonialist Christianity, and then

to seek a wider lay audience both in Asia and the West." Similarly, Smith minimized differences between secular Buddhism and his local sangha, noting that it was rare to hear dharma talks on the metaphysical and cosmological aspects of Buddhism at the New York Insight Meditation Center. Hence, while Batchelor and Higgins's vision for secular Buddhism shows clear evidence of the critical turn, the SBA does not.

In short, secular Buddhism, similar to secular mindfulness and Buddhist Geeks/Meditate.io, should be seen as the continuation and radicalization of Buddhist modernism. It is unsurprising, then, that many of the key figures across these fields have personal and professional connections. Batchelor and Meissner have been featured on the Buddhist Geeks platform, and in Batchelor's keynote speech at the 2015 Buddhist Geeks conference he praised their lay-centered and nonhierarchical platform. He has also borrowed their technological metaphors in his casting of secular Buddhism as Buddhism 2.0. As mentioned in chapter 2, Meissner works at the Center for Mindfulness at the University of Massachusetts and has been one of the most vocal supporters of secular mindfulness in response to traditionalist critiques; and Jenny Wilks, who coteaches the Secular Dharma course with Batchelor, is a mindfulness-based cognitive therapy teacher and supervisor at Exeter University and also facilitated the "What Does Mindfulness Mean for Buddhists?" forum for *Lion's Roar*. While the depth of engagement with Buddhist canonical literature and ethics marks secular Buddhism as distinct from secular mindfulness, Batchelor also ties the two together analytically:

> I cannot think of a single meditative discipline from any other world religion that could be utilized outside a religious setting in the way mindfulness is being used today. This leads one to wonder whether, in its essence, what we call "Buddhism," is best described as a religion at all. While the secularization of mindfulness is deplored by some classic Buddhists as a dumbing down or commodification of a revered practice within their tradition, one could also argue that the discovery of the effectiveness of mindfulness in reducing suf-

fering allows Buddhism to recover its secular soul that has long been obscured by the encrustation of religious beliefs.[58]

Here Batchelor enacts an inversion of the standard terms of the "mindfulness debates" by casting mindfulness less as a revisioning and more as a recovery of the dharma. He further links the two projects together by noting, "Just as Jon Kabat-Zinn and others have secularized Buddhist mindfulness, the challenge now is to secularize Buddhist ethics and philosophy in a way that can address the current conditions of our world."[59] A similar approach is resonant in the Buddhist Geeks rebundling into Meditate.io and their call for an unbundling and a rebundling of different components of the path and not just mindfulness.

Emerging Turns in American Buddhism: Critical, Collective, and Contextual

The scholarship reviewed in chapter 1 presented a clear picture of American convert Buddhism at the turn of the twenty-first century. Convert lineages were heavily lay-oriented and characterized by a strong focus on meditation practice. They downplayed the cosmological, ritual, and communal aspects of Buddhism and presented it through a psychologized therapeutic lens. They were highly individualistic, with participants showing little interest in community building. A democratization of power structures had been seen in both a move toward gender equality, with an increasing number of women in positions of authority, and the blurring of authority between monastic and lay populations. Convert communities were marked by a broad-ranging eclecticism, which included a borrowing of teachings across Buddhist and non-Buddhist lineages. Finally, demographically, participants were overwhelmingly white, middle-class or upper-middle class, highly educated, and politically liberal.

On one hand, the case studies in this book confirm and show the continuation of these trends. The continued emphasis on meditation can be seen in the textual/technical current in the Insight community as well as in the explosion of interest in mindfulness outside of Buddhist contexts. The secularization of Buddhism is continued in secular Buddhism and radicalized in the rebirth of Buddhist Geeks as Meditate. io as well as the mindfulness movement begun by the first generation. Buddhist convert communities often draw on non-Buddhist discourses such as psychology, science, social justice, and critical race theory as much as on canonical Buddhism in adapting the tradition to the social and cultural contexts of twenty-first-century North America. Feminist perspectives have played a major role in the Zen Buddhist response to sex scandals, and intersectional feminist analyses have been crucial to diversity and inclusion work, which has moved beyond the second-wave feminism of the first generation of American Buddhist teachers to more nuanced and critical considerations of the intersections of race, class, gender, and sexuality. Democratic and egalitarian sensibilities can be seen across the case studies, such as a democratization of Buddhist knowledge and practice in virtual communities.

On the other hand, the case studies also complicate this picture and show some new patterns emerging, which, in certain cases, are a reaction against core modernist characteristics. I have identified three distinct, but often interrelated, emerging "turns" or sensibilities within meditation-based convert lineages: critical, collective, and contextual. The critical turn, as discussed above, refers to the development of a reflexive and critical sensibility within these communities. First-generation practitioners tended to celebrate "American Buddhism," enthusing that they were creating new, more modern, and "essential" forms of Buddhism that were nonhierarchical, gender-egalitarian, and free of the cultural and religious "baggage" of their Asian predecessors. While the modernization and secularization of Buddhism certainly continues, there is now much more discussion about the problems and pitfalls of these processes. More voices, for instance, are exposing the Western ethnocentrism that has operated behind the "essential" versus "cultural" distinction and acknowledging that meditation-based convert Buddhism is as culturally shaped as any other form of Buddhism. Some go further in targeting specific aspects of that culture: its individualism, racism, classism, and neo-liberalism. Others call for a reengagement with neglected aspects of the tradition and promote dialogical rather than assimilative encounters between Buddhism and (post)modernity.

The collective turn signifies the multiple challenges to the individualism of meditation-based convert lineages.[60] One expression of this is the increasing efforts toward building inclusive sanghas, or "beloved communities." Another is the development of relational forms of Buddhist and mindfulness practices such as external mindfulness. A third expression is the concept of "collective awakening," hinted at in Thich Nhat Hanh's suggestion that "the next Buddha might take the form of a community," as well as the application of Buddhist principles and practices to the collective dukkha caused by racism and capitalism.[61]

The contextual turn refers to an awareness of how Buddhist practice is shaped and limited by the specific historic and sociocultural contexts in which it occurs. On a basic level, it is the recognition that *context matters.*[62] More specifically, it has two overlapping but distinct dimensions. One of these is a basic historical understanding of how Buddhist meditation has been progressively decontextualized from its larger religious matrix since colonialism and some of the problems caused by that decontextualization. For example, there is much more acknowledgment of the need for meditation to be grounded in and integrated into wider contexts. There is also the beginning of attempts to modify certain "universal" meditation practices to specific contexts or populations. The SBA, for instance, has been experimenting with refashioning the popular body scan meditation to make it more inclusive for trans* and disabled practitioners.[63]

The other dimension of the contextual turn is an understanding of the particular formations of power and privilege operating within various Buddhist contexts. I have explored the politicized aspect of the contextual turn in relation to critiques of the neo-liberal assimilation of mindfulness and in the illumination of white privilege in racial justice work. Another example of it can be seen in Against the Stream teacher Pablo Das's response to Buddhist teachers' thoughts on the US presidential election, in which he critiques their perspectives reflecting a privileged social location that negates the trauma of marginalized communities. Das suggests that calls to meditate and to "sit with what is" are not sufficient to create safety for vulnerable populations, and he warns against misusing Buddhist teachings on impermanence, equanimity, and anger to dismiss the realities of such groups.[64] Shortly after, Against the Stream published a Statement of Commitment echoing many of Das's points.[65] In the conclusion, I consider the significance of these three turns and the other patterns documented across the case studies in terms of the status of Buddhist modernism in the United States.

Conclusion: American Buddhism in a "Post" Age

In a recently published survey of Buddhism in the United States, Scott Mitchell concludes correctly that to understand Buddhism in America, one has to understand the modern trends that have produced it.[1] I extend Mitchell's conclusion to suggest that to understand recent patterns and turns in American meditation-based convert Buddhism, one has to go beyond theories of modernity and explore what has come *after* it—as indicated by sociocultural signifiers such as postmodern, postcolonial, and postsecular. As the case studies should have demonstrated, new developments often explicitly and implicitly assert pressure on modernist characteristics and cannot be fully explained within the parameters of Buddhist modernism. How, then, are we to name such emerging trends and turns? What theoretical model best accounts for these? Should one now talk of Buddhist postmodernism rather than Buddhist modernism? Below I review a number of frameworks that either change the category of Buddhist modernism slightly—such as "multiple modernities"—or introduce a new analytical paradigm—such as "global Buddhism"—and consider how well these alternatives attend to and account for emerging trends identified in this book.

Multiple Modernities

Not long after legitimating Buddhist modernism as a new historic form of Buddhism, David McMahan warned scholars against thinking of it as a monolithic, unitary, static entity. He noted that just as different cultures had been subject to various forces of colonization and modernity and had themselves selectively adopted components of modernity, so Buddhist modernism appeared in unique and distinct ways in different cultural contexts. Considering differences between modernist adaptions in China, Tibet, and Sri Lanka, McMahan concluded, "we should be cautious about defining Buddhist modernism too narrowly or about positing a fixed distinction between modernity and 'tradition.'"[2] Other scholars have also identified other nuances and complexities to Buddhist modernism in different cultural contexts. In her research on Zen in Brazil, for example, Cristina Rocha shows how many of the characteristics that mark Buddhism in the West, such as divisions between immigrant and convert populations and practices, are not as operative in a Brazilian context. She found much fluidity between tradition and modernity in Brazilian Zen and analyzed the complex ways in which tradition was implicated in modernity through the categories of hybridity and creolization. Drawing on Arjun Appadurai's globalization theory, Rocha asserted that the interplay between local and global material and imaginary resources had resulted in the "indigenization of modernity" and the production of "plural modernities" across the world.[3]

Scholars have also drawn attention to multiplicity within American Buddhist modernism. In his research on increasing interest in *jhana* meditation and cosmological elements of Buddhism among American converts, Erik Braun finds a disruption of the standard narrative of what counts as "modern Buddhism" and evidence that Buddhism in North America is not following a linear modernization process. As with my observation of the textual/technical current within the Insight community, Braun highlights both modern and traditional sensibilities within *jhana* practice and concludes that multiple varieties of Buddhist modernism have emerged in the United States.[4]

Natalie Quli and Scott Mitchell go further in providing a nuanced, sophisticated analysis of "multiple Buddhist modernities" through a comparative study of Zen and Jodo Shinshu Buddhism in the United States. They draw on Charles Taylor's distinction between acultural and cultural models of modernity to show that creative and strategic activity within both of these Buddhist communities disrupts any monolithic or acultural notion of modernity. Hence, they suggest redefining modernity as "*a set of narratives,* which when selectively appropriated and embedded in a larger set of narratives, produces a variety of configurations of 'modern' and 'traditional,' yielding multiple Buddhist modernities."[5]

From a variety of geographical locations, therefore, scholars of contemporary Buddhism have demolished any static, essentialist, and linear notion of modernity and illuminated the numerous ways that modernity and tradition are culturally constructed and context dependent. The various analytic models they have produced that pluralize Buddhist modernism—"multiple modernities," "plural modernities," and "Buddhist modernisms"—are useful for indicating the multiple configurations of the traditional and modern strands that appear in my case studies. However, they are limited on two related counts: they do not identify any of the particular discourses shaping these distinct modern configurations, and, most pressingly, they do not acknowledge the critiques of Buddhist modernism central to some of these developments. Other scholars have also observed the limits of the category "Buddhist modernism" to capture contemporary developments in Buddhism and have offered alternative interpretive paradigms.

Global Buddhism

In 2001, Martin Baumann argued that new and unique forms of Buddhism were emerging, forms that displayed characteristics—such as hybridity, plurality, ambivalence, and globality—that were more associated with the postmodern than the modern. Hence, he concluded, "To my mind, there are good reasons to argue that, at least in Western industrial countries, Buddhism has acquired a post-modern shape."[6] Baumann felt, however, that the concept of postmodernity was vague, so he suggested the designator "global Buddhism" rather than "postmodern Buddhism." The advantage of "global" was that it highlighted one of the main characteristics of contemporary Buddhism, namely, the transnational and transcontinental flow of Buddhist teachers, students, thoughts, and practices. Although transnational movement had occurred during colonialism and the formation of Buddhist modernism, advances in transport and technology had enabled an unprecedented degree of mobility and communication. Within this new global period of world history, a number of highly pluralist and heterogeneous Buddhist groups have emerged, some of which reinterpret traditional and modern forms of Buddhism to such a degree that they have produced "postmodern content." Hence, Baumann concluded that there was compelling evidence for thinking of four major and distinct developmental stages in Buddhist history: canonical, traditional, modern, and global. He saw global Buddhism as a continuation and radicalization of the modernization processes begun under modernity. As he explained:

> As modernist Buddhists have demythologized and rationalized traditionalist Buddhism—in a related way certain postmodernist Buddhists secularize and psychologize modernist Buddhism. In whatever way the current period—following that of modernist Buddhism—might be labeled, an important part is constituted by approaches and understandings that no longer refer to themselves as Buddhist. Future developments will show whether this period of Buddhism in its appropriation to individualized and secularized contexts—at least in parts—will cease to be Buddhist.[7]

Baumann was prescient is observing the emergence of new forms of Buddhism that are not fully explainable by the categories of "traditional" or "modern," but his analysis is somewhat underdeveloped and limited. To begin with, he does not sufficiently articulate differences between Buddhist modernism and global Buddhism. Two communities he gives as examples of global Buddhism—the Insight community and Shambhala—have been commonly presented by scholars as forms of Buddhist modernism and fit neatly into that category. Baumann's analysis of what makes them global and postmodern rather than modern is somewhat superficial and unconvincing.

Similarly, how does one distinguish between the global spread of modern Buddhist discourses and the global spread of postmodern Buddhist discourses? As Baumann himself acknowledges, globalization has been central to the formation and dissemination of modernist strands of Buddhism. In an early anthology on modern Buddhist texts, Donald S. Lopez, for example, noted that transnational networks were key to the formation and spread of Buddhist modernism. More recently, Mitchell has discussed the effects of globalization in relation to Buddhism in the United States. He points to the entanglements between modernity and globalization, with their shared roots in colonialism, industrialization, and capitalism. Like Baumann, he recognizes that while modernity and colonialism laid the foundations for globalization, it has accelerated intensely in our current age. Nonetheless, Mitchell retains a foundational link between modernity and globalization, positioning the latter as the operative means by which the discourses of modernity are spread cross-culturally via networks of trade, travel, and digital communications. As he puts it, "U.S. Buddhism is the result of modernist discourses made possible through the apparatuses of globalization."[8]

Finally, as with Buddhist modernism, Baumann's global Buddhism does not identify enough of the key features emerging in contemporary American Buddhism. Although his analysis accounts for the radical secularization of Buddhism seen in the mindfulness movement and the post-Buddhism of Meditate.io, it does not include the historical and critical consciousness seen in what I have called the "critical turn" or the recovery of traditional elements discarded in the modernization process advocated by certain Gen X teachers. Given the above considerations, I suggest that the term "global Buddhism" is insufficient to capture current developments in North American convert lineages and works better in conjunction with other signifiers, such as "modern Buddhism," than alone.

Ultramodern Buddhism

Sociologist Anna Halafoff has also suggested that while "Buddhist modernism" describes well the ways in which Buddhism has been shaped and disseminated in the modern era, the period of "thick globalization" from the 1960s onward requires new frameworks for understanding Buddhism at the turn of the twenty-first century.[9] In coauthored articles with Praveena Rajkobal and with Emma Tomalin and Caroline Starkey, she draws on French sociologist Jean-Paul Willaime's theory of the ultramodern and aspects of Ulrich Beck's cosmopolitan theory to advance the category of "ultramodern Buddhism" as an interpretative paradigm for new developments in Buddhist social activism.[10]

Willaime coined the term "ultramodern" in 1998 as an overall hermeneutical framework to account for changes in Western modernity. The two premises of ultramodernity are "(a) we have not left modernity behind and (b) we are actually in a phase of the radicalization of modernity."[11] For Willaime, the prefix "ultra" is able to indicate both discontinuity and continuity with modernity in a way that "post" cannot. He sees the discontinuity as a shift from a logic of certainty to a logic of uncertainty. Whereas modernity was marked by a strong confidence in progress in science, ethics, and politics, ultramodernity is characterized by a strong feeling of doubt and criticism toward the future and the past. Within ultramodernity, the modern principle of reflexivity has become radicalized. The amplification of reflexivity has resulted in the demythologization of modernity in which "nothing escapes close examination," including the enchantments of modernity. Ultramodernity is the "disenchantment of the disenchanters."[12]

The ultramodern interrogation of secular ideals such as science, universalism, and progress has resulted in new configurations of religion. Religion has "become a symbolic resource" and regained social significance in resisting the extreme ethical relativism and individualism of modernity. New relationships have been forged between religion and politics in which they are no longer positioned as competing arbiters of ultimate meaning but come together in various configurations and mutually beneficial ways. As Halafoff and Rajkobal note, this has resulted in religiously inspired social movements playing an increasingly critical role in the public sphere. They draw on José Casanova to frame such religious movements as "immanent critiques of particular forms of modernity from a modern religious point of view."[13]

Halafoff and Rajkobal argue that the ultramodern provides a useful interpretative lens for the Sakyadhita International Association of
Buddhist Women founded in 1987, which is committed to improving
conditions for Buddhist women worldwide and promoting gender equity in global Buddhism. They demonstrate that Buddhist women within
Sakyadhita display the radical reflexivity that marks the ultramodern
and that the organization illustrates the mix of religious and political
discourses that constitute ultramodern religiously inspired social justice movements. For example, while participants problematize gender
inequality within Buddhism, they also resist the Eurocentric ideals of
liberal feminism and turn attention to resources within the tradition
itself. Hence, Halafoff and Rajkobal conclude that Sakyadhita is a religious social movement that critiques both problematic Buddhist and
liberal secular ideas through a transnational feminist and ultramodern
Buddhist framework.[14]

Halafoff, Tomalin, and Starkey apply the framework of ultramodern Buddhism to Buddhist women's digital activism. They note that since
the late 1980s, a number of organizations have emerged that attempt to
link diverse groups of Buddhist women, including nuns and lay practitioners, scholars and activists, across the globe. Much of this gender
activism has occurred online through websites and social media. While
gender egalitarianism is a characteristic of Buddhist modernism, the authors suggest it cannot account for the hybridity and pluralism within
these new international cyber-driven formations of Buddhist gender activism. Divisions between Western/Asian Buddhism, laypeople/sangha,
traditional/modern, and scholar/practitioner are being increasingly
blurred in the period of ultramodernity and this digital activism. They
conclude that we need new frameworks to understand global Buddhism
in the twenty-first century, and the ultramodern is useful because it
transcends binaries and emphasizes pluralism as well as denoting the
radical reflexivity that is characteristic of emerging Buddhist networks
and communities.[15]

The interpretative paradigm "ultramodern" has significant value in
illustrating current developments in North American convert lineages
in that it captures both the continuity and discontinuity of Buddhist

modernist processes and the radical reflexivity of practitioners found in the critical turn. My main hesitation with the term is that it is somewhat obscure and to my mind does not offer more than the more popular term "postmodern." For Willaime, the prefix "post" indicates that modernity has come to an end and does not convey enough of the continuity between modernity and contemporary culture.[16] Similarly, Halafoff prefers "ultramodern" because we are transcending dualistic modern paradigms, and "ultra" is not a dualistic prefix in the way that "post" is. She suggests that ultramodernity enables "an examination that isn't necessarily a linear progression, but it is more multi-directional, applying reflexive principles to what has come before, what is happening now and what is yet to come."[17] She concedes, however, that the disadvantage to using Willaime's term "ultramodernity" is that it has not gained much academic currency. In the next section, I explore how some theorists have adopted "postmodernity" as a signifier of the same patterns pointed to by ultramodernity, namely, as both an extension *and* a critique of modernity.

Postmodern Buddhism

In the introduction to this book, I defined my work as a continuation and fleshing out of Baumann's and McMahan's respective suggestions that emerging patterns in Western Buddhism were more suggestive of late or postmodern conditions than modern conditions. At the end of each case study, I identified how certain current trends within American convert Buddhist lineages appear to reflect the wider cultural shift from the modern to the postmodern. I have also discussed how the terms "postmodern" and "postmodernity" are contested. Much of the debate revolves around the exact relationship of postmodernity to modernity. Some theorists argue that postmodernity signals a definitive break from modernity; others hold that it continues and further radicalizes the emphases of modernity. I agree with sociologist David Lyon, who sees postmodernity as indicating a reshaping rather than a replacing of modernity, with this restructuring including both an extension and interrogation of modernity.[18] As with Willaime's "ultramodern," therefore, I understand the signifier "postmodernity" to indicate both continuity and discontinuity with modern trends.

Hence, I adopt the term cautiously and strategically as a general signifier to draw attention to the effect of the significant economic, sociocultural, and intellectual shifts under way since the 1970s in which Western society is seen to have transitioned from a modern industrial age to a postmodern postindustrial age—an age marked by increasing globalization, the rapid development of new communication and information technologies, the restructuring of capitalism, and the rise of consumer culture. Some of the characteristics of postmodernity that are particularly relevant to understanding developments within North American convert lineages that I examine in this book are its suspicion of the modern meta-narratives of science and universalism; its revaluing of religious epistemologies, practices, and communities discarded and denigrated in modernity and its celebration of difference, diversity, and hybridity; and its challenge to assimilative modern liberalism.

In addition to Baumann, other scholars have found the framework of postmodernity useful and fitting for understanding changes in contemporary Buddhism. Anthropologist James Taylor applies postmodern social theory to interpret changes occurring in Theravada Buddhism in Thailand. He defines postmodernity as a cultural epoch characterized by reenchantment, desecularization, and the reemergence of religion as a culturally visible and relevant force. He focuses specially on the concept of postmodern space, in which religious forms resist the privatization of religion brought about by the differentiations of modernity through occupying public space and blurring boundaries between the religious and the secular. Through a series of case studies, Taylor shows a resurgence of sacred space in urban Thailand through which new hybrid articulations or "assemblages" of Thai Buddhism have manifested.[19]

Taylor's study demonstrates a blurring of boundaries between the religious and the secular that is similar to the one seen in certain iterations of the mindfulness movement and the Buddhist Geeks/ Meditate.io community. Further support for the postmodern thesis comes from Mitchell's book *Buddhism in America,* which follows chapters on Theravada, Mahayana, and Vajrayana traditions with one titled "Postmodern Horizons?" The chapter opens with the observation that the modern age, which was grounded in the grand narrative of universal reason and empiricism, has given rise to the postmodern era, in which all meta-narratives—premodern and modern—have become culturally contextualized and relativized. Similar to myself, Mitchell highlights two particular features of postmodernity: (1) its critical skepticism toward modern narratives of scientific rationalism, universal truth, and human progress; and (2) its embrace of diversity in contrast to the modern tendency toward the erasure of difference.

Mitchell explores how new emerging groups and trends within US Buddhism can be seen as reflecting and responding to these postmodern conditions. His exploration cites my research into American Buddhism and postmodernity and includes many of the traditions and trends treated in this book: the formation of new nonsectarian and pan-sectarian communities; the secularization of mindfulness and Buddhism; the proliferation of Buddhist digital discourses, practices, and communities; and the "online dissent" expressed by popular bloggers such as David Chapman and the Speculative Non-Buddhists. He ends the chapter by differentiating between the modernist forms of Buddhism that were forged in Asia and brought to North America and these new postmodern articulations.[20]

Zack Walsh offers a sociocultural critique of the effects of core aspects of postmodernity on contemporary Buddhism. Walsh draws on Gerhard Lenski's theory of postmodernity, Fredric Jameson's theory of late capitalism, and Jean Baudrillard's model of hyperreality to situate and critique decontextualized, superficial postmodern iterations of Buddhism such as corporate mindfulness practices, the commodification of Buddhism, and Asian Buddhist theme parks. As he puts it, "In technologically advanced post-modern societies, this confusion between reality and simulations of reality creates a hyper-real world in which cultural traditions like Buddhism are reduced to meaningless representations without reference to their original value."[21] However, Walsh also observes that there are more constructive and mature postmodern adaptions of the tradition that retain its essential religious features while adapting to progressive changes. Among these he includes the Buddhist Geeks network and the "new scientific dialogue" led by contemplative neuroscientists who have introduced more culturally sophisticated and phenomenologically rich paradigms for investigating Buddhist meditation.

Although I find the concept of postmodernity to have great utility in explaining new developments in North American convert lineages, I also have some reservations in fully embracing it. The major disadvantage to the term is its indisputable multivalent and slippery nature. As well as the disagreements on its exact relationship to modernity, many readers will primarily associate it with specific iterations that are not particularly relevant to or helpful in illuminating the major patterns tracked here. Some, for instance, will likely associate it primarily with postmodern philosophers such as Derrida and Lyotard. Others will identify it solely with a heightened sense of irony, skepticism, and nihilism or what some theorists have differentiated as deconstructive rather than constructive postmodernity or skeptical rather than affirmative postmodernism.[22] The emic perspective is worth noting here in that even though certain practitioners have adopted the term "postmodern," others have rejected it. For example, in response to my framing of Buddhist Geeks as postmodern, David Chapman recommended against using the term on the grounds that participants associated it with vacuous and pretentious academic theory. When I quoted his objection during my presentation at the Buddhist Geeks conference, it was met by raucous laughter and applause, which suggested he was on point.[23]

Similarly, as shown above, Buddhist scholars have emphasized different aspects of the postmodern. Whereas both Mitchell and I highlight its rejection of modernist narratives of scientism and its embrace of difference, Taylor and Walsh move in different directions, focusing on postmodern space and commodification. Another primary challenge is that the term has fallen out of fashion and common usage in much of sociology and cultural theory. One way to negotiate the problems faced by adopting postmodernity as a category is to talk of the more fluid "American Buddhism in postmodernity" rather than the more definitive "American postmodern Buddhism." Another is to qualify and nuance the term by distinguishing interpretative frameworks and discourses closely related to but not identical with postmodernity. Here I suggest that two other "post" developments are particularly relevant and helpful to understanding emerging patterns in North American convert lineages: postcolonialism and postsecularism.

Postcolonial Buddhism

Buddhist modernism, as examined in chapter 1, was intricately linked to the colonization of Asia by European nation-states. Asian Buddhist modernism was formed under and in response to colonialism and both extended Western modernity and challenged Western hegemonic forces. How, then, has postcolonialism affected and shaped Buddhism? "Postcolonialism" refers both to the historic period following colonialism—also called "decolonization," as colonized nations established independence from their colonizers—and to a set of theories that critique the continuing legacies of imperialism and colonialism. The main themes of postcolonial theory include a critical examination of the ways in which Asia has been constructed as "other" to the West and the social, cultural, and political dimensions of such representations. Edward Said's 1978 book *Orientalism,* a seminal work in postcolonial theory, examined how Western representations of the "Orient," and the Islamic world in particular, were shaped by and inextricable from Western colonial interests and functioned to extend and legitimate Western imperialism.[24] Said's work has been extended by multiple thinkers to explore the origins and legacy of such "othering" through the ongoing cultural appropriation of Asian religious practices and cultures.[25]

Another central theme within postcolonialism is the examination of the legacy of the Enlightenment, during which the modern celebration of reason and empiricism resulted in the denigration of indigenous religious epistemologies and communities. Postcolonial theorists have revealed how certain Enlightenment discourses and values are inherently Eurocentric and privilege Western experience and interests under the guise of universalism. For example, postcolonial theorists have questioned the supposed objectivity of science, revealing the various ways in which its discourses and practices are bound up in and serve specific political and sociocultural agendas. Similarly, postcolonial feminists have destabilized the universal, homogenous category of "women," pointing to the multiplicity of women's experiences being dependent upon racial, ethnic, and class differences.

As a counter to the multiple operations of this false objectivity and universalism, postcolonial thinkers highlight and promote the local and the particular and celebrate cultural difference over assimilation. This has often resulted in renewed respect for traditional worldviews and cultures that had been dismissed as "primitive" and "superstitious" through the lens of modernity. Closely related is the postcolonial concern for formerly colonized subjects to reestablish their autonomy and agency. As David Tracy notes, one of the marks of postcolonialism is the recovery of those voices that have been muted, forgotten, and erased by Eurocentric modernity.[26]

In what ways have these postcolonial currents affected Buddhist modernism? A number of scholars have observed how postcolonial theory and sensibilities have had an impact on gender equality activism in contemporary Buddhism. Liz Wilson offers a useful overview of such scholarship. She observes that while liberal Western Buddhist female practitioners brought second-wave feminist concerns to Buddhism, third-wave, intersectional, and postcolonial feminists have illuminated some of the shortcomings of the earlier project by drawing attention to how differences in race, ethnicity, class, and sexuality shape the formation of gender identity. Postcolonial feminists have also highlighted the racism and ethnocentrism operative in Western Buddhist liberal feminist projects, which often patronize and exclude Asian women in adopting Western middle-class experience as normative and universal. Karma Lekshe Tsomo has criticized the Eurocentric view that Western liberal feminism has "saved" Buddhist women from Asian patriarchal institutional structures, and Sharon Suh has observed that Western Buddhist feminists tend to privilege meditation practice and dismiss Asian laywomen's ritually based devotional practices as less authentic or merely cultural.[27]

In earlier fieldwork on the East Bay Meditation Center in Oakland, California, I identified a postcolonial sensibility at work in the center's attention to multiple intersections of identity as well as its questioning of the implicit racist, colonial underpinnings of the distinction between essential and cultural Buddhism.[28] It should be clear that postcolonial discourses and sensibilities are also evident in new developments in North American convert lineages, particularly in what I have identified as the "contextual turn" and the "critical turn." Postcolonial perspectives are central to Buddhist diversity and inclusion work as well as operative in critiques of the mindfulness movement and secular Buddhism. Bloggers such as the Angry Asian Buddhist and Richard Payne draw explicitly on postcolonial theory to critique racist and neocolonial dimensions of American convert lineages. The network of Engaged Buddhists involved with the Buddhist Peace Fellowship are at the heart of postcolonial critiques of American Buddhism. In August 2013, BPF published a series under the title "Decolonizing Our Sanghas," which interpreted the five precepts through a postcolonial lens.[29] At the "Dharma and Direct Action" workshop that I attended, a number of participants reflected on the presence of racism and neocolonialism in American Buddhism.[30]

It is important to note how these still marginal perspectives within American convert lineages are affecting the wider community. One example can be seen in the Gen X teachers network. The 2017 conference included among its three goals exploring the impact of colonialism on teaching the dharma, and a number of teachers demonstrated awareness of postcolonial perspectives when I interviewed them.[31] Another is an article in *Buddhadharma* by Funie Hsu in which she took aim at how the distinction between essential and cultural Buddhism functioned to promote white Buddhists as "the erudite saviors and purifiers of Buddhism." In positioning meditation-based Buddhism as being superior to the "baggage Buddhism" of Asian Americans, white Buddhists are guilty of cultural appropriation of an indigenous Asian tradition. Hsu calls on them to reflect on the politics of appropriation as part of their Buddhist practice and offers an essentially postcolonial hermeneutic of the five precepts and the teachings of dukkha for such as reflection.[32] Hsu's "challenging but important article" was supported by a follow-up piece by Tynette Deveaux, *Buddhadharma*'s editor, who said that there had been an unusual number of critical responses from *Buddhadharma*'s readers, ranging from outright anger to more tempered defensiveness.[33]

The above examples should demonstrate that postcolonialism is of great utility in illustrating certain trends within North American convert Buddhism. However, although it captures many of the critiques of Buddhist modernist characteristics, it does not capture the continuities of Buddhist modernism, such as the acceleration of secularization processes. Hence, it is more useful to recognize both the emergence of postcolonial sensibilities within American convert Buddhist lineages and the considerable opposition to them rather than claim that such communities have fully embraced a postcolonial paradigm.

Postsecular Buddhism

As Michele Dillon observes, many scholars agree that there is something qualitatively different enough about the post-1970s era to legitimate a new term that differentiates it from the modern era. She notes that the term "postsecular" had become popular, following the terms "postmodern" and "postcolonial." Although the term had been used before, it began to gain currency after it was adopted by Jürgen Habermas around the turn of the twenty-first century. Acknowledging that the Eurocentric project of modernization had gotten derailed, Habermas suggested that religion had an important cultural role to play in the revitalization of modern democracy and citizenship. He adopted the signifier "postsecular" to denote secularized societies in which religion plays a public role and has an increasing social relevance.[34]

Like Habermas, a number of sociologists and cultural theorists picked up the term to draw attention to the continued or renewed relevance of religion in the public sphere, as seen, for example, in the global rise of religious fundamentalism. This led a number of sociologists, such as Peter Berger, to either abandon or mitigate the "secularization thesis," which had claimed that religion was steadily declining and would eventually disappear under the progressive forces of Western modernity. Sociologists adopted the term "postsecular" or "postsecularity" to denote an historic sociocultural period that was marked by a revival of religion in social and political life as well as a proliferation of deinstitutionalized spiritualities. Others, such as Courtney Bender, have used the term to illuminate how new forms of religious expression undermine and blur the boundaries between the "religious" and "secular" spheres in ways that render their analytic distinction redundant. In certain cases, the term "postsecular" is used to draw attention to the limits and inconsistencies within secularization; in others, the emphasis is on the revitalization of traditional religions or the emergence of new hybrid forms of religious and spiritual expression. As with the postmodern, therefore, the term is multivalent and remains a source of debate among theorists.[35]

A few scholars have applied the category of the postsecular to contemporary Buddhism and particularly the mindfulness movement. In an attempt to determine whether mindfulness is a religious or a secular practice, Liselotte Frisk found both categories unhelpful as explanatory frameworks. Practitioners saw mindfulness as a way to explore various aspects of being human and could not neatly situate this as either a religious or a secular pursuit. Frisk concluded that the distinction between the religious and secular had lost relevance and meaning, which she stated was "part of what it means to live in a postsecular age."[36]

While Frisk did not expand on her use of "postsecular" beyond the disruption of the binary of the religious and the secular, Phra Nicholas Thanissaro incorporated a renewed commitment to traditional religious identity and religious truth claims in his adoption of the term as a helpful sociological paradigm for explaining Buddhist teen identity. In a qualitative study of sixty-five heritage Buddhist youths in Britain, Thanissaro found that while Buddhist teens demonstrated fluidity and hybridity in their negotiation of Asian and Western cultures, they were insistent on their identity as Buddhists and countered relativism with Buddhist truth claims. Such features, Thanissaro maintained, "seem symptomatic of a post-secular reinvention of Buddhism."[37]

Sociologists Jinting Wu and Mario Wenning offer a particularly compelling adoption of the category of the postsecular to interpret the secular mindfulness movement. They use the term "postsecular" to denote an episteme that is distinct from both premodern religious faith and the decline of religions that marked the Eurocentric project of secularization. Offering a comparative study of two educational movements—the mindfulness movement in the West and the revival of Confucian education in China—they argue that education, and society at large, is witnessing a "postsecular turn" in which both religious and nonreligious discourses are seen as valuable learning resources. Whereas modernity has always been marked by hybridity, the postsecular amplifies pluralism and consciously attempts to ameliorate various "pathologies of modernity," such as scientism, false universalism, and the loss of spiritual meaning. As they put it:

Here the "post" indicates not a return to religion, but a form of yearning, searching, and enlightened attitude about the shortcomings of both religion and secularity. The "post" indicates the continual self-critique and reflexivity to acknowledge diverse forms of spiritual, religious, belief systems and wisdom traditions as enduring global cultural forces that give hybrid meanings to educational spheres today. However, the "post" also indicates that secularism has not been fully replaced by a radically different age. In a sense post-secularism is perhaps best understood as an act of second reflection, which curtails the one-sided domination of the secular over the nonsecular without falling back to an age of a naive immersion in religion.[38]

Wu and Wenning's use of the postsecular has much to offer as an interpretative framework for the case studies in this book. Both the mindfulness critiques and diversity and inclusion work problematize aspects of the secularization of Buddhism, particularly those rooted in Eurocentric assumptions. The critical turn dovetails well with what Wu and Wenning identify as an "act of second reflection" among participants. Similarly, across my case studies, there are illustrations of the type of hybrid, pluralist approaches to diverse cultural resources—religious and secular alike—that mark their educational examples. For instance, the textual/technical meditation lineage adopts both canonical Buddhism and neuroscientific studies as valuable learning resources in its project to map meditation development, and the Zen communities under analysis have incorporated psychoanalytic discourse and practices within their broader religious frameworks. It is also of note that Wu and Wenning position the postsecular as a subset of the postmodern. According to them, "Postsecularism is postmodernism applied to the world of religious and spiritual beliefs and forms of life."[39]

On the other hand, one disadvantage of the term is that it runs counter to secular Buddhism, which tends to proudly proclaim its secularity and, at times, positions itself in clear distinction from (and sometimes opposition to) traditional forms of Buddhism. Such a move would clearly be at odds with the blurring of boundaries, hybridity, or reclaiming of tradition seen in other iterations of postsecular religious expression, such as Thanissaro's study of Buddhist teens. Another objection is that similar to the term "postmodern" there is disagreement on the exact meaning of "postsecularity" as well as debate on whether it has staying power as an explanatory framework or is destined to be "yet another fleeting epochal descriptor."[40]

Future Trajectories

Each of the above theoretical paradigms and signifiers has value and limitations in capturing what is currently at play in North American convert Buddhism. As the well-known Zen Buddhist story of the finger pointing to the moon illustrates, however, it is not the signifier that is of ultimate importance but that which it signifies, and scholars of religion have long recognized that religious expression is taking new and distinctive forms in the cultural period that has followed modernity. Likewise, the case studies in this book demonstrate that developments in American convert lineages cannot be captured adequately within the parameters of Buddhist modernism, discourses originally forged under the historical conditions of colonialism, which have resulted in both a radical secularization of Buddhism and some pushback to this secularization. Given the slippery nature of the terms "postmodern" and "postmodernity," it is understandable why some scholars of Buddhism might be reluctant to embrace them. One alternative is to harness the related frameworks of the postcolonial and postsecular in a three-forked "post-" analysis that helps identify the specific currents of modernity that are undergoing transformation in American Buddhism. Another, perhaps, is to simply talk of the new sensibilities and turns occurring in American Buddhism *after* Buddhist modernism.

How much will these emerging shifts and turns affect future formations of American Buddhism? In his consideration of American Buddhist postmodern movements and trends, Mitchell concludes that some will form future Buddhist articulations, others will be absorbed into existing Buddhist or secular narratives, and others will vanish.[41] I suggest that much depends on the continued dissemination and establishment of what are still marginal if increasingly visible viewpoints into the American Buddhist convert mainstream. Five related but distinct areas are particularly important in determining the extent to which this occurs: cross-lineage initiatives, teacher training, the Buddhist mainstream press, the translation of discourse into practices, and the changing demographics of practitioners.

1. The formation of *cross-lineage gatherings, organizations, and initiatives* will be important to implementing long-term changes within meditation-based convert lineages. At present, for example, much evidence suggests that diversity and inclusion initiatives are being shared and further developed across lineages. One way this is occurring is through nonsectarian conferences such as the Dharma Teacher Gathering. While still Theravada/Insight heavy, the organizing committee for the 2017 Dharma Teaching Gathering included teachers from a number of lineages, such as Won Buddhism and Soto Zen Buddhism. One of the four days of the conference was devoted to "Realizing Diversity: Understanding and Undoing Racism and Other Oppressions" and examined cultural power and privilege and how to understand and tackle the dynamics of racism. Another avenue for forming cross-lineage initiatives is through organizations such as the North American Buddhist Alliance, which developed from the 2015 International Dharma Teacher Gathering at the Omega Institute. Twenty-nine teachers from that conference developed an interactive website, group directory, and quarterly newsletter and are coordinating initiatives among Buddhists of multiple traditions. One of these is Buddhists for Racial Justice, which was discussed in chapter 5.[42] Another cross-lineage example is the "Healing Racism Retreat" organized by a small group of teachers from the Shambhala, Thich Nhat Hanh, and Insight communities. Kaira Jewel Lingo explains that the group formed after the 2015 Dharma Teacher Gathering and wanted to develop "a multi-tradition Buddhist movement to begin to share our insights, shine light on our blind spots, and build a strong community to act for racial justice as a maha-sangha."[43]

2. A second area that will be essential in shaping future iterations of American meditation-based lineages is the *training of teachers*. Teacher training differs dramatically from lineage to lineage, with some done in the context of individual teacher-student relationships and others through wider institutional settings. As discussed in chapter 5, the

Insight community runs a four-year Teacher Training program. One requirement of this program is that trainees undergo a year of training in one of three therapeutic modalities, including Peter Levine's somatic experiencing. This has undoubtedly fostered the relational/integrative current tracked in chapter 4 and produced a more context-sensitive approach to meditation. Similarly, Noah Levine began a teaching certification program for the Against the Stream community, through which participants have reported learning about relational practices and attachment theory, thus supporting the communal turn. Moreover, both the current Insight Teacher Training programs, but particularly the one at Spirit Rock, will have a significant impact on spreading the contextual turn in the wider Insight world as trainees lead groups in various communities and locations. Closely related is the training of teachers not only vertically through their particular lineage but also horizontally through peer-to-peer contact. Many Gen X interviewees, for instance, said that they had learned new strategies and approaches to teaching at the Gen X gatherings that they had initiated in their own communities.

3. A third major factor will be *the role of the Buddhist mainstream press* in making visible, disseminating, and legitimating new perspectives. The role of the Buddhist press in shaping American meditation lineages has been significant, and it is able to reach a much wider audience than one community or organization. In 2000, academic Douglas M. Padgett listed *Tricycle*'s subscription at 30,000, with a newsstand draw of 15,000 and estimated readership of 150,000; *Shambhala Sun*'s readership was 35,000.[44] In 2017, James Shaheen, editor and publisher of *Tricycle,* reported the magazine's paid subscription at 30,000, and Tynette Deveaux, *Buddhadharma*'s editor, gave the readership for *Lion's Roar* at about 140,000 and *Buddhadharma*'s readership at 32,000.[45]

There are two developments of note in the Buddhist press that reflect the trends tracked in this book: an increase in articles on diversity, inclusion, and social justice, which reflect the contextual turn, and the publication of articles with academic perspectives on the modernization of Buddhism, which participate in the critical turn. Deveaux, for instance, said that *Buddhadharma* had been intentionally attempting to procure more articles on diversity and inclusion and that the topic had gained momentum as potential contributors saw that the magazine was committed to publishing them.⁴⁶ *Buddhadharma*'s summer 2016 issue contained a number of pieces interrogating white privilege in American Buddhism under the unequivocal title "Free the Dharma: Race, Power, and White Privilege in American Buddhism," and in the accompanying editorial, Deveaux noted that far from being a "one-off," the issue was "the start of a conversation."⁴⁷ *Lion's Roar* has also shown an increased commitment to diversity and inclusion, which was intentionally symbolized by its "New Face of Buddhism" cover for its relaunch. When the cover came under a progressive racialized critique by the BPF, it is noteworthy that the editor, Melvin McLeod, immediately responded publicly.⁴⁸ Similarly, Shaheen pointed to the "considerable time and resources" devoted to a recent online-based project at *Tricycle* that featured thirteen teachers of color in a dharma video series in honor of Black History Month, which was proposed by Vimalasara Mason-John, who teaches in the Triratna Order. Further, Shaheen evidenced a critical sensibility in noting that while *Tricycle* addressed the increasingly secular nature of many dharma schools, "we do not see Buddhism as separate from culture, but understand, rather, that secularism carries with it its own cultural assumptions and blind spots." Hence, alongside Linda Heuman's popular series on Buddhism and modernity, *Tricycle* has published a number of articles that "critique the assumptions that come with modernization and secularization," such as scholar-practitioner Anne C. Klein's "Revisiting Ritual" and Robert Sharf's "The R Word."⁴⁹

4. Given the centrality of practice to meditation-based North American convert lineages, a fourth major factor will be *the development of practices and retreats* as well as the promotion of discourses that support the emerging communal and contextual turns. In chapters 2 and 4, I discussed the growth of relational and interpersonal meditative practices, such as external mindfulness, in the Insight and mindfulness communities. The continuation and popularization of these practices will be one avenue by which the communal turn is further established. One example of the translation of the contextual turn into a practice modality is "Next Step Dharma," a six-week course developed by Insight teachers Oren J. Sofer and Jaya Rudgard that provides ongoing practice support for the transition from meditation retreat to daily life. It

aims to counter the decontextualization of meditation by emphasizing that "Dharma practice is more than sitting" and focusing on the integration of meditative experiences.[50] Similarly, practice formats that integrate sociocultural contextual awareness into Buddhism are beginning to emerge. One example is a Barre Center for Buddhist Studies course called "Buddha's Teaching and Issues of Cultural Spiritual Bypassing." Taught by Sebene Selassie and Brian Lesage, this retreat explores how cultural spiritual bypassing manifests both individually and in spiritual communities in the context of early Buddhist teachings.[51] Another is "Invisible Edge: Unmasking Social Bias, Creating Vibrant Community," a weekend program at the Boulder Shambhala Center, led by Shastri Charlene Leung that focuses on unconscious social bias and the intersectionality of multiple social identities.[52] Along similar lines, Jan Willis led a retreat called "Making the Visible Invisible: Exploring Bias and Racism Through a Buddhist Lens" at the Vajrapani Institute.[53] If such retreats become regular offerings on meditation and retreat center calendars, they will play a role in disseminating and legitimating the contextual turn.

5. Finally, *changing demographics* will be key to the future shaping of North American convert Buddhism. As documented, a number of high-profile Gen X and millennial teachers and communities have already had a significant impact on shaping new forms of American Buddhism, and this is likely to increase as boomers retire and die. Interviews with Gen X teachers revealed the ample presence of critical, collective, and contextualist sensibilities. As well as being more demographically diverse, Gen X teachers demonstrate a strong desire for peer community, an interrogation of social structures such as racism that produce collective suffering, and an awareness of the historic and sociocultural processes that have shaped Buddhism in the United States. Dharma Punx and its affiliated Against the Stream network was one of the first Gen X communities to distinguish itself from the boomer "hippie" generation. A similar rhetoric can be found in the Pragmatic Dharma community, which Daniel Ingram has explicitly framed as a punk-inspired hardcore alternative to the "dharma bums" therapeutic approach to Buddhism. Rogue Zen punk teacher Brad Warner, whose 2003 book *Hardcore Zen*

Chapman dates as marking the beginning of the end for consensus Buddhism, also belongs here.

Millennials Vince and Emily Horn have had a significant influence on shaping new iterations of Buddhism and post-Buddhism. Their Buddhist Geeks project brought new populations to Buddhism, and as we have seen, they are now expanding the secularized trajectory with Meditate.io. Self-professed "dharma brats" are also producing new popular secular forms of practice. Lodro Rinzler has written a number of books with provocative titles such as *The Buddha Walks into a Bar: A Guide to Life for a New Generation* that speak directly to second-generation practitioners whom he sees as being more pluralistic, pragmatic, and technologically immersed than their predecessors.[54] As well as teaching in the Shambhala Buddhist lineage in which he grew up, Rinzler is cofounder and guiding teacher at MNDFL, marketed as "the premier meditation studio in New York City" and modeled around the rhetoric of happiness, with no mention of Buddhism at all.[55]

Other self-identified dharma brats from the Shambhala community have produced *The Arrow: A Journal of Wakeful Society, Culture and Politics*, which explores the relationship between contemplative practice, politics, and activism and has featured a number of articles demonstrating all three emerging turns.[56] Similarly, Loncke and Haney of the Buddhist Peace Fellowship have built a thriving diverse and critically orientated practice community—both actual and virtual—that is increasingly highlighting the voices of third-generation and millennial Asian American Buddhists. Just as the boomers brought psychological theory, liberal feminism, and science into their encounter with an already modernized Buddhism, these Gen X and millennial populations are bringing to the table the perspectives of critical theory, cultural studies, and postcolonial thought, as well as an ease and familiarity with digital media platforms.

It is ultimately these populations that will determine the future of North American meditation-based convert Buddhism, particularly as they move into positions of authority and leadership. Tenku Ruff and Koun Franz, two Gen X teachers interviewed in chapter 7, have recently become president and vice president, respectively, of the Soto

Zen Buddhist Association Board of Directors.[57] Research into how they transmit Gen X sensibilities into the organization, which has more than three hundred members, would be illuminating. Future studies will also be needed to discover how these new demographics and developments are affecting local Buddhist communities across North America and not just in the Buddhist convert "hotspots" on the West and East Coasts. As Jeff Wilson cautions, there has been a tendency to overgeneralize claims about American Buddhism on the basis of studies undertaken primarily in California. He suggests that it is high time to introduce and apply a regional lens to the study of Buddhism in North America.[58] One useful research project would be to track the geographic distribution of teacher trainees in the current Spirit Rock and IMS training programs and observe how they implement their inclusion and equity trainings in different regional contexts.

Nonetheless, while being sensitive to differences between the multiple contexts in which they will operate, if the patterns documented in this book continue to unfold, North American Buddhism will be marked as much by the discourses that have come after modernity—the postmodern, the postcolonial, and the postsecular—as by the discourses that constitute modernity. This will not necessarily result in the complete erasure of Buddhist modernism but rather the appearance of multiple forms of American Buddhisms and post-Buddhisms: enlightenments *beyond* the Enlightenment, ones still imprinted but not as circumscribed by the parameters of Western modernity.

Appendix

An "Explanation of Research" was given to potential Gen X interviewees and interviewees from the Insight Meditation Community of Washington. Each group then received a list of interview questions.

For Gen X Teachers

EXPLANATION OF RESEARCH

Title of Project: American Buddhism in a Postmodern Age
Principal Investigator: Ann Gleig
You are being invited to take part in a research study. Whether you take part is up to you.

- The project is for a book on recent patterns and themes in American convert Buddhism. The specific chapter is focused on emerging differences between American Buddhist "baby boomer" teachers and Gen X teachers (who have been called the NextGen).
- You will be asked some questions regarding your experience and participation with the Gen X conferences (Garrison Institute 2011, Deer Park 2013, and upcoming 2015) and also your own life experience as regards being a self-identified Gen X teacher.
- You may feel some anxiety if you critique the baby boomer generation teachers. You are free to discontinue the interview at any time.
- The questions are mostly open-ended so as not to predetermine the results of the conversation. However, I have prepared some questions as a starting off point. Interviews will take 1–2 hours. They can be done via Skype, cell phone, or written correspondence, as you prefer. There is a

possibility that I will ask you some follow-up questions after I return the transcription. You are free to deny this request.

- Skype interviews will be audio recorded, if consent is given. Cell phone interviews will not.
- If you wish to remain anonymous, you will be provided with a pseudonym and your interview will be destroyed immediately after transcription if it was recorded.

You must be 18 years of age or older to take part in this research study. You must also have attended one or more of the Gen X conferences, be a member of the Gen X Facebook group, or self-identify as a Gen X Buddhist teacher.

Study contact for questions about the study or to report a problem: If you have questions, concerns, or complaints, Dr. Ann Gleig, Faculty Supervisor, Department of Philosophy, UCF, 281-857-1236 or by email at Ann.Gleig@ucf.edu.

IRB contact about your rights in the study or to report a complaint: Research at the University of Central Florida involving human participants is carried out under the oversight of the Institutional Review Board (UCF IRB). This research has been reviewed and approved by the IRB. For information about the rights of people who take part in research, please contact: Institutional Review Board, University of Central Florida, Office of Research and Commercialization, 12201 Research Parkway, Suite 501, Orlando, FL 32826-3246 or by telephone at (407) 823–2901.

INTERVIEW QUESTIONS

Ann Gleig, University of Central Florida

1. Demographic Details: Year of birth/ethnicity/race/class identification/gender identity/sexual orientation
2. Biography: Family background/previous religious affiliations, if any
3. First Exposure to Buddhism
4. Deeper Buddhist Experience: First formal teacher, lineage(s), strong influences, etc.
5. Connection with the Gen X Network: How did you get involved? What is the extent of your involvement?
6. What do you see as the main concerns and characteristics of Gen X? How do you see its relationship to earlier forms of Buddhism, both traditional Asian Buddhism and the Buddhism of the baby boomers?
7. What are your thoughts on the guru scandals that have inflicted many convert communities and how they have shaped understandings of Buddhism in the US?

8. What are your thoughts on the status and understanding of "enlighten-ment" in American Buddhism? For example, has enlightenment been revisioned or cast aside?
9. What are your thoughts on the secularization of Buddhist practice, such as the mindfulness movement?
10. What are your predictions for the future development of convert American Buddhism?

Do you have any recommendations for other potential research participants? Thank you.

For the Insight Meditation Community of Washington
EXPLANATION OF RESEARCH

Title of Project: American Buddhism in a Postmodern Age
Principal Investigator: Ann Gleig
You are being invited to take part in a research study. Whether you take part is up to you.

- The project is for a book on recent patterns and themes in American convert Buddhism. The specific chapter is focused on diversity, equality, and inclusion work in American Buddhism.
- You will be asked some questions regarding your involvement in diversity, equality, and inclusion initiatives in American Buddhism.
- You are free to discontinue the interview at any time.
- The questions are mostly open-ended so as not to predetermine the results of the conversation. However, I have prepared some questions as a starting off point. Interviews will take 1–2 hours. They can be done via Skype, cell phone, or written correspondence, as you prefer. There is a possibility that I will ask you some follow-up questions after I return the transcription. You are free to deny this request.
- Skype and cell phone interviews will be audio recorded, if consent is given.
- If you wish to remain anonymous, you will be provided with a pseudonym and your interview will be destroyed immediately after transcription if it was recorded.

You must be 18 years of age or older to take part in this research study.

Study contact for questions about the study or to report a problem: If you have questions, concerns, or complaints, Dr. Ann Gleig, Faculty Supervisor, Department of Philosophy, UCF, 281-857 1236 or by email at Ann.Gleig@ucf.edu.

IRB contact about your rights in the study or to report a complaint: Research at the University of Central Florida involving human participants is carried out under the oversight of the Institutional Review Board (UCF IRB). This research has been reviewed and approved by the IRB. For information about the rights of people who take part in research, please contact: Institutional Review Board, University of Central Florida, Office of Research and Commercialization, 12201 Research Parkway, Suite 501, Orlando, FL 32826–3246 or by telephone at (407) 823–2901.

INTERVIEW QUESTIONS

Ann Gleig, University of Central Florida

1. How did you begin practicing Buddhism?
2. When and why did you start thinking about racial diversity, justice, and inclusion in the group?
3. Can you tell me about the history of the POC group and its main characteristics and concerns?
4. What is the relationship like between the POC group and the main group(s)?
5. What do you see as the main challenges to diversity, justice, and inclusion work within your sangha?
6. What do you see as the main challenges to diversity, justice, and inclusion work within the wider Insight network?
7. What are you most optimistic about in terms of the diversity, justice, and inclusion work happening in American Buddhism?
8. Do you see any noticeable differences across American Buddhist lineages in terms of diversity work?
9. How do you see the relationship between Buddhist teachings and diversity, justice, and inclusion work?
10. What Buddhist teachings and practices do you draw on to frame diversity, justice, and inclusion work?
11. What Buddhist teachings and practices or structures are (or have been) potential obstacles to diversity work?

Do you have any recommendations for other potential research participants? Thank you.

Notes

Introduction

1. See, e.g., David Hochman, "Mindfulness: Getting Its Share of Attention," *New York Times*, November 1, 2013; and Tony Schwartz, "More Mindfulness: Less Meditation," *New York Times*, January 31, 2014.

2. Barry Boyce, ed., *The Mindfulness Revolution* (Boston: Shambhala, 2011).

3. See, e.g., Nancy Thompson, "Dharma Connect: Are Blondes Better Meditators?," The Interdependence Project, January 27, 2014, http://65.75.130.248/blog/nancy-thompson/2014/01/27/dharma-connect-are-blondes-better-meditatorsruntsk.

4. Joanna Piacenza, "*TIME*'s Beautiful, White, Blonde 'Mindfulness Revolution,'" HuffPost, January 29, 2014 (updated December 6, 2017), http://www.huffingtonpost.com/joanna-piacenza/Time mindfulness-revolution_b_4687696.html.

5. See, e.g., David Loy and Ron Purser, "Beyond McMindfulness," HuffPost, July 1, 2013 (updated August 31, 2013), http://www.huffingtonpost.com/ron-purser/beyond-mcmindfulness_b_3519289.html; and Joshua Eaton, "Gentrifying the Dharma: How the 1 Percent Is Hijacking Mindfulness," Salon, March 5, 2014, http://www.salon.com/2014/03/05/gentrifying_the_dharma_how_the_1_is_hijacking_mindfulness/.

6. David L. McMahan, *The Making of Buddhist Modernism* (Oxford: Oxford University Press, 2008).

7. Robert Sharf, "Experience," in *Critical Terms for Religious Studies*, ed. Mark C. Taylor (Chicago: University of Chicago Press, 1998), 94–116; and Robert Sharf, "Losing Our Religion," *Tricycle* (Summer 2007). Donald S. Lopez Jr., *The Scientific Buddha: His Short and Happy Life* (New Haven, CT: Yale University Press, 2012). Joseph Cheah, *Race and Religion in American Buddhism* (Oxford: Oxford University Press, 2011).

8. James William Coleman, *The New Buddhism: The Western Transformation of an Ancient Tradition* (London: Oxford University Press, 2002).

9. Richard Hughes Seager, *Buddhism in America* (New York: Columbia University Press, 2012), 65–71, 211–14.

10. Jay Michaelson, *Evolving Dharma: Meditation, Buddhism and the Next Generation of Enlightenment* (Berkeley, CA: Evolver Editions, 2013).

11. Martin Baumann, "Global Buddhism: Developmental Periods, Regional Histories, and a New Analytic Perspective," *Journal of Global Buddhism* 2 (2001): 1–43, 4.

12. See Paul Numrich, *Old Wisdom in the New World: Americanization in Two Immigrant Theravada Communities* (Knoxville: University of Tennessee Press, 1996); and Charles S. Prebish, "Two Buddhisms Reconsidered," *Buddhist Studies Review* 10, no. 1 (1993): 187–206.

13. See, e.g., Michaelson, *Evolving Dharma*, 10–11.

14. An earlier critique of the lack of distinction among convert communities comes from Jan Nattier, "Who Is a Buddhist? Charting the Landscape of Buddhist America," in *The Faces of Buddhism in America*, ed. Charles Prebish and Kenneth Tanaka (Berkeley: University of California Press, 1998), 188. Another threefold typology is offered in Seager, *Buddhism in America*, 9–11.

15. Cheah, *Race and Religion in American Buddhism*, 5–6.

16. McMahan, *The Making of Buddhist Modernism*, 23.

17. Coleman, *The New Buddhism*, 13–18.

18. E.g., Kenneth Tanaka has shown how the Buddhist Churches of America has adopted many Protestant reforms. Kenneth Tanaka, "Issues of Ethnicity in the Buddhist Churches of America," in *American Buddhism: Methods and Findings in Recent Scholarship*, ed. Duncan Ryuken Williams and Christopher S. Queen (Honolulu: Curzon, 1999), 3–19. Natalie Quli offers an excellent critique of the mapping of modern and traditional to convert and immigrant communities. Natalie E. Quli, "Western Self, Asian Other: Modernity, Authenticity, and Nostalgia for 'Tradition' in Buddhist Studies," *Journal of Buddhist Ethics* 16 (2009), http://blogs.dickinson.edu/buddhistethics/files/2010/05/quli-article.pdf.

19. Colin Campbell, "Modernity and Postmodernity," in *The Blackwell Companion to the Study of Religion*, ed. R. A. Segal (Hoboken, NJ: Wiley-Blackwell, 2006), 309–20.

20. David Lyon, *Jesus in Disneyland: Religion in Postmodern Times* (Cambridge: Polity Press, 2000), 7.

21. Campbell, "Modernity and Postmodernity," 318.

22. Jin Y. Park, *Buddhism and Postmodernity: Zen, Huayen, and the Possibility of a Buddhist Postmodern Ethics* (Lexington, MA: Lexington Press, 2008). Carl Olson, *Zen and the Art of Postmodern Philosophy* (Albany: State University of New York Press, 2000).

23. Lyon, *Jesus in Disneyland*, x–xi, 37.

24. Jean-François Lyotard, *The Postmodern Condition: A Report on Knowledge*, trans. Geoff Bennington and Brian Massumi (Manchester: Manchester University Press, 1986).

25. James K. Smith, "A Little Story About Metanarratives: Lyotard, Religion, and Postmodernism Revisited," *Faith and Philosophy* 13, no. 3 (2001): 354–55.

26. Lyon, *Jesus in Disneyland*, 37–39.

27. Jean Baudrillard, "Simulacra and Simulations," in *Jean Baudrillard, Selected Writings,* ed. Mark Poster (Stanford, CA: Stanford University Press, 1988), 166–84.

28. Pui-Lan Kwok, *Postcolonial Imagination and Feminist Theology* (Louisville, KY: Westminster John Knox, 2005).

29. David Tracy, *On Naming the Present: God, Hermeneutics, and Church* (New York: Orbis, 1994).

30. J. Ranilo B. Hermida, "The Resurgence of Religion in the Advent of Postmodernity," *Logos* 11, no. 4 (2008): 94–110.

31. Lyon, *Jesus in Disneyland,* 105–13; and Mark C. Taylor, "Reframing Postmodernism," in *Shadow of Spirit: Postmodernism and Religion,* ed. Philippa Berry and Andrew Wornick (London: Routledge, 1992).

32. Lyon, *Jesus in Disneyland,* 49; and Paul Heelas, *Religion, Modernity and Postmodernity* (Oxford: Blackwell, 1998), 4–5.

33. Heelas, *Religion, Modernity and Postmodernity,* 4–5.

34. Lynne Hume and Kathleen McPhillips, eds., *Popular Spiritualities: The Politics of Contemporary Enchantment* (Burlington, VT: Ashgate, 2008), xvi–xvii.

35. Lyon, *Jesus in Disneyland,* 136–38.

36. Courtney Bender and Ann Taves, eds., *What Matters? Ethnographies of Value in a Not So Secular Age* (New York: Columbia University Press, 2012).

37. Campbell, "Modernity and Postmodernity," 316–17.

38. George E. Marcus, "Ethnography in/of the World System: The Emergence of Multi-Sited Ethnography," *Annual Review of Anthropology* 24 (1995): 95–117.

39. Mark-Anthony Falzon, ed., *Multi-Sited Ethnography: Theory, Praxis and Locality in Contemporary Research* (London: Routledge, 2009), 7–10.

40. The results of that research are published in Ann Gleig, "Wedding the Personal and Impersonal in West Coast Vipassana," *Journal of Global Buddhism* 13 (2012): 129–46.

41. For example, the founders of Spirit Rock, such as Jack Kornfield and Sylvia Boorstein, have stated that their motivation for establishing the center was to create a wider "dharma stream" that focused on how to integrate meditation practice with daily householder life. This emphasis on integration can be read as a counter to the modernist emphasis on intensive meditative retreat practice that marks the Burmese Theravadin lineages that strongly influenced the structure and ethos of the Insight Meditation Society in Barre, Massachusetts. See Chapter 3 of Ann Gleig, "Enlightenment After the Enlightenment: American Transformations of Asian Contemplative Traditions" (PhD diss., Rice University, 2011).

42. Karen McCarthy Brown, *Mama Lola: A Voodoo Priestess in Brooklyn* (Berkeley: University of California Press, 2001), 13.

43. Ruth Behar, *The Vulnerable Observer: Anthropology That Breaks Your Heart* (Boston: Beacon Press, 1996), 10.

44. Nancy Scheper-Hughes, "The Primacy of the Ethical: Propositions for a Militant Anthropology," in *Anthropology in Theory: Issues in Epistemology,* ed. Henrietta Moore and Todd Sanders (Oxford: Blackwell, 2006), 506–12.

45. Charles S. Prebish, *Luminous Practice: The Practice and Study of Buddhism in America* (Los Angeles: University of California Press, 1999), 180.

46. See, e.g., Sharf, "Losing Our Religion"; Lopez, *The Scientific Buddha;* and Richard Payne, "Individuation and Awakening: Romantic Narrative and the Psychological Interpretation of Buddhism," in *Buddhism and Psychotherapy Across Cultures,* ed. Mark Unno (Somerville, MA: Wisdom, 2006), 31–51.

47. Quli, "Western Self, Asian Other," 1–6.

48. Coleman, *The New Buddhism.*

49. Ann Gleig, "From Theravada to Tantra: The Making of an American Tantric Buddhism," *Contemporary Buddhism: An Interdisciplinary Journal* 14, no. 2 (2013): 221–38.

50. See, e.g., Erik Braun, "BG 319: The Making of a Mass Meditation Movement," Buddhist Geeks, podcast audio, link no longer available; and David L. McMahan, "Episode 72: The Making of Buddhist Modernism," Secular Buddhist Association, podcast audio, July 8, 2011, http://secularbuddhism.org/2011/07/08/episode-72-david-mcmahan-the-making-of-buddhist-modernism/.

51. See, e.g., Linda Heuman, "Context Matters: An Interview with Buddhist Scholar David McMahan," *Tricycle* (Winter 2013), https://tricycle.org/magazine/context-matters/; Linda Heuman, "Pursuing an American Buddhism: An Interview with Charles Prebish," *Tricycle* (Spring 2012): 68–71.

52. Examples of Buddhist scholars who have blogs on contemporary Buddhism include Richard K. Payne, *Critical Reflections on Buddhist Thought: Contemporary and Classical* (blog), http://rkpayne.wordpress.com/reflections-on-buddhist-thought-posts/; and Scott Mitchell, *DJB* (blog), http://www.djbuddha.org. Justin Whitaker blogs at *American Buddhist Perspectives* for Patheos, http://www.patheos.com/blogs/americanbuddhist/.

53. See, e.g., Buddhist scholar Glenn Wallis's critique of contemporary Buddhism and his vitriolic exchanges with Western Buddhist practitioners at Glenn Wallis, *Speculative Non-Buddhism* (blog), http://speculativenonbuddhism.com, accessed March–November 2014.

54. Courtney Bender, *The New Metaphysicals: Spirituality and the American Religious Imagination* (Chicago: Chicago University Press, 2010), 8–12.

ONE   Buddhist Modernism from Asia to America

1. Anagarika Dharmapala, "The World's Debt to Buddhism," in *Asian Religions in America: A Documentary History,* ed. Thomas A. Tweed and Stephen Prothero (Oxford: Oxford University Press, 1998), 133–37.

2. David L. McMahan, *The Making of Buddhist Modernism* (Oxford: Oxford University Press, 2008), 92.

3. Richard Hughes Seager, *Buddhism in America* (New York: Columbia University Press, 1999), 37.

4. Stephen Prothero, *The White Buddhist: The Asian Odyssey of Henry Steel Olcott* (Bloomington: Indiana University Press, 2010).

5. Donald S. Lopez Jr., *A Modern Buddhist Bible: Essential Readings from East and West* (Boston: Beacon, 2002), xi.

6. Martin Baumann, "Global Buddhism: Developmental Periods, Regional Histories, and a New Analytic Perspective," *Journal of Global Buddhism* 2 (2001): 3.

7. George Bond, *The Buddhist Revival in Sri Lanka: Religious Tradition, Reinterpretation and Response* (Columbia: University of South Carolina Press, 1988), 23.

8. Paul Williams, *Buddhist Thought: A Complete Introduction to the Indian Tradition* (New York: Routledge, 2000), 17.

9. Malalgoda quoted in Bond, *The Buddhist Revival in Sri Lanka*, 23.

10. Tambiah in ibid.

11. Williams, *Buddhist Thought*, 12.

12. Bond, *The Buddhist Revival in Sri Lanka*, 24–25.

13. Pali: nibbāna; Sanskrit: nirvāṇa. Throughout this book I use the familiar "Nirvana" for consistency.

14. Michael Ames, "Magical-Animism and Buddhism: A Structural Analysis of the Sinhalese Religious System," *Journal of Asian Studies* 23 (1964): 28.

15. Erik Braun, *The Birth of Insight* (Chicago: University of Chicago Press, 2013); Brooke Schedneck, *Thailand's International Meditation Centers: Tourism and the Global Commodification of Religious Practices* (New York: Routledge, 2015).

16. Heinz Bechert, *Buddhismus, Staat und Geselschaft in den Ländern des Theravāda Buddhismus* (Berlin: Alfred Metzner, 1966).

17. Donald Swearer, *The Buddhist World of South-East Asia* (Albany: State University of New York Press, 1995).

18. David L. McMahan, "Buddhist Modernism," Oxford Bibliographies, last modified March 30, 2015, http://www.oxfordbibliographies.com/view/document/obo-9780195393521/obo-9780195393521-0041.xml.

19. Braun, *The Birth of Insight*, 124.

20. Ibid., 139.

21. Ibid., 127.

22. Ibid., 123.

23. For more details on these Burmese lineages and their relationship to Insight practice in the US, see Braun, *The Birth of Insight*, 155–69.

24. Ibid., 157–59.

25. Vipassana Meditation, http://www.dhamma.org/, accessed August 2, 2016.

26. Braun, *The Birth of Insight*, 161.

27. Ingrid Jordt, *Burma's Mass Lay Meditation Movement: Buddhism and the Cultural Construction of Power* (Athens: Ohio University Press, 2007), 17–24.

28. Ibid., 65.

29. Braun, *The Birth of Insight*, 123.

30. Schedneck, *Thailand's International Meditation Centers*, 10–15.

31. Ibid., 16.

32. Swearer, *The Buddhist World*, 131–32.

33. Schedneck, *Thailand's International Meditation Centers*, 37.

34. Biographical details of Ajahn Chah from "Ajahn Chah Biography," Forest Sangha, https://forestsangha.org/ajahn-chah/biography, accessed January 20, 2017.

35. Peter Jackson, *Buddhadasa: Theravada Buddhism and Modernist Reform in Thailand* (Chiang Mai: Silkworm, 1987), 119–21.

36. Robert H. Sharf, "The Zen of Japanese Nationalism," in *Curators of the Buddha: The Study of Buddhism Under Colonialism*, ed. Donald S. Lopez Jr. (Chicago: University of Chicago Press, 1995), 107.

37. Ibid., 109.

38. Ibid., 112.

39. Ibid., 113.

40. Ibid., 110.

41. Ibid., 124.

42. Ibid., 108.

43. Ibid., 135–42.

44. Donald S. Lopez Jr., ed., *A Modern Buddhist Bible: Essential Readings from East and West* (Boston: Beacon, 2002), xxix.

45. Ibid., xxix–xxxi.

46. For a nuanced analysis of the Dalai Lama's relationship to Buddhist modernism, see Georges B. Dreyfus, "From Protective Deities to International Stardom: An Analysis of the Fourteenth Dalai Lama's Stance Towards Modernity and Buddhism," in *The Dalai Lamas: A Visual History*, ed. Martin Brauen (Chicago: Serinda, 2005), 172–79.

47. Sarah Jacoby and Antonio Terrone, "Tibetan and Himalayan Buddhism," in *Buddhism in the Modern World*, ed. David L. McMahan (New York: Routledge, 2012), 105–6.

48. Ibid., vii–xi.

49. Ibid., xxxii–xxxviii.

50. Ibid., xxxix.

51. McMahan, *The Making of Buddhist Modernism*, 4–6.

52. Ibid., 42.

53. Ibid., 113.

54. Ibid., 51–59.

55. Ibid., 23.

56. Emma Layman, *Buddhism in America* (Chicago: Nelson-Hall, 1976); Charles S. Prebish, *American Buddhism* (North Scituate, MA: Duxbury, 1979).

57. Prebish, *American Buddhism*, 51, quoted in Charles S. Prebish, *Luminous Passage* (Berkeley: University of California Press, 1999), 57.

58. Charles S. Prebish, "Two Buddhisms Reconsidered," *Buddhist Studies Review* 10 (1993): 187–206, quoted in Prebish, *Luminous Passage*, 58.

59. Paul David Numrich, *Old Wisdom in the New World: Americanization in Two Immigrant Theravada Buddhist Temples* (Knoxville: University of Tennessee Press, 1996), 144, quoted in Prebish, *Luminous Passage*, 63.

60. Seager, *Buddhism in America*, 234.

61. Jan Nattier, "Buddhism Comes to Main Street," *Wilson Quarterly* (Spring 1997): 72–80; 75

62. Wakoh Shannon Hickey, "Two Buddhisms, Three Buddhisms, and Racism," in *Buddhism Beyond Borders: New Perspectives on Buddhism in the United States,* ed. Scott A. Mitchell and Natalie E. F. Quli (Albany: State University of New York Press, 2015), 44–46.

63. Chenxing Han, "Diverse Practices and Flexible Beliefs Amongst Young Adult Asian American Buddhists," *Journal of Global Buddhism* 18 (2017): 1–24.

64. Natalie Quli, "Western Self, Asian Other: Modernity, Authenticity, and Nostalgia for 'Tradition' in Buddhist Studies," *Journal of Buddhist Ethics* 16 (2009): 18.

65. For a comparison of modernist traits in Buddhist Churches of America associated with Zen converts and with immigrants, see Scott A. Mitchell and Natalie E. F. Quli, "Buddhist Modernism as Narrative," in *Buddhism Beyond Borders,* ed. Mitchell and Quli, 197–215.

66. Layman, *Buddhism in America,* xiii, xvi.

67. Rick Fields, *How the Swans Came to the Lake: A Narrative History of Buddhism in America,* 3rd ed. (Boston: Shambhala, 1992), 379.

68. Rick Fields, "Divided Dharma: White Buddhists, Ethnic Buddhists and Racism," in *The Faces of Buddhism in America,* ed. Charles S. Prebish and Kenneth Tanaka (Berkeley: University of California Press, 1998), 197.

69. Ibid., 204.

70. Ibid., 202.

71. Prebish, *Luminous Passage,* 55.

72. Ibid., 57.

73. Helen Tworkov, "Many Is More," *Tricycle* 1, no. 2 (Winter 1991): 4, quoted in Prebish, *Luminous Passage,* 57.

74. Pointed out by Kenneth Tanaka, "Epilogue: The Colors and Contours of American Buddhism," in *The Faces of Buddhism in America,* ed. Prebish and Tanaka, 288, quoted in Prebish, *Luminous Passage,* 57.

75. Prebish, *Luminous Passage,* 63.

76. Ibid., 66.

77. Ibid., 69–81.

78. Ibid., 81–85.

79. Lenore Friedman, *Meetings with Remarkable Women: Buddhist Teachers in America* (Boston: Shambhala, 1987), 33–34, quoted in Prebish, *Luminous Passage,* 88.

80. Victor Sogen Hori, "Sweet-and-Sour Buddhism," *Tricycle* (Fall 1994): 48–52.

81. Seager, *Buddhism in America,* 235.

82. Ibid., 234.

83. For further ethnographic work on American convert Buddhism, see David L. Preston's comparative study of two American Zen groups in Southern California in the late 1980s (*The Social Organization of Zen: Constructing Transcultural Reality* [Cambridge: Cambridge University Press, 1988]), Daniel Capper's examination of Tibetan Buddhism in the US (*Guru Devotion and the American Buddhist Experience,* Studies

in Religion and Society, Vol. 57 [Lewiston, NY: Edwin Mellen Press, 2002]), and Franz Metcalf's study of the Zen Center of Los Angeles ("Why Do Americans Practice Zen Buddhism?" [PhD diss., University of Chicago, 1997]).

84. James William Coleman, *The New Buddhism: The Western Transformation of An Ancient Tradition* (New York: Oxford University Press, 2002), 13–18.

85. Ibid., 218.

86. Ibid., 20–21.

87. Ibid., 54.

88. Quli, "Western Self, Asian Other," 18.

89. Coleman, *The New Buddhism*, 5.

90. Ibid., 8.

91. Wendy Cadge, *Heartwood: The First Generation of Theravada Buddhism in America* (Chicago: University of Chicago Press, 2005), 190–97.

92. Ibid., 197.

93. Ibid., 201.

94. Joseph Cheah, *Race and Religion in American Buddhism* (New York: Oxford University Press, 2011), 1–5.

95. Lori Ann Pierce, "Constructing American Buddhisms: Discourses of Race and Religion in Territorial Hawai'i" (PhD diss., University of Hawai'i, 2000), 6, quoted in Cheah, *Race and Religion*, 3.

96. bell hooks, "Waking Up to Racism," *Tricycle* 4, no. 1 (Fall 1994), quoted in Cheah, *Race and Religion*, 5.

97. Michael Omni and Howard Winant, *Racial Formation in the United States: From the 1960s to the 1990s*, 2nd ed. (New York: Routledge, 1994), 163 n.8, 195 n.11.

98. Cheah, *Race and Religion*, 60.

99. Ibid., 59–60.

100. Ibid., 32.

101. Hickey, "Two Buddhisms," 45.

102. Daniel Goleman, *Inquiring Mind* 2, no. 1 (Summer 1985): 7, quoted in Cheah, *Race and Religion*, 71.

103. Cheah, *Race and Religion*, 129.

104. Ibid., 130.

105. Mitchell and Quli, *Buddhism Beyond Borders*, vii.

106. Jay Michaelson, *Evolving Dharma: Meditation, Buddhism and the Next Generation of Enlightenment* (Berkeley: Evolver, 2013), 53.

107. Ann Gleig, "Dharma Diversity and Deep Inclusivity at the East Bay Meditation Center: From Buddhist Modernism to Buddhist Postmodernism?," *Contemporary Buddhism: An Interdisciplinary Journal* 15, no. 2 (2014): 312–31.

108. McMahan, *The Making of Buddhist Modernism*, 265.

TWO   From the Mindfulness Revolution to the Mindfulness Wars

1. Amanda Ream, "Why I Disrupted the Wisdom 2.0 Conference," *Tricycle*, February 19, 2014, http://tricycle.org/trikedaily/why-i-disrupted-wisdom-20-conference/.

2. "Wisdom 2.0 2014: Google Handles Protesters with Mindfulness and Compassion," Wisdom 2.0, http://wisdom2conference.tumblr.com/post/76757167725/wisdom-20-2014-google-handles-protesters-with, accessed September 15, 2016.

3. Barry Boyce, *The Mindfulness Revolution: Leading Psychologists, Scientists, Artists and Meditation Teachers on the Power of Mindfulness in Daily Life* (Boston: Shambhala, 2011), xii.

4. Norman Fischer, "Mindfulness for Everyone," in *The Mindfulness Revolution*, ed. Boyce, 49–56, 50.

5. Jeff Wilson, *Mindful America: The Mutual Transformation of Buddhist Meditation and American Culture* (Oxford: Oxford University Press, 2014), 9.

6. Ibid., 31–42.

7. Kornfield quoted in Gil Fronsdal, "Life, Liberty and the Pursuit of Happiness in the American Insight Community," in *The Faces of Buddhism in America*, ed. Charles S. Prebish and Kenneth K. Tanaka (Los Angeles: University of California Press, 1998), 167.

8. Ann Gleig, "Wedding the Personal and Impersonal in West Coast Vipassana: A Dialogical Encounter Between Buddhism and Psychotherapy," *Journal of Global Buddhism* 13 (2012): 129–46.

9. Jo Confino, "Thich Nhat Hanh: Is Mindfulness Being Corrupted by Business and Finance?" *Guardian*, March 28, 2014, https://www.theguardian.com/sustainable-business/thich-nhat-hanh-mindfulness-google-tech.

10. Mary Sykes Wylie, "How the Mindfulness Movement Went Mainstream and the Backlash That Came with It," AlterNet, January 29, 2015, http://www.alternet.org/personal-health/how-mindfulness-movement-went-mainstream-and-backlash-came-it.

11. Jeff Wilson, *Mindful America: The Mutual Transformation of Buddhist Meditation and American Culture* (Oxford: Oxford University Press, 2014), 42.

12. Alice Robb, "How 2014 Became the Year of Mindfulness," *New Republic*, December 31, 2014, https://newrepublic.com/article/120669/2014-year-mindfulness-religion-rich.

13. Brigid Delaney, "If 2014 Was the Year of Mindfulness, 2015 Was the Year of Fruitlessly Trying to Debunk It," *Guardian*, October 18, 2015, https://www.theguardian.com/commentisfree/2015/oct/19/if-2014-was-the-year-of-mindfulness-2015-was-the-year-of-fruitlessly-trying-to-debunk-it.

14. Justin Whitaker, "Mindfulness: Critics and Defenders," Patheos, *American Buddhist Perspectives* (blog), December 21, 2013, http://www.patheos.com/blogs/americanbuddhist/2013/12/2013-as-the-year-of-mindfulness-critics-and-defenders.html.

15. Per Drougge, "Notes Towards a Coming Backlash: Mindfulness as an Opiate of the Middle Class," *Speculative Non-Buddhism* (blog), March 4, 2016, https://specu

lativenonbuddhism.com/2016/03/04/notes-towards-a-coming-backlash-mindfulne-as
-an-opium-of-the-middle-classes/.

16. B. Alan Wallace and Bhikkhu Bodhi, "The Nature of Mindfulness and Its Role
in Buddhist Meditation: A Correspondence Between B. Alan Wallace and the Venerable
Bhikkhu Bodhi," International Shamatha Project, 2006, http://shamatha.org/sites/
default/files/Bhikkhu_Bodhi_Correspondence.pdf; B. Alan Wallace, "A Mindful Balance," *Tricycle* (Spring 2008), https://tricycle.org/magazine/mindful-balance-0/.

17. Wallace and Bodhi, "The Nature of Mindfulness," 14.

18. Danny Fisher, "Frozen Yoga and McMindfulness: Miles Neale on the Mainstreaming of Contemplative Religious Practices," *Lion's Roar*, December 15, 2010,
http://www.lionsroar.com/frozen-yoga-and-mcmindfulness-miles-neale-on-the-main
streaming-of-contemplative-religious-practices/.

19. David Loy and Ron Purser, "Beyond McMindfulness," HuffPost, July 1,
2013 (updated August 31, 2013), http://www.huffingtonpost.com/ron-purser/beyond
-mcmindfulness_b_3519289.html.

20. Thanissaro Bhikkhu, *Right Mindfulness: Memory and Ardency on the Buddhist
Path*, 2012, available at Access to Insight, http://www.accesstoinsight.org/lib/authors/
thanissaro/rightmindfulness.pdf.

21. Michael Stone, "Abusing the Buddha: How the U.S. Army and Google Co-
Opt Mindfulness," *Salon*, March 17, 2014, http://www.salon.com/2014/03/17/abusing
_the_buddha_how_the_u_s_army_and_google_co_opt_mindfulness/.

22. Robert Sharf, "Is Mindfulness Buddhist? (And Why It Matters)," *Transcultural
Psychiatry* 52, no. 4 (2015): 479. See also Robert Sharf, "Mindfulness and Mindlessness in
Early Chan," *Philosophy East and West* 64, no. 4 (October 2014): 933–64.

23. Slavoj Žižek, "From Western Marxism to Western Buddhism," *Cabinet Magazine* 2 (2001), http://www.cabinetmagazine.org/issues/2/western.php.

24. Edwin Ng and Ronald Purser, "Corporate Mindfulness Is Bullsh*t: Zen
or No Zen, You're Working Harder and Being Paid Less," *Salon*, September 27, 2015,
http://www.salon.com/2015/09/27/corporate_mindfulness_is_bullsht_zen_or_no_zen
_youre_working_harder_and_being_paid_less/.

25. See, e.g., Linda Heuman, "Don't Believe the Hype," *Tricycle*, October 11, 2014,
and Linda Heuman, "A New Way Forward," *Tricycle* (Spring 2015).

26. Andrew Cooper and Ron Purser, "Mindfulness' Truthiness Problem: Sam
Harris, Science and the Truth About Buddhist Tradition," *Salon*, December 6, 2014,
http://www.salon.com/2014/12/06/mindfulness_truthiness_problem_sam_harris
_science_and_the_truth_about_buddhist_tradition/.

27. Edwin Ng and Ron Purser, "White Privilege and the Mindfulness Movement,"
Buddhist Peace Fellowship, October 2, 2015, http://www.buddhistpeacefellowship.org/
white-privilege-the-mindfulness-movement/.

28. Edo Shonin and Jon Kabat-Zinn, "This Is Not McMindfulness by Any Stretch
of the Imagination," *Psychologist*, May 18, 2015, https://thepsychologist.bps.org.uk/not
-mcmindfulness-any-stretch-imagination.

29. Barry Boyce, "It's Not McMindfulness," *Mindful,* September 12, 2015, http://www.mindful.org/its-not-mcmindfulness/.

30. Lion's Roar Staff, "Forum: What Does Mindfulness Mean for Buddhism?" *Lion's Roar,* May 5, 2015, http://www.lionsroar.com/forum-what-does-mindfulness-mean-for-buddhism/.

31. All quotations from ibid.

32. Lynette M. Monteiro, R. F. Musten, and Jane Compson, "Traditional and Contemporary Mindfulness: Finding the Middle Path in the Tangle of Concerns," *Mindfulness* 6, no. 1 (2015): 1–13.

33. Ajahn Amaro, "A Holistic Mindfulness," *Mindfulness* 6, no. 1 (2015): 63–73.

34. Doug Smith, "On Some Criticisms of Modern Mindfulness," Secular Buddhist Association, May 16, 2016, http://secularbuddhism.org/2016/05/16/on-some-criticisms-of-modern-mindfulness/.

35. John Dunne, "Toward an Understanding of Non-Dual Mindfulness," *Contemporary Buddhism: An Interdisciplinary Journal* 12, no. 1 (2011): 71–88.

36. Rod Meade Sperry, "Mindfulness: It's All Good," *Lion's Roar,* July 29, 2016, https://www.lionsroar.com/mindfulness-its-all-good/.

37. Seth Zuiho Segall, "The Politics of Mindfulness," *Existential Buddhist: Dharma Without Dogma* (blog), April 23, 2015, http://www.existentialbuddhist.com/2015/04/the-politics-of-mindfulness/.

38. C. Pierce Salguero, "Translating Meditation in Popular American Culture," Patheos, March 2, 2014, http://www.patheos.com/blogs/americanbuddhist/2014/03/translating-meditation-in-popular-american-media.html.

39. Jeff Wilson and Wendy Joan Biddlecombe, "On Mindfulness: Two New Perspectives," *Tricycle* (Fall 2016), https://tricycle.org/magazine/the-religion-mindfulness-essay-jeff-wilson/.

40. Emma Varvaloucas, "An Interview with Chris McKenna," *Tricycle* (Spring 2014), https://tricycle.org/magazine/interview-chris-mckenna/.

41. Seth Zuiho Segall, "In Defense of Mindfulness," *Existential Buddhist: Dharma Without Dogma* (blog), December 19, 2013, http://www.existentialbuddhist.com/2013/12/in-defense-of-mindfulness/.

42. Mark Knickelbine, interview with the author, September 22, 2016.

43. Ted Meissner, interview with the author, September 22, 2016.

44. Knickelbine interview.

45. Sperry, "Mindfulness: It's All Good."

46. Sharf, "Is Mindfulness Buddhist?"

47. For details about my interviews with Gen X Buddhist teachers, see chapter 7 and the appendix.

48. Knickelbine interview.

49. Meissner interview.

50. "Working with Mindfulness: An Interview with Mirabai Bush," *Tricycle,* October 10, 2012, https://tricycle.org/trikedaily/working-mindfulness-interview-mirabai-bush/.

51. Trudy Goodman, "BG 331: Stealth Buddhism," Buddhist Geeks, podcast audio, 2014, accessed September 20, 2016, link no longer available.

52. Ajahn Sujato, "Mindfulness Is What It Is," *Sujato's Blog* (blog), August 7, 2014, https://sujato.wordpress.com/2014/08/07/mindfulness-is-what-it-is/.

53. Segall, "The Politics of Mindfulness."

54. Phillip Moffitt, "The Mindfulness of the Buddha," *Tricycle,* May 24, 2016, https://tricycle.org/trikedaily/the-mindfulness-of-the-buddha/; Danny Fisher and Joseph Goldstein, "Uncovering the Meaning of Mindfulness: A Conversation with Joseph Goldstein," *Lion's Roar,* August 29, 2016, https://www.lionsroar.com/uncovering-the-meaning-of-mindfulness-joseph-goldstein-in-conversation-with-danny-fisher/.

55. Fleet Maull and angel Kyodo williams, "Beyond Mindfulness: Explore Mindfulness as a Path to Wisdom and Transformation," conference topic, Shambhala Mountain Online, May 13–17, 2015.

56. Diana Winston, "The 12 Myths of the Mindfulness Movement," Dharma Seed, podcast audio, June 27, 2014, http://dharmaseed.org/teacher/53/.

57. Vince Horn, personal correspondence with the author, December 12, 2016.

58. Maia Duerr, "Towards a Socially Responsible Mindfulness," *World We Live In* (blog), May 16, 2015, http://maiaduerr.com/toward-a-socially-responsible-mindfulness/.

59. Bhikkhu Bodhi, "Conscientious Compassion: Why Mindfulness Alone Is Not Enough," presentation for "Beyond Mindfulness" conference, Shambhala Mountain Online, May 13–17, 2015.

60. Bhikkhu Bodhi, *The Buddha's Teachings on Social and Communal Harmony: An Anthology of Discourses from the Pali Canon* (Somerville, MA: Wisdom, 2016).

61. Ruth King, "Mindful of Race Training: A Stimulus for Social Healing and Leadership," RuthKing.net, http://ruthking.net/mindful-of-race-2/, accessed September 21, 2016.

62. Mushim Patricia Ikeda, comment on Justin Whitaker, "On Modern Mindfulness, Buddhism and Social Ethics," Patheos, *American Buddhist Perspectives*, May 24, 2016, http://www.patheos.com/blogs/americanbuddhist/2016/05/on-modern-mindfulness-buddhism-and-social-ethics.html.

63. Jessica Morey, interview with the author, May 26, 2015.

64. Ted Meissner, "Episode 229: Dave Smith: Ethical Mindfulness," Secular Buddhist Association, podcast audio, August 13, 2015, http://secularbuddhism.org/2015/08/13/episode-229-dave-smith-ethical-mindfulness/.

65. Dave Smith, *Ethical Mindfulness* (Las Vegas: Central Recovery Press, 2015).

66. Lama Karma Justin Wall, interview with the author, September 21, 2016.

67. "Open Mindfulness," Altruistic Open Mindfulness, http://www.openmindfulness.net/en/, accessed September 21, 2016.

68. Lisa Dale Miller, *Effortless Mindfulness: Genuine Mental Health Through Awakened Presence* (London: Routledge, 2014), and Lisa Dale Miller, "Universal Dharma . . . Not," Dharma Wisdom, July 2014, http://dharmawisdom.org/blogs/psychology-and-buddhism/universal-dharma-not-dharma-talks-available-now.

69. Robert Meikyo Rosenbaum and Barry Magid, eds., *What's Wrong with Mindfulness (And What Isn't): Zen Perspectives* (Somerville, MA: Wisdom, 2016), 4.

70. Barry Magid and Marc R. Poirier, "The Three Shaky Pillars of Western Buddhism," in ibid., 41–42.

71. Marc. R. Poirier, "Mischief in the Marketplace," in *What's Wrong with Mindfulness*, ed. Rosenbaum and Magid, 21.

72. Martin Aylward, interview with the author, July 23, 2016.

73. Morey interview.

74. Craig Hase, personal correspondence with the author, May 26, 2016.

75. Megan Cowan, interview with the author, March 2, 2015.

76. Caverly Morgan, interview with the author, July 7, 2017.

77. David L. McMahan, *The Making of Buddhist Modernism* (Oxford: Oxford University Press, 2008), 51–59.

78. Bhikkhu Bodhi, quoted in Duerr, "Towards a Socially Responsible Mindfulness."

79. Linda Heuman, "The Science Delusion: An Interview with Cultural Critic Curtis White," *Tricycle* (Spring 2014), https://tricycle.org/magazine/science-delusion/.

80. Linda Heuman, "The Embodied Mind: An Interview with Philosopher Evan Thompson," *Tricycle* (Fall 2014), https://tricycle.org/magazine/embodied-mind/.

81. Willoughby Britton, "Mindful Binge Drinking and Blobology: The Promises and Perils of Contemplative Neuroscience," presentation at the Buddhist Geeks conference 2012, University of Colorado, Boulder, August 9–11, 2012.

82. Bhikkhu Bodhi, "Sati Center: Compassionate Vision, Conscientious Action, with Ven. Bhikkhu Bodhi," Benefit for Buddhist Global Relief, October 30, 2010, Insight Meditation Center, http://www.insightmeditationcenter.org/2010/09/compassionate-vision-conscientious-action-with-ven-bhikkhu-bodhi/.

THREE   Sex, Scandal, and the Shadow of the Roshi

1. Shinge Chayat, Lama Palden, Pamela Rubin, Alan Senauke, and David Whitehorn, "Confronting Abuse of Power," Forum, *Buddhadharma: The Practitioner's Quarterly Magazine* (Winter 2014): 46–81, 47.

2. Rob Preece, "Our Teachers Are Not Gods," *Buddhadharma: The Practitioner's Quarterly Magazine* (Winter 2014): 43–45.

3. Grace Schireson, "Zen Teachers Issue Open Letter on Abuse," *Lion's Roar,* January 13, 2015, http://www.lionsroar.com/openletteronabuse/.

4. Grace Schireson, "A Zen Woman's Personal Perspective on Sexual Groping, Sexual Harassment, and Other Abuses in Zen Centers," Sweeping Zen, Blogs, November 21, 2012, http://sweepingzen.com/a-zen-womans-personal-perspective-on-sexual-groping-sexual-harassment-and-other-abuses-in-zen-centers/.

5. David L. McMahan, *The Making of Buddhist Modernism* (Oxford: Oxford University Press, 2008), 51–59.

6. Thanissaro Bhikkhu, "Romancing the Buddha," *Tricycle* (Winter 2002), http://www.tricycle.com/feature/romancing-buddha).

7. Stephen Butterfield, *The Double Mirror: A Skeptical Journey into Buddhist Tantra* (Berkeley: North Atlantic, 1994).

8. Kathy Butler, "Encountering the Shadow in Buddhist America," in *Meeting the Shadow: The Hidden Power of the Dark Side of Human Nature*, ed. Connie Zweig and Jeremiah Abrams (New York: Jeremy P. Tarcher/Putnam, 2001), 137–47.

9. June Campbell, "The Emperor's Tantric Robes," *Tricycle* (Winter 1996), http://www.tricycle.com/interview/the-emperors-tantric-robes.

10. Mary Finnigan, "Lama Sex Abuse Claims Calls Buddhist Taboos into Question," *Guardian*, July 1, 2011, http://www.theguardian.com/commentisfree/belief/2011/jul/01/lama-sex-abuse-sogyal-rinpoche-buddhist.

11. Scott Carney, *A Death on Diamond Mountain: A True Story of Death, Madness and the Path to Enlightenment* (New York: Gotham, 2015).

12. Michael Downing, *Shoes Outside the Door: Desire, Devotion and Excess at San Francisco Zen Center* (Berkeley: Counterpoint, 2002).

13. James William Coleman, *The New Buddhism: The Western Transformation of an Ancient Tradition* (London: Oxford University Press, 2002), 168–69.

14. James Ford, "Zen Teachers Respond to the Genpo Merzel Scandal," Patheos, *Monkey Mind* (blog), February 16, 2011, http://www.patheos.com/blogs/monkey mind/2011/02/zen-teachers-respond-to-the-genpo-merzel-scandal.html.

15. Mark Oppenheimer, *The Zen Predator of the Upper East Side*, Kindle ed. (Boston: The Atlantic Books, 2013).

16. Mark Oppenheimer, "Zen Buddhists Roiled by Accusations Against Teacher," *New York Times*, February 11, 2013, http://www.nytimes.com/2013/02/12/world/asia/zen-buddhists-roiled-by-accusations-against-teacher.html.

17. Stephanie Kaza, "Finding Safe Harbor: Buddhist Sexual Ethics in America," *Buddhist Christian Studies* 24 (2004): 23–35.

18. "An Olive Branch," Zen Center of Pittsburgh, http://an-olive-branch.org, accessed March 27, 2015.

19. Scott Edelstein, *Sex and the Spiritual Teacher: Why It Happens, When It's a Problem and What We Can All Do* (Boston: Wisdom, 2011).

20. Schireson, "Zen Teachers Issue Open Letter on Abuse."

21. Grace Schireson, "Combating Zen Zombies," Sweeping Zen, Blogs, April 2, 2015, http://sweepingzen.com/combating-zen-zombies/.

22. Empty Nest Zen Group: Zen Meditation Groups in the California Central Valley, http://emptynestzendo.org, accessed March 12, 2018.

23. Grace Schireson, "Education for Zen Students on Misconduct in Sanghas: Studying Personal, Interpersonal and Transpersonal Levels," Sweeping Zen, Blogs, February 21, 2011, http://sweepingzen.com/education-for-zen-students-on-misconduct-in-sanghas-studying-personal-interpersonal-and-transpersonal-levels/.

24. Grace Schireson, "How the West Won Creating Healthier Zen Sanghas,"

Sweeping Zen, Blogs, March 1, 2013, http://sweepingzen.com/how-the-west-won -creating-healthier-zen-sanghas/.

25. Grace Schireson, personal correspondence with the author, October 17, 2014.

26. Schireson, "How the West Won."

27. John Welwood, *Toward a Psychology of Awakening: Buddhism, Psychotherapy, and the Path of Personal and Spiritual Transformation* (Boston: Shambhala, 2002).

28. Grace Schireson, "Those Misbehaving Zen Monks," Sweeping Zen, Blogs, August 24, 2012, http://sweepingzen.com/those-misbehaving-zen-monks/.

29. Ibid.

30. All quotations from Schireson, "A Zen Woman's Personal Perspective."

31. Grace Schireson, "Blaming Dharma Transmission Is Like Blaming a Driver's License for an Accident," Sweeping Zen, Blogs, February 10, 2011, http://sweepingzen.com/ blaming-dharma-transmission-is-like-blaming-a-drivers-license-for-an-accident/.

32. Grace Schireson, "Zen Centers, Sexual Liaisons, and Delusion: One Stop Shopping?," Sweeping Zen, Blogs, December 8, 2012, http://sweepingzen.com/zen-centers -sexual-liaisons-and-delusion/.

33. Grace Schireson, "Zen Training in the Wild West," Sweeping Zen, Blogs, February 15, 2014, http://sweepingzen.com/zen-training-in-the-wild-west/.

34. While this book was being written, the SPOT program ended. Schireson explained that this was "mostly due to the death of two faculty and the difficulty of running a retreat center in the mountains as I was ageing." Grace Schireson, personal correspondence with the author, November 9, 2017.

35. Shogaku Zen Institute website, accessed January 17, 2015, no longer available. See previous note.

36. Grace Schireson, personal correspondence with the author, October 29, 2014.

37. Ibid.

38. Ibid.

39. Schireson, "Combatting Zen Zombies."

40. Grace Schireson, personal correspondence with the author, April 21, 2015.

41. Schireson, "Those Misbehaving Zen Monks."

42. Barry Magid, *Nothing Is Hidden: The Psychology of Zen Koans* (Somerville, MA: Wisdom, 2013), 3.

43. Ordinary Mind Zendo, http://www.ordinarymind.com, accessed March 10, 2015.

44. Barry Magid, *Ordinary Mind: Exploring the Common Ground of Zen and Psychotherapy* (Somerville, MA: Wisdom, 2002), 8.

45. Amy Goss, "Life's Not a Problem: An Interview with Charlotte Joko Beck," *Tricycle* (Summer 1998), https://tricycle.org/magazine/lifes-not-a-problem/.

46. Charlotte Joko Beck, Foreword, in Magid, *Ordinary Mind*, x.

47. Charlotte Joko Beck, *Everyday Zen: Love and Work* (New York: Harper & Row, 1989).

48. "Charlotte Joko Beck," Ordinary Mind Zendo, http://www.ordinarymind.com/charlotte-joko-beck, accessed March 10, 2015.

49. Magid, *Ordinary Mind*, 8. Italics mine.

50. Magid, *Nothing Is Hidden*, 25.

51. Magid, *Ordinary Mind*, 64-65.

52. Barry Magid, *Ending the Pursuit of Happiness: A Zen Guide* (Somerville, MA: Wisdom, 2008), 17-18.

53. Magid, *Nothing Is Hidden*, 59.

54. Magid, *Ordinary Mind*, 151.

55. Ibid., 15-23.

56. Barry Magid, "There Is No Zen, Only Zen Teachers," Sweeping Zen, February 25, 2011, http://sweepingzen.com/there-is-no-zen-only-zen-teachers/, and Magid, *Nothing Is Hidden*, 38-39.

57. Magid, *Ending the Pursuit of Happiness*, 41.

58. Kestrel Slocombe, "Everyone Comes to Meditation Practice for the Wrong Reason: A Conversation with Psychoanalyst Barry Magid," Wisdom Publications, "The Wisdom Blog: Classic & Contemporary Buddhism," March 3, 2014, https://www.wisdompubs.org/blog/201403/everyone-comes-meditation-practice-wrong-reason-conversation-psychoanalyst-barry-magid.

59. Magid, *Ordinary Mind*, 106.

60. Magid, *Nothing Is Hidden*, 113-16.

61. Magid, *Ending the Pursuit of Happiness*, 30-32.

62. "About Ordinary Mind Zendo," Ordinary Mind Zendo, http://www.ordinarymind.com/about-ordinary-mind-zendo, accessed April 20, 2015.

63. Magid, *Ending the Pursuit of Happiness*, 15-16.

64. Kelly Sosan Bearer, "Getting a Handle on Scandal," presentation at the Buddhist Geeks conference 2013, University of Colorado, Boulder, August 16-18, 2013.

65. Two Arrows Zen, Boulder Mountain Zendo, http://twoarrowszen.org, accessed March 3, 2015.

66. Dennis Genpo Merzel, "Introducing Big Mind," *Tricycle* (Winter 2008), https://tricycle.org/magazine/introducing-big-mind.

67. Dosho Port, "Les Kaye Letter to Kanzeon Board re: Genpo and AZTA History," Patheos, *Wild Fox Zen* (blog), February 14, 2011, http://www.patheos.com/blogs/wildfoxzen/2011/02/les-kaye-letter-to-kanzeon-board-re-genpo-and-azta-history.html.

68. Ford, "Zen Teachers Respond."

69. A copy of this can be found at Alan Senauke, "The Cloud of Knowing & Not Knowing: Sex, Power and the Sangha," *Clear View Blog* (blog), February 23, 2011, http://clearviewblog.org/2011/02/23/the-cloud-of-knowing-not-knowing-sex-power-and-sangha/.

70. Michael Zimmerman, "Ameland Reflection I—The Elements of a Healthy Sangha," *Mugaku Sensei's Blog* (blog), January 28, 2011, http://mugaku-sensei.blogspot.com/2011/01/reflection-about-sangha-from-ameland.html.

71. Nicolee Jikyo McMahon, *Student and Teacher: A Zen Perspective* (Del Mar, CA: Three Treasures Zen Community, 2001), http://ttzc.org/docs/student-teacher.pdf.

72. Michael Zimmerman, "The Last Word from the White Plum Asanga—Addressing Shadow in Lineage," *Mugaku Sensei's Blog* (blog), June 10, 2011, http://mugaku-sensei.blogspot.com/2011_06_01_archive.html.

73. Michael Zimmerman, "Ameland Reflection III—The Role of Individual Practice in Healthy Sangha," *Mugaku Sensei's Blog* (blog), January 31, 2011, http://mugaku-sensei.blogspot.com/2011_01_01_archive.html.

74. Zimmerman, "The Last Word."

75. Ken Wilber, *Integral Spirituality: A Startling New Role for Religion in the Modern and Postmodern World* (Boston: Shambhala, 2007), 42–49.

76. Ibid., 88–98.

77. Diane Musho Hamilton, *Everything Is Workable: A Zen Approach to Conflict Resolution* (Boston: Shambhala, 2014), 74.

78. Robert Augustus Masters and Ken Wilber, "Knowing Your Shadow: Healing the Broken Self," Integral Life, October 21, 2013, https://www.integrallife.com/ken-wilber-dialogues/knowing-your-shadow-healing-broken-self.

79. Diane Musho Hamilton, "Shadow," Two Arrows Zen, May 9, 2014, http://twoarrowszen.org/dharma-talk/shadow.

80. Diane Musho Hamilton, "BG 168: Integral Zen," Buddhist Geeks, podcast audio, accessed March 13, 2015, link no longer available.

81. William B. Parsons, "Psychoanalysis Meets Buddhism: The Development of a Dialogue," in *Changing the Scientific Study of Religion: Beyond Freud?*, ed. Jacob A. van Belzen (New York: Springer, 2009), 179–209.

82. Magid, *Ordinary Mind*, 7–8. The same feminization is seen in psychotherapeutic approaches within the American Insight Community. See Ann Gleig, "Wedding the Personal and Impersonal in West Coast Vipassana: A Dialogical Encounter Between Buddhism and Psychotherapy," *Journal of Global Buddhism* 13 (2012): 34–35.

83. Joan Halifax, "Why Buddhism? Violations of Trust in the Sexual Sphere," Upaya Zen Center, January 2, 2011, https://www.upaya.org/2011/01/why-buddhism-violations-of-trust-in-the-sexual-sphere-roshi-joan-halifax/.

84. G. E. Stinson, "A Response to Barry Magid's Article on sweepingzen.com," Sweeping Zen, February 28, 2011, http://sweepingzen.com/there-is-no-zen-only-zen-teachers/.

85. Adam Tebbe, personal correspondence with the author, November 3, 2014.

86. Adam Tebbe, "An Interview with Shinge Roko Sherry Chayat," Sweeping Zen, February 29, 2012, http://sweepingzen.com/shinge-roko-sherry-chayat-interview/.

87. Jay Michaelson, "The Shocking Scandal at the Heart of American Zen," Daily Beast, November 13, 2014, http://www.thedailybeast.com/articles/2013/11/14/the-shocking-scandal-at-the-heart-of-american-zen.html.

88. "Sex, Gender, Power: The Study Guide," Buddhist Peace Fellowship, July 1, 2013, http://www.buddhistpeacefellowship.org/sex-gender-power-the-study-guide/. Also see

Brad Warner, *Sex, Sin and Zen: A Buddhist Exploration of Sex from Celibacy to Polyamory and Everything in Between* (Novato, CA: New World Library, 2010).

89. "Sex and the Sangha: Out of Touch," *Smiling Buddha Cabaret* (blog), March 30, 2011, https://enlightenmentward.wordpress.com/2011/03/30/sex-and-the-sangha-out-of -touch.

90. Brad Warner, "On Grace Shireson's Open Letter," Hardcore Zen, January 16, 2015, http://hardcorezen.info/on-grace-schiresons-open-letter/3261.

91. Jun Po Kelly Roshi, "In Defense of Promiscuity," Integral Life, February 7, 2011, https://www.integrallife.com/integral-post/defense-promiscuity.

92. William B. Parsons and Diane Jonte-Pace, Introduction, *Religion and Psychology: Mapping the Terrain,* ed. William B. Parsons and Diane Jonte-Pace (London: Routledge, 2001), 1–29.

93. McMahan, *The Making of Buddhist Modernism,* 51–59.

94. Richard Payne, "Individuation and Awakening: Romantic Narrative and the Psychological Interpretation of Buddhism," in *Buddhism and Psychotherapy Across Cultures,* ed. Mark Unno (Somerville, MA: Wisdom, 2006), 31–51.

95. Thanissaro Bhikkhu, "Romancing the Buddha."

96. Noah Levine, *Refuge Recovery: A Buddhist Path to Recovering from Addiction* (San Francisco: HarperOne, 2014).

97. Gleig, "Wedding the Personal and Impersonal."

98. Parsons, "Psychoanalysis Meets Buddhism."

99. Jeffery Rubin, *Psychotherapy and Buddhism* (New York: Plenum, 1996); Harvey Aronson, *Buddhist Practice on Western Ground* (Boston: Shambhala 2004). Other examples of a dialogical approach include Joseph Bobrow, *Zen and Psychotherapy: Partners in Liberation* (New York: W. W. Norton, 2010); Daijaku Kinst, *Trust, Realization and Self in Soto Zen Practice* (Honolulu: University of Hawaii Press, 2015); and Franz Metcalf, "An Object-Relations Psychology of Zen Practice," in *Buddhist Studies from India to America: Essays in Honor of Charles S. Prebish,* ed. Damien Keown (London: Routledge, 2010), 191–206.

100. David Loy, *A New Buddhist Path: Enlightenment, Evolution and Ethics in the Modern World* (Boston: Wisdom, 2014), 26–33.

101. Robert Sharf, "Experience," in *Critical Terms for Religious Studies,* ed. Mark C. Taylor (Chicago: University of Chicago Press, 1998), 4.

FOUR   Meditation and Awakening in the
American Vipassana Network

1. Dharma Overground, http://www.dharmaoverground.org, accessed multiple time January–April 2016.

2. Daniel Ingram, *Mastering the Core Teachings of the Buddha: An Unusually Hardcore Dharma Book* (London: Aeon, 2008), 15.

3. One teacher who bridges this divide is George Haas. He combines a systematic approach to Vipassana with attachment theory. See Mettagroup, "About," http://www .mettagroup.org/about/.

4. Insight Meditation Society, https://www.dharma.org, accessed July 2, 2009.

5. Steve Armstrong, "The Practical Dharma of Mahasi Sayadaw," Buddhist Geeks, accessed May 15, 2016, link no longer available.

6. For an in-depth discussion of the founding of IMS, see Ann Gleig, "Enlightenment After the Enlightenment: American Transformations of Asian Contemplative Traditions" (PhD diss., Rice University, 2011), 102–8. See also Jack Kornfield, *Bringing Home the Dharma: Awakening Right Where You Are* (Boston: Shambhala, 2011), 216–18.

7. James William Coleman, *The New Buddhism: The Western Transformation of an Ancient Tradition* (London: Oxford University Press, 2002), 178–79.

8. Ann Gleig, "Wedding the Personal and Impersonal in West Coast Vipassana: A Dialogical Encounter Between Buddhism and Psychotherapy," *Journal of Global Buddhism* 13 (2012): 129–46.

9. Jack Kornfield, "A Vision for Spirit Rock," Spirit Rock, accessed May 15, 2016, link no longer available.

10. Kornfield, *Bringing Home the Dharma*, xiii.

11. Jack Kornfield, "Changing My Mind Year After Year" Declara, February 28, 2018, https://declara.com/content/21bmYYan.

12. Jack Kornfield, *A Path with Heart* (New York: Bantam, 1993), 6–7.

13. Interviews were between one and three hours long and were conducted in the Bay Area between May and August 2008.

14. Kornfield, *A Path with Heart*, 246.

15. Jack Engler, "Promises and Perils of the Spiritual Path," in *Buddhism and Psychotherapy: Across Cultures,* ed. Mark Unno (Boston: Wisdom, 2006), 23–24.

16. Ibid., 24.

17. Kornfield, *A Path with Heart*, 245.

18. Engler, "Promises and Perils," 23.

19. Kornfield, *A Path with Heart*, 286–91.

20. Kornfield, *Bringing Home the Dharma*, 19, 162.

21. Ann Gleig, "From Theravada to Tantra: The Making of an American Tantric Buddhism," *Contemporary Buddhism: An Interdisciplinary Journal* 14, no. 2 (November 2013): 221–38.

22. Kornfield, *Bringing Home the Dharma*, 222.

23. Ibid., 252.

24. Ibid., 197.

25. Ibid., 260.

26. Ibid., 133–48.

27. Ibid., 126–27, 211–15.

28. This was repeated in interviews with teachers and is reiterated by Kornfield in "American Buddhism," in *The Complete Guide to Buddhist America* (Boston: Shambhala, 1998), xxix, and Kornfield, *Bringing Home the Dharma*, 208.

29. Kornfield, "American Buddhism," xxvii–xxviii.

30. Kornfield, *Bringing Home the Dharma*, 225–32.

31. Jack Kornfield, "Tending the Garden of the Dharma for Twenty Five Years,"

Jack, https://jackkornfield.com/tending-garden-dharma-25-years-interview-jack-korn
field/, accessed May 15, 2016.

32. All information on Josh Korda is taken from Ann Gleig, "External Mindfulness, Secure (Non)-Attachment, and Healing Relational Trauma: Emerging Models of
Wellness for Modern Buddhists and Buddhist Modernism," *Journal of Global Buddhism*
17 (2016): 1–21.

33. Josh Korda, personal correspondence with the author, February 2, 2016.

34. Josh Korda, "Don't Believe the Hype," Dharma Punx NYC, August 8, 2013,
http://www.dharmapunxnyc.com/blog/2013/08/dont-believe-hype.html.

35. Kornfield, "Changing My Mind."

36. Josh Korda, "Spiritual Bypass," Dharma Punx NYC, podcast audio, October 8,
2013, http://dharmapunxnyc.podbean.com/e/the-spiritual-bypass/.

37. Josh Korda, "Mindfulness Is Not Enough," Dharma Punx NYC, March 7, 2014,
http://dharmapunxnyc.blogspot.com/2014/03/mindfulness-is-not-enough.html.

38. Josh Korda, personal correspondence with the author, May 26, 2015.

39. Josh Korda, "Broken Pickers: Understanding the Need to Compulsively
Choose Unsuitable Partners," Dharma Punx NYC, October 23, 2013, http://dharma
punxnyc.blogspot.com/2014/03/mindfulness-is-not-enough.html.

40. Josh Korda, "One Teacher's Perspective: The Rewards and Risks of Seclusion
and Extended Silent Retreats," Dharma Punx NYC, June 2, 2014, http://dharmapunxnyc
.blogspot.com/2014/06/one-teachers-perspective-rewards-and.html.

41. Josh Korda, personal correspondence with the author, March 20, 2015.

42. Josh Korda, "Cultivating Security in Relationships," Dharma Punx NYC,
podcast audio, November 29, 2014, http://dharmapunxnyc.podbean.com/e/cultivating
-security-in-relationships/.

43. Bhikkhu Analayo, *Satipatthana: The Direct Path to Realization* (Birmingham:
Windhorse, 2004), 94–96.

44. Jessica Morey, interview with the author, May 22, 2015.

45. Gregory Kramer, *Insight Dialogue: The Interpersonal Path to Freedom* (Boston:
Shambhala, 2007).

46. Haas combines a systematic approach to Vipassana with attachment theory.
See Mettagroup, "About," http://www.mettagroup.org/about/.

47. Josh Korda, "Noble Truths Three and Four and the Nature of Liberation,"
Dharma Punx NYC, podcast audio, June 25, 2014, http://dharmapunxnyc.podbean
.com/e/noble-truths-three-and-four-and-the-nature-of-liberation/; Josh Korda, "What
Is Liberation," Dharma Punx NYC, February 27, 2014, http://dharmapunxnyc.blogspot
.com/2014/02/what-is-liberation.html.

48. Korda, personal correspondence with the author, May 26 2015.

49. Korda, personal correspondence with the author, March 20, 2015.

50. Josh Korda, "Why I'm a Buddhist," Dharma Punx NYC, December 6, 2013,
http://www.dharmapunxnyc.com/blog/2013/12/6/why-im-a-buddhist.

51. Sayadaw U Pandita, *In This Very Life: The Liberation Teachings of the Buddha*
(Boston: Wisdom, 1992).

52. Gleig, "Wedding the Personal and Impersonal," 136.

53. Steve Armstrong, "Insight Meditation in America," Wisdom Publications, podcast audio, April 15, 2016, https://learn.wisdompubs.org/podcast/steve-armstrong/.

54. Erik Braun, "United States of Jhana: Varieties of Modern Buddhism in America," in *Buddhism Beyond Borders: New Perspectives on Buddhism in the United States,* ed. Scott A. Mitchell and Natalie E. F. Quli (New York: SUNY Press, 2015), 165.

55. Kornfield, *Bringing Home the Dharma,* 128–29.

56. Natalie F. Quli, "Multiple Buddhist Modernisms: Jhana in Convert Theravada," *Journal of the Institute of Buddhist Studies* (2008): 239.

57. Ajahn Brahm, *Mindfulness, Bliss, and Beyond: A Meditator's Handbook* (Boston: Wisdom, 2006), 104, quoted in Braun, "United States of Jhana," 169.

58. Leigh Brasington, "Sharpening Manjushri's Sword: An Interview with Leigh Brasington," *Insight Journal* 28 (2007): 94–98, quoted in Braun, "United States of Jhana," 170.

59. Braun, "United States of Jhana," 176.

60. Ibid., 169.

61. Shaila Catherine, interview by Daniel Aitken, "Shaila Catherine: Mastering the Jhanas," Wisdom Publications, podcast audio, May 2, 2016 http://learn.wisdompubs.org/podcast/shaila-catherine/.

62. Shaila Catherine, *Focused and Fearless: A Meditator's Guide to States of Deep Joy, Calm, and Clarity* (Boston: Wisdom, 2008), and Shaila Catherine and Pa-Auk Sayadaw, *Wisdom Wide and Deep: A Practical Handbook for Mastering Jhana and Vipassana* (Boston: Wisdom, 2011).

63. "Shaila Catherine: Founder and Principle Teacher," Insight Meditation South Bay, http://www.imsb.org/about-us/founder-and-principal-teacher-shaila-catherine/, accessed May 16, 2016.

64. Shinzen Young, "enlightenment, Enlightenment and the Age of Enlightenment," *Shinzen's Blog,* October 16, 2015, http://shinzenyoung.blogspot.com/2015/10/enlightenment-enlightenment-and-age-of.html.

65. Quotations from Kenneth Folk, all personal correspondence with the author, October 2012.

66. Daniel Ingram, "BG 006: You Can Do It!," Buddhist Geeks, podcast audio, accessed March 10 2015, link no longer available.

67. Ingram, *Mastering the Core Teachings,* 96–98.

68. Ibid., 102.

69. Ibid., ix.

70. Ibid., 188.

71. Jeff Warren, "The Anxiety of the Long-Distance Meditator," *New York Times* December 17, 2012.

72. Daniel Ingram, "BG 119: The Dharma Overground," Buddhist Geeks, podcast audio, accessed March 14, 2016, link no longer available.

73. "Welcome to the DhO Dharma Wiki," Dharma Overground, http://www.dharmaoverground.org/web/guest/dharma-wiki, accessed March 9, 2016.

74. "Welcome to the Dharma Overground," Dharma Overground, http://www
.dharmaoverground.org, accessed March 9, 2016.

75. Ron Crouch, Aloha Dharma, https://alohadharma.com, accessed March 10,
2016.

76. Ron Crouch, personal correspondence with the author, March 9, 2016.

77. Ron Crouch, "The Path," Aloha Dharma, https://alohadharma.com/the-map/,
accessed March 10, 2016.

78. Daniel Ingram, "BG 118: An Unusually Hardcore Dharma Book," Buddhist
Geeks, podcast audio, accessed March 14, 2016, link no longer available.

79. "Back to Suffragette City?," Smiling Buddha Cabaret, July 28, 2010, https://
enlightenmentward.wordpress.com/2010/07/28/back-to-suffragette-city/.

80. "DhO Male Gender Skew," Dharma Overground, http://www.dharmaover
ground.org, accessed March 15, 2016.

81. Ron Crouch, personal correspondence with the author, March 9, 2016.

82. Robert Sharf, "Experience," in Critical Terms for Religious Studies, ed. Mark C.
Taylor (Chicago: University of Chicago Press, 1998), 94.

83. Thanissaro Bhikkhu, "Romancing the Buddha," Tricycle 12, no. 2 (Winter
2002): 45–47, 106–12.

84. Ron Crouch, "What Is Pragmatic Dharma?," Aloha Dharma, https://aloha
dharma.com/2015/11/03/what-is-pragmatic-dharma/, accessed March 13, 2018.

85. Quli, "Multiple Buddhist Modernisms," 227.

86. Braun, "United States of Jhana," 176.

87. Daniel Ingram, "BG: 356 A Pragmatist Take on the Powers," Buddhist Geeks,
podcast audio, link no longer available.

88. Vipassana Meditation, http://www.dhamma.org/, accessed August 2, 2016.

89. David A. Treleaven, "Meditation, Trauma and Contemplative Dissociation,"
Somatics 16, no. 2 (2010): 20–22. Jane Compson comes to a similar conclusion as Treleaven and explicitly attributes the appearance of psychological symptoms in meditators
to the dislocations of Buddhism wrought during modernity. Jane Compson, "Meditation,
Trauma and Suffering in Silence: Raising Questions About How Meditation Is Taught
and Practiced in Western Contexts in the Light of a Contemporary Trauma Resilience
Model," Contemporary Buddhism: An Interdisciplinary Journal 15, no. 2 (2014): 274–97.

90. Jared R. Lindhal, Nathan E. Fisher, David J. Cooper, Rochelle J. Rosen, and Willoughby Britton, "The Varieties of Contemplative Experience: A Mixed Methods Study
of Meditation-Related Challenges in Western Buddhism," PLoS One 12, no. 5 (May 24,
2017), http://journals.plos.org/plosone/article?id=10.1371/journal.pone.0176239. Britton
has presented her research at conferences such as Buddhist Geeks and the Mind and Life
Institute; see also the podcast "#79: Willoughby Britton, Jared Lindhal—Does Meditation Have a Dark Side?," 10% Happier, May 24, 2017, http://www.10percenthappier.com/
podcast/willoughby-britton-jared-lindahl-does-mediation-have-a-dark-side.

91. David A. Treleaven, Trauma-Sensitive Mindfulness: Practices for Safe and
Transformative Healing (New York: W. W. Norton, 2018). Willoughby Britton wrote the

Foreword, and the book contains effusive blurbs from Tara Brach and Rick Hanson, two popular figures in American Buddhist networks. Also of note is that three of my Gen X interviewees, all from the Insight Community, said that they felt trauma awareness was a common feature of Gen X teachers in their communities. For a longer discussion of trauma approaches in the Insight network, see Gleig, "External Mindfulness," 10–11.

FIVE   The Dukkha of Racism

1. See "Two 'Calls'—One Goal," North American Buddhist Alliance, https://north americanbuddhistalliance.org/calls-to-buddhists/, accessed March 15, 2018. In early 2017, the group Buddhists for Racial Justice was integrated into the North American Buddhist Alliance.

2. "Statement on Racism from Buddhist Teachers & Leaders in the United States," Jack Kornfield, Jack, May 14, 2015, https://jackkornfield.com/statement-on-racism -from-buddhist-teachers-leaders-in-the-united-states/.

3. The booklet is available electronically at http://static1.1.sqspcdn.com/static/f/ 636447/10751208/1297739615160/MTIV+3rd+ed.pdf?token=SvfuIzMO9pxzmA9Q2bTJ VBAXbF0%3D.

4. Hilda Gutiérrez Baldoquín, ed., *Dharma, Color, and Culture: New Voices in Western Buddhism* (Berkeley: Parallax, 2004).

5. "Free the Dharma: Race, Power, and White Privilege in American Buddhism," *Buddhadharma: The Practitioner's Quarterly* (Spring 2016).

6. Lawrence Pintak, "'Something Has to Change': Blacks in American Buddhism," *Lion's Roar*, September 1, 2001, https://www.lionsroar.com/something-has-to-change -blacks-in-american-buddhism/.

7. "Sangha and Diversity," New York Insight Meditation Center, https://www .nyimc.org/sangha-diversity/, accessed March 29, 2017.

8. Zenju Earthlyn Manuel, *The Way of Tenderness: Awakening Through Race, Sexuality and Gender* (Boston: Wisdom, 2015).

9. angel Kyodo williams, Lama Rod Owens, and Jasmine Syedullah, *Radical Dharma: Talking Race, Love, and Liberation* (Berkeley: North Atlantic Books, 2016).

10. Travis M. Spencer, interview with the author, October 15, 2015.

11. Travis M. Spencer, "The Color of the Buddha Heart," *Dharma of A Man* (blog), May 25, 2010, http://dharmaofaman.blogspot.com/search?updated-min=2010-01-01 T00:00:00-05:00&updated-max=2011-01-01T00:00:00-05:00&max-results=19.

12. Tara Brach, "Beloved Community," Insight Meditation Community of Washington, podcast audio, June 17, 2015, http://imcw.org/Talks/TalkDetail/TalkID/812.

13. Information from IMCW website, http://imcw.org, and Tara Brach, interview with the author, August 30, 2015.

14. La Sarmiento, interview with the author, September 14, 2015.

15. Hugh Byrne, interview with the author, October 14, 2015.

16. Larry Yang, interview with the author, October 20, 2011.

17. La Sarmiento interview.

18. People of Color/POC Sangha, Insight Meditation Community of Washington, http://imcw.org/Community/Affinity-Groups, accessed September 14, 2015.

19. La Sarmiento interview.

20. Ibid.

21. Byrne interview.

22. Information on the friendship group came primarily from interviews with La Sarmiento and Tara Brach.

23. La Sarmiento interview.

24. Klia Bassing, interview with the author, September 4, 2015.

25. Ibid.

26. White Awake, https://whiteawake.org, accessed multiple times September–December 2015.

27. Eleanor Hancock, interview with the author, August 28, 2015, and discussion with the author, December 7, 2015.

28. Brach interview.

29. La Sarmiento interview.

30. Byrne interview.

31. Harrison A. Blum, "Mindfulness Equity and Western Buddhism: Reaching People of Low Socioeconomic Status and People of Color," *International Journal of Dharma Studies* 2, no. 10 (2014), https://doi.org/10.1186/s40613-014-0010-0.

32. Brach interview.

33. Ibid.

34. Ruth King, interview with the author, December 2, 2015.

35. La Sarmiento interview.

36. Jonathan Foust, "The World Is One Family: Healing the Wounds of Racism and Discrimination," video, Insight Meditation Community of Washington, June 8, 2015, http://imcw.org/Talks/TalkDetail/TalkID/822.

37. Ann Gleig, "From Theravada to Tantra: The Making of an American Tantric Buddhism," *Contemporary Buddhism: An Interdisciplinary Journal* 14, no. 2 (November 2013): 221–38.

38. Brach interview.

39. La Sarmiento interview.

40. Brach interview.

41. Bassing interview.

42. Brach interview.

43. Ibid.

44. La Sarmiento interview.

45. Ibid.

46. Byrne interview.

47. La Sarmiento interview.

48. "Beloved Community: Healing What Separates Us": BuddhaFest 2015,

White Awake, https://whiteawake.org/2015/12/28/beloved-community-panel-discussion-buddhafest-2015/, accessed March 29, 2017.

49. *Lion's Roar* Staff, "The Road to Diversity," *Lion's Roar*, November 10, 2011, https://www.lionsroar.com/road-to-diversity/.

50. Pintak, "'Something Has to Change.'".

51. "Commitment to Diversity," Insight Meditation Society, https://www.dharma.org/about-us/diversity/, accessed December 28, 2017.

52. "Diversity, Equity and Inclusion," Spirit Rock, https://www.spiritrock.org/diversity-initiative.

53. Larry Yang, Appendix 4, "The History of Diversity-Related Events in the Western Insight Meditation Community," in *Awakening Together: The Spiritual Practice of Inclusivity and Community* (Boston: Shambhala, 2017), 237–40.

54. Jaweed Kaleem, "Buddhist 'People of Color Sanghas,' Diversity Efforts Address Conflicts About Race Among Meditators," HuffPost, November 18, 2012, https://www.huffingtonpost.com/2012/11/18/buddhism-race-mediators-people-of-color-sangha_n_2144559.html.

55. Kathryn Arnold, discussion with the author, November 3, 2015.

56. Jan Willis, "On Conferences: A New Spirit at Spirit Rock," *Tricycle* (Winter 2000).

57. Dawn Yun, "Spirit Rock's New Mantra—Diversity," SFGate, September 17, 2004, https://www.sfgate.com/bayarea/article/COMMUNITY-Spirit-Rock-s-new-mantra-diversity-2724842.php.

58. *Lion's Roar* Staff, "Buddhist Teacher Marlene Jones Dies, Will Be Remembered as "Singular Pioneer," for Sangha Diversity," *Lion's Roar*, January 9, 2013, https://www.lionsroar.com/buddhist-teacher-marlene-jones-suffers-cardiac-arrest/.

59. Ann Gleig, "East Bay Meditation Center," World Religions and Spirituality, December 9, 2014, https://wrldrels.org/2016/10/08/east-bay-meditation-center/; Ann Gleig, "Dharma Diversity and Deep Inclusivity at the East Bay Meditation Center: From Buddhist Modernism to Buddhist Postmodernism?," *Contemporary Buddhism: An Interdisciplinary Journal* 15 (2014): 312–31.

60. For an inside account of EBMC, see Yang, *Awakening Together*, 165–71.

61. Rachel Uris, personal correspondence with the author, December 14, 2017.

62. "Sangha and Diversity," New York Insight Meditation Center, https://www.nyimc.org/sangha-diversity/, accessed December 29, 2017.

63. Larry Yang and Gina Sharpe, "Diverse World, Diverse Sangha," Dharma Seed (audio), June 4, 2010, http://dharmaseed.org/talks/audio_player/75/15966.html.

64. Larry Yang and Gina Sharpe, personal correspondence with the author, December 6, 2017.

65. Bhikkhu Analayo, *Satipatthana: The Direct Path to Realization* (Birmingham: Windhorse, 2004).

66. Yang, *Awakening Together*, 118–26.

67. This text is a key part of Yang's multicultural hermeneutics of Buddhism.

See Larry Yang, "Buddha Is Culture," HuffPost, June 19, 2012, https://www.huffington post.com/larry-yang/buddha-culture_b_1192398.html; Larry Yang, "Dharma Is Culture," HuffPost, June 27, 2012, https://www.huffingtonpost.com/larry-yang/dharma -culture_b_1599969.html; and Larry Yang, "Sangha Is Religion," HuffPost, July 10, 2012, https://www.huffingtonpost.com/larry-yang/sangha-culture_b_1600095.html.

68. Joseph Goldstein, interview with Noam Sandweiss-Back (audio), May 5, 2015.

69. Joseph Goldstein, "Reflections on Race and Diversity," Dharma Seed, December 12, 2014, http://dharmaseed.org/teacher/96/talk/25655/.

70. Bob Agoglia, "Visions and Aspirations," Insight Meditation Society Sangha News (Summer 2008), https://www.dharma.org/wp-content/uploads/2017/02/Sangha News-Summer_2008.pdf.

71. "IMS's Commitment to Diversity and Inclusion—Our Work and Aspirations," August 2016, https://www.dharma.org/wp-content/uploads/drupal-archive/Diversity _and_Inclusion_Our_Work_and_Aspirations.pdf.

72. IMS Guiding Teachers email of July 26, 2017; shared with permission of Bonnie Duran, December 2, 2017.

73. Don Lattin, "Dalai Lama in Marin to Shape Future of American Buddhism," SFGate, June 24, 2000, https://www.sfgate.com/bayarea/article/Dalai-Lama-in-Marin -to-Shape-Future-of-American-2715917.php.

74. Over the course of writing this chapter, in addition to my interviewees at IMCW, I interviewed ten POC who attended and/or led POC retreats or sitting groups.

75. Larry Yang, personal correspondence with the author, December 20, 2017.

76. "Teacher Training at Spirit Rock," Spirit Rock, https://www.spiritrock.org/ teacher-training-2016, accessed December 30, 2017.

77. Yang personal correspondence.

78. For an inside account of teacher demographics in the Insight Community, see Yang, Awakening Together, 191–214.

79. "Increasing POC Leadership in Our Sanghas," Insight Meditation Society Sangha News, July 2015, https://www.dharma.org/about-us/current-news/sangha-news/ july-2015/.

80. "Diversity, Equity and Inclusion Initiative: A Message from the Board of Directors," Spirit Rock, March 16, 2016, https://www.spiritrock.org/board-letter-march -2016.

81. Linda Spink, "The Next Phrase of Our Diversity Work," Insight Meditation Society Sangha News, February 2016, https://www.dharma.org/about-us/current-news/ sangha-news/february-2016/#diversity.

82. Ed Hong, "Teacher Training Program Update," Insight Meditation Society Sangha News, August 2016, https://www.dharma.org/about-us/current-news/sangha -news/august-2016/#TTP.

83. "New Teacher Training Program," Insight Meditation Society Sangha News, December 2016, https://www.dharma.org/about-us/current-news/sangha-news/ december-2016/.

84. "IMS's 2017–2021 Teacher Trainees," Current News, Insight Meditation Society, http://www.dharma.org/about-us/current-news/.

85. "Spirit Rock Teacher Training Update: Empowering Future Dharma Teachers," Spirit Rock, https://www.spiritrock.org/about/about-teacher-training-update, accessed March 18, 2918.

86. René Rivera, interview with the author, December 23, 2017.

87. Larry Yang, Gina Sharpe, and Kate Lila Wheeler, personal correspondence with the author, December 6, 2017.

88. Rachel Uris, personal correspondence with the author, December 6, 2017.

89. Michelle Latvala, "Hearts Breaking Open: Mudita & Karuna—A message from Michelle Latvala, Executive Director" (originally published Summer 2016), Spirit Rock, "Diversity, Equity and Inclusion," https://www.spiritrock.org/diversity-initiative.

90. Bonnie Duran was the only IMS teacher to respond to my interview requests. She forwarded my request to other teachers and also sent me the IMS booklet *Understanding Race and Racism*. On October 28, 2015, which was before Yang, Sharpe, and Wheeler resigned from the teacher training process, I interviewed Linda Spink, the executive director at IMS, on general diversity work at IMS but with little specifics on the teacher training program. Between November and December 2017, Inger Forland, the current executive director at IMS, and I made two interview dates but were unable to keep them. Therefore, I have had to rely solely on public documentation for IMS's part in and perspective on the teacher training proposal process.

91. Yang and Sharpe personal correspondence.

92. Sharon Suh, for instance, has produced a potent analysis of the intersections between elite, patriarchal Asian Buddhist monasticism and Western Orientalism and white privilege. Sharon A. Suh, *Silver Screen Buddha: Buddhism in Asian and Western Film* (London: Bloomsbury, 2015).

93. Goldstein interview with Sandweiss-Back.

94. Ann Gleig, "Wedding the Personal and Impersonal in West Coast Vipassana: A Dialogical Approach Between Buddhism and Psychotherapy," *Journal of Global Buddhism* 13 (2012): 129–46.

95. Gleig, "Dharma Diversity and Deep Inclusivity."

96. Mushim Patricia Ikeda, "Daylighting the Hidden Streams: Why Our Stories Matter," podcast, August 15, 2012, http://media.sfzc.org/mp3/2012/2012-08-15-cc-mushim-ikeda.mp3.

97. Natalie E. Quli, "Western Self, Asian Other: Modernity, Authenticity, and Nostalgia for 'Tradition' in Buddhist Studies," *Journal of Buddhist Ethics* 16 (2009): 16, http://blogs.dickinson.edu/buddhistethics/files/2010/05/quli-article.pdf.

98. Yang interview.

99. Rod Meade Sperry, "Open Hearts, Open Doors at Brooklyn Zen Center," *Lion's Roar*, December 1, 2014, https://www.lionsroar.com/open-hearts-open-doors-brooklyn-zen-center/; Greg Snyder, interview with the author, July 2015.

SIX Buddhism Unbundled

1. Bodhipaksa, "Debugging the Source Code of the Dharma," presentation at the Buddhist Geeks conference, Boulder, CO, October 16–19, 2014.

2. Mikey Siegel, "Enlightenment Engineering," presentation at the Buddhist Geeks conference, Boulder, CO, October 16–19, 2014.

3. Robin Arnott, "Game Design for Meditation," presentation at the Buddhist Geeks conference, Boulder, CO, October 16–19, 2014.

4. Ann Gleig, "#Hashtag Meditation, Cyborg Buddhas, and Enlightenment as an Epic Win: Buddhism, Technology, and the New Social Media," in *Religion, Technology, and Science in South and East Asia,* ed. Istvan Keul (London: Routledge, 2015), 199.

5. Email from Vince and Emily Horn, September 20, 2016.

6. Vincent Horn, "Buddhist Geeks Death Poem," Medium, December 12, 2016, accessed April 7, 2017, link no longer available. The Buddhist Geeks website has been removed, so all podcasts and articles are no longer available, and URLs are not given in the notes in this chapter.

7. "Our Koan," Buddhist Geeks, accessed April 2, 2013.

8. Information from "BG 001: Meet the Geeks," Buddhist Geeks, podcast audio, accessed November 7, 2012; and Vince Horn interview with the author, September 20, 2012.

9. "Our Koan," Buddhist Geeks.

10. Horn interview, September 20, 2012.

11. These interviews are all available at "Buddhist Geeks: Ethics," SoundCloud, https://soundcloud.com/buddhistgeeks/sets/ethics, accessed April 17, 2017.

12. Because Buddhist Geeks has used multiple tools to capture the metrics over the years, these are not representative of the total statistics. However, they are representative of what was most popular, in terms of new episodes, during this time. Vince Horn, personal correspondence with the author, April 25 2017.

13. "BG 001: Meet the Geeks," Buddhist Geeks.

14. Mitchell Landsberg, "Buddhist Wonks? No, Buddhist Geeks," *Los Angeles Times,* August 8, 2011, http://articles.latimes.com/2011/aug/08/local/la-me-buddhist-geeks-20110808; Ed Halliwell, "Buddhist Geeks and the Virtual Path to Enlightenment," *Guardian,* August 9, 2011, https://www.theguardian.com/commentisfree/belief/2011/aug/09/buddhist-geeks-enlightenment-online.

15. David Chapman, "The Buddhist Geeks Conference Rocks," *Vividness* (blog), July 31, 2011, https://vividness.live/2011/07/31/the-buddhist-geeks-conference-rocks/.

16. Vince Horn, interview with the author, December 10, 2015.

17. Hokai Sobol, personal correspondence with the author, April 17, 2017.

18. "Life Retreat: Awakening Is a Team Sport," Buddhist Geeks, February 22, 2013 available at YouTube, https://www.youtube.com/watch?v=Z3DAgv4hSxY.

19. Horn interview, December 10, 2015.

20. Ibid.

21. Horn personal correspondence with the author, April 17, 2017.

22. Horn interview, December 10, 2015.

23. Ibid.

24. Daniel Thorson, interview with the author, April 21, 2017.

25. Vince and Emily Horn, "When Rebels Mature," Buddhist Geeks, September 15, 2015.

26. Horn interview, December 10, 2015.

27. Vince and Emily Horn, "The Buddhist Geeks Dojo," Buddhist Geeks, September 13, 2015.

28. Horn interview, December 10, 2015.

29. See Ken McLeod, "Why the Buddhist Geeks Conference Is Unique," Buddhist Geeks, accessed September 20, 2012.

30. For more details, see Gleig, "#Hashtag Meditation," 193–96.

31. Ken McLeod, "BG 250: Crossing the Generational Divide," Buddhist Geeks, podcast audio, accessed March 29, 2013.

32. Tami Simon, "Selling the Dharma," presentation at the Buddhist Geeks conference, University of Colorado, Boulder, August 9–11, 2012.

33. "Life Retreat," Buddhist Geeks.

34. Rohan Gunatillake, "Practice, Play and Products," Buddhist Geeks, accessed March 25, 2013.

35. Ibid.

36. Daniel Ingram, "BG 118: An Unusually Hardcore Dharma Book," Buddhist Geeks, podcast audio, accessed June 28, 2012.

37. Kenneth Folk, "Contemplative Fitness," presentation at the Buddhist Geeks conference, University of Colorado, Boulder, August 16–18, 2013. See also Kenneth Folk, "BG 156: Ordinary People Can Get Enlightened," Buddhist Geeks, podcast audio, accessed March 29, 2013.

38. Vince and Emily Horn, "The Buddhist Geeks Dojo."

39. Gleig, "#Hashtag Meditation," 199.

40. Vince and Emily Horn, "The Buddhist Geeks Dojo."

41. Sobol, personal correspondence, April 17, 2017.

42. See, e.g., McLeod, "Crossing the Generational Divide."

43. Lodro Rinzler, "BG 244: The Buddha Walks into a Bar," Buddhist Geeks, podcast audio, accessed July 29, 2013.

44. Rohan Gunatillake, "BG 217: The Aesthetic of Meditation Is Broken," Buddhist Geeks, podcast audio, accessed March 13, 2012.

45. Ingram, "An Unusually Hardcore Dharma Book."

46. Buddhist Geeks 2012 preconference discussion thread on "generational differences." No longer available online.

47. Thorson interview, April 21, 2017.

48. Vince Horn, interview with the author, December 13, 2016.

49. Horn personal correspondence, April 17, 2017.

50. Email from Vince and Emily Horn, September 20, 2016.

51. Vince Horn, "Buddhism Unbundled," Keynote Speech, Buddhist Geeks conference, Boulder, CO, October 16–19, 2014.

52. Ibid.

53. Vince Horn, "Making Meditation Modular," Medium, August 16, 2016, https://medium.com/@meditateio/making-meditation-modular-567b3e5cd68d; and Vince Horn, "A New Spiritual Immune System," Medium, December 21, 2016, https://medium.com/@vincenthorn/a-new-spiritual-immune-system-7a4ea68179b9.

54. Meditate.io, http://programs.meditate.io/p/mindplusplus, accessed multiple times March–April 2017.

55. Horn interview, December 13, 2016.

56. Ibid.

57. Vince Horn, "The Second Generation of Mindfulness," Medium, January 12, 2017, https://medium.com/@meditateio/the-second-generation-of-mindfulness-e669318c03fc.

58. Horn interview, December 13, 2016.

59. In a further twist of the plot, Vince restarted the Buddhist Geeks podcast in August 2017. One of the factors he gave for this decision was, "I was also kind of missing podcasting (after a year-long break) and I guess, in some ways, have started to re-integrate some of my post-non-trans-buddhist tendencies with my inner conservative monk." Vince Horn, personal correspondence with the author, November 29, 2017.

60. Horn interview, December 13, 2016.

61. Ibid.

62. Ibid.

63. J. Carl Gregg, conversation with the author, April 23, 2017.

64. Francis J. Lacoste, conversation with the author, April 23, 2017.

65. "Who We Are," Meditate.io, accessed April 27, 2017, link no longer available

66. "Great Uncertainty Calls for Great Practice," Meditate.io, http://programs.meditate.io/p/mindplusplus, accessed April 27, 2017.

67. This conclusion draws significantly on Ann Gleig, "From Buddhist Hippies to Buddhist Geeks," Journal of Global Buddhism 15 (2014): 24–29.

68. Donald S. Lopez Jr., Buddhism and Science: A Guide for the Perplexed (Chicago: University of Chicago Press, 2008); and Donald S. Lopez Jr., The Scientific Buddha: His Short and Happy Life (New Haven, CT: Yale University Press, 2012).

69. Shinzen Young, "Towards a Science of Enlightenment," Buddhist Geeks, accessed March 22, 2013.

70. Vincent Horn, "Mind Hacking: Upgrading from Windows ME," Buddhist Geeks, accessed March 25, 2013.

71. Jean-François Lyotard, The Postmodern Condition: A Report on Knowledge, trans. Geoff Bennington and Brian Massumi (Manchester: Manchester University Press, 1986).

72. Vince Horn and Rohan Gunatillake, "BG 275: Buddhism, Technology and Quarter-Pounders," Buddhist Geeks, podcast audio, 2013, accessed March 29, 2013.

73. Horn interview, September 20, 2012.

74. Kelly Sosan Bearer, "The Scientist and the Contemplative," Buddhist Geeks, accessed March 29, 2013.

75. David L. McMahan, *The Making of Buddhist Modernism* (Oxford: Oxford University Press, 2008), 246; Jeff Wilson, *Mourning the Unborn Dead: A Buddhist Ritual Comes to America* (Oxford: Oxford University Press, 2009).

76. Paul Heelas, ed., *Religion, Modernity and Postmodernity* (Oxford: Blackwell, 1998), 4–5.

77. Lynne Hume and Kathleen McPhillips, *Popular Spiritualities: The Politics of Contemporary Enchantment* (Aldershot: Ashgate, 2008), xvi–xvii.

78. Donna Haraway, "A Cyborg Manifesto: Science, Technology, and Socialist-Feminism in the Late Twentieth Century," ch. 8 in *Simians, Cyborgs and Women: The Reinvention of Nature* (New York: Routledge, 1991), 149–81, 181.

79. Vincent B. Letich, "Postmodern Theory of Technology," *Symploke* 12, nos. 1 and 2 (2004): 209–15, 214.

80. It is worth noting that the community, on the whole, was receptive to my etic analysis of Buddhist Geeks as postmodern. They invited me to present my academic research at the 2013 conference. Ann Gleig, "From Buddhist Hippies to Buddhist Geeks," presentation at the Buddhist Geeks conference, University of Colorado, Boulder, August 16–18, 2013.

81. Horn interview, December 10, 2015.

82. Thorson interview, April 21, 2017.

83. David L. McMahan, "Repacking Zen for the West," in *Westward Dharma: Buddhism Beyond Asia,* ed. Charles S. Prebish and Martin Baumann (Berkeley: University of California Press, 2002), 218–29, 227–28.

84. McMahan, *The Making of Buddhist Modernism,* 242.

SEVEN　From the Boomers to Generation X

1. "Three Statements of Next Gen," unpublished document in the author's possession.

2. "About Dharma Teacher Gathering," Dharma Teacher Gathering, http://dharmateachergathering.org/about/, accessed July 5, 2016.

3. Danny Fisher, "The Great American Buddhist Teachers Council," Dharma Dew, The Buddhist Channel, June 24, 2011, http://www.buddhistchannel.tv/index .php?id=6,10263,0,0,1,0#.V1X6wumqNW3.

4. Nick Ribush, "Teachers Discuss the Future of Buddhism in the West: The 2011 Garrison Institute Conference," Mandala Publications, October–December 2011, http://fpmt.org/mandala/archives/mandala-issues-for-2011/october/teachers-discuss -the-future-of-buddhism-in-the-west-the-2011-garrison-institute-conference/, accessed July 5, 2016.

5. Quoted in Fisher, "The Great American Buddhist Teachers Council."

6. Rachel Zoll, "At the Crossroads: Buddhism in America Is Facing a Generation Shift," TuscaloosaNews.com, July 16, 2011, http://www.tuscaloosanews.com/article/

20110716/NEWS/110719820. Tenku Ruff points out that Zoll's framing of the boomers as having spent many decades training in Asia is lineage specific and not representative of senior American Zen teachers, of whom very few trained in Asia. She points out that only 8 (out of 176) American Soto Zen Buddhist Association pre-1960 full-time members trained in Japan for more than a year.

7. Martin Aylward, discussion with the author, March 10, 2014.

8. Interviews lasted between one and two hours, with any needed follow-up clarification via written correspondence. Most of the interviews were undertaken via Skype, a smaller percentage were conducted over the phone, and one interview was conducted entirely in writing. I used a set question format as the starting point but encouraged interviewees to discuss issues that were most relevant to them. Interviewees were also given the option of using a pseudonym, and three of the thirty-three opted to do this.

9. Sumi Loundon Kim, discussion with the author, July 26, 2016.

10. Eshu Martin, discussion with the author, February 2, 2015.

11. Sumi Loundon Kim, Lama Rod Owens, Nina La Rosa, Tenku Ruff, and Dave Smith, "Forum: The Road Ahead," *Lion's Roar,* January 31, 2016, http://www.lionsroar .com/forum-the-road-ahead/.

12. Loundon Kim discussion.

13. Martin Aylward discussion with the author, July 23, 2016.

14. Ibid.

15. Martin Aylward, discussion with the author, August 8, 2014

16. Martin Aylward, "BG 226: The Buddhist Teachers Council," podcast audio, no longer available.

17. David Brazier, "American Buddhism or American Culture for Buddhists?," Flotsam & Jetsam, June 10, 2011, http://amidatrust.typepad.com/dharmavidya/2011/06/ american-buddhism-or-american-culture-for-buddhists.html.

18. David Chapman, "Brad Warner vs. the Maha Teachers," *Vividness* (blog), June 9, 2011, https://meaningness.wordpress.com/2011/06/09/brad-warner-vs-the-maha -teachers/.

19. Loundon Kim et al., "Forum."

20. Ibid.

21. "Deer Park Monastery Hosting Gathering for Generation X Dharma Teachers in June," *Lion's Roar,* April 26, 2013, http://www.lionsroar.com/deer-park-monastery -hosting-gathering-for-generation-x-teachers-in-june/.

22. "Official Conference Announcement," Generitech, http://us3.campaign-archive 2.com/?u=31fa74bf023170322cb0cd809&id=a4a7c3135c.

23. "'Gen X' Teachers Address Western Buddhism's Future," *Lion's Roar,* June 23, 2015, http://www.lionsroar.com/gen-x-teachers-address-western-buddhisms-future/.

24. Gen X Dharma, "Apply to the Conference," accessed November 30 2017, link no longer available.

25. Hemera Foundation website, https://hemera.org, accessed November 30, 2017.

26. Loundon Kim et al., "Forum."

27. Heather Sundberg, interview with the author, February 23, 2015.

28. Aylward discussion, March 10, 2014.

29. Anonymous, interview with the author, March 2, 2015.

30. Anonymous, interview with the author, March 3, 2015

31. Michael Stone, interview with the author, April 6, 2015. Michael, who had lived with bipolar disorder much of his life, died during the time this manuscript was being written. Rod Meade Sperry, "Remembering Buddhist Teacher Michael Stone," July 20, 2017, *Lion's Roar*, https://www.lionsroar.com/remembering-buddhist-teacher-michael-stone/.

32. Viveka Chen, interview with the author, March 30, 2015.

33. Jay Rinsen Weik, interview with the author, July 16, 2014.

34. Jessica Morey, interview with the author, May 26, 2015.

35. Ji Hyang Padma, interview with the author, October 26, 2015.

36. Lama Rod Owens, interview with the author, February 9, 2015.

37. Lama Karma Justin Wall, interview with the author, July 29, 2014.

38. angel Kyodo williams, interview with the author, July 2, 2015.

39. Tempel Smith, interview with the author, March 13, 2015.

40. Aylward discussion, July 23, 2016.

41. Ryushin Hart, interview with the author, April 5, 2015.

42. Anushka Fernandopulle, interview with the author, June 29, 2015.

43. Tenku Ruff, interview with the author, February 1, 2015.

44. Kokyo Henkel, interview with the author, March 20, 2015.

45. Koshin Paley Ellison, interview with the author, July 24, 2014.

46. Koun Franz, interview with the author, February 6, 2015.

47. Matthew Brensilver, interview with the author, April 13, 2015.

48. Deborah Eden Tull, interview with the author, April 6, 2015.

49. Oren J. Sofer, interview with the author, June 12, 2015.

50. Vimalasara Mason-John, interview with the author, March 25, 2015.

51. "Free the Dharma: Race, Power and White Privilege in American Buddhism," *Buddhadharma: The Practitioner's Quarterly* (Summer 2016).

52. Koun Franz, interview with the author, February 6, 2015.

53. Jeffrey Zlotnik, interview with the author, May 26, 2016.

54. Sumi Loundon Kim, interview with the author, April 8, 2015.

55. Justin von Bujdoss, interview with the author, July 22, 2015.

56. "About Us," Against the Stream Buddhist Meditation Society, http://www.againstthestream.org/about-us/our-tradition/, accessed July 16, 2016.

57. Kenley Neufield, interview with the author, March 30, 2015.

58. Sean Feit, interview with the author, April 1, 2015.

59. Aylward discussion, July 23, 2016.

EIGHT Critical, Collective, and Contextual Turns

1. "The New Face of Buddhism," *Lion's Roar,* March 2016.

2. "5 Responses to the Awkwardly Titled 'New Face of Buddhism,'" Buddhist Peace Fellowship, January 27, 2016, http://www.buddhistpeacefellowship.org/5-responses-to-the-new-face-of-buddhism/. For the response of *Lion's Roar,* see Melvin McLeod, "Buddhist Peace Fellowship's Comments on Buddhism, Diversity, and *Lion Roar's* cover," *Lion's Roar,* January 27, 2016, http://www.lionsroar.com/buddhist-peace-fellowship-comments-on-buddhism-diversity-and-first-lions-roar-cover/.

3. Katie Loncke, "10 Principles of Our Radical Rebirth," Buddhist Peace Fellowship, October 29, 2013, http://www.buddhistpeacefellowship.org/10-principles-of-our-radical-rebirth/.

4. Della Z, "Episode 13: Dawn Haney," *Interviews with Della Z,* podcast audio, March 13, 2015, http://dellazinterviews.blogspot.com/2015/03/episode-thirteen-dawn-haney.html.

5. "Gathering Greeting," Buddhist Peace Fellowship, http://www.buddhistpeace fellowship.org/gathering-greeting/.

6. Dawn Haney, personal correspondence with the author, April 21, 2017.

7. Dawn Haney and Katie Loncke, interview by Danny Fisher, "Off the Cushion with Danny Fisher," September 2014, available at https://archive.org/details/Offthe CushionwithDannyFisher_201511.

8. Ibid.

9. Ibid.

10. Ibid.

11. "Heal Racism in Our Body + Mind + Soul with Be More," workshop, Brooklyn Zen Center, July 19, 2015.

12. "Welcome to Transbuddhists.org," https://transbuddhists.org, accessed April 24, 2017.

13. Dharma and Direct Action, workshop, New York Insight Meditation Center, November 7–8, 2015.

14. "Block Build Be," Buddhist Peace Fellowship, http://www.buddhistpeace fellowship.org/block-build-be/, accessed March 27, 2018; Haney personal correspondence, April 21, 2017.

15. Haney personal correspondence, April 21, 2017.

16. Haney and Loncke, "Off the Cushion with Danny Fisher."

17. Follow-up video to "Build, Block, Be," August 2016.

18. "Bodhisattva Work: Interview with Turning Wheel Media," *Tricycle,* August 14, 2012, https://tricycle.org/trikedaily/bodhisattva-work/.

19. Katie Loncke, "Episode 6: Katie Loncke—Confrontational Compassion," Mindful Cranks, podcast audio, http://www.mindfulcranks.com/episode-6-katie-loncke-confrontational-compassion/, accessed April 24, 2017.

20. Haney personal correspondence, April 21, 2017.

21. David Chapman, "BG 239: Consensus Buddhism and Mindful Mayo," Bud-

dhist Geeks, podcast audio, accessed March 10, 2017, link no longer available; and David Chapman, "Consensus Buddhism: What Is Left," *Vividness* (blog), October 25, 2015, https://vividness.live.

22. David Chapman, "10.0: David Chapman on Stages of Maturation, Dzogchen, Imperfection & the Future of Buddhism," Imperfect Buddha Podcast, podcast audio, SoundCloud, https://soundcloud.com/post-traditional-buddhism/100-imperfect -buddha-david-chapman-on-stages-of-maturation-dzogchen-the-future-of-buddhism.

23. Aaron Lee, the writer of *Angry Asian Buddhist*, died of cancer during the period this manuscript was being revised. Chenxing Han, "In Memory of a Refuge: Aaron Lee, the 'Angry Asian Buddhist,'" November 2, 2017, *Lion's Roar,* https://www.lionsroar .com/in-memory-of-a-refuge-aaron-lee-the-angry-asian-buddhist/.

24. *Angry Asian Buddhist* (blog), http://www.angryasianbuddhist.com/, accessed February 24, 2017.

25. Richard Payne, "White-Washing the Buddhisms," *Critical Reflections on Buddhist Thought: Contemporary and Classical* (blog), December 12, 2016, https://rkpayne .wordpress.com/2016/12/12/white-washing-the-buddhisms-unacknowledged-privilege -and-the-making-of-a-white-safe-buddhism/.

26. Shaun Bartone, "Neoliberal Buddhism," Engage!, January 31, 2015, https:// engagedbuddhism.net/2015/01/31/neoliberal-buddhism/.

27. Shaun Bartone, "6.2: Shaun Bartone on Engaged Buddhism," Imperfect Buddha Podcast, SoundCloud, podcast audio, https://soundcloud.com/post-traditional -buddhism/62-imperfect-buddha-podcast-shaun-bartone-from-engage-interviewed -on-engaged-buddhism, accessed March 13, 2017.

28. Brent R. Oliver, "White Trash Buddhist," *Tricycle* (Fall 2014), https://tricycle .org/magazine/white-trash-buddhist/.

29. The Tattooed Buddha, http://thetattooedbuddha.com, accessed March 13, 2017.

30. Brent R. Oliver, interview with the author, February 24, 2016.

31. *Speculative Non-Buddhism: Ruins of the Buddhist Real* (blog), https:// speculativenonbuddhism.com, accessed March 10, 2017; Glenn Wallis, Tom Pepper, and Matthias Steingass, *Cruel Theory–Sublime Practice: Toward a Revaluation of Buddhism* (Denmark: Eyecorner, 2013).

32. Glenn Wallis, "What Is Non-Buddhism," *Speculative Non-Buddhism* (blog), https://speculativenonbuddhism.com/why-non-buddhism/, accessed March 29, 2017.

33. Seth Segall, "Glenn Wallis," *Existential Buddhist* (blog), September 7, 2011, http://www.existentialbuddhist.com/tag/glenn-wallis/.

34. Patricia Ivan, personal correspondence with the author, January 2, 2017.

35. Scott A. Mitchell, *Buddhism in America: Global Religion, Local Contexts* (Oxford: Bloomsbury, 2016), 168.

36. "Post-Traditional Buddhism?," Post-Traditional Buddhism, https://post traditionalbuddhism.com/about/, accessed February 22, 2017.

37. Stewart M. Hoover and Nabil Echchaibi, "Media Theory and the Third Spaces of Digital Religion," quoted in Emma Tomalin, Caroline Starkey, and Anna Halafoff,

"Cyber Sisters: Buddhist Women's Online Activism and Practice," in *Religion and Internet*, ed. Daniel Enstedt, Göran Larsson, and Enzo Pace (Leiden: Brill, 2015), 11–33, 20.

38. Winton Higgins, "The Coming of Secular Buddhism," *Journal of Global Buddhism* 13 (2012): 109–26, 110.

39. Ibid., 111.

40. Stephen Batchelor, "A Secular Buddhism," *Journal of Global Buddhism* 13 (2012): 87–107, http://www.globalbuddhism.org/jgb/index.php/jgb/article/view/127.

41. B. Alan Wallace, "Distorted Visions of Buddhism: Agnostic and Atheist," FPMT, October 2010, https://fpmt.org/mandala/archives/mandala-issues-for-2010/october/distorted-visions-of-buddhism-agnostic-and-atheist/; Stephen Batchelor, "An Open Letter to B. Alan Wallace," FPMT, January 2011, http://fpmt.org/mandala/archives/mandala-issues-for-2011/january/an-open-letter-to-b-alan-wallace/.

42. Stephen Batchelor, "A Secular Buddhist," *Tricycle* (Fall 2012), https://tricycle.org/magazine/secular-buddhist/.

43. Batchelor, "A Secular Buddhism."

44. Stephen Batchelor, "Buddhism 2.0: A Secular Manifesto" and "Resources," *Against the Stream Nashville TN* (blog), https://againstthestreamnashville.files.wordpress.com/2012/06/buddhism2.pdf, accessed March 10, 2017.

45. "Stephen Batchelor on the Four Noble Tasks," Upaya Institute and Zen Center, February 2, 2015, https://www.upaya.org/2015/02/stephen-batchelor-four-noble-tasks/.

46. Bodhi College, Mission Statement, https://bodhi-college.org/mission-statement, last updated February 28, 2018.

47. Stephen Batchelor, personal correspondence with the author, March 8, 2017.

48. Bhikkhu Bodhi, "Facing the Great Divide," Secular Buddhism in Aotearoa New Zealand, http://secularbuddhism.org.nz/resources/documents/facing-the-great-divide/, accessed March 10, 2017.

49. Batchelor personal correspondence, March 8, 2016.

50. Ted Meissner, personal correspondence with the author, March 12, 2017.

51. "Episode 270: Stephen Batchelor, Secular Buddhism: Imaging the Dharma in an Uncertain World," Secular Buddhist Association, March 5, 2017, http://secularbuddhism.org/2017/03/05/episode-270-stephen-batchelor-secular-buddhism-imagining-the-dharma-in-an-uncertain-world/.

52. Ted Meissner, interview with the author, September 22, 2016.

53. Jennifer Hawkins, interview with the author, March 17, 2017.

54. Doug Smith, interview with the author, September 22, 2016, and Mark Knickelbine, interview with the author, September 22, 2016.

55. Amy Balentine, interview with the author, March 8, 2017.

56. Hawkins interview.

57. Dana Nourie, "What Is a Secular Buddhist, and What Do They Believe?," Secular Buddhist Association, July 12, 2009, http://secularbuddhism.org/2012/07/09/what-is-a-secular-buddhist-and-what-do-they-believe/.

58. Stephen Batchelor, *Secular Buddhism: Imagining the Dharma in an Uncertain World* (New Haven, CT: Yale University Press, 2017), 168.

59. Ibid., 169.

60. In earlier research, I identified these patterns as part of a "relational turn," but I have since come to feel that "collective turn" captures more of what is at play here. For more details on the relational turn in the Insight network, see Ann Gleig, "External Mindfulness, Secure (Non)-Attachment and Healing Relational Trauma: Emerging Models of Wellness for Modern Buddhists and Buddhist Modernism," *Journal of Global Buddhism* 17 (2016): 1–21."

61. Thich Nhat Hanh, "The Next Buddha May Be a Sangha," *Inquiring Mind* 10, no. 2 (Spring 1994).

62. "Context matters" is a direct quotation from Vince Horn's 2015 Buddhist Geeks conference keynote speech. It is also the title of an interview with David McMahan in *Tricycle*: "Context Matters: An Interview with David McMahan," *Tricycle* (Winter 2013), https://tricycle.org/magazine/context-matters/.

63. Mark Knickelbine, "Practice Circle: The Benefactor Body Scan," Secular Buddhist Association, October 20, 2017, http://secularbuddhism.org/2017/10/20/practice-circle-the-benefactor-body-scan/.

64. Pablo Das, "Why This Gay Buddhist Teacher Is Dubious About Buddhist Refuge in the Trump Era," *Lion's Roar,* November 17, 2016, https://www.lionsroar.com/commentary-why-this-gay-buddhist-teacher-is-dubious-about-buddhist-refuge-in-the-trump-era/.

65. "Statement of Commitment," Against the Stream Buddhist Meditation Society, https://www.againstthestream.org/statement-of-commitment/, accessed January 3, 2018.

Conclusion

1. Scott A. Mitchell, *Buddhism in America: Global Religion, Local Contexts* (London: Bloomsbury, 2016), 233.

2. David L. McMahan, "Buddhist Modernism," in *Buddhism in the Modern World,* ed. David L. McMahan (New York: Routledge, 2012), 173.

3. Cristina Rocha, *Zen in Brazil: The Quest for Cosmopolitan Modernity* (Honolulu: University of Hawaii Press, 2006), 196.

4. Erik Braun, "United States of Jhana: Varieties of Modern Buddhism in America," in *Buddhism Beyond Borders: New Perspectives on Buddhism in the United States,* ed. Scott A. Mitchell and Natalie E. F. Quli (New York: SUNY Press, 2015), 174–76.

5. Natalie E. F. Quli and Scott A. Mitchell, "Buddhist Modernism as Narrative: A Comparative Study of Jodo Shinsu and Zen," in *Buddhism Beyond Borders,* 197–215, 198.

6. Martin Baumann, "Global Buddhism: Developmental Periods, Regional Histories, and a New Analytic Perspective," *Journal of Global Buddhism* 2 (2001): 4.

7. Ibid., 32.

8. Donald S. Lopez Jr., ed., *A Modern Buddhist Bible: Essential Readings from East and West* (Boston: Beacon, 2002), vii–xi; xxxv; Mitchell, *Buddhism in America,* 231–49, 231.

9. The term "thick globalization" comes from Manual A. Vasquez and Marie F. Marquardt, *Globalizing the Sacred: Religion Across the Americas* (New Brunswick, NJ: Rutgers University Press, 2003), 36.

10. Anna Halafoff and Praveena Rajkobal, "Sakyadhita International: Gender Equity in Ultramodern Buddhism," *Feminist Theology* 23, no. 2 (2015): 111–27; and Emma Tomalin, Caroline Starkey, and Anna Halafoff, "Cyber Sisters: Buddhist Women's Online Activism and Practice," in *Religion and Internet,* ed. Daniel Enstedt, Göran Larrson, and Enzo Pace (Leiden: Brill, 2015), 11–33.

11. Jean-Paul Willaime, "Religion in Ultramodernity," in *Theorizing Religion,* ed. James A. Beckford and John Wallis (Aldershot: Ashgate, 2008), 77–89, 78.

12. Ibid., 79.

13. Halafoff and Rajkobal, "Sakyadhita International," 119.

14. Ibid., 120.

15. Tomalin, Starkey, and Halafoff, "Cyber Sisters,"13.

16. Willaime, "Religion in Ultramodernity," 78.

17. Anna Halafoff, personal correspondence with the author, November 28, 2016.

18. David Lyon, *Jesus in Disneyland: Religion in Postmodern Times* (Cambridge: Polity Press, 2000), x–xii, 6–8, 37–41.

19. James Taylor, *Buddhism and Postmodern Imaginings in Thailand: The Religiosity of Urban Space* (Burlington, VT: Ashgate, 2008).

20. Mitchell, *Buddhism in America,* 155–72.

21. Zack Walsh, "A Sociocultural Critique of Post-Modern Buddhism and Meditation" unpublished paper, 2004, 6, available at http://cst.academia.edu/ZackWalsh/Unpublished-Drafts.

22. David Ray Griffin, William A. Beardslee, and Joe Holland, eds. *Varieties of Postmodern Theology* (Albany: State University of New York Press, 1989).

23. Ann Gleig, "From Buddhist Hippies to Buddhist Geeks," presentation at the Buddhist Geeks conference, University of Colorado, Boulder, August 16–18, 2013.

24. Edward Said, *Orientalism* (New York City: Pantheon, 1978).

25. Richard King, *Orientalism and Religion: Post-Colonial Theory, Orientalism and "the Mystic East"* (London: Routledge, 1999).

26. David Tracy, *On Naming the Present: God, Hermeneutics, and Church* (New York: Orbis, 1994).

27. Liz Wilson, "Buddhism and Gender," in *Buddhism in the Modern World,* ed. David L. McMahan (New York: Routledge, 2012), 261–63.

28. Ann Gleig, "Dharma Diversity and Deep Inclusivity at the East Bay Meditation Center: From Buddhist Modernism to Buddhist Postmodernism?," *Contemporary Buddhism: An Interdisciplinary Journal* 15, no. 2 (2014), 312–31.

29. "Welcome to a Month of Decolonizing Our Sanghas," Buddhist Peace Fellowship, August 2013, http://www.buddhistpeacefellowship.org/welcome-to-a-month-of-decolonizing-our-sanghas/.

30. "Dharma and Direct Action," workshop, New York Insight Meditation Center, November 7–8, 2015.

31. GENXDHARMA, https://genxdharma.wordpress.com/conferencegoals/, accessed December 12, 2017, link no longer available; however, information on the 2019 conference can be found at GENXDHARMA, https://genxdharma.com, accessed April 11, 2018.

32. Funie Hsu, "We've Been Here All Along," *Buddhadharma: The Practitioner's Quarterly* (Winter 2016): 24–31.

33. Tynette Deveaux and Ajahn Amaro, "A Response to Critics of 'We've Been Here All Along' from the Winter 2016 *Buddhadharma*," *Lion's Roar,* December 1, 2016, http://www.lionsroar.com/a-response-to-critics-of-weve-been-here-all-along-from-the-winter-2016.

34. Michelle Dillon, "Jürgen Habermas and the Post-Secular Appropriation of Religion: A Sociological Critique," in *The Post-Secular in Question: Religion in Contemporary Society,* ed. Philip S. Gorski, David Kyuman Kim, John Torpey, and Jonathan VanAntwerpen (New York: NYU Press, 2012), 249–78.

35. Gregor Thuswaldner, "A Conversation with Peter L. Berger: 'How My Views Have Changed,'" *Cresset* 77, no. 3 (2014): 16–21; Courtney Bender, "Things in Their Entanglements," in *The Post-Secular in Question,* 43–76; Philip S. Gorski, David Kyuman Kim, John Torpey, and Jonathan VanAntwerpen, "The Post-Secular in Question," in *The Post-Secular in Question,* 1–22.

36. Liselotte Frisk, "The Practice of Mindfulness from Buddhism to Secular Mainstream in a Post-Secular Society," *Post-Secular Religious Practices* (2012): 48–61, 59.

37. Phra Nicholas Thanissaro, "Almost a Proper Buddhist: The Post-Secular Complexity of Buddhist Teen Identity in Britain," *Journal of Global Buddhism* 15 (2014): 10.

38. Jinting Wu and Mario Wenning, "The Postsecular Turn in Education: Lessons from the Mindfulness Movement and the Revival of Confucian Academies," *Studies in Philosophy and Education* 35, no. 6 (2016), 551–71, 566.

39. Ibid., 553 n.1.

40. "(Post)secular: Imagining Faith in Contemporary Cultures," Warwick University, June 8–10, 2017, http://www2.warwick.ac.uk/fac/arts/modernlanguages/research/german/conferences/postsecular/, accessed January 20, 2017.

41. Mitchell, *Buddhism in America,* 170.

42. North American Buddhist Alliance, https://northamericanbuddhistalliance.org.

43. Kaira Jewel Lingo, interview with the author, January 16, 2017.

44. Douglas M. Padgett, "'Americans Need Something to Sit On,' or Zen Meditation Materials and Buddhist Diversity in North America," *Journal of Global Buddhism* 1 (2000): 61–81, 72.

45. Tynette Deveaux, personal correspondence with the author, March 30, 2017.

46. Tynette Deveaux, personal correspondence with the author, February 6, 2017.

47. True to her word, the fall 2016 issue featured an article on intersectionality by Lama Rod Owen and one on self-care for social justice activists by Mushim Patricia Ikeda; and the spring 2017 issue contained two articles, one by Doshin Nathan

Woods and another by Bhikkhu Bodhi, calling for solidarity with marginalized peoples. Lama Rod Owen, "Do You Know Your True Face?," *Buddhadharma: The Practitioner's Quarterly* (Fall 2016): 30–33; Mushim Patricia Ikeda, "I Vow Not to Burn Out," *Buddhadharma: The Practitioner's Quarterly* (Fall 2016): 53–55; Doshin Nathan Woods, "The Path of Solidarity," *Buddhadharma: The Practitioner's Quarterly* (Spring 2017): 61–65; Bhikkhu Bodhi, "Let's Stand Up Together," *Buddhadharma: The Practitioner's Quarterly* (Spring 2017): 9–10.

48. Melvin McLeod, "Buddhist Peace Fellowship Comments on Buddhism, Diversity, and *Lion's Roar* Cover," *Lion's Roar,* January 27, 2016, https://www.lionsroar.com/buddhist-peace-fellowship-comments-on-buddhism-diversity-and-first-lions-roar-cover.

49. James Shaheen, personal correspondence with the author, March 2, 2017.

50. Next Step Dharma, http://www.nextstepdharma.org/#home, accessed March 10, 2017.

51. "Buddha's Teaching and Issues of Cultural Spiritual Bypassing," Barre Center for Buddhist Studies, May 18–21, 2017, https://www.bcbsdharma.org/course/buddhas-teachings-and-issues-of-cultural-spiritual-bypassing/; Sebene Selassie, personal conversation with the author, December 29, 2017.

52. "Invisible Edge: Unmasking Social Bias, Creating Vibrant Community," Shambhala, April 1–2, 2017, https://boulder.shambhala.org/program-details/?id=309914/feed/feed/.

53. "Making the Visible Invisible: Exploring Bias and Racism Through a Buddhist Lens," Vajrapani Institute, December 7–10, 2017, https://vajrapani.org/retreat/dharma-and-activism/.

54. Lodro Rinzler, "BG 244: The Buddha Walks into a Bar," Buddhist Geeks, podcast audio, accessed July 29, 2013, link no longer available.

55. MNDFL, http://www.mndflmeditation.com, accessed March 12, 2016.

56. *The Arrow: A Journal of Wakeful Society, Culture and Politics,* "About," https://arrow-journal.org/about/, accessed January 3 2017.

57. "SZBA Board Member Profiles," Soto Zen Buddhist Association, http://szba.org/szba-board-member-profiles/, accessed January 3, 2018.

58. Jeff Wilson, *Dixie Dharma: Inside a Buddhist Temple in the American South* (Chapel Hill: University of North Carolina Press, 2012), 17–21.

Index

adaptation or acculturation, as one of
five main developmental issues in
American Buddhism delineated by
Prebish, 40

Against the Stream network, as a Gen X
Buddhist community, 302

Aloha Dharma, 133–34

American Buddhists: defined as a term,
7; "neoliberal sangha" associated with,
262–63; and social shifts in America,
247–48. *See also* white Buddhism

American Insight Community, femi-
ninization of psychotherapeutic approaches of, 325n82

American Romantic lineage of Buddhism, 12, 33–34, 49, 85

American Zen Buddhism: feminine
approach to practices of, 105; teach-
ers (*see* Beck, Charlotte Joko; Fischer,
Norman; Hamilton, Diane; Kabat-
Zinn, Jon; Magid, Barry; Merzel,
Genpo; Rosenbaum, Robert Meikyo;
Ruff, Tenku; Schireson, Myoan Grace;
Shimano, Eido); training programs (*see*
Shogaku Priest Ongoing Training)

Angelou, Maya, 165, 258; and Owens's
interpretation of the iconography of
Green Tara, 249

Angry Asian Buddhist: critique of "White
Buddhism," 261; as a platform for Buddhist "discourses of dissent," 265, 294

Armstrong, Steve, 113, 126, 128

Asian American Buddhists, defined as an
umbrella term, 7

Asian American immigrants: dismissal
by mainstream convert Buddhism,
174. *See also* Japanese Buddhist
communities

Aylward, Martin, 211, 214, 224–25, 227,
247; Mindfulness Training Institute
cofounded by, 78–79

Bainbridge, William, model of "audience
client," 38

Bartok, Josh, 214

Bartone, Shaun, 262–63

Batchelor, Stephen: Buddhist Geeks
podcast by, 180; mindfulness cast as recovery of the dharma by, 276–77; nonhierarchical "ground-up approach" to